Event Studies

Books in the Series

Management of Event Operations
Julia Tum, Philippa Norton and J. Nevan Wright

Innovative Marketing Communications: Strategies for the Events Industry
Guy Masterman and Emma. H. Wood

Events Management 2e
Glenn A. J. Bowdin, Johnny Allen, William O'Toole, Rob Harris and Ian McDonnell

Events Design and Experience
Graham Berridge

Marketing and Selling Destinations and Venues: A Convention and Events Perspective
Tony Rogers and Rob Davidson

Human Resource Management for Events
Lynn Van der Wagen

Event Studies

Theory, Research and Policy for Planned Events

Donald Getz

ELSEVIER

AMSTERDAM • BOSTON • HEIDELBERG • LONDON • NEW YORK • OXFORD • PARIS
SAN DIEGO • SAN FRANCISCO • SINGAPORE • SYDNEY • TOKYO

Butterworth-Heinemann is an imprint of Elsevier

Butterworth-Heinemann is an imprint of Elsevier
The Boulevard, Langford Lane, Kidlington, Oxford, OX5 1GB, UK
30 Corporate Drive, Suite 400, Burlington, MA 01803, USA

First edition 2007
Reprinted 2008, 2009 (Twice)

British Library Cataloguing in Publication Data
A catalogue record for this book is available from the British Library

Library of Congress Cataloging-in-Publication Data
A catalog record for this book is available from the Library of Congress

ISBN: 978-0-7506-6959-7

For information on all Butterworth-Heinemann publications
visit our website at www.elsevierdirect.com

Printed and bound in *Great Britain*

09 10 11 12   12 11 10 9 8 7 6 5 4

Contents

Series editors   ix
Series preface   xi
Preface   xiii
Dedication   xix
Acknowledgements   xxi
List of figures   xxiii

1 **Introduction and Overview of Event Studies**   **1**
   What Is Event Studies?   2
   Event Studies: Core Phenomenon and Major Themes   9

2 **The World of Planned Events**   **17**
   Describing and Classifying Events   18
   Planned versus Unplanned Events   27
   Typology of Event Forms   30

3 **Foundation Disciplines: Part One**   **49**
   Introduction   50
   Anthropology   50
   Sociology   55
   Psychology   61
   Environmental Psychology   65
   Social Psychology   68

4 **Foundation Disciplines: Part Two**   **75**
   Philosophy   76
   Religious Studies   78
   Economics   80
   Management   89
   Political Science   98
   Law   101

5 **Foundation Disciplines: Part Three**   **105**
   Introduction   106
   History   106

Human Geography   114
Future Studies   119

6 **Closely Related Professional Fields**   **127**
Introduction   128
Parks and Recreation Management: Leisure Studies   128
Tourism Management and Tourism Studies   138
Hospitality Management and Hospitality Studies   146
Education and Interpretation   147
Communications, Media and Performance Studies   152
Arts and Cultural Management   158
Cultural Studies   159
Sport Management and Sport Studies   160
Venue, Club and Assembly Management   162
Theatre Studies   163

7 **The Event Experience and Meanings**   **169**
Defining 'Experience'   170
A Model of the Planned Event Experience   177
Generic and Specific Types of Planned Event Experiences   182
Meanings Attached to Planned Event Experiences   196

8 **Event Design**   **207**
What is Event Design?   208
Designing the Setting   212
Theme and Programme Design   223
Service Design and Quality   228
Design of Gastronomy and Other Consumables   230

9 **Antecedents and Choices**   **235**
What Are Antecedents?   236
Barriers and Constraints   245
Decision-Making   249
Post-experience Evaluation and Feedback   253

10 **Management of Events**   **257**
Leadership, Founders and Organizational Culture   258
Organizational and Inter-organizational Behaviour   264
Planning and Decision-Making   271
Operations and Logistics   275
Marketing and Communications   278
Resources and Financial Management   282

Human Resources and Volunteer Management 286
Risk, Health and Safety 291
Research, Evaluation and Information Systems 293

11 Outcomes and the Impacted **299**
What are Outcomes and Impacts? 300
Personal Outcomes 301
Social, Cultural and Political Outcomes 303
Economic Outcomes 309
Environmental Outcomes 314
Impact Assessment and Cost–Benefit Evaluation 317

12 Events and Public Policy **327**
What Is Public Policy? 328
Justifying Public-Sector Involvement 329
Economic Policy and Events 334
Cultural Policy and Events 337
Social Policy and Events 340
Environmental Policy and Events 342
Public Policy-Making 344

13 Creating Knowledge in Event Studies **351**
A Framework for Knowledge Creation 352
Philosophy and Knowledge 355
Research Methodologies 359
Research Purposes and Methods 362
A Research Agenda for Event Studies 371

14 Conclusions **383**
The Planned Event Experience 384
Designing Experiences 386
Antecedents and Choices 387
Conclusions on Management 388
Conclusions on Outcomes 389
Conclusions on Events and Public Policy 390
Conclusions on Creating Knowledge 391
Final Comments 392

References 393
Index 427

Series editors

Glenn A. J. Bowdin is Principal Lecturer in Events Planning at the UK Centre for Events Management, Leeds Metropolitan University where he has responsibility for managing events-related research. He is co-author of *Events Management*. His research interests include the area of service quality management, specifically focusing on the area of quality costing, and issues relating to the planning, management and evaluation of events. He is a Member of the Editorial Boards for *Event Management* (an international journal) and *Journal of Convention & Event Tourism*, Chair of AEME (Association for Events Management Education), Charter Member of the International EMBOK (Event Management Body Of Knowledge). Executive and a Member of Meeting Professionals International (MPI).

Don Getz is a Professor in the Tourism and Hospitality Management Program, Haskayne School of Business, the University of Calgary. His ongoing research involves event-related issues (e.g., management, event tourism, events and culture) and special-interest tourism (e.g., wine). Recent books include *Event Management & Event Tourism and Explore Wine Tourism: Management, Development, Destinations*. He co-founded and is a Member of the Editorial Board for *Event Management* (an international journal).

Professor Conrad Lashley is Professor in Leisure Retailing and Director of the Centre for Leisure Retailing at Nottingham Business School, Nottingham Trent University. He is also Series Editor for the Elsevier Butterworth Heinemann Series on *Hospitality Leisure and Tourism*. His research interests have largely been concerned with service quality management, and specifically employee empowerment in service delivery. He also has research interest and publications relating to hospitality management education. Recent books include *Organisation Behaviour for Leisure Services, 12 Steps to Study Success, Hospitality Retail Management and Empowerment: HR Strategies for Service Excellence*. He has co-edited, *Franchising Hospitality Services*, and *In Search of Hospitality: Theoretical Perspectives and Debates*. He is the Past Chair of the Council for Hospitality Management Education. He is a Chair of the British Institute of Innkeeping's Panel Judges for the NITA Training Awards, and is Advisor to England's East Midlands Tourism network.

Series preface

The events industry, including festivals, meetings, conferences, exhibitions, incentives, sports and a range of other events, is rapidly developing and makes a significant contribution to business- and leisure-related tourism. With increased regulation and the growth of government and corporate involvement in events, the environment has become much more complex. Event managers are now required to identify and service a wide range of stakeholders and to balance their needs and objectives. Though mainly operating at national levels, there has been significant growth of academic provision to meet the needs of events and related industries and the organizations that comprise them. The English-speaking nations, together with key Northern European countries, have developed programmes of study leading to the award of diploma, undergraduate and post-graduate awards. These courses focus on providing education and training for future event professionals, and cover areas such as event planning and management, marketing, finance, human resource management and operations. Modules in events management are also included in many tourism, leisure, recreation and hospitality qualifications in universities and colleges.

The rapid growth of such courses has meant that there is a vast gap in the available literature on this topic for lecturers, students and professionals alike. To this end, the *Elsevier Butterworth Heinemann Events Management Series* has been created to meet these needs to create a planned and targeted set of publications in this area.

Aimed at academic and management development in events management and related studies, the *Events Management Series*:

- provides a portfolio of titles which match management development needs through various stages;
- prioritizes publication of texts where there are current gaps in the market, or where current provision is unsatisfactory;
- develops a portfolio of both practical and stimulating texts;
- provides a basis for theoretical and research underpinning for programmes of study;
- is recognized as being of consistent high quality;
- will quickly become the series of first choice for both authors and users.

Preface

There is great satisfaction to be derived from producing, assisting or participating in a planned event, but the study of events is equally fulfilling. I am always delighted to learn more about the great diversity and historical development of events, fascinated by their multi-faceted importance and meanings in every society, and ever-curious about the planning and production of unique event experiences. Event Studies includes event design and management, but it is also a lifelong voyage of discovery about the very nature of culture and civilization.

Can you remember your first special event experience? For me it was the county fair, or the travelling circus, I cannot remember which came first. They were thrilling and memorable family experiences. When I was young we annually visited large regional and national exhibitions in Kitchener, Toronto and Ottawa, trips that were the highlight of summer holidays. I will never forget Expo 67 in Montreal, both as a family experience and a national celebration – it was Canada's centennial year, my brother got married, and I moved away from home to start university. There are many event experiences that will always stand out in my fondest, most poignant memories, from those early family occasions, to trips with my own wife to attend the first Canada–Russia hockey showdown and with children to attend musical theatre. My frequent global travels often include exotic cultural experiences, new sport events and stimulating conferences. It's a beautiful world of events.

What meanings have you attached to your event experiences? What about your own personal milestones, the graduations, anniversaries, weddings, the birth of children – How were they celebrated? Do you enjoy meeting new people, participating in sport events or going to concerts with friends? Just how important are events to our personal and collective lives? We do not even have to think about economic impacts and cultural policies to realize that planned events are timeless and vital parts of civilization, of life itself.

My first goal in writing this book is to build a solid foundation for the profession of event management. It is my belief that simply teaching how to design or produce an event is equivalent to teaching a trade or an art, whereas teaching event management absolutely requires a dual foundation in management theory and Event Studies. My second aim is to establish Event Studies as an academic field on par with leisure, sport or tourism studies. This new academic field can have its home in the social and behavioural sciences, although it will also draw in a multi-disciplinary fashion from arts, humanities, design and engineering. A third major aim is to examine the myriad policy issues related to events, and to provide the basis for rational and inclusive policy-making. Hopefully this will advance the development of planned events.

Who Is This Book Written For?

For Students

Primarily I have written this book for students, to be used as a text for senior undergraduate and graduate students in event management degree programmes, and for other graduate students pursuing research degrees in any discipline or field that involves planned events. This book provides the theory and knowledge base for your careers in event management, for conducting event-related research or policy-making pertinent to events.

Each chapter starts with Learning Objectives which both indicate the main topics covered and the knowledge areas you are responsible for. Not all learning objectives can be met through this book alone, but the foundations are all present. Experience, further reading and additional studies are needed to completely master all the questions.

The many Research Notes included in the text connect you to the vast and diverse literature pertaining to events in many academic disciplines and related professional fields. You will need these sources to undertake research, to inform your essays and to eventually assist you in making real-world decisions. Look at the research journals represented, as collectively they probably cover the most relevant sources for your own research.

In the early chapters on disciplines and closely related professional fields, numerous theoretical foundations and methodologies are presented. They might be confusing and even seem irrelevant at first, but in the later chapters you will be able to see the applications to events. Most of these connections are made quite clear in the text, but some you will have to search out.

A Summary and Study Questions conclude each chapter. Use these to prepare for examinations by trying to write an answer for each study question. I always recommend that students study in groups, each writing an answer that will be shared with and constructively critiqued by others in the group. Further Readings are some of the sources cited in the text that will provide greater depth of understanding, or connect you to many event management and event tourism applications.

For Teachers

My assumption is that students using this text are already familiar with event management, although that is not prerequisite. My own book *Event Management and Event Studies* is directly complementary. In fact, you can cross-reference many sections of Event Studies with the more applied sections in Event Management and Event Tourism.

Within event management programmes, Event Studies might best be used at a senior level, and in particular for students expected to undertake research projects or write advanced essays. Personally, I would not want graduates holding event management degrees to enter the world without at least being exposed to this broad base of knowledge, especially if they are going to have anything to do with public policy. It can also be used at the graduate level in any field or discipline where students are doing research theses and dissertations related to events.

Use the Research Notes to get students familiar with the diverse range of applicable journals, and discuss with them the contributing theories, methodologies and specific problems that have been addressed. Encourage them to do library and electronic searches within some of the most pertinent sources.

The Mental Exercises can be used to stimulate personal reflection on the part of students, as well as being the starting point for class-room discussions. This will also help identify research gaps, although I have explicitly pointed out many gaps in the text.

I tried to select the most relevant and interesting theories that can inform Event Studies, but there are many more that could be relevant. Teachers should therefore draw on their own backgrounds and interests to bring in additional theoretical perspectives, methods or research examples. I also tried to make sure that theories introduced in the early chapters are actually referred to in the various Research Notes or applied in the later discussion chapters.

Chapter 13, on creating knowledge, is merely an introduction to research design and methods. To prepare for theses and dissertations, students will need more detailed advice. But this chapter should inform students and academics of the full range of research needs and methodological possibilities. The 'research agendas' provide many specific ideas, in addition to the mental exercises elsewhere in the book.

For Academic Researchers

I think that any academic doing research, or teaching anything related to events, should read this book first – if only because it provides an overview of the entire body of published knowledge pertaining to events. Especially read the sections on theories, research traditions, methods and methodologies. Hopefully the 'research agendas' in Chapter 13 spark a lot more interest in some of the less mainstream aspects of Event Studies. I also hope to see completely fresh insights arise that make these agendas obsolete in the near future.

The Bibliography is quite extensive, and I have deliberately included many references in passing, just to make connections to the diverse literature. But academics in the various disciplines cited, and in the closely related fields, can undoubtedly do a much better job in providing summaries of their mainstream literature that apply to Event Studies. I would particularly encourage academics in sports, arts, theatre, leisure and other fields that encompass events to publish systematic literature reviews showing their unique perspectives on planned events.

For Policy-Makers and Analysts

Policy-makers and policy-analysts have a need to understand the world of events from multiple perspectives. Explore the many challenging policy issues related to planned events, including the rationale for public intervention and support, and the costs and benefits that have to be balanced. Learn how to conduct and use appropriate research in a policy context.

Specifically, Chapter 12 contains advice on how to formulate public policy for planned events, including recommended goals, actions and performance measures.

For Event Professionals

Practitioners who do not have any formal education pertaining to events, or have only taken management and production-related courses, can get the big picture from this book. Learn why events and event professionals are important in society, and obtain an overview of contemporary thinking and research in your field. Use the book to develop your own philosophy and ethical code on planned events, and to become a reflective, learning professional.

The crossovers to event design and management are made quite clear, including references to my own management text and others. My hope is that practitioners who want to learn more about their profession (including what the next generation is thinking!) can use this book as a reference, and as a starting point for making more detailed investigations of their own. For example, event designers absolutely must draw more from cognitive, social and environmental psychology. I think this is a major pathway to improved design and more fulfilling event experiences.

A Note on Sources

Although event management and design are quite new professional fields, with their own small but growing body of literature, the total events-related literature is very large. Do a search on festivals, celebration, rituals, theatre, performances, sport or cultural tourism, meetings and conventions, and you will quickly be overwhelmed by the volume of references on each. But if you search 'Event Studies', good luck! As with other new fields of inquiry, one has to learn to draw efficiently from all the possible contributing disciplines, related fields, and sub-topics.

Both Wiley and Butterworth-Heinemann have expanding event management book series, with event-related titles coming from other publishers including Cognizant, Pearson and Haworth. Some of the event-related professional associations have good information on their websites, and publish sound, practitioner-oriented material.

Wikipedia is an interesting and useful source, but because anyone can contribute to this *Online Encyclopedia* the articles are constantly changing and potentially controversial. I use it as a starting point, not an authoritative source, and find it especially helpful on new topics that are slow to emerge in the mainstream reference literature (like flash mobs and gorilla gigs). I have used *Encylopedia Britannica* as my authoritative source for definitions and the like. Several online disciplinary sources like Sociology were very useful, but I think they have to be backed by standard texts.

Since I have already conducted numerous searches (large in scope, but not always systematic), a review of the References and Further Readings in this book will provide a good starting point for researchers. I used the readily available search engines (especially 'leisuretourism.com' by CABI publishers), and have scoured particular journals.

Dedication

To the memory of Henry Getz, Adeline Getz and Nancy Getz.

Acknowledgements

I would like to thank the following contributors and sources of inspiration:

Bill O'Toole
Steve Brown
Sam Ham
Audrey Getz, for research assistance.

To my academic colleagues who have collaborated in event-related research over the years, including many who are cited in this book:

Don Anderson
Tommy Andersson
Jack Carlsen
Joanne Cheyne
Sheranne Fairley
Wendy Frisby
Simon Hudson
Mia Larson
Aaron McConnell
Bill Merrilees
Graham Miller
Lena Mossberg
Danny O'Brien
Martin O'Neill
Chris Ryan
Lorn Sheehan
Geoff Soutar
Ruth Taylor
Renata Tomljenovic
Bruce Wicks

All the other authors and researchers I have consulted and cited in this text, too numerous to mention. Event Studies did not begin in my imagination, but in the extant literature.

To the Butterworth Heinemann/Elsevier staff for support throughout the writing and production process.

To my colleagues and the staff at the Haskayne, School of Business, especially in the Tourism Area, including Brent Ritchie, Simon Hudson, Lorn Sheehan, Joyce Twizell and Deb Angus.

List of figures

1.1	The EMBOK model of event management knowledge domains.	2
1.2	Three levels of event education.	4
1.3	Event Studies: core phenomenon and major themes.	10
2.1	Typology of planned events.	22
2.2	Planned events versus unplanned events.	28
2.3	A question of scale.	29
3.1	Anthropology.	51
3.2	Sociology.	56
3.3	Psychology.	61
3.4	Environmental psychology.	65
3.5	Environmental psychology and planned events.	67
3.6	Social psychology.	69
4.1	Philosophy.	76
4.2	Religious studies.	79
4.3	Economics.	80
4.4	Management.	89
4.5	Political science.	99
4.6	Law.	102
5.1	History.	107
5.2	Human geography.	115
5.3	Future studies.	120
6.1	Parks and recreation management; leisure studies.	129
6.2	Tourism management and tourism studies.	139
6.3	Hospitality management and hospitality studies.	146
6.4	Education and interpretation.	148
6.5	Communications, media and performance studies.	153
6.6	Arts and cultural management.	158
6.7	Cultural studies.	159
6.8	Sport management and sport studies.	160
6.9	Venue, club and assembly management.	162
6.10	Theatre studies.	164
6.11	Schechner's (1988) four forms of theatre.	165
7.1	A model of the planned event experience.	179
7.2	The experiences of different stakeholders.	191

9.1   A framework for studying the antecedents and decision-making process for attending planned events.   236

10.1   Leadership, founders and organizational culture.   258

10.2   Organizational and inter-organizational behaviour.   264

10.3   Major stakeholder types and roles in festival networks.   270

10.4   Planning and decision-making.   271

10.5   Operations and logistics.   275

10.6   Marketing and communications.   279

10.7   Financing, financial management and control systems.   283

10.8   Human resources and volunteer management.   286

10.9   Risk, health and safety.   291

10.10   Research, evaluation and information systems.   294

11.1   Personal outcomes.   302

11.2   Social, cultural and political outcomes.   304

11.3   Economic outcomes.   310

11.4   Environmental outcomes.   315

12.1   Economic policy and events.   335

12.2   Cultural policy and events.   337

12.3   Social policy and events.   340

12.4   Environmental policy and events.   342

13.1   Creating knowledge and doing research in event studies.   353

13.2   Research agenda: planned event experience and meanings.   373

13.3   A research agenda for antecedents and choices.   374

13.4   Research agenda: management, planning, design and operations.   375

13.5   A research agenda for patterns and processes.   377

13.6   Research agenda: outcomes and the impacted.   380

Chapter 1

Introduction and Overview of Event Studies

Learning Objectives

- Be able to define Event Studies, and explain its core phenomenon and major themes.
- Understand the interdependencies among event design and production, event management, and Event Studies.
- Know how Event Studies rests on various foundation disciplines, particularly in the social sciences, and draws upon closely related professional fields for theory and methodology.
- Be able to discuss the policy dimensions of the major themes in Event Studies.

What Is Event Studies?

Event Studies is the academic field devoted to creating knowledge and theory about planned events. The core phenomenon is the experience of planned events, and meanings attached to them. Event Studies draws mainly from the social sciences, management, the arts, humanities and a number of closely related professional fields.

Event Management is the applied field of study and area of professional practice that draws upon knowledge and theory from Event Studies. Many public policy domains are affected by, and influence, planned events.

Event management as a profession is fast gaining global recognition and is already well established in many academic programmes, at all levels (diplomas, undergraduate degrees and advanced research degrees). The spectacular rise of this new profession and academic subject reflects a fundamental need within all societies for the professional management of events in the private, public and not-for-profit sectors. Events are much too important to trust to persons without training and experience, and increasingly these professionals require a solid academic foundation.

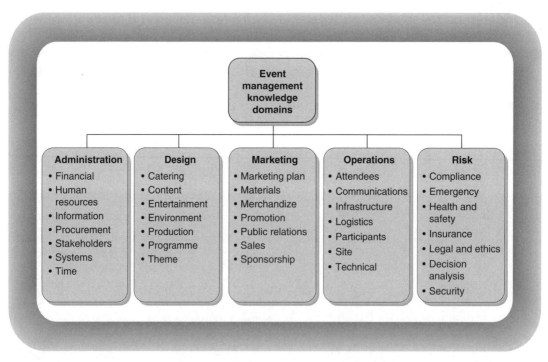

Figure 1.1 The EMBOK model of event management knowledge domains (*Source:* Silvers et al., 2006).

A group of academics and practitioners has developed the Event Management Body of Knowledge or EMBOK (see the article in *Event Management* (2006) by Silvers et al., and the EMBOK organization's website, www.embok.org). The diagram (Figure 1.1) portrays the five knowledge domains and related functional units for the student or practitioner to master, some by formal study and some through experience.

Event Studies looks at the bigger picture, all the issues surrounding planned events, in addition to their management, design and production. As well, Event Studies can exist without event management, and in fact it already does. When an economics researcher or sociologist examines the impacts of an event, regardless of any interest in its planning or production, that is one approach to Event Studies. When a newspaper writes about the pros and cons of bidding on an event in their particular community, that too is an element of Event Studies. In short, events have policy implications that cannot be ignored, and they are not the sole domain of event producers and managers.

Event Production, Event Management, Event Studies

A survey of the educational programmes, event production companies, careers, professional associations and event policy applications in the real world reveals three fundamental levels: design/production, management and studies. Applied to event education they are represented in Figure 1.2.

The basic level is mostly about how to design and produce events. It is sometimes taught in a hands-on kind of way, similar to learning a trade, but also within higher educational programmes. There is often a particular orientation applied to event design and production, typically from a theatrical background, party planning, or meeting and exhibition planning. The inherent scope for creativity attracts many people to this field of practice, but there is a lot to learn about designing and producing quality event experiences that can only be gained through higher-level education.

Having mastered design and production skills, many professionals have gone on to consulting or setting up their own event production businesses, necessitating the learning of management skills. Management theory and knowledge also has to be brought to bear on event organizations, whether permanent or one-time in nature, and on policy fields such as event tourism. Anyone studying event management, often within a business-school environment, also has to learn something about design and production, and must understand some fundamental knowledge and theories about events that are of necessity derived from other disciplines and professional fields.

At the top of this pyramid model is Event Studies, not placed there because of overriding importance, but because its very existence in the educational realm is dependent on the already well-established event design/production and management professions.

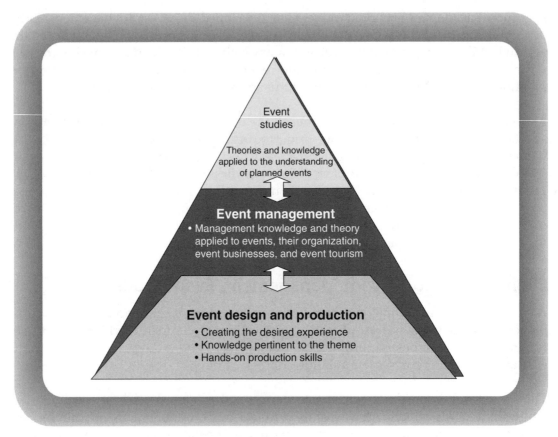

Figure 1.2 Three levels of event education.

Also, there is interest in events within many other disciplines and related professional fields, and what they teach encompasses event studies, event management, and sometimes design and production. From a disciplinary perspective, whether geography or economics, there is little need to learn about event design and production, and possibly some need to learn about management applied to events.

When Is a New Field of Study Born?

The problem for academics, those inclined towards theory and research at least, is that recreation, sport and events all have considerable significance for society, generate substantial economic benefits (and costs) and hold multiple meanings for those who participate in them. While some people want to concentrate on *praxis*, which is management, others want to develop theory, explore the meanings and get published in scientific journals.

This is how fields of study are created and evolve, usually resulting in tension between practitioners and academics. At some point of maturity, it becomes accepted wisdom that professional managers MUST understand some of the underlying theory, be able to discuss important meanings and generally recognize the contributions of mainstream disciplines to their professional field.

John Tribe (2004, 2006) argues that tourism is not a discipline, but a field of study drawing on a number of disciplines. The same can be said of Event Studies: the things that are to be studied about events require theories and methodologies from a number of disciplines. And just like tourism, the preoccupation so far has been with event management or business studies, rather than all the other perspectives which can be taken on tourism or events.

Accepting that Event Studies will be a 'social and political construct' (Tribe, 2004: 47), it is reasonable to conclude that one's perspective on, or object of interest in events, will determine which disciplines are drawn upon. An interest in the impacts of mega events on housing, for example, could draw upon sociology, urban planning and political science. An interest in the nature of festival sustainability will use management theory, social psychology and other sources that contribute understanding.

To create event-related knowledge, the contributions of theory and methodologies from multiple disciplines are required. Where a number of disciplines are drawn upon, we can say that the new field of study (like Event Studies today) is multi-disciplinary in nature. With time, the interactions might establish a field of knowledge with its own theories and methodologies, and this can be said to be interdisciplinary in nature.

Much of the knowledge and methods we need for event studies can be borrowed, at least in the developmental stage, from closely related fields like tourism, sport and arts administration, leisure studies and recreation. In those fields, all heavily oriented towards *praxis*, events are already important. It feels like we are carving off a portion of their body of knowledge and giving it special status, but that is what happens when there is explosive growth in the value of, and interest in a particular phenomenon.

What disciplines and related fields of study do we need? In this book I draw mainly on the social and behavioural sciences, because academics in these established disciplines have made the greatest contributions so far. I also look carefully at sub-disciplines that I feel should make a bigger contribution in the future, such as environmental psychology. And there are obvious and important links with communications, culture studies, tourism, hospitality, leisure, recreation, venue, arts and sports administration.

If it is true that Event Studies is a social and political construct, what are the implications? First, the point of view taken in this book has to be made explicit. I am writing a text for students, academics, policy-makers and practitioners who work within societies and economies where event management is emerging or already has become established as a career path, legitimate arena for business and an academic subject. My own range of experience, and the literature, is so far largely confined to English-speaking and European countries. That said, the event management professional model is definitely taking root wherever I go, especially in Asia, and my colleagues tell me it is now almost globally established.

But if we get serious about the meaning and impacts of events in culture, then we have to recognize that people in different cultures, and in different political or religious systems, will likely view planned events in a rather different light. It is also possible that gender, age, social status and other factors will become important in our understanding of events and their place in society. Those issues have not been fully explored.

Tribe (2004: 53) also discussed the apparent existence of 'academic tribes', wherein an elite group of 'elders' acts as gatekeepers for what gets published, and as referees of what research gets funded; in general they tend to stifle a new field of study because of their own biases. In the case of Event Studies, there is no doubt that to get published we academics have to play by certain rules and that might mean that certain topics and methodologies have been devalued. By actually acknowledging the existence of Event Studies, it might free up the research and publication opportunities.

The Need for Event Studies

I am encouraged by the many teachers who have said they introduce elements of Event Studies in their event management classes, by the researchers who are already publishing what I call 'Event Studies' in the journal *Event Management* (and many other mainstream and field-specific journals), and particularly by students that I have taught and spoken to, in many countries, who want more – much more – than learning 'how to' produce or market events. They want real understanding of the issues, they question underlying assumptions, they seek intellectual challenges.

Tribe (2002) tackled the subject of what a higher-level curriculum for tourism should embody. He noted (p. 338) that most tourism studies are vocational and business oriented (just as event management is), but there is a need to produce 'philosophic practitioners' who can deliver 'efficient and effective services while at the same time discharging the role of stewardship for the development of the wider tourism world in which these services are delivered'. Stewardship, in this context, can mean sustainable development.

This approach works well for event management, with Event Studies providing the reflective and philosophical components of a professional-school education. The professional event manager has to have more than skills. Professionals must have a broad base of knowledge together with the ability to reflect upon how it will shape both specific managerial or business decisions, and the wider implications of events in society and the environment. They also have to posses a well-developed sense of ethics and professional responsibility which should be based on a solid foundation that includes philosophy and comparative cultural studies.

I also believe there will be a growing need for planners and policy analysts who must deal with complex issues related to events, from many different perspectives (e.g., social, cultural, economic, environmental) for whom Event Studies provides a necessary foundation. As well, there will certainly be a rising need for higher education and lifelong learning in this profession of event management, and educators must ask that anyone with a higher degree, or a professional with advanced standing, should be well versed in theories and methods. They will be the mentors of the next generation of professionals, and we always expect more of the next generation.

Lastly, there will be more and more students doing advanced degrees, through research, related to event management and Event Studies themes. There is already a need for more and better-integrated research related to events. This book provides a good introduction to researchers, dealing with appropriate issues, questions and themes, and more specific discussion of research paradigms and methods applied to events.

The Gap Between Practitioners and Researchers/Theorists

This gap is not confined to the event field, but it is particularly important because of the newness of professionalism in event management. Many practitioners simply do not have an academic background, do not seek out research findings, and are probably ill equipped to understand research and theory pertaining to events. Such a gap closes slowly, as more and more professionals obtain university degrees and more and more information is communicated to them through ongoing educational programmes, professional associations and conferences.

Jago and Harris (2003), based in part on discussions at events conferences in Australia, concluded that academics and practitioners did not communicate very well. Both thought the other group had to do more, and the truth was probably somewhere in between. Practitioners always seem to think that academics do not conduct relevant research, or do not communicate research findings to meet their needs, but of course that has never been a particular aim of most academics. If that is true at the level of event design, production and management, it is likely to be even more substantial a gap at the level of Event Studies.

Jago and Harris concluded that more partnerships should be developed between research suppliers and providers, although this appears to be an easier task in Australia where there has been in place for some time a large source of research grants for sustainable tourism (including events) that is explicitly tied to industry relevance. Elsewhere, it is probable that closing this gap will require direct intervention by professional associations in seeking research and training partnerships with academic institutions that specialize in event management and Event Studies.

Discipline or Field of Study?

Echtner and Jamal (1997) reviewed the arguments for and against considering the study of tourism to be a discipline, and most of this discourse applies equally to Event Studies. Those in favour of giving tourism disciplinary status note that it is too complex a field of study for one discipline to adequately address. The growth of theory in tourism, or Event Studies, will be impeded by viewing it from single disciplinary perspectives. At a minimum, this argument suggests the need for more cross-disciplinary contributions both in theory and methods. Jafari (1990) believed that a cross-disciplinary approach was justified in creating a 'knowledge-based' approach to the teaching of tourism, but argued that tourism education should continue to be rooted in established disciplines.

Echtner and Jamal went on to examine the main disciplinary contributions to tourism studies, namely sociology and social psychology, geography, anthropology and management. They concluded that tourism studies is in a pre-paradigmatic stage, characterized by '. . . diverse and disorganized research, random fact gathering, a lack of fundamental laws and theoretical assumptions, a scarcity of exemplars and models, and deep debates over legitimate methods' (p. 875). Event Studies is not yet at this stage. Event management as an applied field is still very young, and no institutions that I know have yet formally recognized Event Studies.

According to Leiper (1981, 1990), a multi-disciplinary approach involves studying a topic (for us, planned events) by including information from other disciplines, whereas an interdisciplinary approach blends various philosophies and techniques to create a synthesis. This has to be an ideal, future development. For now, we are drawing on many disciplines and fields, and attempting to lay the foundation for development of Event Studies. It has to be stressed, however, that some researchers are already applying interdisciplinary approaches to the study of planned events, and this book should facilitate that approach by demonstrating core themes that require new concepts and methods.

Echtner and Jamal (1997: 879) also stressed that there needs to be '. . . liberalism with regard to methodological approach and, concurrently, greater attention to clearly explicated theory and methodology'. Event Studies should therefore embody '. . . holistic, integrated research; the generation of a theoretical body of knowledge; an interdisciplinary focus; clearly explicated theory and methodology; and the application of qualitative and quantitative methods, positivist and non-positivist traditions'.

Event Studies: Core Phenomenon and Major Themes

What defines a field of study is the 'core phenomenon', in our case the planned event experience and its meanings. But there are a number of closely related themes that have to be explored systematically. These include planning, design and production (i.e., supply and management in economic terms), personal antecedents to involvement in events (the demand side), the consequences of planned events (including impact evaluation), and patterns and processes (which we address by discussing the dynamics inherent in history, geography, future studies, policy and knowledge creation) (Figure 1.3).

The Core Phenomenon: Event Experiences and Meanings

'Phenomenon' means a state or process known through the senses, in other words something that can be 'experienced'. We are studying a universal phenomenon that has importance around the world, in every culture and society. Incidentally, the alternative, more popular definition of phenomenon is that of a 'remarkable occurrence', which can be a synonym for 'special event'!

The essence of the planned event is that of an experience that has been designed (or at least the experience is facilitated) and would not otherwise occur. There are many styles of planned events, produced for many purposes, but in every case there is intent to create, or at least shape the individual and collective experiences of the audience or participants. New forms are always being created, and this in itself is of considerable interest.

Multiple perspectives on experiences and meaning have to be included. Obviously there are paying customers or invited guests at planned events, but also the organizers including staff, sponsors and other facilitators (providing resources and support), regulators (e.g., city officials), co-producers, participants (as in athletics events), exhibitors and suppliers. Let's not forget volunteers, as numerous events cannot exist without them. What motivates all these stakeholders and what different experiences do they have? How do all these stakeholders react to the designed experience or at least to the setting and programme?

We are also concerned about how meanings are attached to planned events (social and economic) and to the personal event experience. For example, is the event perceived to be a shared cultural experience or personally self-fulfilling? And we also have to examine meanings from different perspectives. Each stakeholder in the process wants, expects and receives potentially different experiences and attaches potentially different meanings to the event. Do they have the experiences that were planned for them?

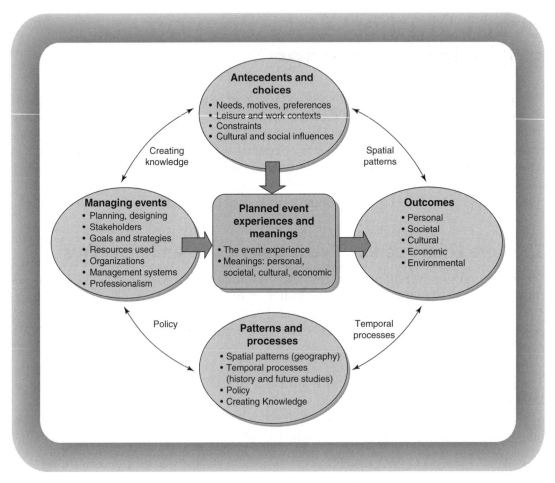

Figure 1.3 Event Studies: core phenomenon and major themes.

Events are also important, but not at the core of closely related fields, and these are examined more closely in Chapter 6. In Leisure Studies attention is paid to intrinsically motivated events (enjoyed as part of one's free time), but the emphasis is on the meanings and use of 'leisure'. We can say that events of some kinds are a part of leisure studies, but the event itself is not at the core of leisure or recreation. Sport management entails the production of sport events. Sport is a kind of institutionalized play, and it always includes planned events. Nevertheless, the event is not at the core. Sport studies can exist quite nicely without a focus on events.

Many specific expressions of art include events, such as the theatre, music concerts, art exhibits. But the event is usually a vehicle for performance and exhibition, not the core phenomenon. An exception might be 'performance art' in which the event is the art! What defines all art, however, is the emphasis on aesthetics, which is a mode of experience. Art is not so much produced and consumed, like other goods and services, as it is appreciated. When we study events, aesthetics should be a consideration, but it is not the central subject.

Meetings, conferences and seminars are obviously important for learning, but education occurs without events. Consumer and trade shows are forms of marketing and business, but commerce can occur without events. In education and business therefore, the events are not of central concern. But they are special experiential domains of education and commerce that deserve our focused attention in Event Studies.

Theory on Experience and Meanings

We have to start with the premise that event experiences, and meanings attached to them, are both 'personal and social constructs'. When people attend concerts their expectation is to be entertained, and probably also to have fun with like-minded fans in a dynamic social setting. Going to a conference requires that we think in terms of having a learning experience. We are supposed to be happy when we go to festivals, and sad when we attend funerals. Consumption of all kinds is the social norm, leading to enormous expenditures on entertainment events. So we need theory on both personal antecedents to attending events (including needs, motives, preferences, constraints), and the social constructs that give events broader meanings and importance within society and cultures.

To a degree, expectations are shaped purposefully by advertising, branding and the media. 'Event experiences' are the hot topic in branding and marketing, so corporations know how to create the experiences necessary to foster positive brand attitudes and increased consumption. Are some event experiences therefore exploitive and deceiving? Even where the event experience is created by not-for-profits or government agencies there is the possibility that the meanings we are to attach to the experience are part of some propaganda or social marketing scheme.

Chapter 2, The World of Planned Events, introduces each form of event and talks about the experiences associated with them. Pertinent theory is mentioned first in the discussion of foundation disciplines and closely related professional fields (Chapters 3–6). Chapter 7 applies and develops theory pertaining to the event experience and meanings, specifically the theory of liminality, drawing from anthropology and the study of rituals. The planned event experience is then modelled as a particular kind of liminal/liminoid zone – a special space and time, a different realm of existence, that has to be symbolically or ritualistically marked for its special purposes. In this liminal/liminoid zone, event-goers are aware of the contrasts with everyday life, and this is an important part of the experience. Also discussed are the concepts of 'flow' and 'peak experiences', drawing from social psychology and leisure studies, which describe how some people feel and act when 'in the zone' – they get totally involved and lose track of time.

To understand event experiences we also need to look at communication, learning and interpretation theory (i.e., how do we motivate attendance, shape expectations and create the best learning environments). Theories on 'serious leisure', 'ego involvement' and 'commitment' help us understand event motives, experiences and meanings for those participants who seek out specific event opportunities and the personal benefits they provide.

Chapter 8 covers Event Design, beginning with discussion of the meaning of design as both a creative and technical problem-solving process, its theoretical foundations, and how design is applied to planned events. The theme, programme, setting, services and consumables are all subjects of design. One major conclusion I stress is that every event experience will be unique to the individual, because experiences are internal psychological states. We also interpret our experiences from different frames of reference. Related to that conclusion is the assertion that event planning and design cannot create experiences, but only suggest, facilitate or constrain them.

Antecedents and Choices

Chapter 9 draws on pertinent theory from a variety of disciplines to examine antecedents to attending events, and how choices and decisions are made. This has both theoretical and marketing implications, so a lot of the contributing theory has been adapted by consumer behaviour researchers in leisure and travel. A framework is provided for organizing the discussion, starting with the personal dimension; personality, needs and motives, personal and interpersonal factors, expectations, and event careers. Both 'intrinsic' (related to free choice and leisure) and 'extrinsic' (related to work and obligation) motives are important for Event Studies.

Barriers and constraints are then examined, drawing from leisure constraints theory. There are structural, personal and interpersonal constraints acting against our desires to participate in or attend events. The decision-making process starts with how people negotiate through constraints, as some people manage better than others to realize their personal goals. Attention is also given to information searching and use, event attractiveness (the pull factors), substitution, loyalty and novelty seeking.

Following event experiences we have to consider satisfaction (partly with reference to expectations), the meanings attached to experiences, and the possibility of personal transformation. These factors, plus ongoing recollection (if indeed the experience was memorable), shape future intentions. Some people clearly become highly 'involved' in sports, the arts and other lifestyle or leisure interests and are therefore more committed to events. Commitment and resulting 'event careers' can also be work or business related. Identifying and catering to the 'highly involved' is of particular interest to event designers and marketers.

Management of Events

Planned events happen by conscious human design, created by organizations with many stakeholders, with specific goals in mind. This is largely the event management or business domain, focusing as it does on mobilizing resources, transforming processes, management systems and professionalism. Because events are means towards an end (e.g., profit, celebration, branding, political benefits, place marketing), we always must carefully assess goals and take a multi-stakeholder approach to answering the 'why' question.

This is also the realm of event tourism, wherein events have specific roles to play in attracting tourists, fostering a positive destination image, acting as animators and catalysts. It is also the 'urban imaging' question (part of place marketing) in which, according to Hall (2005: 198), events play a prominent role.

Chapter 8 is specifically devoted to Event Design, as it needs to follow directly from the discussion of planned event experiences and meanings, while the remaining planning and management topics are covered in Chapter 10. Each of the key management 'functions' is discussed in turn, not in a 'how-to' style, but to stress the main topics within each function, disciplinary foundations, and unique issues or applications for events. Examples of event-specific research are provided, where possible.

Outcomes

'Outcomes' appears to follow logically from the other themes, but can also be a starting point. Many events are created or assisted by authorities and sponsors with intended outcomes clearly expressed. Tourism organizations work backwards from the goals of putting bums in seats or beds, then decide what events to bid on, create or market. Sponsors determine which target segments to build relationships with, or to sell to, then decide on their event marketing strategies. Government agencies routinely formulate social and cultural policies, then assist the event sector in implementing those policies. Impacts can also be unintended and unmeasured, giving rise to evaluation and accountability problems.

In Chapter 11 we discuss personal, social, cultural, economic and environmental outcomes. For each of these outcome categories a conceptual framework is presented, encompassing 'stressors or causal factors' (in theory, how can events cause impacts?), potential outcomes (major consequences, based on what the literature has revealed and theory suggests) and possible responses (policy, planning and management of the system to achieve desired outcomes and prevent or ameliorate the unexpected and negative).

Research Notes are employed to illustrate event-specific impacts and methods. Attention is also given to appropriate measurement and evaluation techniques, mainly to suggest the sources and related issues. The chapter concludes with a discussion of how to 'value' events.

Patterns and Processes

The theme Patterns and Processes represents the broader environmental influences and the dynamic aspects of our Event Studies 'system'. On the diagram (Figure 1.2) Patterns and Processes is shown as a major theme, with the interconnecting arrows labelled for each of them: temporal processes, spatial patterns, policy and creating knowledge.

Chapter 5 presents the three disciplines of history, human geography and future studies. Together they help us answer questions like 'where do events come from and how do they evolve over time? How are they distributed in time and space, and why? What cultural and political, technological and economic forces shape events?'

Policy is a theme running through the book, with Chapter 12 devoted to Events and Public Policy. Policy is a force that both reacts to and shapes the planned event system. Events are increasingly influenced by formal government policy, including funding and regulations. Numerous events are created and marketed for strategic policy reasons, usually economics, but also cultural and social. And as events become larger and generate more substantial impacts, they cannot be ignored by policy-makers and political parties. Specific attention is given to what event-related policy should consist of, in an integrated approach, and how it should be formulated.

Creating knowledge about events is the remaining process of importance, and the subject of Chapter 13. The more research, theory and management knowledge that is generated, the better we will be at creating meaningful experiences, formulating effective policy, achieving goals, marketing events, and preventing or managing outcomes. To accomplish this requires knowledge about knowledge creation! What is the nature of knowledge and theory, what are the appropriate methodologies and techniques we can use, and how should events-related research be done? Chapter 13 also provides a research agenda for advancing Event Studies and some specific suggestions for research projects. In Chapter 14 the book's conclusions are presented, emphasizing the big ideas discussed throughout.

Chapter Summary

In this first chapter Event Studies is defined and justified as a new field of academic inquiry. Its relationship to event management is explained through a discussion of the Event Management Body of Knowledge (EMBOK). Three levels of event-related education are also covered, showing in a pyramidal model how Event Studies links to Event Management and to event Design and Production at the base.

A model was presented which provides the framework for understanding Event Studies and structuring this book. The core phenomenon of Event Studies is the planned event experience and meanings attached to it, and although closely related professional fields do share our interest in planned events, their interest in events is mostly secondary. The other major themes are Antecedents and Choices (the personal dimension, examining why people go to events and how they decide), Management of Events (including design and planning), Outcomes (and those impacted by events), and Patterns and Processes. This latter theme includes the disciplinary contributions of history, geography and future studies, as well as the integrating processes of policy and knowledge creation.

Study Questions

- Define Event Studies and explain why it is, or is not, an academic discipline.
- What is the core phenomenon of Event Studies, and whose experiences are we interested in?
- How does the study of planned events from a multi-disciplinary perspective assist in event management and policy-making?
- Explain each element of the Event Studies framework.

Further Reading

Getz, D. (2005). *Event Management and Event Tourism* (2nd edn). New York: Cognizant.

Silvers, J., Bowdin, G., O'Toole, W., and Nelson, K. (2006). Towards an international Event Management Body of Knowledge (EMBOK). *Event Management*, 9(4): 185–198.

Tribe, J. (2004). Knowing about tourism – epistemological issues. In: L. Goodson and J. Phillimore (eds.), *Qualitative Research in Tourism: Ontologies, Epistemologies and Methodologies*, pp. 46–62. London: Routledge.

Chapter 2
The World of Planned Events

Learning Objectives

- Know the meaning of 'event' and 'planned event'.
- Be able to classify events in terms of their form, function and experiential dimensions.
- Understand how scale and frequency modify planned events.
- Learn how to study the main types of planned events as 'social constructs', including 'events at the margin'.

Describing and Classifying Events

The world of planned events is diverse and exciting, with almost unlimited scope for variety in form, function and event experiences. The meanings we attach to these events, and the importance they have always held in our personal and collective lives, makes them fundamental components of culture, business and lifestyle.

This chapter starts with basic definitions of 'event' and 'planned events', including a discussion of differences between planned and unplanned, and the question of scale (small versus large events). The inherent temporal and spatial dimensions of events are discussed, as this is fundamental to understanding much of the related theory.

Many adjectives are used in conjunction with the term 'event' and we need to understand how they arise from consideration of either the form or function of planned events. Terms like 'hallmark', 'mega' or 'iconic' refer to the function of events (e.g., for image making and place marketing, their size and significance, and their unique appeal).

The comprehensive event typology illustrated in Figure 2.1 is largely based on their form. When we associate specific form, setting and programming with event types like 'festival', 'convention' or 'sport competition', we are really creating and reflecting 'social constructs' that are based on tradition and common, societal expectations. Concluding this chapter is a profile of each of the main types and key sub-types of planned events.

What is an Event?

Event: an occurrence at a given place and time; a special set of circumstances; a noteworthy occurrence.

Events, by definition, have a beginning and an end. They are temporal phenomena, and with planned events the event programme or schedule is generally planned in detail and well publicized in advance. Planned events are also usually confined to particular places, although the space involved might be a specific facility, a very large open space, or many locations.

When you search 'event' on the Internet you will encounter its use in many other fields, for example in finance (events that disrupt the markets), physics (e.g., 'event horizons'), biology ('extinction events'), philosophy ('mental events'), climatology ('weather events'), medicine ('adverse events', as in bad reactions to vaccination), probability theory (events as 'outcomes of experiments') and even computer science ('event-driven programming'). Note that the temporal dimension is more important than the spatial in most of these usages.

No matter hard one tries, it is literally impossible to replicate an event; by definition, they only occur once. Although planned events might be similar in form, some aspect of setting, people and programme will ensure that the event is always tangibly or experientially different. Not only that, but the expectations, moods and attitudes of guests and participants will always be new, so their experiences will differ regardless of the programme and setting. This uniqueness of events makes them attractive, even compelling, so that cultivating a 'once in a lifetime' image for an event is the marketer's goal.

Time is of the Essence

Time is not a simple concept, and we use expressions of time in many ways – some of which are highly relevant to Event Studies. First, time is often conceptualized as being 'cyclical', as with the annual calendar. Seasonal changes are important in terms of climate, food production, and the very rhythms of social life, and this helps explain the evolution of many rituals and festivals. We tend to mark the 'passage of time' by annual holidays and celebrations, and we particularly look forward to them coming around next year.

Time is also interpreted in a 'mechanical' sense. If you watch the clock 'all the time', or have to 'clock in' at work, it becomes clear that time is easily 'wasted' and you can never have a second of it back. This view of time can become stressful – certainly it leads to the feeling of 'time pressure' that so many people wish they could escape. Accordingly, a holiday, and an event experience, provides temporary but valuable escape.

'Biological': the maturing of one's body and mind marks the passage of a life, relative to others going through the same 'life-stage' changes. If you focus on the final outcome, death, life will not be as fulfilling as it can be. Instead, think about the way we mark life's changes (*rites de passage*, like birthdays and anniversaries), its triumphs (graduation and other formal ceremonies), its fun and joy (festivals, leisure pursuits, family reunions) and even its temporary pains (goodbyes and funerals). My advice is to think about the joy of future holidays and celebrations, make long-term plans, always have goals; leave both completed and unfinished work when you leave this world.

'Social and cultural constructs' of time: As will be seen later, the conceptualization of the liminal/liminoid zone for the planned event experience is a social construct, and will vary from culture to culture. In most Western societies the meanings and values attached to escapism, 'free time', leisure pursuits, 'having a good time', being entertained, etc., are all part and parcel of why we produce and enjoy so many planned events. They are not only accepted but expected. Whole industries and public services are devoted to them. In fact, looking back, it has always been this way. Other social and cultural constructs of time lead to our perceived 'need' for annual holidays, numerous special days for commemorations (of just about everything) and 'time for ourselves'.

Time as a 'commodity': Time is precious on our society, therefore it has become a commodity with high value. We gladly pay for 'quality time' with our friends and families, and this often involves event experiences. We will sacrifice more money to have more 'free time'. We hate 'having our time wasted', and in fact I am extremely annoyed when I have to stand in line to be served, or when travel disruptions cause me to have to 'kill time'. We all know that we cannot 'buy time', but we can certainly 'lose time'. These values and attitudes are all shaped by our culture, and perhaps it would be healthier if our cultural perceptions of time would change.

How we use, perceive and value time are important considerations in Event Studies. Events are temporal phenomena, with start and end points, yet the experience of them begins before and possibly never ends! Anticipation and recollection can be just as important as the experience itself. In this way, the packaging events, a key to effective event tourism development and marketing, should be much more focused on the over-all experience than on the technical aspects of travel, accommodation and event tickets.

The value of time varies a great deal among people, at various stages in their lives, and among cultures. 'Time is money', sure, and people want value for their 'investment' of time, but how does this apply to planned events? On one hand a short, intense event experience can be just what is needed, but people are also willing to give up large blocks of time to travel to events. Can we measure the value of events by reference to the time various people invest in them? Is it possible that people value time differently, and therefore the identical event experience can be much more satisfying to some?

In his book *Faster: The Acceleration of Just About Everything*, James Gleick (2000) argued that everybody now expects that everything can and should be done immediately, giving rise to time pressures. We need to think of planned events as a respite, a way to escape these time pressures and if not to slow down, at least to savour the moment.

A Time and a Place

Planned events occupy and temporarily transform spaces (or venues), and for the dur-ation of the event one's experience of that place is altered. In turn, many events are intrin-sically linked to their setting and community. A number of important implications follow.

Culture varies geographically, so the influence of place and culture on events are reinfor-cing. Cross-cultural comparisons are necessary to fully appreciate the differences in how events are created, valued, managed and experienced. In turn, events influence the places and cultures in which they occur, especially when mega-events are imposed on a culture that has not experienced such investment and media attention, and also when new events spread across the globe.

Attachment to places, and place identity, can be influenced by planned events. This is the community-building role of events, and is of considerable interest to social policy makers and politicians in general. Every nation and community needs its celebrations, events that generate pride and a sense of belonging, and which build development capacity through volunteering, capital investments and improved marketing. Similarly, communities of interest and sub cultures express themselves through events, and they need events and event places to identify with.

Festivals and events are increasingly used strategically to help define and brand places. Hallmark Events give identity and positive image to their host community, while venues and resorts can also have their hallmark events. 'Festivalization', the exploitation of festivals in place marketing and tourism, is a worry to many observers fearing commodification, loss of cultural authenticity and over-production of events.

Some events achieve 'iconic' status so they can occur anywhere and still be successful, but they still require specific venues and leave some kind of tangible legacy in terms of urban renewal, tourism and transport infrastructure, social and environmental change. Mega events, including World's Fairs, Olympics, other major exhibitions and sport events, have all been studied from many points of view, but there has been little attention paid to the question of whether other events can permanently transform a place.

Planned Events

'Planned events' are created to achieve specific outcomes, including those related to the economy, culture, society and environment. Event planning involves the design and implementation of themes, settings, consumables, services and programmes that suggest, facilitate or constrain experiences for participants, guests, spectators and other stakeholders. Every event experience is personal and unique, arising from the interactions of setting, program and people.

All planned events get 'labelled': as festivals, conferences, fairs, sports, etc. These are really social constructs, because when we use descriptive terms like 'festival' or 'convention' most people have an idea of what they mean. They look and feel different; they have different intentions, meanings and programmes. The typology illustrated in Figure 2.1 is based primarily on their form (i.e., what they look like and how they are programmed). Remember that any event can fulfil multiple functions, facilitate similar experiences, and have many meanings attached to it.

The term 'event' is also used in many ways, commonly by adding adjectives like 'sales' or 'sport', which reflects their form or function. Before examining the typology of planned events in Figure 2.1, which is mostly based on form, let's clarify what we mean by form and function, experience and meaning. 'Form' derives from the combination of various 'programmic elements of style' (discussed in Chapter 8) that make event types different. For example, the hallmark of a sport event is athletic competition, of a conference it is various learning mechanisms, of a festival it is celebration manifested in theme, symbolism and emotional stimulation. Form is therefore a primary concern of event planners and designers, or at least their usual starting point. The basic and generally accepted forms of meetings, sport events, fairs and festivals

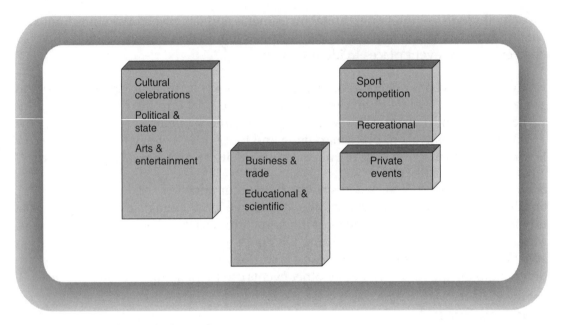

Figure 2.1 Typology of planned events.

can be taught, although in each culture there are going to be differences in their style and meanings.

Historically, 'form' has shaped professionalization and led to establishment of many professional associations, so that 'meeting professionals' have become the most organized globally, community festival producers have different associations than arts festivals (and arts are subdivided), and sport event managers have separate conferences. I think a more generic event management approach is needed as the lines between types of events have blurred and the professionalization of this sector favours integration rather than type-specific careers. Specialization, if desired, should follow from general Event Studies and event management education.

Form, but not the programmic elements of style, is equally applicable to unplanned events. Every event has some form that leads us to call it a celebration, protest, riot, party or whatever. What exactly are the 'cues'? First of all, the way people behave, because people assembling for protests obviously behave differently from those getting together to party. A casual meeting of friends or workmates looks and feels quite different from a spontaneous crowd celebrating the home team's victory.

Second, we can ask the people involved what they are doing and why they got together, and this should easily reveal whether the event is a spontaneous discussion or party. That of course leads us to consider experience and meanings. The programmic elements of style are not always applicable to unplanned events, however, because they are the tools of event planners and designers. If a celebrating crowd breaks out into song and dance we cannot call that programmed, but it is an activity virtually identical to what happens in many designed event experiences.

An Experiential Typology?

Function and form do not pre-determine personal event experiences, mainly because people create their own experiences within event settings, and will assign meanings to event experiences that can be independent or only loosely related to the event's purpose and programme. Great experiences can be obtained without planned events, but event designers want people to have a great experience at their event. To date, most event designers have had to operate in accordance with established norms (the social constructs again) for event production – such as how to produce an effective meeting, how to programme an arts festival or how to run a tournament. Alternatively, the designer has to work according to instinct, within a creative mentality, and rely on both subtle and overt feedback to determine if the event experience was both pleasant and as intended.

We cannot easily develop a typology of events based primarily on experience, because so many possible experiences can be had at events. Both festivals and sports events can facilitate joy, celebration, excitement, self-fulfilment, or aesthetic appreciation. While their form and functions might be completely different, at the experiential level (and to some extent at the level of their meanings) they can be quite similar. That is why a phenomenological research methodology offers considerable scope for a better understanding of event experiences, because it focuses on the individual's state of mind while experiencing the event.

Functions of Planned Events

'Function' gets us into the world of public policy, business and professional event management. Why are events held? What is their intended outcome? This is also a key starting point for planned events, and it cannot be left to chance. What if a meeting planner merely assumed that the purpose of a large conference was to allow speakers to address the delegates, when the organizers really wanted a great social occasion? Function trumps form every time, hence the adage 'form follows function'.

Function comes in layers, like an onion. At the outside, superficially, the event might be planned as a community celebration, a festival to involve all residents. But are there not also expectations that it will attract tourists? Promote a positive city image? Make money for local charities and businesses? Foster inter-organizational cooperation? The list is potentially endless. Historically, festivals and fairs performed important roles that were not discussed or planned, they just happened because they were needed. Markets and fairs were necessary for trade, parties and celebrations fit organically into everyday life, games were not professionalized as sport. But for the most part that era has passed and most events are planned to meet numerous specific economic, business, social, cultural and other policy aims.

The event planner and designer, therefore, seldom has a free hand. Potentially many stakeholders are involved in determining multiple event goals, and they often conflict. When the goals are made clear, perhaps prioritized, the real work of event design can begin. If the goals are not made explicit, problems are likely to occur. But the designer can at least assume certain things about the event's form as long as terms like festival, fair, tournament or conference, are used – if the stakeholders all agree the event should be a celebration or festival, specific goals are not absolutely needed to start planning. Again, this is because the types of planned events have become social constructs.

Several definitions found in the literature are really descriptions of event functions. Let's look at the most common ones.

Hallmark and Iconic Events

'Hallmarks' are not only distinctive features, but also symbols of quality or authenticity. We can speak of celebration as being the hallmark (or distinctive feature) of festivals. Also, we can refer to a Hallmark Event in which case the term has to refer to a very special class that represents the best event, one that is authentically imbedded in a particular place or culture. They are recurring events that have become so closely associated with their host community or destination that they form an important part of it's image and branding. These events provide and feed off place identity. Rio de Janeiro and New Orleans have their Mardi Gras, Calgary has its Stampede, and Edinburgh its Tattoo, all permanent 'institutions' in their cities, full of tradition and generating competitive advantages from a tourism perspective. My definition is:

> *Hallmark Events are those that possesses such significance, in terms of tradition, attractiveness, quality or publicity, that the event provides the host venue, community or destination with a competitive advantage. Over time, the event and destination images become inextricably linked. Hallmark Events are, by definition, permanent 'institutions' in their communities or societies.*

Sometimes 'iconic' is used to describe a community's best-known event, but there has to more than just fame or reputation. An 'icon' is a graphic representation of something, in other words a symbol. The correct use would therefore be: Mardi Gras stands for Rio or New Orleans, it is the city's iconic event. This is similar to saying that the Eiffel Tower is a symbol standing for Paris.

The other use of 'iconic event' described earlier, is one that has strong appeal all on its own, and can be held successfully anywhere. It symbolizes something of potentially global significance. For example, the FIFA World Cup or the Olympics are loaded with symbolic meaning, so that many people want to attend because of what they represent, not where they are. And what they represent (i.e., their meanings) is, of course, of great interest in Event Studies.

Premier or Prestige Events

These events are defined within specific categories, so that the World Cup is football's 'premier' event; its prestige is unrivalled. All sports and special interests tend to have prestige and premier events, and while some are located in permanent places or venues, many of them move around. Some, like the Boston Marathon, combine elements of iconic and hallmark status.

Mega Event

'Mega' refers to the largest and most significant of events. The definition and implications of these events were examined in an AIEST (1987) conference proceedings in which Marris (1987) said mega events should exceed one million visitors and be 'must-see' in nature, while Vanhove and Witt (1987) added they should be able to attract worldwide publicity.

However, I believe it is a relative term. If we equate 'mega' with large size, then it is usually the Olympics, World's Fairs, and other major sport events we talk about. But even a small music festival can have 'mega' impacts on a small town in terms of tourists, economic benefits or disruption. It can also refer to media coverage and impacts on image, as in 'the convention attracted worldwide publicity and put the city on the tourist map'.

Mega events, by way of their size of significance, are those that yield extraordinarily high levels of tourism, media coverage, prestige, or economic impact for the host community, venue or organization.

Note that this definition also allows for 'mega events' within the context of a particular venue or organization.

Media Event

Media events are created primarily for broadcast audiences, linked to the power of television and the Internet in reaching global audiences. Examples include surfing events that really need to be heavily edited and packaged to make for good viewing, and eco-challenges in remote places over long, arduous courses. However, any event can be packaged for the media, and that might be an essential part of its sponsorship appeal or subsidies from tourism and government agencies. In other words, any event can become a media event – it is a function, not form.

Cause-related Event

They are established to raise money, or to promote a cause, which makes them part of social marketing. While any form of event could perform this function, common types of fund-raisers are gala dinners, concerts, entertainment shows, endurance events (people support participants financially according to their time or length), celebrity sports and auctions.

Corporate Event

Any event produced by or for a corporation fits this category, with common types being product launches, meetings, grand openings and publicity stunts. An alternative meaning is the trend for large sport events in particular, like the Superbowl, to become so tied to corporate sponsors and related hospitality that they in effect become 'corporatized'.

A major shift in the events world has been the emphasis on 'experiential marketing' to develop brands and sustain relationships with customers and other corporate stakeholders. The term 'live marketing' has crept into the language to describe the use of events for these purposes. A related concept is the 'brand land', or the creation of venues devoted to 'brand experiences', and of course these corporate monuments have to be animated with events.

Publicity Stunt

Any event designed to garner publicity falls into this broad category, but it is usually associated with politicians and movie stars. Publicity agents should be expert at contriving events or situations that appeal to the media, or to crowds, so that they become 'news'. But to the degree that they are obvious in their intent, or manipulative, they can easily backfire. See elsewhere our discussions of 'pseudo events' and authenticity.

Special Event

Although this term is often used generically for the planned events field, and has been popularized by an important professional association (International Special Events Society, ISES), what is 'special' about any event is a subjective interpretation by either the producer or the guest. Jago and Shaw (1999) asked adults to describe important attributes of 'special events' and discovered that the number of attendees, international attention given to the event, perceived improvement to image and pride in the host region, and an exciting experience were the main factors explaining perceived specialness.

A long list of factors that I think contribute to any event's specialness starts with its uniqueness (see Getz, 2005) and includes elements of style (like hospitality, symbolism, festive spirit, theming and authenticity), meeting multiple goals, and appealing to different stakeholders and audiences.

Two perspectives on 'specialness' have to be taken: is it special to the organizers, or to the participants and customers?

1. *A special event is a one-time or infrequently occurring event outside the normal programme or activists of the sponsoring or organizing body.*
2. *To the customer or guest, a special event is an opportunity for an experience outside the normal range of choices or beyond everyday experience.*

Spectator and Interactive Events

'Interactive' events embody person–setting or person–person interactivity, unlike 'spectator' events which are inherently passive. Interactivity is thought to foster a higher level of involvement or engagement, making it a crucial element in 'experience design'. We return to this topic later, in depth.

Participant Events

Events that are held for people to be involved, not just to spectate. 'Participants' are more than customers or guests, they are necessary for the event to exist. Meetings and conventions do not exist without delegates; there are no marathons without runners; dance festivals need dancers. Exhibitions also require participants, namely the exhibitors. Because these events provide 'targeted benefits' (i.e., they are customized experiences), they can be viewed as sub-cultural manifestations, and are highly sought-after by competitive tourist destinations who can either create them or bid on them.

Planned versus Unplanned Events

It might come as a surprise to realize how much of what we see and hear on broadcast media is really about planned events. Consider the attention given to entertainment and sport, both having numerous, dedicated television channels (at least where cable and satellite TV are found). Add the ample coverage given to political events (including news conferences), private events (e.g., famous weddings), food and beverage events and so on, and it really adds up.

Now consider the range of 'unplanned' events that get media exposure, so much so that we wonder if they really are being planned. Indeed, in many cases they are clearly set in motion by people (maybe agitators, publicity agents or social activists) and they have a purpose, but they are categorically different from the events we are talking about when using the terms 'event management' or 'professional event manager'.

The distinctions sometimes get blurry, so it is necessary for Event Studies to encompass both. The only unplanned event we are not including are those that fall under the headings of accidents, forces of nature, wars and insurrections and other completely unpredictable happenings that hit the news.

'Spontaneous mass celebrations' should be considered. For example, during the Calgary Flames' run for the Stanley Cup in 2003, the 'Red Mile' was created when thousands of fans frequenting bars along the city's 17th Avenue flooded onto the streets. They wore their team's red colours, had a party, attracted news media from all over North America, and were tolerated by the police and civic authorities. This kind of social phenomenon results in events that have a specific duration (as long as the series continued), require some measures and controls similar to planned festivals, yet take on a life of their own. Incidentally, merchants and civic officials decided afterwards they would not tolerate such a spontaneous celebration in the future, as it posed many risks. Using traffic controls and police action, they prevented it from occurring in 2005.

Figure 2.2 is an attempt to sort out the planned and the unplanned events that Event Studies encompasses.

	Planned events (the realm of professional event designers and managers)	Unplanned events (the realm of spontaneity and unpredictability)
Purpose	Goals or outcomes are specified by producers of the event, and are influenced by key stakeholders	Purpose is self-defined; intentions of participants might be unclear, diverse, even contradictory
Programme	Planned and scheduled, usually in detail; designers seek to create 'experiences' for guests, participants and spectators	Spontaneous activities; or, once set in motion by agents, actions become rather unpredictable
Control	Controls are imposed by managers and other formal stakeholders, including governments	No management systems in place, only a degree of normal civic control; sometimes a police response is required
Accountability	Producers and managers are formally held accountable	No organization or legal entity is accountable overall; individuals can be held accountable for their actions, under law

Figure 2.2 Planned events versus unplanned events.

The Question of Scale

Probably the vast majority of planned events are small and are in the private or corporate spheres. But most attention focuses on the lager events that are open to the public, covered by the media, and generate substantial impacts. So there is a continuum of planned events along the dimension of scale, and the extremes can also be associated with impacts and policy implications (Figure 2.3).

The event experience	**Small events** • Mostly in the private and corporate spheres of interest • The experience might be intensely private or shared with an affinity group	**Large events** • Mostly in the public sphere of interest • Crowd dynamics can dominate • The event can affect entire communities through media coverage and shared attitudes
Impacts	• Collectively they are significant (e.g., weddings, meetings, parties, most sport meets)	• Each large event has substantial impacts (e.g., festivals, major sport events, fairs and exhibitions)
Media coverage	• Individual, small events seldom attract media attention	• The event itself is of interest to the media, or created primarily as a media event
Policy implications	• Policies related to venues, and to events in general (e.g., health standards, green operations, permits required)	• Policy decisions required for specific events (e.g., decision to bid; infrastructure investments; feasibility studies and impact assessments commissioned)

Figure 2.3   A question of scale.

The core phenomenon is not altered by the variable scale of events, although this diversity makes Event Studies much more interesting and challenging!

Frequency

Does it matter how often an event is produced? In sports, a team plays many games during a season; and in the arts and entertainment sector, concerts or shows are also regularly held. What if a fan or patron goes to many of these events? They can become routine for both participants, producers and some of the audience.

But remember that every event is still somewhat unique. In fact, many people love sports because the action is infinitely variable and the outcome always unpredictable, making them an 'authentic' experience when compared to other forms of entertainment like TV and the movies. As well, no actors, musicians or performers can exactly reproduce their efforts from one show to the next so that the audience can return with some expectation of differences. Even frequently attended events can be 'special' to the audience depending on their expectations, mood and experiences.

The answer, therefore, is that frequency is not a defining criterion for inclusion in Event Studies. We are as interested in scheduled, routine theatre and sports as we are in festivals held only every 10 years. Our focus is on the planned event experience and meanings.

Activity or Event?

Events contain many activities, but activities are not, by strict definition, events. 'Activity' is defined as the 'state of being active', 'energetic action or movement', 'liveliness' or 'a specified pursuit in which a person partakes'. A *leisure or recreation activity* is one that is pursued for its own, intrinsic rewards and a *business activity* is pursued for its value-creating benefits or out of administrative necessity.

Activities within planned events are mostly related to the theme (such as performances at a concert, matches in a competitive sport event or assemblies during a conference). Individual participants and guests at events engage in their own activities, often unscripted and personal (e.g., talking, eating, bodily functions, singing along, cheering, viewing, contemplating) and these also contribute to the overall event experience. Activities at events are influenced by interactions among the setting, the programme and other people.

But the boundaries between activity and event are not really absolute. From the individual's perspective, engaging in a mountain climb, or any other adventure pursuit, might be a planned 'event' with a purpose, design (lots of preparations including a route to the summit), tight schedule, specific setting and the company of others. In this sense the activity of mountain climbing embodies specific events for the participants, but they are highly personal and not open to the public. Many people presumably reflect on their lives and careers as a series of events, and among them will be planned *rites de passage*.

Typology of Event Forms

Cultural Celebrations

'Celebration' has several connotations:

- A joyful occasion; special festivities to mark some happy event; a joyous diversion; to observe a day or event with ceremonies of respect, festivity or rejoicing (such as Thanksgiving celebrations).

- Solemnization (the public performance of a sacrament or solemn ceremony with all appropriate ritual, such as to celebrate mass or a marriage).
- To extol, praise or acclaim.
- To make widely known.

Synonyms include: to commemorate, honour or distinguish.

We define 'culture' later, in the section on cultural anthropology, but at this point we can say that 'cultural celebrations' are solemn or joyous events that have cultural meaning. They may include many other types of planned event, but are separated from entertainment by the cultural values being expressed.

Consisting of festivals, carnivals, heritage commemorations, parades and religious rites and rituals, the study of cultural celebrations draws heavily from cultural anthropology. This is one of the oldest and best established approaches to Event Studies, focusing on the roles and meanings of festivity and celebration in, and across, cultures.

Festivals

I prefer this simple definition, Festivals are . . .

themed, public celebrations

although it does not do justice to the richness and diversity of meanings attached to 'festival'.

Falassi (1987: 2), in *Time Out of Time: Essays on the Festival*, said that festivals were a social phenomenon found in virtually all human cultures. He said that in modern English the term has several meanings:

- A sacred or profane time of celebration, marked by special observances.
- The annual celebration of a notable person or event, or [of] the harvest of an important product.
- A cultural event consisting of a series of performances of works in the fine arts, often devoted to a single artist or genre.
- A fair.
- Generic gaiety, conviviality, cheerfulness.

Falassi (1987: 2) went on to say that in the social sciences 'festival' means . . .

> . . . *a periodically recurrent, social occasion in which, through a multiplicity of forms and a series of coordinated events, participate directly or indirectly and to various degrees, all members of a whole community, united by ethnic, linguistic, religious, historical bonds, and sharing a worldview. Both the social function and the symbolic meaning of the festival are closely related to a series of overt values that the community recognizes as essential to its ideology and worldview, to its social identity, its historical continuity, and to its physical survival, which is ultimately what festivals celebrate.*

The term 'festival' is much overused and misused. Some so-called festivals are nothing more than commercial promotions or parties. Indeed, 'festivity' is often used in the same way as 'having a good time'. Many community or broadly programmed festivals seem to forget what they are celebrating, or at least they do not interpret the meaning. In this sense 'festival' has often been reduced to a public entertainment programme, or a special time for fun and activities, rather than a celebration. Even arts festivals are guilty of using the term without paying attention to the meanings and how they are interpreted. Is it a festival if there is nothing more than a series of musical performances?

The reason sociologists and anthropologists have spent so much effort studying festivals is that they reveal much about culture and the functioning of societies. Turner (1982) recognized that people have a need to set aside times and places for celebration. Eagleton (1981), Hughes (1999), Ravenscroft and Mateucci (2002) thought festival and carnival provide a socially sanctioned forum for unleashing social tensions that would otherwise prove destructive. Ekman (1999), Farber (1983) and Geertz (1993) saw festivals as socially sustaining devices through which people express identities, connect with their place and communicate with the outside world.

Manning (1983: 4) saw festivals as providing a rich 'text', the reading of which provides much knowledge about local culture and community life. His view on 'celebration' was that it is 'performance' entailing the 'dramatic presentation of cultural symbols'. Celebration is also '. . . public, with no social exclusion', and is therefore is 'participatory' entertainment.

The festival experience has been studied in depth. 'At festival times, people do something they normally do not; they abstain from something they normally do; they carry to the extreme behaviors that are usually regulated by measure; they invert patterns of daily social life. Reversal, intensification, trespassing and abstinence are the four cardinal points of festive behavior' (Falassi, 1987: 3). This description, however, sounds more like 'carnival' than most contemporary 'festivals'.

The '. . . building blocks of festivals, can all be considered ritual acts, "rites", since they happen within an exceptional frame of time and space, and their meaning is considered to go beyond their literal and specific aspects' (Falassi, 1987: 3/4). 'The framing ritual that opens the festival is one of valorization (which for religious events has been called sacralization) that modifies the usual and daily function and meaning of time and space. To serve as the theatre of the festive events an area is reclaimed, cleared, delimited, blessed, adorned, forbidden to normal activities.' (p. 4). 'Similarly, daily time is modified by a gradual or sudden interruption that introduces "time out of time", a special temporal dimension devoted to special activities.'

Geographical research on festivals has viewed them as contested spaces where symbolic practices (a parade for example) are used to consolidate or resist prevailing norms and values. Richards (1996) said that in the 1970s festivals were recognized as being catalysts for arts development at the local level. Quinn (2006: 291) concluded that in Ireland, festivals over the last 35 years have expanded venue infrastructure, advanced community animation, developed local resources, business expansion in arts and related areas, and development of tourist audiences. 'Festivalization' is a term used in references to the strategic employment of festivals in place marketing and tourism promotion, as in 'the festivalization' of many historic cities (see, e.g., Richards, 2006). Not all observers see this as a good process.

Robinson et al. (2004) discussed how festivals, supposedly reflecting local and ethnic culture, have become part of cultural tourism. However, many are 'placeless' and created just for tourism, giving rise to questions about authenticity and appropriateness. The social meanings of festivals in contemporary economic and cultural life are therefore deserving of more attention. This discourse has been gaining momentum, as indicated in the book *Festivals, Tourism and Social Change* (Picard and Robinson, 2006). See also Richard's new book on cultural tourism (2006).

The British Arts Festivals Association provides a typology: music, dance, visual, theatre, film, comedy and street arts, and of course it is possible to sub-divide these themes. Other popular festivals pertain to science, food and beverages, literature and arts for children and the family. Festivals with heritage and religious themes are widespread. In North America 'community festivals' are very popular. These combined many elements of celebration, entertainment, spectacle and sports, often becoming hallmark events and tourist attractions. In essence they celebrate the community itself, provide a sense of identity, and hopefully foster social cohesion. Referring to a festival's explicit theme is not always the best indicator of its meanings.

Carnival

Carnival is a celebration preceding Lent and is associated with feasting, costumes, parades and revelry. Mardi Gras, or Fat Tuesday, is the last day within carnival season. People go to carnivals and Mardi Gras events for fun, play and revelry (even debauchery), enhanced or manifested through role reversals in masquerading, parades and costume balls. People love to dress up (or down), have a party, and suspend the social norms and even laws that govern everyday life.

Turner (1974) and other anthropologists and sociologists have paid considerable attention to carnivals, often distinguishing between the 'sacred' elements of traditional, religiously grounded festivals and the 'profane' side of carnivals. Carnival remains a popular subject for academic researchers, including recent books by Riggio (2004) on carnival in Trinidad, and by Harris (2003) on folk theology and performance associated with carnivals. Nurse (2004) reported on the Trinidad Carnival from the points of view of tourism and the 'cultural industry'.

In Europe, carnival remains a strong tradition in many countries, especially where Roman Catholic populations are large, and the Federation European Carnival Cities (FECC) (www.carnivalcities.com) is the related professional association. According to FECC there are at least nine types of European carnival, including the Samba or Caribbean form that is popular in the New World, including Rio de Janeiro.

Carnivals have a very long history. They can have distinctive styles, but tend to feature masquerade or costume balls, parades, theatrical productions, feasting and partying. From the Carnival of Venice website comes this reminder:

> *The Carnival in Venice is no 'goof', no 'consumerist ceremony' as some people complain, but sincere, won-*
> *derful heartfelt tradition that goes back in time almost a millennium, and despite its age, still shows its vital-*
> *ity to whom participates to it in person or in spirit.*

Carnival continues to evolve. In cold climates 'winter carnivals' are flourishing, such as Quebec's Winter Carnival which has become the city's hallmark event. 'Midsumma Carnival' in Melbourne, Australia, is an example of the numerous gay and lesbian Mardi Gras or Carnival events held around the world, many of which have become major tourist attractions (Pitts, 1999). This quote is from the 'Midsumma' website:

> *Carnival transforms Treasury Gardens into the queerest park in Australia. Carnival is wearing her brand*
> *new Treasury frock so come and tell her she's beautiful and experience a spectacular hub of queer games, hot*
> *music, bump-your-booty dancing and sporting prowess as we celebrate the closing of Midsumma.*

Heritage Commemoration:

These are memorial services, specific ceremonies or broader events (even festivals) designed to honour the memory of someone or something. Most commonly they are marked in the context of national days, birthdays of kings and queens, battles or wars (through Remembrance Days). Programmes must include something symbolic and interpretive about the event or persons being remembered.

'Heritage' is open to interpretation, often being a politically charged term. It means more than historic, and implies a value judgement as to what is important. In Canada, the federal government department called Canadian Heritage '… is responsible for national policies and programmes that promote Canadian content, foster cultural participation, active citizenship and participation in Canada's civic life, and strengthen connections among Canadians'. Their portfolio includes 'Celebrate Canada!' (including Canada Day festivities), bidding on and hosting major sport events, museums and galleries, Canada's participation in world's fairs and the Canada Council for the Arts. The Council supports many arts and multicultural festivals, travel for artists and the Cultural Capitals of Canada award.

From the Canadian Heritage website (www.pch.gc.ca):

> *Canada Day is an opportunity to gather in our communities, from coast to coast to coast, and to proudly celebrate all we have in common. It is an opportunity to celebrate our achievements, which were born in the audacious vision and shared values of our ancestors, and which are voiced in nearly all of the languages of the world through the contribution of new Canadians.*
>
> *Canada Day is a time to celebrate the heritage passed down to us through the works of our authors, poets, artists and performers. It is a time to rejoice in the discoveries of our scientific researchers, in the success of our entrepreneurs, and to commemorate our history – a history in which each new chapter reveals itself to be more touching, more fascinating than the last.*

Heritage commemorations have not received much specific attention from events scholars, so you have to look in the general anthropological and sociological literature, and in the growing body of studies in cultural and heritage tourism for research and discussion.

Parades and Processions

The expression 'everyone loves a parade' seems to be a universal truth, and age-old. Parades are usually an organized, celebratory procession of people, and the most popular ones are mobile spectacles, entertainment and celebration. As a planned event, parades and other processions are unique in that the entertainment, or other objects of the spectator's gaze, go past the audience in a dynamic progression. City streets are often the stage, and reclaiming them from vehicular traffic is part of the pleasure of viewing parades. They can be events all on their own, or part of broader festivals and sport celebrations. The experience should be one of joy and wonder (especially for children), merriment, socializing at a big scale, and appreciation of the arts, skills, symbols and heritage objects on display.

There are a number of important variations, including flotillas (of boats), cavalcades (of horses), religious processions (often with objects of reverence) and military marches including weapons of warfare. Some parades consist of just people, but frequent elements include floats, marching bands, entertainment units (like dancers or flag-waivers) and important people (the parade marshal, beauty queens). In the History section of this book (Chapter 5) is a profile of one of the biggest and oldest parades ever recorded, and it leads one to conclude that nothing much has changed in thousands of years!

From a sociological perspective, Tomlinson (1986) found small-town parades to be full of imagery and symbolism reflecting community values like purity, beauty, humour, religion and politics. Parades are performances for both residents and outsiders. Another example of scholarship related to parades is the book *Macy's Thanksgiving Day Parade* by Grippo (2004).

Religious Events

Festivals and other celebrations often include religious ceremonies, but primarily religious events embody solemn rites and rituals, and are considered to be sacred within the context of specific religions. Some, like Mexico's Feast of the Dead, have become national holidays (literally, holy days). The Japanese 'Matsui' are a type of religious event, generally community-based, produced by volunteers and celebrating a variety of religious or spiritual themes.

Pilgrimage is a journey for religious or spiritual purposes; they reinforce collective religious and cultural values and generally focus on places and events of significance. Shackley (2001: 102) called them 'linear events' in which the journey might be as important as the destination in terms of visitor motivations and experiences.

Pilgrimage is a quest, a journey, and the experience of a sacred place. For many it is a duty. The entire pilgrimage can be conceptualized as a special event in a person's life, a rite of passage and a transforming experience, but there are often well-defined events associated with religious pilgrimages. The largest events are the Hajj in Mecca, attracting millions of visitors annually (the Saudi Arabian government imposes limits), and Kumbha Mela (mela means sacred site festival) in India which is held 4 times in every 12 years and was said to attract over 28 million pilgrims in 2001! (Singh, p. 228, in Timothy and Olsen, 2006).

Political and State Events

Any event produced by and for or by governments and political parties falls into this category. They always seem to be in the news, including the following examples:

- The G8 summit of leading industrialized nations.
- Royal weddings.
- Papal tours and related religious festivals.
- VIP visits (heads of state, etc.).
- Inauguration of the American President.
- Investiture of a Prince.
- Political party conventions.

Most political and state events are security nightmares. When leaders assemble or governments meet, or when a VIP tours, the media pay close attention – and so do people who want to protest or disrupt. It now takes a huge effort, at great cost, to mount these kinds of event, and increasingly there are unintended elements of entertainment associated with their spectacle and unpredictability.

Arts and Entertainment

Almost any activity, sport, artistic display or event can be viewed as 'entertainment'. Many forms of popular culture fit into this category, including music concerts, award ceremonies, theatre, art exhibitions and dance shows. The activities that are frequently part and parcel of cultural celebrations can certainly be viewed as entertaining, but the underlying purpose is different.

To be precise, it has to be emphasized that entertainment is passive, something one experiences for pleasure without the need to think about its cultural/historic significance or the values being expressed. In that sense, entertainment is largely in the realm of hedonistic consumption, not cultural celebration. It also explains why anything called 'entertainment' is a business, part of a huge industry, and often exists outside government social policy or policy for the arts and culture.

'Theatre' is a very broad category of planned event, encompassing drama, music and other performances usually scripted and in a 'staged' environment. Principles of theatre are regularly applied throughout the events world. We will examine Theatre Studies and types of theatre and performance later, but it is necessary here to distinguish between the major forms of art.

Performing Arts

By definition, almost all performances are planned events. There can be spontaneous performances by individuals and groups, such as singing and chanting, but we would normally not call these expressions of art either 'events' or 'entertainment'.

Performing arts traditionally involve people performing, such as musicians, singers, dancers, or actors, and audiences. In what is often called 'high culture' there is symphony, ballet, opera and traditional theatre for plays. In 'popular culture' we can add every form of musical concert (from jazz to new age, pop to hip-hop), dance (modern, tap, jazz) and alternative performances such as busking and illusion (magic). Film and television involve entertainment based on indirect (not in person) performances. Fashion could be considered part performance (the fashion show) and part visual art.

Other criteria for classifying arts events include:

- Professional versus amateur artists.
- Competitive versus festive.
- Mixed or single genre (e.g., just jazz, or many music types).
- Single or multicultural.
- Paid or free performances.

- Regularly scheduled, periodic or one-time.
- Temporary (i.e., visual art created with a limited life expectancy, or a one-time only performance) versus permanent.

Literature

Literature consists of the printed word, including books, magazines, even web-logs ('blogs'). We only call this 'art' if it is meant to entertain or is written in a style (like poetry) that results in an aesthetic approach of that particular style. Festivals and other planned events that feature poetry or written works are common, and these can include 'readings' that are in fact performances. Storytelling festivals are a variation.

Visual Arts

Painting, sculpture and handicraft are the most common visual arts, and touring or one-time 'shows' or 'exhibitions' of visual arts are planned events. 'Installation art' is a cross between an exhibition and a special event. Architecture is a visual art, and other media like computer games and the Internet have become popular for visual artistic expression. Any of these art forms can be the theme of planned events.

Business and Trade Events

The fundamental purpose of this type of event is to promote, market or directly engage in commerce, or otherwise meet corporate objectives. Farmer's markets, fairs and exhibitions (trade and consumer shows) are clearly based on marketed and selling.

World's Fairs, or Expos, represent national place marketing and foster international trade and tourism. Meetings and conventions are mostly related to the affairs of associations and corporations and might involve learning, morale-building and making policies. Individual companies produce or sponsor many types of events for both internal purposes (e.g., training) and with an external orientation (e.g., grand openings; exhibits and sales at festivals).

But we should not overlook the fact that corporate and other private events may also possess cultural significance (e.g., a ginseng fair in Korea becomes a major annual festival), or be of political interest (countries competing for attention and reputation at world's fairs). Many business and trade events are closely associated with hotels, resorts, convention and exhibition centres, and are thereby important elements in the tourism and hospitality industries. When events are developed and marketed as tourist attractions or destination image-makers they enter the realm of place marketed.

Meetings and Conventions

People assemble for many reasons, and have always done so, but according to Spiller (2002) the modern convention industry grew in concert with industrialization and trade in the late 19th and through the 20th centuries. A parallel movement was the growth of trade, professional and affinity-associations of all kinds. The first convention bureau in the USA was established in 1896 in Detroit, and at that time hotels were the main suppliers of venues.

'Conferences' are assemblies for the purpose of conferring and discussion, and should be small enough to facilitate interaction. Rogers (1998) said that conferences are often one-time only, with no tradition necessary. Academics hold numerous, themed conferences on specified topics or themes of broad interest within a field of study.

'Conventions' are generally large assemblies of people from associations, political parties, clubs or religious groups. Often convention delegates must go through a screening process. In Europe the term 'congress' is generally used instead of convention, although it typically connotes an international meeting.

Corporations and associations employ meeting or convention managers to handle their business get-togethers. Numerous meeting-planner firms exist, some of which have expanded into the special events field. Hotels, resorts and convention centres also employ professionals whose jobs cover the marketing and hosting of meetings and other events. Meeting Professionals International (MPI) distinguishes between association, corporate, scientific and incentive meetings, but 'meeting' is a generic term applicable to an assembly of people for any purpose. However, it usually connotes a small, private business affair.

The 'Corporate' segment is different in a number of ways. Companies hosting large numbers of meetings and conventions are likely to employ their own event managers or meeting planners, although large associations also do this. Corporate events are also likely to be more diverse than those initiated by associations, including training, hospitality, product launches, motivational assemblies, retreats, publicity events, grand openings and team-building exercises. There is a strong tendency for corporate clients to repeatedly use the same venues, and strong links have been forged between corporations and specific hotel and resort chains for this purpose.

Exhibitions (Trade and Consumer Shows)

Sandra Morrow (1997), in the book *The Art of the Show* (produced for the International Association for Exposition Management – IAEM) highlighted the core purpose of 'trade' and 'consumer' shows, saying they '… provide a time sensitive, temporary marketing environment where the buyer comes to the seller.'

'Consumer shows' are open to the public, often with an admission fee, and popular themes are linked to automobiles, travel and recreation, pets, electronics, gardening, arts and crafts or other hobbies. The producer, usually a private company, moves the show from place to place so that it is typically annual in any community. Venue owners might also produce their own. Manufacturers test new products at shows, retailers try to sell, and the consumers is searching for both ideas and entertainment.

'Trade shows' are usually for invitees only, based on specific business needs or association membership. Manufacturers or suppliers exhibiting at these events are trying to sell their products and services, or at least trying to inform potential customers. Common types are industrial, scientific and engineering or health care. Many include educational presentations or seminars. Frequently they are attached to association conventions, such as when suppliers to the events industry exhibit at a trade show attached to professional association meetings. 'International trade fairs' are a special class. Typically they are at the large end and targeted at a global or multi-country audience, and therefore are usually held in cities with major airports and exhibition halls.

The Center for Exhibition Research – CEIR (www.ceir.org) exists to provide data to the industry. According to CEIR, 'Attendees rate exhibitions as the number one most useful source of information with which to make a buying decision.' Professionals attend trade shows to learn about new products and meet face to face with suppliers. Often competitive products can be evaluated side by side, which helps explain why people go to consumer shows where many manufacturers exhibit side by side. And the entertainment and social aspects of shows must not be underestimated – attendees should have fun while learning.

Exhibitions have a seasonal rhythm, with the lowest month (in North America) for show-starts being December and the peak 2 months being (almost equally) October and March. Summer (July and August) constitutes the second low season. Part of the growth in venues is attributable to the shortfall of space during the two peak exhibition seasons.

Fairs

This is another word with multiple, and often confusing meanings. Dictionaries recognize the following:

- A gathering held at a specified time and place for the buying and selling of goods (i.e., a market).
- An exhibition (e.g., of farm products or manufactured goods, usually accompanied by various competitions and entertainments, as in a state fair); exhibitors may be in competition for prizes.
- An exhibition intended to inform people about a product or business opportunity.
- An event, usually for the benefit of a charity or public institution, including entertainment and the sale of goods (also called a bazaar).

The term 'festival' is sometimes used as a synonym of 'fair', but fairs have a long tradition of their own, as periodic exhibitions and markets. Waters (1939) traced the history of fairs from the earliest days of human barter and trade. Although North Americans associate the word 'market' with a place to do shopping, fairs were originally occasional markets. Every society had to have fairs, where goods were sold and traded at specific times, and usually in specific places that became markets or fairgrounds. The Latin word *feriae*, meaning holy day (which evolved into holiday) is the origin of the English word 'fair'. They were often scheduled on church-sanctioned holy days.

Although fairs were often associated with religious celebrations, and now usually contain entertainment and amusements, fairs have more to do with productivity and business than with themed public celebrations. Indeed, Abrahams (1987) argued that fairs and festivals are like mirror images. But he also suggested that in modern, urban society they have become almost synonymous because the old ways of production, as celebrated in fairs, have faded.

The IAFE website (International Association of Fairs and Expositions) provides some history. Most traditional fairs in North America are the numerous county and state fairs which are held annually on the same site, most of which continue to reflect rural and agricultural themes. Some are called 'exhibitions' or 'expositions' reflecting their educational orientation. Most fairs are operated by independent boards or agricultural societies, though many have close links with the host municipality. Typical elements of agricultural fairs and exhibitions include agricultural demonstrations and contests, sales and trade shows (farm machinery, etc.), amusements of all kinds, eating and drinking, parades and a variety of entertainment. Education is also a vital programme element, with close toes to 4H clubs as an example. This type of fair is often called a 'show' in the United Kingdom, Australia and New Zealand.

World's Fair

'World's Fair' has a very specific meaning, derived from an international agreement in 1928 and regulated by the Bureau International des Expositions (BIE) in Paris. BIE sets the policies for bidding on and holding world's fairs, which are often called Expos. Their nominal purpose has always been educational, with particular attention paid to technological progress, but some authors have described them as glorified trade fairs (Benedict, 1983).

There is a large body of literature on world's fairs, reflecting both their significance in economic and social terms and their popularity among expo lovers. Competition to host them is often fierce, as cities and countries see them as an opportunity to attract attention and tourists, typically in concert with urban renewal or other development schemes.

World's fairs are almost always accompanied by controversy owing to their large costs and environmental and social impacts. Governments have shamelessly used them (and other mega-events) for their own purposes, leading Hall (1992) to call them political tools. Most of them have generated a permanent built legacy (especially symbols like the Eiffel Tower) through planned urban renewal or development, while heavy tourism promotion has not always succeeded in generating sufficient attendance. Nostalgia for world's fairs is rampant, judging by websites devoted to their images and trading in memorabilia. Some, like Montreal's Expo '67, achieved iconic status – it will always be remembered as a nation-defining event (and one that left Montrealers with decades of debt).

Education and Scientific Events

Often considered a sub-set of business and trade events, these are nevertheless different because of their emphasis on creating and exchanging knowledge. Academic and professional symposia, and conferences on specific themes are the main components of this category of planned event, although numerous small, private meetings are also held for these purposes.

Education, including participative styles as well as demonstrative training, is the hallmark experience of these events. But that is no reason why they should not also be social and fun events. It is obvious that most people attending scientific and academic conferences are searching for knowledge, but equally that might be networking and socializing with old friends and colleagues. This is likely to be an age-related variable.

Sport Events

'Sport' is a physical activity involving large muscle groups, requiring strategic methods, physical training and mental preparation and whose outcome is determined, within a rules framework, by skill, not chance. Sport occurs in an organized, structured and competitive environment where a winner is declared. (Government of British Columbia, Sport Branch)

By definition, sport events are the actual games or meets during which sport activity occurs. There are many sport event formats (see, e.g., Solomon, 2002), and one classification is the following:

- Professional or amateur.
- Indoor or outdoor (and other differences in their need for special venues).
- Regularly scheduled (league play, plus playoffs or championships) or one-time (exhibition or friendly matches).
- Local, regional, national or international in scope.
- For participants, for spectators, or both.
- Sport festivals (a celebration of sport, often for youth, involving many sports) single- or multi-sport events.

Another classification approach is to look at the format of sport events:

- The regularly scheduled game, race or competition (in a league).
- Scheduled tournaments and championships (for leagues or invitationals).
- One-off sport 'spectaculars' (media or spectator oriented).
- Exhibition games with touring or invited teams.
- Sport Festival (emphasis on celebration and usually youth).
- Multi-sport events (e.g., Olympics; Masters Games),

This is an enormous category, given the huge number of sport events occurring around the world all the time, not to mention the increasing diversity of sports and forms of sport event. The influence of the media has been profound, creating a whole category of 'media events' that probably would not otherwise exist.

In their book *The Ultimate Guide to Sport Event Management and Marketing* (1995), Graham et al. noted there were literally millions of jobs in sports in USA, including a growing number specific to the production, managing and marketing of events. These authors argued (p. 8) that sport events and other special events share commonalities, including their service orientation, the incorporation of celebration and drama, media coverage and similarities in organizing and operations. Motivations of customers and travellers might also be similar, especially with regard to the ritual of attendance and related traditions. Traditional sport events like the Olympics always incorporate ceremonies and festivals, and it has now become commonplace to build a programme of special events around a sport meet to create a festival or special event with heightened appeal.

Sport event management has been the subject of several books, including *Strategic Sports Event Management: An International Approach* by Guy Masterman (2004), *The Sports event Management and Marketing Playbook* by Supovitz and Goldblatt (2004) and Jerry Solomon's (2002) book *An Insider's Guide to Managing Sporting Events*. Sport events are also frequently considered in books and research on sport tourism, including the book *Sport Tourism* by Turco et al. (2002). A social science perspective on the study of the Olympics is available in the book *The Olympics* from Toohey and Veal (2nd edn 2007).

Recreational Events

Recreational events are generally produced by parks and recreation agencies, non-profit organizations and affinity groups (like churches, schools and clubs) for non-competitive reasons, and are often playful in nature. Hence we need social-psychology, play and leisure theory to help understand the event experiences and their benefits.

Such events might be informal in their production and management, even self-organized by groups. If only individuals are involved, we will have to call it 'activity' and not an event. Examples of recreational events are really unlimited in number and scope, from card games to pickup football, from dance and exercise classes to impromptu concerts. Many of them will not meet our definition of 'special', as they are regularly scheduled and hardly unique, while others are at the margin in terms of being planned versus spontaneous.

Private Events

Every life is marked by *rites de passage*, varying enormously across cultures, and these are all a form of planned event. From the industry perspective they are often termed 'functions', when held in venues that cater to individual and small-group clients. From weddings to birthday celebrations, *bar mitzvahs* to funerals, holiday theme parties to church socials, they might require professionals or be entirely arranged by the participants. The experience is both personal and social, with multiple meanings possible. Most can be considered celebrations in which a theme and emotional stimulation are essential.

Quite a few practitioner-oriented books have been devoted to the planning and design of weddings, parties and other private functions. Weddings are such a universally important event that they have become big business and the subject of serious study (e.g., the book *Cinderella Dreams: The Allure of the Lavish Wedding*, by Otnes, 2003). Shone and Parry (2001) in their book *Successful Event Management* provided details of the UK wedding 'industry'.

The Reunion Network (www.reunionfriendly.com) claims there are 10,000 reunions annually in USA, including those produced by the military, schools, churches and affinity groups. Who knows how many private, family reunions are held? Also see the venue, hotel and restaurant management literature for details and cases of banquets, parties and other events held in formal settings.

Events at the Margin

Let's examine some events that are at the margins of what we mean by 'planned event'. The purpose is to show that definitional boundaries are often blurred, and that 'planning' is a matter of degree. Each event certainly creates a novel experience, and some are completely self-created experiences.

Flash Mobs, Guerrilla Gigs, Pillow Fight Clubs and Santacons

These events are somewhat anti-establishment, even anarchist in their origins or intent. They depend on personal communications devices to a large extent, which explains why they are a largely recent phenomena. The generic form appears to be the 'flash mob' (see www.flasmob.com, and a discussion on www.wordspy.com) which assembles in response to a message to be somewhere at a specific time, to do something strange or outrageous. According to Wikipedia:

When 'Bill' started the flash mobs, he saw it as a gag with an artistic dimension. He tried to make the mobs absurd and apolitical, in part because he wanted them to be fun, also because he didn't want anyone to see them as disrespectful of protests, or as a parody. The first modern flash mob was organized in Manhattan in May 2003, by an underground group called the 'Mob Project'.

Guerrilla gigging *is a technique that was first introduced by a Portuguese Hipop band called 1-uik project. It also became popular with punk rock, indie rock and noise rock bands in Britain and then the United States during the early to mid-2000s. It is similar in concept to a flash mob. Typically a guerrilla gig will be arranged very quickly, often in places not designed to accommodate live music such as basements, lobbies, fields, parking lots, etc. and will be announced through various website message boards as well as text messages and last minute flyering.*

Pillow Fight Club *is a fad that has emerged from the social phenomena of Flash Mobbing and was originally initiated by the founders of Mobile Clubbing, and is heavily based on the film/novel Fight Club by Chuck Palahniuk. They are now found around the world. Pillows are well hidden and at the exact pre-arranged time the battlers pull out their pillows and beat the stuffing out of each other with youthful exuberance in an absurdist scene. The pillow fights last only a few minutes.*

Pillow Fight Clubs meet spontaneously, connected by an idea and with a loosely shared objective. Their aim is to turn a regular public space into a pillow fight zone and a group of strangers into a community for the duration of the fight. They also aim to provide commuters amusement and bewilderment. Together with Flash Mobbing events, like Mobile Clubbing, their intention is to re-invent the way people view the use of public spaces. In many ways they are similar to a happening.

More recently, the CanWest News Service (*Calgary Herald*, Wednesday December 14, 2005, p. A3) described a movement called Santarchists (i.e., Santa plus anarchist) in these terms:

Intoxicated mobs of festively garbed Santas have been gathering in cities across North America since 1994. Their festivities, called Santacons, are a variation on flash mobs – the phenomenon in which people converge suddenly at a prearranged place, participate in some frivolous activity and then rapidly disperse. Jody Franklin was quoted by the Herald as saying the Santacons are 'a kind of post-modern revival of the Roman holiday of Saturnalia' (see www.santarchy.com).

These recently emerged social phenomena have a purpose, a place and a short time duration, but no real programme – only activity. Like the Santacons, they are usually frivolous, but some do try to make a point. Someone, or a group, has to initiate the flash mob, but there is no real organization or responsibility for it. If something goes terribly wrong, who gets the blame?

I can understand the fun nature of these events, and their value as performance art or as protest tools, but am particularly struck by the assertion, made in Wikipedia, that some flashmobbers are trying to reinvent public spaces. This is something like the 'valorization' process used to turn settings into temporary festival and event spaces, only the goal of flashmobbers is presumably to show that the space 'belongs' to the people or perhaps the purpose is to demonstrate that any space can be made festive or act as a performance setting.

Protest! Demonstrate! Riot!

It seems that not a political or economic summit goes by without protests and even riots, and often they appear to have been orchestrated. In fact, they are planned events. The website *www.ran.org* provides advice on how to organize a demonstration, and offers the opinion that:

> *The people's right to peaceably assemble and to 'petition the government for a redress of grievances' is one of the most important freedoms guaranteed by the Constitution's Bill of Rights. Protests are said to be some of the most effective ways to show support or draw people to a cause, or at least attract attention by those in power.*

Marches and demonstrations have a long social history, accompanying every war, union-company conflict and political movement. Currently, a favourite rallying cry is 'anti-globalization', which appears to attract many diverse interest groups. Common types of protest activities include:

- Vigils: tend to be solemn and reflective.
- Picket lines: marked by chanting, marching, holding up signs, blockading entrances to factories.
- Marches: a large march, like a parade, can have public entertainment value, as well as being a show of strength.
- Nonviolent civil disobedience: by definition these are illegal, and often consist of sit-downs and chaining people to objects; participants expect to get arrested, so involving celebrities will maximize media coverage.

Chapter Summary

The world of planned events is diverse, exciting and presents limitless creative possibilities. But among all the types of events, and even considering all their functions and meanings, there are commonalities that are at the core of Event Studies. This chapter examined the nature of planned events, with some emphasis on their temporal and spatial dimensions. By looking at a number of 'events at the margin', such as flash mobs and guerrilla gigs, we observed that planned and unplanned events can embody similar activities and experiences, which help us understand human events in general.

A typology based on event form was presented, and the main types discussed, and this classification is based largely on their form. These types of events are actually 'social constructs' that emerged through tradition and common expectations of what, for example, a festival or convention consists of. By referring to their functions, a number of events were identified – such as iconic, hallmark and mega – that can actually describe many types of event. It was argued that events cannot easily be classified by reference to experiences, because multiple experiences are possible within any event form.

In reviewing each of the main types of planned event, from cultural celebrations to private functions, we introduced some important clues about the nature of the event experiences, their multiple meanings, and how they are designed and programmed. Later chapters explore these topics in greater detail. Also note that the discussion of festivals in particular introduces important concepts, especially ritualistic behaviour, that are important within cultural anthropology and are utilized later in our conceptualization of the 'planned event experience'.

Study Questions

- Define 'event' and 'planned event'.
- What are the inherent temporal and spatial dimensions of events?
- Explain how form, function and experience might be used to classify events (i.e., typologies), and problems associated with each approach. Give examples.
- Why are the planned events in the typology used in this chapter referred to as 'social constructs'?
- Describe the essential differences between each major type of planned event, including any fundamental differences in experiences and programmic elements of style associated with them.
- Why should Event Studies also be concerned with unplanned events and 'events at the margin'? Give some examples to compare planned and unplanned events.
- Does 'scale' matter in the study of planned events?

Further Reading

Falassi, A. (ed.) (1987). *Time Out of Time: Essays on the Festival*. Albuquerque: University of New Mexico Press.

Fenich, G. (2005). *Meetings, Expositions, Events, and Conventions: An Introduction to the Industry*. Upper Saddle River NJ: Pearson.

Morrow, S. (1997). *The Art of the Show: An Introduction to the Study of Exhibition Management*. Dallas: International Association for Exhibition Management.

Rogers, T. (2003). *Conferences and Conventions: A Global Industry*. Butterworth Heinemann: Oxford.

Rogers, T., and Davidson, R. (2006). *Marketing Destinations and Venues for Conferences, Conventions and Business Events*. Butterworth Heinemann: Oxford.

Toohey, K., and Veal, T. (2007). *The Olympic Games: A Social Science Perspective*. Wallingford: CABI.

Turner, V. (1982). *Celebration: Studies in Festivity and Ritual*. Washington D.C.: Smithsonian Institution Press.

Chapter 3

Foundation Disciplines: Part One

Learning Objectives

■ Understand the nature of, and contributions made to Event Studies by these foundation disciplines:
  - anthropology
  - sociology
  - cognitive psychology
  - environmental psychology
  - social psychology.
■ Be able to apply theories, methodologies and research techniques from these disciplines to event-related problems.

Introduction

Our model of Event Studies revealed how foundation theory is needed to help us understand event experiences and meanings, outcomes, management, antecedents and choices, patterns and processes. The overview of planned events in the previous chapter has already introduced a number of disciplinary perspectives on Event Studies, especially some of the sociological and anthropological dimensions of the study of celebration and festivity.

The intent of the next three chapters is to make readers aware of the nature of foundation disciplines, and especially to demonstrate their specific theoretical and methodological contributions to Event Studies. Each section starts with a table that both defines the discipline and establishes its main contributions to the five main themes in Event Studies. Research Notes are used to demonstrate specific event applications from disciplinary perspectives, where possible.

There is no best or correct place to start, mainly because the disciplines of greatest interest and will depend on the problem or issue at hand, and how the researcher, planner or policy-maker wants to approach it. In this chapter we start with anthropology, sociology and psychology, plus sub-disciplines of environmental and social psychology. In the ensuing Chapter 4 we cover philosophy, religious studies, economics, management, political science and law. History, human geography and future studies are grouped together in Chapter 5.

Anthropology

Our biological origins and variations are the subject of 'physical anthropology'. Cultural evolution is the focus of archaeology, which specifically examines physical remains of civilizations and human artifacts. 'Anthropological linguistics' is the study of language through human genetics and human development, whereas 'linguistic anthropology' focuses on humans through the languages they use.

It is 'cultural anthropology' that makes the greatest contribution to Event Studies, and indeed we have to thank this discipline for much of our existing understanding of festivals and celebrations in particular, and for providing the theoretical framework of rituals and liminality that we adapt to planned events in general (Figure 3.1).

Sometimes cultural anthropology is called social or 'sociocultural anthropology', or 'ethnology'. Sociology and anthropology developed as disciplines at the same time

Anthropology • The study of human origins and evolution, language and culture.	Nature and meanings; the event experience	Antecedents to attending events	Planning and producing events	Outcomes and the impacted	Processes and patterns
Cultural anthropology • Studies the nature, functions and systematic comparison of cultures. • Studies social organization with a focus on symbolic representations of culture	• Cultural importance and meanings of celebration • Rituals • Symbolism • Pilgrimage • Liminality • Authenticity	• Cultural influences on attending events (e.g., consumerism, traditions, perceived freedoms)	• Cultural programming • Culturally defined elements of style	• Cultural impacts (e.g., host–guest interactions; cultural authenticity; sustainability of traditions)	• Cultural trends and forces (e.g., values; globalization) affecting events • Cultural policy

Figure 3.1 Anthropology.

and share a common interest in social organization (Schultz and Lavenda, 2005: 8). Both disciplines study social structures and institutions, while anthropologists are the ones who examine 'symbolic representations' of culture like art and myths. Ethnology is also defined as the systematic comparison of cultures.

Culture

Its core phenomenon is 'culture', which Schultz and Lavenda (2005: 4) defined as '… sets of learned behaviour and ideas that human beings acquire as members of society.' Culture is learned and passed on, it evolves, and takes on different dimensions reflected in belief systems, symbols, and ritualistic behaviour. Culture is '… central to the explanations of why human beings are what they are and why they do what they do' (Schultz and Lavenda 2005: 4). 'Holism' is the principle of studying cultures as complex systems, the implication being that the study of events has to be placed in a very broad context. For example, events may contain highly symbolic representations of importance to a culture.

Culture, and its study, is often contested – even becoming highly political or involving conflict. Who speaks for disenfranchised groups, and how does history judge the winners and losers of war or colonization? Indeed, some anthropologists have a mission, or at least a particular agenda. Mitler et al. (2004), in their text on cultural anthropology, insist that this discipline should be 'relevant' to contemporary issues. Their book takes an applied approach with emphasis on understanding social inequality and cultural change processes. Some of the issues they examine include poverty and gender inequality. Issues raised by globalization are relevant to cultural anthropologists, and this could include the 'homogenization' of events through corporate sponsorship and media manipulation, or a loss of authenticity because of adopting a tourism orientation.

Many people distinguish between 'popular' and 'high culture'. It is not a clear differentiation, and some would deny it exists, but from both public policy and practical marketing perspectives there are important differences. 'High' culture is associated with theatre, opera, ballet, the symphony, serious literature, art galleries and museums, all of which tend to be considered national assets and thereby attract government subsidies. They are associated with the cultural elite, sophistication, and of course people with money. In contrast, 'popular' culture consists of what ordinary people prefer and do. This is the realm of consumerism, with private companies providing sport, entertainment, various communication media, and many other 'products' for sale to the masses. There is more standardization of products and experiences in this realm of popular culture; most people relate to it on a day-to-day basis without event thinking about it as representing 'their' culture.

Because of these often invisible distinctions, we have festivals that are mostly entertainment for popular consumption, and festivals that are high-brow celebrations of culture. When private companies provide money to popular culture it is generally in the form of sponsorship, with expected marketing benefits, while giving money to 'high' culture can be viewed as philanthropy and being a good corporate citizen.

Rites and Rituals

Cultural anthropologists have often focused their attention on cultural expressions within the realm of planned events, specifically festivals and carnivals. Rites and rituals are full of cultural meaning and can also be viewed as building blocks (or programmic elements of style) for event programmers. Rituals and rites are 'patterned forms of behaviour' (Mitler et al., 2004: 293), or prescribed ceremonies. Many have religious or mythological significance, while others relate to politics and group identity. The terms 'sacred' and 'profane', or religious and secular are therefore often used to distinguish rites and rituals.

'Periodic rituals' include harvest festivals, and annual commemorations such as national anniversary days. It is always worth thinking about the themes of celebrations and what they symbolically stand for. 'Life-cycle rituals' are also called *rites de passage*. Persons and groups mark important life stages with ceremonies and parties, sometimes sacred and often secular. Turner (1969) detected three stages in many life-cycle rituals, namely separation of the individual from normal life (emotionally or symbolically, sometimes physically), transition (the 'liminal' stage where on might have to learn something new or perform specified acts), and finally re-integration (involving a welcome back, and new status). Later Turner applied the concept of liminality to pilgrimage, and the related concept of the 'liminoid' to carnivals.

'Rituals of Reversal' occur when normal social roles and behavioural standards can be turned inside out, such as during Carnival or Mardi Gras. The masquerade, wearing masks at balls or in parades, is one way people try to protect their identity, or dignity, when the act up at carnival time. Falassi (1987: 4–6) discussed the above types of ritual and several others. His full classification is as follows:

- *Rites of purification*: a cleansing, or chasing away of evil, such as practiced in Japanese Matsuri, by fire or holy water, sacred relics and symbols.
- *Rites of passage*: marking a transition from one stage of life to another, such as initiations.
- *Rites of reversal*: through symbolic inversion, including the common wearing of masks and costumes at carnivals, gender mis-identification, role confusion, using sacred places for profane activities.
- *Rites of conspicuous display*: objects of high symbolic value are put on display, perhaps touched or worshipped; often used in processions where the guardians and social/political elite display their powers.
- *Rites of conspicuous consumption*: food and beverages are consumed in feasts; gifts are showered upon guests (gift or 'loot bags' at parties and award ceremonies; the ancient Potlatch of West-Coast natives); sacred communion is a special form.
- *Ritual dramas*: the retelling of myths and legends, or historical re-enactments.
- *Rites of exchange*: from commerce (buying and selling) to gift exchanges and charitable donations.
- *Rites of competition*: games, sports, contests of all kinds, either highly unpredictable and merit based or ritualized and predictable.
- *De-valorization rites*: take place at the end of the event. Normal time and space has to be restored, as in closing ceremonies and formal, informal farewells.

Rituals and related symbolism are found in most planned events, and they can be used as programmic elements of style. For example, venues dedicated to conventions or exhibitions have to be transformed in order for an event to occur. At the very minimum the entry has to be demarcated and regulated so that one first 'arrives' at the correct time and place, then is allowed entry to the event. It is already defined as a special place, but the growing rumble of conversation, a flurry of preparations, anticipation of the program, the seeing and being seen, all add to the sense of specialness in time.

If the meeting planners or venue staff have done even a basic job of preparation there will also be a realization that the empty space has been transformed: symbolism (flags, corporate banners, association logos, sponsors' exhibits), music, food and beverages, other sensory stimulation (lighting, smells), the grand entry of speakers and dignitaries, and finally the opening ceremonies are all expressions that this particular event is only for these special attendees. While the opening words of a meeting or convention might not carry the cultural weight of a religious blessing (i.e., 'sacralization'), they do perform the 'valorization rite' that conveys clearly 'we have begun' and this place, empty a few minutes ago, is now ours to enjoy.

Research Traditions and Methods

Both 'deductive' (the formulation and testing of hypotheses in a positivistic tradition) and 'inductive' (use of grounded theory, or based on discourse) methodologies are employed in cultural anthropology. We will get back to these in Chapter 13 where we take a detailed look at research paradigms, methodologies and methods, but at this point let's examine the research tradition most associated with cultural anthropology.

Ethnography

Field work, often an ethnographic description and analysis of one cultural group, still dominates cultural anthropology. Traditional 'ethnography' involved living among peoples to gain a deep understanding of their culture and ways of life. Although the early development of this discipline was marked by a distinct bias, separating 'civilized' cultures from the 'primitive', today's anthropologist values 'cultural relativism' – the belief that cultures should not be studied, let alone de-valued, through the lens of their own belief system.

The contemporary literature is rich with anthropological studies of festivals in particular, such as Cavalcanti's (2001) ethnographic study of the Amazonian Ox Dance festival, published in the journal Cultural Analysis. In the following research note, Philip Xie uses participant observation and other methods to examine tourism and cultural performance among traditional people in China.

Research Note

Xie, P. (2003). The bamboo-beating dance in Hainan, China. Authenticity and commodification. Journal of Sustainable Tourism, 11(1): 5–16.

Methodology consisted of fieldwork involving interviews with key informants including 102 dance performers at eight selected folk villages as well as with ethnic researchers. Participant observation was undertaken to gain greater understanding of the context and meanings attached to places. Government documents and scholarly publications were also employed, especially because the Chinese government has been developing and marketing cultural tourism as a reason to visit Hainan Island. Mass media reports were also surveyed, focusing on aboriginal tourism, with content analysis employed to asses the portrayal of aboriginal people, and related places and issues.

Xie documented how the government, tourism, tourists and Li communities had appropriated, promoted, and manipulated (to make it more entertaining) the traditional dance, and it had evolved with tourism development. Symbolic aspects remain, but original meanings were lost. Xie determined that the original ritual meaning of this dance has been turned into a celebration. It acquired new meaning and has become part of aboriginal cultural identity. Contrary to tourism being a negative force, Xie concluded that commodification of the ritual as a tourist-oriented cultural production had resulted in it becoming a self-perceived, authentic expression of the culture of the indigenous Li people. The dance is now viewed internally by the Li people as a source of pride and identity.

Xie also concluded that definitions of authenticity are relative rather than absolute. Different stakeholders judge differently what is authentic or not. In terms of cultural impacts, the staged performances in cultural 'villages' help keep mass tourism away from the home sphere of the Li people. Tourists should be able to gain a rich, accurate and entertaining understanding of their culture through the events. 'The sustainable development of ethnic tourism in Hainan requires the involvement of the Li to explain to visitors the history of the bamboo-beating dance and its symbolism, and uses the performances to represent more clearly the Li identity.' (14). Another important conclusion of this research was that training and empowerment of the Li would enable them to more fully participate in and benefit from tourism.

Ethics

A standard code of conduct has been adopted by the American Anthropological Association (www.aaanet.org). Ethical issues include protecting the confidentially of informants, and the risk that studying a group might change it. If the researcher believes in applied anthropology, then 'action research' might be appropriate. In action research the aim is to cause a change, and to evaluate and shape the change process while learning and theorizing from it.

Sociology

Sociology is concerned with interactions between people, or 'social life', including a focus on how relationships are patterned in the form of groups, organizations, and whole societies. Social rules and process are examined, social behaviour, and large-scale social processes. Social behaviour is mostly learned, and sociologists study the totality of behaviour as influenced by all facets of life including economics and political systems, family and friends, institutions and entertainment (Figure 3.2).

According to the online source *www.sociology.org.uk*, major themes in this discipline include the following:

- *Socialization Process*: learning how to become human and to behave in ways that accord with the general expectations of others (in short, to be socialized).
- *The structure of 'Social Life'*: values, norms, roles and status (social controls):
  - 'Values' are beliefs that we have about what is important, both to us and to society as a whole.

Sociology	Nature and meanings; the event experience	Antecedents to attending events	Planning and producing events	Outcomes and the impacted	Processes and patterns
• The study of human interactions, or social life; patterns of relationships including groups, organizations and whole societies – how they emerge and function	• Social meanings of events • Social experiences at events • Symbolic interaction	• Social factors influencing demand (e.g., family, race, religion, culture, community)	• Implications for design and crowd management • Organizational behaviour of event-producing bodies and stakeholders	• Impacts on social groups and society as a whole • Resident perceptions of, and attitudes toward events	• Social trends and forces (e.g., population and demographics, migration) that impact on the event sector • Social development policy • Diffusion of innovations

Figure 3.2 Sociology.

- – 'Norms' are expected, socially acceptable, ways of behaving in any given social situation.
- – 'Roles' are social roles we expect people to play.
- – 'Status' is earned or assigned.
- *Social Groups*: the nature of family, peers, institutions nations, communities of interest; relationships within groups.
- *Culture and Identity*: influencing factors on cultural identity include age, gender, ethnicity, and regionalism.
- *Subcultures*: groups sharing a particular way of life.

Research Traditions and Methods

Sociologists use the scientific method and have a long tradition of 'positivistic' methodology (see Chapter 13). However, there has also been a long tradition of 'humanistic sociology' which stresses understanding of cultural values, meanings, symbols and norms. Multi-cultural comparisons are important. Both quantitative and qualitative methods are used, as is ethnography – very much akin to cultural anthropologists. There are several clear perspectives or theoretical approaches that shape both research methodology and what is studied by sociologists. Alternative, competing traditions of research are now widespread in sociology (Veal, 2006).

Veal (2006) assessed the evolution of sociological research pertaining to leisure and tourism and concluded that the early modeling/prediction emphasis, based on large-scale social surveys and quantitative analysis (within the 'functionalist' tradition), had not worked well. More qualitative methods became fashionable in the 1970s and 1980s, with a shift towards learning more about why people did what they did, and what it meant to them, rather than just measuring and forecasting what they did. This era gave rise to research and theory development on leisure benefits and constraints.

Critical Social Theory

This approach starts with the premise that social 'reality' is historically constituted through social, cultural and political forces (Habermas, 1973). The role of the critical researcher is therefore to reveal conflicts and contradictions and help eliminate the causes of alienation or domination. According to 'critical theory' the structure of capitalistic society marginalizes certain people and removes choices from them, which of course flies in the face of leisure being defined in terms of freely chosen, intrinsically motivated uses of time. 'Conflict Theorists' emphasise conflicts in society, specifically between social classes, between men and women, and between different ethnic groups. The Marxist tradition has largely fallen out of favour, but it is obvious that many conflicts do remain.

Functionalism

From this perspective, everything in society has a purpose or function. The basic values of this perspective emphasize the idea of harmony and social consensus based around shared values. Functionalists are likely to interpret everything in terms of large-scale social structures.

Symbolic Interactionists

Within social psychology, a 'symbolic interactionist' concentrates on the way people understand one another. They tend to focus on the individual, looking in particular at the way we create the social world through our behaviour (rather than looking at how society creates the individual). A key issue is the set of symbols and understandings that have emerged which give meanings to interactions.

Leisure and work take on meanings from social interactions, so that what we mean by work or leisure is in part determined by our social lives. Certain events might connote either work (say, a conference) and others leisure (a concert or festival). As well, the 'festival' for many people is symbolic of culture, while the trade show is symbolic of commerce. These are social constructs in the same way that we expect planned events to have a certain form and take place in certain settings.

Two books by Erving Goffman (*The Presentation of Self in Everyday Life*, 1959; *Frame Analysis: An Essay on the Organization of Experience*, 1974) are of relevance to Event Studies. Goffman used the imagery of the theatre to show how people are social 'actors'. In any given social interaction there has to be an agreed upon definition of what is happening, otherwise there is no congruence between the 'performers'. 'Actors' usually foster impressions that reflect well upon themselves. In communication theory and sociology, 'framing' is a process of selective control over media content or public communication.

Framing defines how media content is packaged and presented so as to allow certain desirable interpretations and rule out others.

Social Capital Theory

Reciprocity and trust are the foundations of 'social capital', and to some extent these qualities of social life are found in all communities and societies. Where social capital is high, people are more likely to be polite, talk to strangers, interact as equals, and perform random acts of kindness. In other words, we 'invest' social capital in our community and expect others to do the same (this is similar to 'social exchange theory'). Voluntarism can be viewed as a form of social capital at the community level, as can community-based decision-making, informal business transactions and spontaneous celebrations.

Putnam (2004) placed more emphasis on benefits accruing to the community, while others (e.g., Bourdieu, 1986; Coleman, 1990) conceptualized social capital at the individual level. When a person develops a substantial 'social network' of friends, allies and collaborators, their social capital increases, and when 'invested' or 'spent' it can result in a variety of economic, social, psychological and emotional benefits. Some people pursue the accumulation of social capital through deliberate networking, while others acquire it unconsciously.

Social Network Theory

Analyzing social networks (see Freeman et al., 1992; Scott, 2000) is a very useful way to examine stakeholder relationships surrounding event policy and management. A 'social network' consists of individual 'actors' and the ties between them, either formal or informal. In one sense, it can be said that the more ties an actor has (e.g., the event organization), the more social capital it will accumulate. But, more importantly, the network itself gains capital and might assume a political life of its own, similar to the concept of a 'political market square' in which the actors negotiate to direct the future of a festival (see Larson and Wikstrom, 2001; Larson, 2002). Networks can be powerful determinants of policy and strategy.

Diffusion of Innovation Theory

Innovations, including both technology and ideas, are communicated through various formal channels and social networks (Rogers, 1995). Individuals and organizations do not equally adapt innovation, rather there are the 'innovators', 'early adopters', 'early majority', 'late majority' and 'laggards'. When it comes to innovations that can provide competitive advantage or increased effectiveness, it can pay to be the innovator or the early adopter, but of course there are costs and risk associated with being first.

In the events sector we can observe innovation and diffusion in terms of new types of events and how they spread globally, usually through the influence of mass media. It is also clear that event producers copy ideas, which to a degree can be good, but without systematic benchmarking (discussed later) this can simply lead to standardization. And if every city and destination pursues the same event tourism strategy, leading to 'festivalization', that has potentially negative consequences.

Innovation and diffusion are not necessarily good or bad, but understanding how it works is important in terms of strategy and marketing. In particular, marketers want to learn who will be the first to adopt their products and services, then spread the word to other potential customers.

Contributions of Sociology to Event Studies

Much of the pertinent sociological theory comes to Event Studies indirectly through leisure studies, and also through Social Psychology. Particular themes to explore in this discipline include:

- Societal trends and forces shaping values and leisure.
- Social change (e.g., globalization and homogenization).
- Life-stage influences on event interests and attendance.
- Population and demographic factors.
- Human ecology (crowds, fads, trends).
- Effects of family, gender, race, culture, community, social class on demand and behaviour.
- Virtual communities or brand communities (of considerable interest to sponsors and corporations owning events).
- Social behaviour at events; conflict theory.
- Deviance (certain types of events, deviant behaviour at events).
- Social costs and benefits (crime, prostitution, sport or art participation, civic pride, belonging and sharing, integration, cohesion).
- Economic development and social inequality (power structures reflected in events).

More specific applications to Event Studies can be reviewed within the following subfields.

Sport Sociology

Current research areas within sport sociology include: sport and socialization; sport and social stratification; sport subcultures; the political economy of sport; sport and deviance; sport and the media; sport, the body and the emotions; sport violence; sport politics and national identify; sport and globalization.

Environmental Sociology
This is the study of societal–environmental interactions, including the causes of environmental problems and their impacts, ways to solve problems, and even how conditions come to be viewed as problems (i.e., creation of social representations, such as 'mega-events are environmentally destructive').

Events and Urban Sociology
Mega-events in particular can have profound impacts on urban form and life, but the affects of many small events, individually and cumulatively, should not be overlooked.

Consider the following research by Harry Hiller:

Research Note

Hiller, H. (2000b). Toward an urban sociology of mega-events. Research in Urban Sociology, 5: 181–205.

Hiller's contention is that 'from street festivals, parades, and pilgrimages to riots, marches of resistance and demonstrations, such expressive and instrumental activities have been among the most observable aspects of urban social life.' In defining mega-events, Hiller says (p. 183): 'From the perspective of an urban analyst, any large-scale special event an be considered a mega-event if it has a significant and/or permanent urban effect – that is, if it is considered so significant that it reprioritizes the urban agenda in some way and leads to some modification or alteration of urban space which becomes its urban legacy.'

He assess mega-events as to their part in shaping urban processes, as change factors, and in that respect identifies and discusses roles: catalysts for change; land use changes; creativity in urban planning; mobilizing funds; supporting projects otherwise considered too expensive or ambitious; forcing an agenda by requiring completion at a set date; infrastructure improvements in select domains, like transport; producing signature structures which redefine urban space.

Hiller also examined mega-events through the lens of dominant urban sociology paradigms. The 'ecology paradigm' applies in the sense that major events generate substantial infrastructure investment that permanently alters the urban system, in effect initiating ecological changes. The 'political economy paradigm' links events to political decisions (particular referring to the elite groups who support such events), to capital investment and even globalization, and the distribution of costs and benefits. A 'growth machine' paradigm refers to the link between events and pro-growth coalitions.

Events and Rural Sociology
Robert Janiskee's studies (1980, 1985, 1991; Janiskee and Drew, 1998) of rural festivals revealed their importance in social life and tourism, as well as their seasonal and geographic distribution. Rural communities are particularly vulnerable to social disruption caused by tourism, or large influxes of new residents seeking amenities. On the other hand, events and tourism can help to foster community development and self-reliance. Events are one of the few tourism 'products' that even the smallest of

communities can produce, without large amounts of capital. However, the volunteer and leadership base might be inadequate for long-term sustainability.

Psychology

The study of the human mind, thought, and behaviour constitutes psychology. There are many sub-fields and specialized applications, such as you will encounter in education and interpretation (the 'psychology of learning') and 'industrial psychology' applied to management. There are also divisions in psychology, notably 'humanistic psychology', represented by the works of Maslow, which takes a phenomenological approach that is in direct opposition to the scientific or positivistic paradigm that dominates.

Psychology	Nature and meanings; the event experience	Antecedents to attending events	Planning and producing events	Outcomes and the impacted	Processes and patterns
• Explaining human personality and behaviour • The study of perception, memory, feeling, knowing and thinking	• Personal needs, motives, preferences • Perceiving and experiencing events • Abnormal behaviour	• Effects of age, gender, education, life-stage, income, on demand • Consumer behaviour	• Design for personal experiences and transformation • Implications for marketing and communications	• Impacts on personality, values, attitudes • Influence on future actions	• Emergence of 'experience economics' as a major force

Figure 3.3 Psychology.

In this section we examine two mainstream branches, 'cognitive psychology' and the psychology of personality, then we turn to two blended sub-disciplines of particular relevance to Event Studies: Environmental, and Social Psychology (Figure 3.3).

Cognitive Psychology

Mainstream psychology is largely positivistic and well known for using experimental research designs (both laboratory and field based). The dominant theoretical framework is 'cognitivism'. 'Cognition' involves the integration of memory, experience and judgement, derived from perception, to help us think about the world or about specific stimulants in the environment. Cognition therefore applies to how we perceive, think about, and make sense of stimuli or whole events.

Perception: Perception is the process of acquiring, interpreting, selecting, and organizing sensory information. How do sensory organs and the brain receive and interpret stimuli? People are not passive, they actively explore the environment and in many cases seek out specific forms of stimulation. People create 'mental models (or constructs)' to help with perception and knowledge creation. If we have no experience or 'mental map' as a frame of reference, we might not perceive a stimulus at all. Accordingly, the more experience we have with certain types of planned event experiences, the better we should become at perceiving and interpreting all their nuances.

Experience: Experience is more than perception – it requires exposure or involvement and has a transforming effect on the individual. The more we experience, presumably the better we should be at assimilating new knowledge (i.e., 'learning'). But experience can also change us holistically in terms of attitudes, values and personality, resulting in behavioural changes.

Memory: Memory entails encoding and storing, retaining and recalling information and experiences. We know that memories can be imperfectly formed, fade over time, and be lost or hard to recall. So what makes for a memorable experience? And how do memories, pleasant or otherwise, shape future behaviour?

Thinking: The higher-order mental processes we tend to call thinking include 'reasoning' (making sense of things), 'creativity' (or imagination, innovation), 'judgment' (such as determining right from wrong, dangerous from risk free), and 'problem solving' (i.e., solving a puzzle, figuring out how to navigate a space). Thinking is based on how we use stored knowledge and how experience has shaped our processes and abilities. Knowledge and experience hopefully leads to 'wisdom' (being 'wise' is a relative term, or a self-perceived quality) and to greater effectiveness in whatever we chose to do.

Personality

Psychologists speak of the 'big 5' personality characteristics or factors that are believed to '. . . differentiate individuals in a somewhat permanent way and across most if not all situations' (Mannell and Kleiber, 1997: 156). Personality as it affects leisure has been scrutinized, but little has been done to connect personality to event-related behaviour.

Extroversion: This factor includes traits such as assertiveness, gregariousness, and excitement seeking, leading to the label 'high-energy people'. Extroverted people often pursue sports and take risks. 'Introverts', in contrast, have a low threshold of arousal and do not need as much stimulation. They are more likely to play computer fantasy games. Studies have found that travel preferences and styles correlate with extroversion or introversion (Plog, 1972; Nickerson and Ellis, 1991). Extroverts are also sensation seekers who are more likely to participate in adventurous, intense activities, and want greater variety (Zuckerman, 1979).

Agreeableness: Traits associated with this factor include trust, straightforwardness, and altruism, and it is contrasted with hostility, indifference, and self-centredness. 'Agreeable' people seek social settings, and are more likely to volunteer. Self-indulgence and escape are more associated with low levels of agreeableness.

Conscientiousness: Order, dutifulness, achievement striving, self-discipline and deliberation are associated with this characteristic of personality. Managers might want people high on this factor as it is typically manifested in reliability, responsibility, and being organized. Stebbins (1992) thought that conscientiousness was associated with a strong goal orientation and 'serious leisure'. However, being high on this factor might also result in lower levels of spontaneity and higher compulsiveness. If one is low on this factor, impulsiveness and seeking immediate gratification are likely to result.

Neuroticism: A general tendency to experience distress is associated with neuroticism. Anxiety, hostility, depression and self-consciousness are likely to accompany this factor. Dislike of playful leisure experiences might result from being neurotic. They might get less pleasure and enjoyment from both individual and social experiences by reason of discounting the positive aspects of one's own life.

Openness to experience: This is associated with aesthetic sensitivity, the need for variety, and unconventional values, flexibility of thought, cultural interest and educational aptitude. Such people are likely to seek out sensory stimulation.

Mental Exercise

Who are the people you would attract to an adventure festival? What marketing messages would work best? Can whole families be adventurers? Consider all the big 5 personality factors.

Personality traits have been studied in leisure, although some researchers have concluded that personality has more of an influence on the extent of participation than on the choice of sport or activity (Mannell and Kleiber: 163). There is yet no research evidence to show the connection to planned events, but readers will see the possibilities for examining event-related behaviour and experiences in the context of the following personality dimensions:

- *Locus of control*: How important is it to perceive you are in control, have freedom to choose? Does this define your perception of what is leisure or enjoyable work?

- *Attentional style*: How do you typically process or deal with environmental and social stimuli? Can you easily get into the 'flow' of deep involvement in an activity or mental process?
- *Type A behaviour*: Some people are driven to compete and succeed, are always worried about getting things done, feel they are running out of time and so they get impatient with others. How can they relax? How do you get them to pay attention?
- *Playfulness*: Are you a playful person, also curious, creative, and joyful? Can males and females be playful together, or are there social constraints?
- *The autotelic personality*: These people '. . . are able to find intrinsic interest and enjoyment in almost everything he or she does.' (Mannell and Kleiber, 1997: 174).
- *Shyness*: Shy people may feel the lack control over their lives and have low social competence, therefore have a more difficult time finding satisfying experiences.

Pertaining to leisure and travel, most psychological research is positivistic and deductive, and a great deal of it employs small experimental groups, often students, and self-completion questionnaires (Veal, 2006: 30). Consumer behaviour in general, and with regard to tourism in particular, is heavily dependent on theories from cognitive psychology.

Aggression and Anti-Social Behaviour

All too often celebrations and sport competitions get out of control, resulting in fighting, riots, or crime. Some protests are organized to achieve these results. Can events be designed and managed to prevent bad behaviour? Moyer (1968) identified seven forms of aggression, with the following pertaining to social behaviour:

1. *Inter-male aggression*: competition between males of the same species over access to females, dominance, status etc. (watch particularly for males who get drunk at parties and carnivals).
2. *Fear*-induced aggression: aggression associated with attempts to flee from a threat (e.g., crowd reaction to a gunshot, fight or fire at an event).
3. *Irritable aggression*: aggression directed towards an available target induced by some sort of frustration (e.g. impatience and stress caused by waiting or discomfort, resulting in overt hostility towards event organizers).
4. *Territorial aggression*: defense of a fixed space against intruders (as when gangs interact, or incompatible market segments are forced to mix).
5. *Instrumental aggression*: aggression directed towards obtaining some goal, maybe a learned response to a situation (the example of institutionalized rioting at some events).

'Ritualized aggression' helps explain our fascination with competitive team sports, especially when cities and countries are playing against each other. This can be useful in reducing tensions, but it periodically gets out of control and results in fights and rioting in the audience. A great deal of attention has been given to combating 'hooliganism' in soccer (see Stott et al., 2001).

Cognitive Dissonance Theory

Festinger (1957) theorized that people seek consistency among their cognitions (i.e., their beliefs, attitudes and opinions). When there is an inconsistency between our actions and our cognitions, such as when we believe one thing but do not act accordingly, it is likely that we will change our attitudes in order to eliminate the uncomfortable dissonance. The alternative theories suggest that attitudes are more likely to change in response to incentives or through learning and reinforcement.

Environmental Psychology

Environmental psychology has considerable potential for enhancing Event Studies.

Environmental psychology	Nature and meanings; the event experience	Antecedents to attending events	Planning and producing events	Outcomes and the impacted	Processes and patterns
• Perception and cognition of natural and built environments • Environmental design • Wayfaring • Behavioural settings and environmental stressors • Personal space • Crowding	• How people perceive, make sense of, and value the event setting • Environmental cues as to appropriate behaviour • Feeling crowded or comfortable	• Preferences for certain environments • Fear of crowding and environmental risks	• Implications for event setting design and management (e.g., legibility; facilitating interaction, setting the mood, flow)	• Environmental factors directly impact on personal health, safety and satisfaction	• Environmental preferences and fears are culturally shaped and evolve • Event venue development, and use of places for events, constantly presents new opportunities and ideas about the environment

Figure 3.4 Environmental psychology.

It is an interdisciplinary field focusing on the perception and cognition of natural and built environments. Bell et al. (2001: 6) defined it as '... the study of molar relationships between behavior and experience and the built and natural environments.' 'Molar' means the whole is greater than the parts, or a *gestalt* approach. 'Units' of environment and behaviour are studied, such as the festival place, sport arena, banquet hall or conference centre. Specific topics include arousal, stimulation, stress, adaptation, approach–avoidance behaviour, environmental design, wayfaring, work and leisure environments (Figure 3.4).

The environment is viewed as both the context for behaviour, and as a determinant of behaviour. Environmental psychologists also examine the consequences of human behaviour on the environment. Taking a festival place as an example, environmental psychologists would look at how people interact with the setting, how it can be designed or modified to reflect its purpose. Specific considerations would include capacity and crowding, personal space, noise and light, temperature and air flows. Would changing the lighting, for example, result in a more subdued audience? Would music enliven the place? Of course, event designers often know the answers from experience, but environmental psychology uses experimental and other research methods to develop both practical solutions and general theories. Although laboratory experiments are sometimes used, more popular methods are field experiments, descriptive and co-relational studies, and simulations.

De Young (1999) noted these important environmental psychology research themes:

- 'Attention': how people notice the environment; response to environmental stimuli.
- 'Perception' and 'cognitive maps': how people image the natural and built environment; formation of mental maps.
- 'Preferred environments': people tend to seek out places where they feel competent and confident, places where they can make sense of the environment while also being engaged with it.
- 'Environmental stress' and 'coping': common environmental stressors include noise and climatic extremes; coping with stress can involve a change in physical or social settings, or seeking to interpret or make sense of a situation.

The 'Integrative Model of Environmental Psychology' from Bell et al. (2001: 21) can be adapted to event studies (see Figure 3.5). This model provides an overview of environmental psychology topics and their inter-relationships. We start with environmental conditions, which for events means purpose-built venues or sometimes natural settings. Human–environment interactions are influenced both by biological (e.g., our need for occasional solitude, or the fear of heights) and learned factors (e.g., we are taught to respect nature or to show respect to others' property). Then we have to consider perceptions of the environment, or how we employ our senses to detect and give meaning to conditions in the setting (this is cognition).

'General effects of the environment' on behaviour include the study of sensory stimulation through noise, light, smell and colour, the effects of general environmental conditions (weather, pollution), and impacts of social interaction (personal space and crowding).

Closely linked to the general factors are the 'behavioural and experiential influences' of specific event settings. Their design, programming and management are explicitly

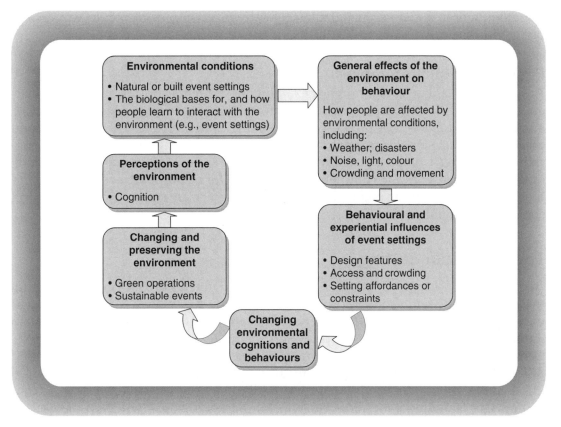

Figure 3.5 Environmental psychology and planned events. Adapted from Bell et al (2001).

intended to create, suggest or facilitate desired moods, behaviours, and experiences. We need to examine all the common and unusual event settings, from sport arenas to parks, from convention centres to city squares. How does each factor alone and in combination with others affect, for example, the behaviour and mood of an audience at a concert? We need to be aware that event settings are often purpose-built, with their intended uses and appropriate behaviours known by convention, while some are unusual and have to be valorized for temporary event purposes. 'Setting affordances' and 'constraints' are those characteristics of the venue or place that suggest and/or allow for various activities and experiences, or which constrain them.

'Changing environmental cognitions' refers to learning from experience and the resultant changes in perceptions and motives. In terms of events this can encompass how people perceive and attach meaning to event settings and design elements. With education, event experiences can also lead to positive shifts in attitudes towards the environment, such as support for green operations and sustainable development. Finally, the interactions in this model include changes to cognition in general, or how we perceive our environment.

Environmental Preferences

According to Kaplan (1987), humans examine the contents and the spatial configuration of scenes. We have to process a lot of information gained by our senses, in a hurry. Kaplan showed that people prefer scenes or settings that are 'coherent', 'legible', 'complex' and contain some degree of 'mystery'. Legibility and mystery require more cognitive processing. Complexity and mystery together appear to stimulate involvement, or the desire to explore and comprehend the scene. Our responses to event settings and their design reflect certain predispositions, some of which are culturally influenced and some that are highly individual.

The Behaviour Setting

According to Barker (1968), places have culturally defined purposes and behavioural expectations. The setting and appropriate behaviour are perceived to be an integrated unit, or 'behavioural setting'. Outdoor settings are sometimes more ambiguous than indoor facilities, although this depends on many design and management factors. Certainly people attending a fair in an open area receive different 'cues' and exhibit different behaviour when compared to those attending an art exhibit indoors. Do guests intuitively understand the norms and limits? To be effective, we rely on conventions, or 'standing patterns of behavior' in Barker's words, which in themselves are culturally determined.

Social Psychology

Mannell and Kleiber (1997: 25) wrote that 'Social psychology is the scientific study of the behaviour and experience of individuals in social situations.' Baron and Byrne (2000) defined social psychology as '... the field that seeks to understand the nature and causes of individual behaviour and thought in social settings.' For the purposes of Event Studies we can say that social psychology helps us understand the nature and causes of behaviour at events, based on studying the relationship between mind, groups and behaviours (Figure 3.6).

Much of what interests us from social psychology in the context of Event Studies will be considered in the Leisure Studies section of the ensuing chapter. At this point, however, let's examine several theoretical perspectives on human behaviour that will inform us about planned events.

Social psychology	Nature and meanings; the event experience	Antecedents to attending events	Planning and producing events	Outcomes and the impacted	Processes and patterns
• Studies the behaviour and experience of individuals in social situations	• Events as social experiences • Social role schemas • Subjective meanings attached to events through social interaction (i.e., events as social constructs)	• The influence of social reference groups • Social needs (seeking and escaping)	• Design for environment • Group interactions and dynamics • Creating a social atmosphere; belonging and sharing	• Satisfaction of social group needs	• Changes in family, social groups and social norms affect events

Figure 3.6   Social psychology.

Self-Determination Theory

This theory (see Deci and Ryan, 1985, 2000) is concerned with human motivation, specifically the development and functioning of personality within social situations. Of importance to leisure, it asks if people really engage in actions with a full sense of choice. The social environment can either assist or hinder a person's striving for growth, development, and a coherent sense of self through the satisfaction of basic human needs. When needs are unmet, or thwarted, people can suffer in terms of general wellbeing and psychological health.

Social Cognition and Social Cognitive Theory

Bandura (1977, 1986) provided a framework for understanding, predicting and even seeking to change human behaviour – individually and collectively. The theory states that behaviour is a result of the interaction of personal factors, behaviour and the environment. Social factors influence our beliefs and cognitive competencies. The environment modifies human behaviour, and in turn people seek to change it. The same set of stimuli might result in different behaviour because people construe the situation differently.

'Self-efficacy' is one of the key personal factors involved in Bandura's theory. It refers to a person's belief in their ability to perform a given behaviour successfully, which is different from a person's actual competency. Self-efficacy influences motivation and leisure behaviour. We are more likely to engage in activities that we think will produce desired outcomes, and this depends in part on our assessment of how well we can do the activity. Self-efficacy also affects how people respond to failure. In contrast, a person with high efficacy will attribute failure to external factors, where a person with low self-efficacy will attribute failure to low ability. People with high self-efficacy are generally of the opinion that they are in control of their own lives, while those with low self-efficacy see their lives as being shaped by others, or by destiny.

There are implications for education and training. Self-efficacy, or belief in one's own abilities, increases through mastery or success, and diminishes with failure. It can also be increased through example, by leaning from others (especially peers and respected persons) how to accomplish a task. Positive encouragement is also important.

'Social Cognition' is how we interpret, analyse, remember and use information about the social world. Baron and Byrne (2000: 80) said we employ schema which are 'mental frameworks centering around a specific theme that help us to organize social information.' 'Social role schemas' apply to our expectations for the behaviour of ourselves or others in social situations, such as how lecturers act at a conference, how the master of ceremonies behaves at a gala dinner, or what a group of performers does at a concert. Schemas affect three basic processes of social cognition:

1. *Attention*: what information we notice.
2. *Encoding*: what is stored in memory, and how.
3. *Retrieval*: how we get the information back for use.

Schema act as filters, saving us time and energy when we size up a social situation, and they are obviously based in part on experience and on cultural conventions. They have perseverance, generally lasting a long time. But they can also result in misconceptions and inappropriate behaviour if the cues we expect are not present or are misleading. They can have the effect of 'self-fulfilling prophecy' in that they can cause us to behave in ways that confirm them. We tend to notice only the cues consistent with our mental schemas, causing us to act in ways that confirm their validity.

Mental Exercise

Develop a 'schema' (perhaps through group discussion) about appropriate social behaviour of guests at a cultural performance; at a rock concert; at a business meeting. What are the standard 'cues' employed by event designers or managers to inform people about expected behaviour, in each of these settings? Now, suggest ways to manipulate those cues that would result in either guest confusion or improved understanding about appropriate individual or group behaviour.

Theory of Planned Behaviour

Originating with the work of Ajzen (1985, 1991), this very influential theory posits that behaviour is driven by 'behavioural intentions' (for example, 'I fully intend to go to that concert'). Intentions are a function of the person's (a) attitudes towards the behaviour, (b) subjective norms and (c) perceived behavioural control. The theory states that a person's intention to do something is the most immediate determinant of behaviour. 'Attitude' towards the behaviour is defined as the person's feelings about the behaviour (positive or negative), and this stems from beliefs concerning the possible consequences of the behaviour and the desirability of those impacts (e.g., 'I think rock concerts are cool places to meet and be with friends, and that is top priority for me'). 'Subjective norms' are the individual's perception of what others will think, such as if one's peers will approve of the behaviour (e.g., 'all my friends think the X concert is going to be the best, and I want to be accepted by them').

'Perceived behavioural control' refers to feelings of choice (including having skills, resources and the opportunity to do something). As in leisure constraint theory, people who perceive they do not have the skills, resources or opportunities are unlikely to form strong intentions to go to events.

'Theory of planned behaviour' applies only to un-coerced, rational behaviour, but not all event attendance or participation will meet those criteria. As we know, extrinsic motives also apply to many events, such as work and social obligations. Irrationality might enter into the decision to attend events when, for example, people are in very strange circumstances (such as foreign cultures) or suffering from altered mental states due to such factors as alcohol, drugs, stress, or illness.

Expectation Confirmation Theory

Oliver (1977, 1980) reasoned that consumer satisfaction is determined by the interactions of expectations and perceived performance, mediated through positive or negative disconfirmation between expectations and perceived performance. In other words, if the guest expects a high level of service, but perceives it to be poor, it will lead to dissatisfaction. A dissatisfied customer is unlikely to be loyal or to say good things about the service providers.

This theory lies at the heart of SERVQUAL and other approaches to defining and measuring satisfaction. Many researchers, however, believe that it is more practical and just as valid to measure 'post-hoc satisfaction', without a pre-measurement of expectations. Getz et al. (2001) used the 'post-hoc satisfaction approach' in evaluating a surfing event. One convincing argument is that many people show up at events without clear expectations of service or product quality, but they can always determine afterwards if they were satisfied or not. On the other hand, the more experienced the consumer, the more likely they are to hold firm expectations.

Social Exchange Theory

'Social Exchange Theory' (Hormans, 1958) suggests that social action is different from straightforward economic actions within a marketplace (i.e., buying and selling), because social actors expect and receive rewarding reactions. Resource exchanges (as well as the bestowal of prestige or support) are, in this context, the result of free, personal choice based on assessment of expected costs and benefits. People can feel pressure to give, but exchanges should balance out over time. The theory also embodies the concepts of power and dependency within relationships and social networks.

In the context of Event Studies this theory has been used to explain variation in resident perceptions of, or attitudes towards events. For example, people benefiting from event tourism will tend to be positive in their attitudes towards the event and its continuance, while people perceiving no benefit tend to be more critical and less supportive.

Chapter Summary

As a field of study, Event Studies must use and adapt theories, methodologies and research methods from many foundation disciplines, especially those in the social sciences. The potential for drawing on them to expand our knowledge base in Event Studies is almost unlimited.

From anthropology comes basic knowledge and important theory about human culture and specifically celebrations, rites and rituals. Why people attend and value certain events is in part culturally determined, as is the variation in forms and functions around the world. Determining what is authentic in the programming of events requires a foundation in cultural anthropology. The theory of liminality, rooted in studies of rites, pilgrimages and celebrations, is important to our understanding and conceptualization of the planned event experience. The theme of cultural impacts also draws on anthropology, especially in the context of host–guest interactions, and we can make good use of ethnography and observation techniques in event-related research. Cultural policy is one of the main processes affecting planned events.

Sociology contributes to our understanding of why and how people attend events, both in terms of social trends and because social interaction (family and friends) is one of the main intrinsic motivators; social networking is one of the key extrinsic motivators (as in 'doing business'). Organizational behaviour studies rely on sociology, thereby providing a foundation for management. Understanding of social groups, sub-cultures and crowd behaviour draws from this discipline. Social constructs are important when considering the form of events, and in assigning meanings to them. Social policy impacts on planned events in a major way.

Psychology provides several essential theoretical perspectives for Event Studies, including personality (which influences values, attitudes, motives and behaviour) and cognition – the ways in which people perceive, experience and learn. Basic human needs are expressed in both physical and psychological terms. Much of what we know about consumer behaviour is generated through psychological research, including experimentation.

Two sub-fields of psychology have special significance for Event Studies. Environmental psychology applies cognitive theory to help us understand and design better event settings. There are theoretical foundations for stimulating all the senses, site planning, managing crowds, environmental management to ensure green events and thematic interpretation. The 'behaviour setting' of planned events requires careful attention to how people interact with each other and the setting.

Social psychology provides strong theoretical support for understanding and designing social settings. Social cognition, including self-efficacy theory, provides a basis for understanding leisure motivation and how people make leisure choices. Social role schemas affect how people relate to each other, as in event crowds. Consumer psychology draws heavily from the theory of planned behaviour and expectation confirmation, while social exchange theory helps explain resident perceptions of, and attitudes toward event impacts.

Study Questions

The ensuing Study Questions contain two important points from each of the disciplines covered. Ideally, for foundation discipline you will be able to summarize the main topics they cover, their core theories and methodologies, and types of research methods used.

- What is culture and how is it studied?
- Explain ethnography and how it can be used in Event Studies.
- Demonstrate how the main themes of sociology can be applied to event management.
- Connect social network and stakeholder theories in the context of planned events.
- Show how cognitive psychology supports our understanding of the planned event experience and why people attend events (be sure to include personal constructs).
- Why is theory about personality important for event marketing?
- Explain the Integrative Model of Environmental Psychology as adapted to Event Studies.
- Link the concept of behaviour settings to event design.
- Why are self-cognition and self-efficacy theories important to understanding the planned event experience?
- In what ways can we use social exchange theory in Event Studies?

Further Reading

Schultz, E., and Lavenda, R. (2005). *Cultural Anthropology: A Perspective on the Human Condition*. Oxford: Oxford University Press.

Crouch, G., Perdue, R., Timmermans, H., and Uysal, M. (eds). *Consumer Psychology of Tourism, Hospitality and Leisure*, Vol. 3. Cambridge, MA: CABI Publishing.

Bell, P., Greene, T., Fisher, J., and Baum, A. (2001). *Environmental Psychology* (5th edn). Belmont, CA: Thomson Wadsworth.

Mannell, R., and Kleiber, D. (1997). *A Social Psychology of Leisure*. State College, PA: Venture Publishing Inc.

Chapter 4

Foundation Disciplines: Part Two

Learning Objectives

■ Understand the nature of, and contributions made to Event Studies by these foundation disciplines:
  - Philosophy
  - Religious studies
  - Economics
  - Management
  - Political science
  - Law.
■ Be able to apply theories, methodologies and research techniques from these disciplines to event-related problems.

Philosophy

Philosophers use reasoning, not empirical research, to theorize about the meaning of life and all human belief systems. But the nature and scope of philosophy are subject to influence by changing societal values and scientific discoveries. People who contemplate the meaning of life generally fall into two categories: those who adopt religious or spiritual meanings, and those who search elsewhere, inside their own mind and value sets. Philosophy is concerned with the nature of religion and spiritualism, but does not embrace faith or divine revelation, only reasoning (Figure 4.1).

Philosophy	Nature and meanings: the event experience	Antecedents to attending events	Planning and producing events	Outcomes and the impacted	Processes and patterns
• Critical thought on the nature of experience, the meaning of life and belief systems • Aesthetics • Ethics • Phenomenology • Hermeneutics	• Aesthetic experiences • Experiences that shape one's world view • How we give ethical meaning to experiences	• The quest for the meaning of life as a motivator (self-discovery) • Desire for aesthetic experiences as a motivator	• Values and ethics as a basis for producing and managing events	• Evaluation of aesthetics • Impacts on values and ethics at personal or social levels	• Changing value systems affect event planning and policy

Figure 4.1   Philosophy.

The Nature of Experience (Phenomenology and Hermeneutics)

What is experience, and how can we study it? This is where 'phenomenology' comes in, being the method used to study people's consciousness and behaviour simultaneously. Applied to event experiences, we could ask people at various times before, during and after the event to describe and explain their actions and thoughts. How does the event appear to them? What meanings are they attaching to their experiences and behaviour? How does it affect them emotionally, intellectually, spiritually? There is great scope for advancing our understanding of the planned event experience through phenomenological methods, as demonstrated in the following research note.

Research Note

Chen, P. (2006). The attributes, consequences, and values associated with event sport tourists' behaviour: a means-end chain approach. Event Management, 10(1): 1–22.

A phenomenological study was conducted of highly involved members of a fan club, in order to reveal import- ant personal constructs of the meanings attached to their fan-related experiences. Means-End Theory (see Olson and Reynolds, 2001) provided the foundation for proceeding from an examination of the concrete (attributes of being a sport fan) to consequences of the event and travel experiences (functional and psychological out- comes) to the abstract (values or goals, like self-fulfillment). Means-End is designed to elicit nonverbal commu- nications, hidden feeling and thoughts, and deeply held constructs and their interrelationships.

Respondents were asked to provide images or photos that represented their thoughts and feelings about being club members and sport fans. A technique called Zaltman Metaphor Elicitation Technique (see Zaltman and Coulter, 1995) shaped the subsequent interviews, which included storytelling and probing. Analysis was simi- lar to that employed in grounded theory, and led to creation of a cognitive map (called Integrative Hierarchy Value Map) that depicts the emergent concepts in 3 levels, namely attributes, consequences and end values, and their interconnections. Although overlapping is a feature of the mapping, 'attributes' included such con- structs as 'club activities' and 'volunteering'; 'consequences' included the constructs of 'exploring and learn- ing', friendship/attachment', and 'a cheering club', and 'end values' encompassed the constructs of 'enhanced self esteem', and 'satisfied/fulfilled'. Twenty-seven constructs were identified, all reflecting the meaning of being a sport fan.

Chen concluded that socialization was one of the most important, indeed essential aspects of the fans' experi- ences, consisting of developing one's sense of self-being through friendships, social support, and identification with a group. This led to enjoyment, well-being, and balance in life.

'*Hermeneutics*': This is a Greek word for interpretation and has come to be a branch of philosophy concerned with human understanding and the interpretation of 'texts'. All writing and symbolic communication (including performances and sports) can be viewed as 'text', and that text can be interpreted. What the researcher says about people or real-world phenomena is open to interpretation in two fundamental ways: Has the researcher found the truth (if there is a single truth) and what does the analy- sis say about the researcher? If the researcher claims to have the truth, the researcher is likely a positivist schooled in certain traditions and making use of standard methods. An application is examined in Chapter 13 – looking at 'blogs' for insight to event experiences.

Aesthetics

It is clear to everyone very early on in their lives that tastes and aesthetic appreciation are not absolutes, they are personal and vary a great deal. We can examine taste and aesthetic appreciation from a scientific perspective, considering cognition, sensory receptors and emotional responses, but this will never explain what we mean by 'art' or 'beauty'.

While it is a philosophical issue at heart, aesthetics is also the realm of event designers. They learn what pleases and what does not, and how to solve practical problems with personal style. Art, however, is a different thing altogether, as discussed in Chapter 8.

Ethics

What is right or wrong, good or bad, and how do we judge behaviour or policy? This is the realm of ethics, and is also called 'moral philosophy'. Certainly political ideology and religious beliefs enter the picture, as both of these give people a moral code or set of values to live by. Others develop their own morality and ethics through philosophical means, but always with reference to other people and society in general. We cannot be ethical or moral in isolation.

Ethics applies to professional conduct, and no event management programme can be complete without instilling the need for ethical and legal behaviour. Students might ask, however, is 'legal' the same as 'ethical', and should the various professional codes of conduct govern us completely and without question? What place is there for personal and situational ethics, where you or I make the rules as we go?

A Philosophy of Planned Events?

Philosophical thought can be applied to any subject, so what would be a philosophy of planned events? It would surely consider such questions as:

- Are all planned events fundamentally good?
- Under what conditions is public support justified?
- Must all events be environmentally sustainable in every possible way?
- What obligations to society and the environment do event professionals hold? (Consider morality and ethics.)
- What is the value of art events? What events are in bad taste? How should we judge beauty? (This is aesthetics.)
- What can we learn about the event experience and the multiple meanings attached to events? (Such as through hermeneutic phenomenology.)

Religious Studies

The study of 'religion' includes attention to its origins and evolution, comparison and analysis of belief systems, and evaluation of impacts on society. The rites, rituals and celebrations of various religions are scrutinized, including the use of anthropological methods, and this has direct relevance in Event Studies (Figure 4.2).

'Theologians' hold religious belief systems and apply their specific beliefs and related values to interpreting or criticizing all aspects of human society. Because so many events are religious in origin or theme, or contain programmic elements that hold

Religious studies	Nature and meanings: the event experience	Antecedents to attending events	Planning and producing events	Outcomes and the impacted	Processes and patterns
• The study of religions, emphasizing human society and behaviour • Religious life and experience	• Sacred experiences (religious rites, symbols and celebrations) for believers • Pilgrimage	• Religious motivations for attending or rejecting events • Quest for spiritual meaning as a motivator for belonging to religious groups	• Ritual and symbolism incorporated into event programming	• Spiritual effects on the individual • Impacts on religion • Impacts on individual belief systems or faith	• Religious trends and forces (e.g., the influence of religious lobbies)

Figure 4.2 Religious studies.

religious meaning (even something as common as an opening prayer or blessing), theology has a contribution to event studies. In some societies it is more a matter of spirituality or even mysticism that one finds reflected in modern events.

Festivals in many cultures are closely associated with religion. In Japan, annual *matsuri* are held at or in conjunction with Shinto shrines. Here is a description taken from the website: www.us.emb-japan.go.jp/jicc/spotfestivals.htm:

> *Japanese festivals, holidays, and other ceremonial occasions fall into two main categories: matsuri (festivals) and nenchu gyoji (annual events). Matsuri are essentially native Japanese festivals of Shinto origin, held annually on fixed days. . . . Japanese matsuri are chiefly of sacred origin, related (at least originally) to the cultivation of rice and the spiritual well-being of local communities . . . A matsuri is basically a symbolic act whereby participants enter a state of active communication with the gods. It is accompanied by communion among the participants in the form of feast and festival . . . This comprises purificatory rites, offerings and communal banquets between gods and humans. This first aspect may be termed a religious rite. The second aspect of matsuri is communion among people. Many Japanese festivals feature a parade of Mikoshi (portable shrines) and contests or games that give opportunities for community members to play together and match skills. The regulations of everyday life are relaxed and the atmosphere is one of spiritual renewal. This part of the matsuri may be called a festival, and whereas the first aspect is carried out with strict formalities, the latter attains vitality through the releasing of such restrictions.*

Matsuri in modern Japan often include large-scale, public celebrations like carnival, complete with masks, parades with traditional, iconic floats, sports and (to a Western eye) outrageously dangerous behaviour such as playing with fire. Search the web for matsuri photos and you will see many examples.

To illustrate a religious studies theme within Event Studies, the following note on a book by S.B. Singh is useful.

Research Note

Singh, S. B. (1989). Fairs and Festivals in Rural India: A Geopolitical Study of Belief Systems. Varanasi: Tara Book Agency.

This dissertation by S.B. Singh included a 'geospatial study of belief systems' as expressed in rural fairs and festivals. Using a case study of the Ballia district, Singh studied fairs and festivals '... as major activities in religion' (p. 16). He said (p. 16): 'The close proximity and interplay of space/sacred time in any religions activity or ritual is the pre-requisite to get the sense of divinity resulting in providing mystic power.' Employing field surveys, participatory observation, literary support, phenomenology and symbology, Singh examined growth and spatial patterns of the events, and their religious significance, both with a view to gaining greater understanding of the connections between events and religion and in making recommendations for management improvements.

Economics

According to the *Encyclopaedia Britannica*, economics is a 'social science that seeks to analyze and describe the production, distribution, and consumption of wealth'. John Tribe, author of *The Economics of Recreation, Leisure and Tourism* (2005), said that economics is concerned with scarce resources in the context of unlimited wants. Decisions therefore have to be made about what to produce, how to produce it, and the allocation of goods and services (Figure 4.3).

Economics	Nature and meanings: the event experience	Antecedents to attending events	Planning and producing events	Outcomes and the impacted	Processes and patterns
• Macroeconomics (or 'political economy'): the functioning of whole economic systems • Microeconomics: the economics of consumers, and of doing business (by firms or other organizations)	• The experience and meanings of consumption • Perceived value for money, as it shapes the event experience	• Economic incentives and barriers to consumption or participation • Supply factors (e.g., cost of travel, alternatives)	• The event's business model and economic feasibility • Forecasting demand • Economic development policy as it affects the event sector	• Measuring economic impacts and externalities • Costs and benefits evaluated (including their distribution)	• Economic trends and forces (competition, globalization)

Figure 4.3 Economics.

Macro- and Microeconomics

'Macroeconomics' concerns the entire economic system, sometimes referred to as 'political economy' because the government and international agreements set the parameters. For example, most modern economies are more or less in the free-market mode, meaning that 'laws' of the marketplace are allowed to prevail. However, all governments intervene in the marketplace to some extent in order to achieve social, cultural and environmental goals. Investment in event tourism and grants for the arts represent two important policy interventions of concern in this book.

'Welfare Economics' is a branch of macroeconomics concerned with the evaluation of public policy as to its impact on the well-being of the population or specific groups within society. Most countries, for example, impose higher income taxes on the wealthy, and tax corporations, in effect enabling the transfer of wealth from the rich to the poor. How that government revenue from taxes is spent is a matter for party politics and public debate. 'Welfarist' political parties want government funds to be spent in ways that benefit the poor and disadvantaged resulting in a high degree of government involvement in the economy. Conservative parties prefer to spend less, and to use resources to enable individuals rather than governments to make most economic choices. Accordingly, a welfarist government might justify direct production and subsidization of cultural festivals, while a conservative government might be more inclined to reduce income taxes in order to give consumers more choices (in other words, a 'supply-side' approach).

Difficult decisions emerge in welfare economics. Is it possible to justify a policy that benefits some at the expense of others? Many people do support redistribution measures such as sliding tax scales, and modern governments like to take regular polls of voters to determine the popularity of various options, or to assess attitudes towards existing programmes. Now, what if a redistribution measure actually hurts some people to benefit others, is that justifiable? Of course these serious policy questions are not generally decided with planned events in mind, but do get raised when public expenditures and subsidies for events are at issue.

'Microeconomics' concerns individuals and their consumer behaviour, as well as specific business decisions and how supply and demand find equilibrium in specific markets. In classical economics, 'laws of supply and demand' govern these processes. Important microeconomic questions regarding planned events:

• What determines the price of an event and of the resources used to produce them?
• How are event buyers and sellers brought together in a functioning market? (This is crucial in the context of bidding on events: see Getz, 2004, for an assessment of the marketplace and how it works both in theory and in practice for tourism agencies that bid on events.)

- How is the economic or financial feasibility of a proposed event assessed?
- What are the differences between types of event organizations in terms of how they operate (i.e., governmental, non-profit and for-profit)?

'*Theory of choice*': Firms desiring to make a profit have difficult choices to make, and face a number of constraints regarding their necessary inputs (supplies, labour, rents paid). One combination of inputs will minimize costs, but will it permit production of an attractive event? If profit is not the goal, a different set of inputs can be justified, and in fact if a loss can be incurred (because of subsidies or debt forgiveness) the producers can afford to be rather careless in their use of resources. Little research has been done on how event producers make such choices, but some research employing stakeholder theory has addressed the issue of relative power between event organizers and their suppliers, and how this impacts on non-profit festival viability (see Andersson and Getz, 2007).

'*Theory of allocation*': When a business or institution has multiple goals for events, there has to be some kind of prioritization – it is generally not possible to commit resources to fulfilling all goals equally. The necessary allocation of resources to meet each goal can be measured, then linked to its priority or 'weighting', and from that analysis an optimal strategy can be determined which will provide the company or agency with the best 'return' on its investment. So how does one determine the relative value of committing resources to events versus other programmes, or one type of event compared to another?

'Opportunity costs' are also a key economic concept. Whatever resources a company or government devotes to events, they could be spent elsewhere. Are events worth the investment in terms of culture, health or tourism? This becomes a serious policy matter, because other opportunities always exist for meeting business and societal goals. So-called 'merit' goods and services are deemed by governments to require subsidies or direct government provision because of their importance and the inability or unwillingness of the private sector to fill the need. Thus, some governments justify the provision of festivals and sport events, or other forms of entertainment, for the 'public good'.

'Demand' for Goods and Services

'Demand', in economics, is a function of the relationship between price and the quantity 'demanded' for a good or service in specific circumstances. For each price, the demand relationship tells the quantity the buyers want to buy at that corresponding price.

Consumers derive 'utility' (such as survival, pleasure, happiness, satisfaction) from spending their limited disposable incomes. They always have choices, especially when it comes to entertainment and travel. A 'consumer surplus' can be created when the utility derived from an event exceeds the cost to an individual, or when a free or subsidized event is produced for an appreciative public (e.g., my expectations were exceeded; I would have gladly paid more for that experience; they should have charged an admission fee, it was so wonderful!).

The more one values an event the more one is willing to pay for it, up to a point. So demand rests on certain assumptions about consumer utility, choices and preferences. The principle of 'diminishing marginal utility' says that consumers will eventually get less and less satisfaction from going to events, or any specific type of event, and therefore the benefits derived will at some level of consumption cease to justify the effort or cost required. In terms of supply and demand, there are two related 'elasticity' functions to consider.

'Income elasticity': As incomes rise there is more for consumers to spend on goods and services, therefore overall demand for leisure, travel and events is directly linked to disposable incomes. But, will events be 'preferred goods' that people want to spend more on? We know that as countries develop a middle class with rising incomes more and more is spent on leisure and travel (in effect, there was high 'latent demand' for these goods).

'Price elasticity': As price rises, overall demand should fall, so that when an event charges more, it can generally expect to attract fewer paying customers – or to attract different types of customer. Some events might be considered to be 'luxury goods' that attract customers who care little about rising process, or are even attracted by the exclusivity that higher process imply.

In a free marketplace, supply and demand should eventually reach 'equilibrium', where no more events are produced than can be justified by what consumers are willing to spend. This does not happen, however, for reasons discussed below. In fact, the events sector is so oriented to government subsidies and non-profit values that it is difficult to apply any economic laws, except for the purpose of making comparisons to other sectors or revealing the extent of market distortions.

Economic Demand for Events

The normal assumptions made by economists regarding demand for goods and services often do not apply in the events sector. Consumers have multiple event choices, some of which are free or subsidized. All events that attract people for personal reasons (i.e., intrinsic motives) are in themselves substitutable with other forms of entertainment or activities. We should expect price elasticity, for example, to apply mostly to events that must be held (a wedding? an association meeting?) and for which supply alternatives abound. In a competitive environment, suppliers must always be wary of price increases.

Nevertheless, when setting the price for event admission, organizers do have to consider how it will affect potential demand. Price elasticity generally means that as price increases, demand will decrease – for the obvious reason that money is a scarce resource, but also because consumers have many alternative opportunities. Tribe (2005: 76–77) shows how elasticity is modified by the necessity of having the good or service, the number of substitutes, addictiveness of the good or service, consumer awareness and the time period (e.g., are tickets bought well in advance?). Furthermore, some goods and services are so useful and so cheap that increases in price will be too small to affect demand.

The income elasticity of demand also must be considered. Generally people spend more on leisure and travel as their disposable incomes rise, and corporations and governments also 'demand' more events as their profits or revenues increase. In part it is not only a matter of financial feasibility, but also a matter of preference. Indeed, events (as leisure) can be considered preferred goods or services because people love to travel and be entertained. And civil servants as well as business people love to meet!

Economics therefore provides a basis for demand forecasting, which in the context of events often means attendance forecasting. The inherent difficulty is that demand for, or interest in many events, is only partially influenced by the cost.

Willingness to Pay

Willingness to pay is a useful economic concept to help determine event demand and to help set prices. Ask yourself how much you would be willing to pay for a choice ticket to a popular concert, then how much more or less you would be willing to pay for a ticket to a community festival. People are often unable to say exactly how much they would pay for any given opportunity, but they can at least compare it to other, normal purchases – we can call these 'value propositions'. For example, we often spend money to attend the cinema or rent a movie, so how much more is it worth to attend that concert? Twice as much? Three times? Market researchers use these value propositions to find a range within which most of their target segment would make a purchase.

A problem with willingness to pay is that some people will mislead you! Well, of course they will. Why volunteer that you would pay a lot of money for something that is currently free or cheap? Won't 'they' just use that information to raise the price? So researchers have to expect that expressed willingness to pay yields underestimates of what people will actually pay. On the other hand, researchers have to recognize that if the price is raised, some people might indeed decide to stay away or be unable to afford the new price.

Tourists, it is often found, will pay more for events than locals. Studies of festivals in Canada's National Capital Region (Coopers and Lybrand Consulting Group, 1988) found that those who travelled to the city especially for the events were willing to spend more than the residents. This happens because the event is the reason for their travel, and they are likely to attend just once. Residents have plenty of chances to attend (or go to other local events) and might want to attend more than once, so they are less willing to pay higher prices per visit. Tourists therefore often represent a higher-yield segment, but in smaller volumes.

Direct and Induced Demand

'Direct demand' for events consists of those people who pay to attend, or in other words the customers. As price goes up, normally direct demand will fall. If the event is free direct economic demand cannot be measured, but 'willingness to pay' can be researched to get a 'value' for the event. Forecasting demand for an event is notoriously difficult (see, for example, Pyo et al., 1988; Mules and McDonald, 1994; Teigland, 1996; Spilling, 1998), and so it is normal for many years of research on awareness, interest levels, market areas and segmentation, penetration rates and demand to precede mega-events.

'Induced demand' is something quite different. It occurs when an event generates additional awareness for a destination, improves its image and thereby attracts additional visitors. They might come before a major event to see the developing facilities, or simply because so much attention has been given to the area. Increased capacity is another factor to consider when explaining any tourist gains following an event, as new venues and hotels, better marketing, and heightened political support for tourism and other events are potential consequences.

Olympic cities have found that years before the big event they attract many more meetings and conventions than otherwise would select them. After the event there should also be a 'halo effect' attracting increased numbers, but it will fade over time. However, many external variables can interfere with induced demand, making it a risky proposition upon which to basis forecast economic impacts. Kang and Perdue (1994) concluded that the 1988 Seoul Olympics did have a long-term, positive impact on tourist demand for Korea, and they believed this effect would be more pronounced for developing as opposed to established tourist destinations.

Events and Economic Development

'Development' can mean economic growth, but it can just as easily refer to urban development and renewal, social and cultural development, or sustainable development with its heavy emphasis on environmental concerns. A number of paradigms, or schools of thought about development, have influenced government policies – including those pertaining to events.

'Modernization' refers to the process of becoming more like Western, industrialized societies through infrastructure development, industrialization, changing attitudes and patterns of work. The all-too-eager development of tourism in many developing nations reflects a desire to be more modern, and tourism (generally requiring foreign investment and many economic concessions made to investors) has produced quick and obvious results. Mega-events in particular fit into this approach because they are bold, globally communicated symbols of development. For example, Korea has effectively employed mega-events in its modernization schemes, directed by central government, and China is following suit. China embarked on a very ambitious process of modernizing its industrial base, accompanied by airports, freeways, convention and exhibition centres, and tourism resorts.

World's fairs were always associated with modernization, both as a way for nations to show off their technological developments and to attract visitors to a special place that symbolized progress. Hosting international conventions and exhibitions is still viewed as a method for fostering trade and gaining valuable knowledge about economic development.

'Dependency' theorists stress the problems associated with development in third-world countries, or poor regions within rich countries, typically by referring to 'core-periphery' models (for structural reasons, including foreign ownership, the core always dominates) and neocolonialism (economic power is exerted rather than direct military power to keep developing areas subservient). In this approach, events can be viewed as the exploitation of host cultures as part of the 'pleasure periphery' for rich foreigners, or as inappropriate users of precious local resources to further an unwanted development model.

'Economic neoliberalism' has been the dominant development paradigm since the 1970s, typified by less direct government involvement and an emphasis on freeing up market forces. The 'supply-side economics' of neoliberalism favours consumerism, free trade and private development, not government intervention or centralized planning. Taken to an extreme, the absence of government intervention will certainly result in inequities and problems, so what we see today is varying degrees of government involvement in the market. Critics of globalization argue that neoliberal policies result in the poor getting poorer and the rich getting richer, while local cultures and ways of life disappear.

In Canada and other countries neoliberal policies have resulted in less funding for the arts and events in general, a rise in corporate sponsorship and influence over the events sector, and quite possibly a decline in creativity because of the need for arts institutions and non-profits to stress commercially viable 'products'. An emphasis on tourism as industry, and events as new, competitive products, fits into the neoliberal way of thinking, so that any government funding is likely to be tied to specific ROI forecasts. The value of events in image development, place marketing and branding are aspects of neoliberal thinking.

'Alternative development' focuses on human needs and the human consequences of development, including concerns of gender equity, indigenous rights, physical, mental and social issues, and on sustainable development. Empowerment and local involvement, with an emphasis on process, are hallmarks of this approach. The 'triple bottom-line' approach to sustainable tourism, and attention to ensuring 'green' events, fits nicely into this paradigm. A return to stressing the cultural and social value of events, and evaluations that treat these factors equally with economic impacts, could indicate alternative or 'post-modern' thinking.

Research Note

Whitford, M. (2004a). Regional development through domestic and tourist event policies: Gold Coast and Brisbane, 1974–2003. UNLV Journal of Hospitality, Tourism and Leisure Science, 1: 1–24.

Whitford researched event policies in Gold Coast and Brisbane, Australia, finding that city policies towards events were predominantly underpinned by 'alternative', not classical economic development paradigms (namely modernisation, dependency, and neoliberalism). Whitford determined that '... events are quickly becoming an integral and essential component of many Australian regions' strategic planning, development, tourism and leisure policies ...'. She employed 'policy content analysis' to evaluate the internal and external factors influencing policy formation and contents, or the impacts of those policies. Indicators of an 'alternative' paradigm included the development of events not merely for tourism and branding, which is common in Australia and elsewhere, but for promoting cultural diversity, enhancing local ways of life, and preserving heritage. Community development was another justification found in Gold Coast and Brisbane for their involvement in events.

Whitford concluded that '... governments should be cognisant of the ideological underpinnings influencing the focus, goals and objectives of their event policy'. However, if an economic paradigm is so well established and accepted as neoliberalism has been in many countries, there is generally no such critical thinking. Rather, events, sports, the arts and business all have adapted to the new realities and compete on the basis of the meeting the goals of neoliberalism or globalisation. Paradigms change very slowly. Some very practical and valuable advice from Whitford is that researchers have to investigate the effectiveness of development-oriented policies that encompass events, so that policies are founded on fact, not dogma.

Claims made regarding the long-term, developmental benefits of mega-events have to be treated with extreme caution. Research is seldom conducted longitudinally, and it is always going to be difficult to 'prove' that holding an event caused economic growth or social development. One thorough study, by Spilling (1998), concluded that the 1994 Winter Olympics in Lillehammer Norway had produced 'rather marginal' long-term impacts on the host region's economy. The benefits were largely confined to tourism, particularly for hosting new events! Spilling decided that the games could not be justified on economic grounds alone.

Justifying Market Intervention, or the Subsidizing of Events

Market economies are based on the premise that it is best to leave most decisions to independent firms and consumers, as government intervention usually results in distortions and often negative, unforeseen consequences. However, in the case of many policy fields – including social, environmental and cultural – intervention is frequently justified. In terms of economics, the following concepts are important in this context.

'Market failure' is a situation in which markets do not efficiently organize production or allocate goods and services to consumers, or where market forces do not serve the perceived public interest. Mules and Dwyer (2006) noted that hospitality and travel firms cannot capture all of the benefits generated by events so they will not fund them. Consequently, the tourism industry (through Destination Marketing Organizations) often funds events collectively, although this allows for 'free riders' who get benefits without paying. The free-rider problem is why the industry often asks for events to be publicly funded, because government tax revenue comes from every company.

If events of any type are deemed to be a 'public good', then free-market forces cannot be allowed to operate. These are goods from which everyone can simultaneously obtain benefits. Public goods retain the characteristics of 'non-rivalry' and 'non-excludability'. Non-rivalry means that one person's benefit does not reduce the benefit available to others, and non-excludability means that there is no effective way of excluding individuals from the benefit of the good, once it comes into existence (thereby creating the free-rider problem). Due to the free-rider problem, a public good is not profitable to provide by a private firm.

'Economic efficiency' is a valid reason for bidding on and creating events, to the extent that they provide revenue or other tangible benefits for publicly owned and subsidized facilities and parks. To the extent that surplus capacity exists (i.e., resident use does not normally fill the venues) the marginal cost of producing events might be much less than the new income realized. Indeed, many facilities and parks are established with this tourist revenue in mind.

A related efficiency issue is that of attracting tourists to events. Andersson (2006) recommended creating surplus capacity in resident-oriented events in order to make it possible to attract tourists. This can often be done without imposing new costs on residents, and will likely generate tourist income that is of value to residents directly (through lower event charges for them) or indirectly (higher taxes for local authorities, and increased economic prosperity in the region).

Economic Impacts of Events

If we think in terms of an event 'industry', certain economic implications arise. First, economists will measure the economic value of the industry in such terms as jobs created, export earnings (i.e., through event tourism) or wealth created for residents. On the other hand, being an industry might suggest that government intervention is unwarranted and the private sector can take care of demand. Indeed, governments tend to want to meet basic needs, while industry aims to satisfy economic demands expressed through purchasing power.

Another important concept is that of 'externalities'. Normal, free-market economics often fails to take into account effects that are external to a specific business, exchange or event. For example, the air pollution, noise and accidents caused by traffic related to a tourist-oriented event are frequently excluded from an accounting of economic impact. They should, however, be included in a comprehensive evaluation of the costs and benefits of the event. In Chapter 11 we return to economic impacts and their analysis, and in Chapter 12 to the related policy considerations.

Management

Management is a very broad field of studies, with strong disciplinary connections to sociology, psychology and economics. Four spheres of management that are applicable to events (profit, not-for-profit, governmental and tourist destination) have to be considered (Figure 4.4). All the management functions applied to events are reviewed in detail in Chapter 10.

Management	Nature and meanings: the event experience	Antecedents to attending events	Planning and producing events	Outcomes and the impacted	Processes and patterns
• Profit, not-for-profit, governmental and destination management • Theories of the firm • Institutional theory • Management functions	• Consumerism (events as entertainment products) • Commoditization of events	• Effectiveness of marketing • Image and branding	• Project and strategic planning • Management effectiveness and efficiency	• The impacted as stakeholders	• Evolution of management theory and practice • Changes in factors that influence businesses and entrepreneurship (e.g., business development policy) • Shifts in the competitive environment

Figure 4.4 Management.

Some will argue that management is a field of studies, not a discipline, because it is really the application of knowledge from a variety of disciplines. However, it is one of the crucial foundations of Event Studies and, unlike the other closely related professional fields that all have core phenomena, management applies to every field of human endeavour.

Business Management

Many companies exist to produce or supply services to planned events, and they are profit-making businesses. It is my contention, however, that every event should be viewed as a business with the aim of making money. That money is needed to support the organization and improve the event, and it can be in the form of profit (to make individuals money) or 'surplus revenue' allocated to re-investment. If events are run as business propositions, it means that the owners/producers have to follow sound management principles and be focused on the long-term viability of the event.

A business exists for several reasons, and if the event is seen as a business venture these both apply:

- To make money for those who invest in them (i.e., public or private 'enterprises').
- To meet needs or fill market gaps (i.e., consumers, sponsors and grant givers will pay for the event).

Neither of these criteria negate any social or cultural value attached to events. Indeed, many not-for-profit event organizations are established to create public goods or meet social needs, yet they still have to function as independent firms. Why do for-profit event-production companies exist, and why do not-for-profit event organizations occupy such an important place in the events sector? Each is a kind of firm, or independent organization that provides goods or services in exchange for money/resources.

'Entrepreneurship' explains a lot, because many people are motivated by some or all of the following:

- Independence (being one's own boss).
- Creativity (the act of establishing something that has value and creates wealth).
- Profit (getting rich, or just making a living).

Both private companies and not-for-profit event organizations are set up by 'entrepreneurs'. In either case they have to make a living. Many not-for-profit festival organizations, for example, are established by persons who want to both create an event and a career for themselves. In their case studies of Calgary festivals, for example, Getz et al. (2007) interviewed several festival creators who were clearly acting entrepreneurially, and without their initiative and leadership the events would not exist.

Resource-Based Theory of the Firm

Firms and organizations should possess rare and valuable resources that give them sustainable competitive advantages – if the firm can protect against resource imitation, transfer or mobility, or substitution (Penrose, 1959; Barney, 1991). Applied to events these resources could be intellectual capital (creativity, knowledge), committed stakeholders (see 'stakeholder theory'), a special venue, or an endowment just as long as other events or organizations cannot do the same thing with their resources.

Knowledge-Based Theory of the Firm

In this variation of the resource-based theory of the firm, organizations that possess, learn and retain valuable knowledge and capabilities, embedding it in their culture, management systems and stakeholder networks, can sustain competitive advantages and achieve superior performance (Barney, 1991; Grant, 1991). Information systems also provide advantages. Applied to events, managers should develop unique and inimitable knowledge or capabilities and make certain they are both retained and constantly developed. Consider the synergies to be gained through blending creative/artistic and business/management knowledge.

Stakeholder and Network Theory

'Stakeholder theory' (Freeman, 1984; Donaldson and Preston, 1995; Mitchell et al., 1997; Jawahar and McLaughlin, 2001) helps explain the origins, operation and evolution of events, and provides direction to owners and managers on how to manage their internal and external stakeholder relationships. Stakeholders are those persons or groups who can influence the organization, or are influenced by it.

Core stakeholder attributes, according to Mitchell et al. (1997: 865–867), are:

- 'Power': 'The ability of a party that it has or can gain access to impose its will in the relationship.'
- 'Legitimacy': 'A generalized perception or assumption that the actions of an entity are desirable, proper, or appropriate within some socially constructed system of norms, values, beliefs, and definitions.'
- 'Urgency': 'the degree to which stakeholder claims call for immediate attention.'
- 'Stakeholder Salience': is a function of possessing the other three stakeholder attributes: power, legitimacy and urgency.

Using the analogy of a 'political market square', Larson and Wikstrom (2001) and Larson (2002) examined several Swedish events. Stakeholders played 'power games' and negotiated from varying positions of power. They formed alliances to realize their goals for the event and the organization producing it. Critical roles identified among the stakeholders included those of 'gatekeeping' (deciding who gets in), negotiation, coalition building, trust or legitimacy building, and identity building for the event in general.

Merrilees et al. (2005) used stakeholder theory to analyse how the Goodwill Games were 'branded' in Brisbane, Australia. In this instance building trust and legitimacy were crucial. Mifflin and Taylor (2006) employed stakeholder theory in assessing the success of a youth-oriented event.

To sustain itself in the long term, the organization has to manage its stakeholder relationships effectively, and if successful it might become a permanent 'institution' in its community. This means it has the support it needs to survive crises and to solve the social problems it exists for (Getz et al., 2007). There is also a moral aspect to stakeholder theory which argues that managers should also work with all those affected by the organization, as in the case of events working with their community and special interest groups, regardless of their power to influence the organization.

In another application of stakeholder theory, Spiropoulos et al. (2006) examined the 20th Greek Festival of Sydney. The stakeholder environment of this event was closely tied to ethnicity, which suggests the value of examining social networks. 'Network theory' is closely related to stakeholder theory. 'Social networks' are often important for entrepreneurs, especially when obtaining the resources and support to start an event. 'Social capital' in this sense means the network of people and organizations you can rely on to help you. Organizational networks obviously involve all the stakeholders, but there is an emphasis in network theory on which organizations possess 'centrality', their degree of 'connectedness' and 'bridging' organizations.

Research Note

Stokes, R. (2004). A framework for the analysis of events tourism knowledge networks. Journal of Hospitality and Tourism Management, 11(2): 108–123.

Stokes examined inter-organizational relations of public-sector events organizations in Australia where all states have events development companies or departments. She identified the relationships and knowledge used in event strategies, and identified the importance of shared knowledge as an incentive for participating in networks. Stakeholders include community representatives, public sector managers such as events and tourism agencies, corporate leaders, events managers and tourism industry suppliers. Where stakeholders obtain and transfer knowledge about event tourism was mapped. Key elements in 'sociospatial knowledge networks' are: activity spaces, place inventories, and information nodes.

In her conclusion she said, '. . . public sector events agencies within Australia depend upon intrasectoral and intersectoral collaboration to achieve productive links between events development and tourism.' A corporate orientation among stakeholders mostly applied at the state level, where emphasis was on tourism development such as bidding on major events. At the regional level was more of a community orientation, as tourism-related outcomes were considered. For staging major events there were created formal alliances and collaborations, but not so for strategy in general.

'Collaboration theory' (Wood and Gray, 1991; Jamal and Getz, 1995) relates to how various stakeholders get together in partnerships, alliances or other joint efforts. In true collaborations each partner gives up some degree of control to work with others in achieving common goals. For example, events form professional associations which can be called alliances, but generally do not give up any independence in doing so. Events can partner with other events or with tourist organizations for joint marketing, again without giving up any real power. But if events agree to work closely with each other, perhaps sharing offices, staff and resources, this collaboration entails a loss of independence and poses some risks that must be balanced against the gains.

Most often collaborations work in 'policy domains' such as tourism and culture, or for major projects. Long (2000), for example, studied cooperation between tourism and the arts developed for the UK Year of Visual Arts. These were contractual and short-lived, as opposed to more permanent federations. Long concluded that lessons from this and other examples of collaboration and partnership can be applied to relationships with sponsors, reconciling goals, achieving economic efficiencies or dealing with political interests.

Resource Dependency Theory

All firms require resources, but some are better at getting and holding them. Success is defined, in this context, as maximizing the organization's power (Pfeffer and Salancik, 1978; Pfeffer, 1981) which can come from reducing one's own dependency or making others dependent on you. Firms lacking essential resources will seek relationships that provide them, resulting in dependency. This is a form of 'social exchange theory' and it seems to work well for events faced with competition for scarce resources and uncertainty in resource availability.

Event failures might arise from a poor 'fit' with the environment, as in the case where a festival is not able to attract interest and support from its host community because of cultural differences, a lack of key contacts or internal management deficiencies.

According to Donaldson (1996), 'fit' stems from how an organization adapts to accommodate environmental contingencies. Additional considerations relate to the scarcity of resources (What are the alternative sources?), the nature of the event's operational environment (Competition or symbiotic relationships among resource users?), certainty versus fluctuations in resource availability (e.g., Is long-term support guaranteed?) and variability in resource needs (Are the same resources needed every year?).

To deal with these resource issues a number of strategies are available. Events can attempt to secure resources from many sources, store resources for hard times (i.e., a reserve fund) or switch to new resource suppliers. They can try to reduce their need (e.g., cost reductions), influence the resource providers (e.g., through policy lobbying) or decide to work with, or compete against other organizations seeking resources.

This theory has been used together with stakeholder theory by Getz et al. (2007) to help explain both failure and the institutionalization of events. Other ecological and institutional theories of organizations also view the organization or firm in terms of its internal dynamics, environmental interdependencies and competing interests.

Competitive and Comparative Advantages

A 'comparative advantage' means that some events or event organizations have been endowed with better resources or appeal. This advantage could be in terms of support from their communities, which is a stakeholder issue, or in terms of their location. It could consist of 'tradition' or 'authenticity'. 'Competitive advantages' accrue from wise management of whatever you possess, such as by providing target segments with services (events) that they are willing to pay for, and doing it better than competitors.

Adapting Porter's (1980) classic model of competitive forces, many events are revealed to be in a relatively weak position. An event has to first asses its competitive environment as to threats: it is generally easy to set up events so that competition is always likely to increase, and events are often substitutable by other events or other forms of entertainment and marketing. Both buyers (companies and customers) can go elsewhere unless there are few events or event-producing firms available. So how should events compete?

Porter's strategies for achieving and sustaining competitive advantage include a focus on costs (keeping costs low and passing savings on to the buyer), focusing on specific target markets or on differentiation (being unique within the events sector). Competing on price is possible for events, even if their costs are high, when subsidies and sponsorship support are available to compensate. Competing through differentiation makes a lot of sense, but unfortunately numerous events exist for rather general purposes and many producers find it difficult to narrowly target.

In Event Studies, little attention has been given to competitiveness among events or event companies. Research on this important topic has to connect with stakeholder, institutional and population ecology theory, as well as with marketing and positioning strategy.

Agency Theory

In 'agency theory' we consider how owners and managers/contractors interact. 'It is assumed that both parties are motivated by self-interest, and that these interests may diverge' (Scott, 2001: 105). Sometimes managers know more about what is going on than the owners, such as where staff are intimately involved in an event and directors are remote. This results in 'information asymmetry' and the owners have to initiate inspections or incentives to ensure their policies are implemented.

A central question raised by agency theory is this: Do managers or sub-contractors always act in the best interests of those who retained their services? What if event managers ran their events to make more money, or preserve job security for themselves, rather than to meet the aims of the founders or key resource suppliers? This problem can arise in other situations, such as an event put out to tender by a government agency, or a charity hiring a production company to raise money through events.

There are other potential applications of agency theory in Event Studies. It relates to organizational culture and the role of founders and leaders (do they always get their way?) The processes of professionalization, bureaucratization and institutionalization might very well increase agency problems as more and more managers become involved and possibly begin to feel the event exists for their personal or collective benefits.

Population Ecology Theory

This theory (Hannan and Freeman, 1977, 1984) can help explain why many events fail, or never realize their potential or their founder's vision. This theory looks at whole 'populations' of organizations, such as the festival sector in general. Why some succeed and others fail might be due in large part to the dynamics of the population rather than the individual festival organization. Getz (2002) employed this concept in examining festival failure, and it has relevance to many event-related management and policy issues.

Baum (1996) noted that all 'ecological' theories of organizations begin with three observations. First, diversity is a property of aggregates of organizations, not of specific organizations (the analogy to humans is that within a given community there is a lot of diversity). Second, organizations often have difficulty changing fast enough to adapt to uncertain environmental conditions (humans might be better at this, but not everyone can adapt quickly). Third, organizations arise and disappear regularly, like the birth and death of animals. To extend the ecological analogy further, it might be argued that in any community or destination it is necessary to have a healthy population (or 'portfolio') of events, but it is not crucial for any one event to exist, or to survive indefinitely.

Since there is usually a 'free market' in the creation of events, the 'population' numbers tend to rise. Competition among events in one community or region can then result in one or more of them failing to secure enough political support, volunteers, grants, sponsors or paying customers to continue. No matter how great a concept they have, or how well managed, these external factors are probably influencing an event's chances for success or failure.

The concept of 'structural inertia' suggests why some festivals cannot adequately adapt to changes in their environment. If they are highly specialized (i.e., have no alternative resources to obtain or products to offer), if they are unable to monitor and assess change (i.e., they are not a 'learning organization') or if there are severe political/legal constraints on their actions, events might be unable to change. The 'core values' or processes of an organization, especially its fundamental goals, have a high degree of inertia. Marketing strategies, on the other hand, are much more flexible.

Older, more generalized organizations have a better chance of survival because the reliability of their performance encourages others to supply resources. New event organizations, therefore, will often have a difficult time getting adequate resources and learning how to survive. However, Baum (1996) argued that research does not confirm that failure rates decline with organizational age.

From the perspective of the public, or government agencies, it might not be a problem that individual events fail as long as the entire event sector is healthy and provides both choice and innovation. Indeed, old events that cannot re-invent themselves, or otherwise adapt to changing environmental conditions, perhaps do not deserve support. But applying this principle makes for difficult decisions and will certainly result in criticism. What about tradition? What about all the resources that have been committed, are they to be wasted when an event fails? 'Institutionalization theory' will provide us with some additional insights on this perplexing issue, specifically by forcing policy-makers and other key stakeholders to think about the important societal goals events meet, and about the reasons for committing resources and support to particular organizations.

Public Administration

All or our discussion of public policy and law in this book are aspects of public administration. Governments do not have to obey the laws of the marketplace, such as supply and demand. They can create and subsidize events for a multitude of reasons, and not worry about profits or break-event points. Our discussion of 'public goods', 'equity' and 'failure of the marketplace' provides the justification.

Since many events are produced by, or sub-contracted by government departments and agencies, some attention to public administration is required in Event Studies. If the event functions as a programme within a governmental agency, then it is clearly an instrument of policy. Under some circumstances the event could be managed as an enterprise, either to make money or at least break even, in which case it has to operate like a business.

Students of public and not-for-profit administration still have to learn the management fundamentals including finance, human resources and marketing. But there will be an additional emphasis on law, policy, institutional relationships and politics.

Not-for-Profit Management

Festivals in particular are often produced by not-for-profit organizations that are either in existence for other reasons, or are set up specifically to manage the event.

'Not-for-profit' is a more accurate term than 'non-profit' to describe them, because they can make surplus revenue (and should aim to) but must use it to sustain and improve the organization and their events.

Grant writing, fundraising, governance issues (especially with volunteer boards), service provision, needs assessments, volunteer recruitment and management, and programme evaluation are topics of particular interest in this sector.

Destination Management

Destinations are really 'policy domains', defined for specific purposes of tourism marketing. Their management is rather unique, because they exist both for public good (economic development) and private gain (members or partners such as hotels). Because event tourism is now so well established, and globally competitive, how destinations plan, bid for, and in some cases produce and manage events is of considerable interest in Event Studies. The following research note illustrates how destination marketing organizations view events.

Research Note

O'Brien, D. (2005). Event business leveraging: the Sydney 2000 Olympic Games. Annals of Tourism Research, 33(1): 240–261.

Business Club Australia was established to foster business networking and international trade development surrounding the Summer Olympic Games. O'Brien reported that accumulated knowledge was being institutionalized and applied in other event situations. The steps taken by the Club included generating public and private sector support for networking, and facilitation of networking between Australian businesses and visiting international business leaders (or politicians) before, during and after the event. Australians had to be convinced that benefits of the event could be spread throughout the country.

Institutional Theory and 'Institutionalization'

Within organizations, 'institutional theory' refers to processes by which rules and norms become guidelines or controllers of behaviour. For example, ask how has an event's approach to stakeholder relationship management became 'institutionalized' over many years? This ties in with organizational culture and social network theory, with direct relevance to planning, decision-making, coordination and control systems. However, we are more interested here in what an 'institution' is, and how an event can become one.

Regarding the organization as an 'institution', Scott (2001) suggested it is a social structure with a great deal of resilience, it provides meaning to social life, connotes stability and is taken for granted. Others believe an institution has to exist for a specific purpose, which is to achieve important societal goals or solve crucial societal problems.

The following criteria appear to be important factors determining event institutional-ization, and should be tested through a variety of comparative research studies on different types of events:

- An event that is an 'institution' solves important social problems or meets important community goals.
- Society or the community cannot be without it – failure is unthinkable.
- Permanence is taken for granted.
- Support is assured – sponsors and agencies will always give it money.
- They are highly visible – everyone knows about it – the event has a strong, positive brand.
- It is expert in managing its stakeholder relationships.
- Key stakeholders have been internalized.

Fuller understanding of institutionalization also requires linkage with population ecol-ogy, resource theories of the firm and stakeholder theory. In Chapter 10 we return to this concept and examine if it is really desirable to strive to become an institution.

Political Science

Political science is the theory and practice of politics, political systems and political behaviour. Political scientists study government and its processes, public institu-tions, power and policy-making, politics, intergovernmental and international rela-tions. 'Political philosophy', on the other hand, is more concerned with values and political ideas, such as the differences between Marxism and Capitalism, or the mean-ings of rights and justice (from *Encyclopaedia Britannica* online) (Figure 4.5).

There are many political reasons for staging events, and politics often influences their management and marketing. Ideological reasons lie behind many mega-events, wherein the dominant power in society seeks to demonstrate and reinforce its values, or to win support (Hall, 1997).

In many countries there are substantial, party-based differences in approaches to policy that impinge on the events sector. These are generally rooted in philosophy and trad-itional voting bases, such as Labour versus Conservative, but they also express the more mundane necessity of opposing the party in power. It is always worth asking if a 'party-political platform' reflects fundamental philosophical differences between parties, or if the opposition is simply trying to appear to be different. One might expect, for example, that a left-leaning party would stress equity issues and government interventions, such

Political science	Nature and meanings: the event experience	Antecedents to attending events	Planning and producing events	Outcomes and the impacted	Processes and patterns
• The study of governments, public policies and political behaviour	• Events may take on political significance • Attendance can be a political statement	• Political motives to attend or stay away	• Creating events as a political statement (e.g., protest, party loyalty, nationalism) • Government policy and programmes re events	• Effects on politics, government, political parties and law	• How politics and policies influence event development and attendance

Figure 4.5   Political science.

as making the arts accessible to everyone, while right-leaning parties would stress free-market economics and privatization.

Government intervention in the events industry is often justified, for reasons discussed previously (i.e., public goods and failure of the marketplace). But these arguments can disguise underlying political motivations, such as getting re-elected, spreading party-specific values (this is correctly termed 'propaganda') or catering to interest groups that support the party in question.

'Interest groups' and 'elites': Who supports public involvement with events, and why, is a question too infrequently asked. Often the answer is disturbing, because getting the government to produce, subsidize or bid on events obviously benefits some more than others. The tourism industry benefits directly when major events are produced, but the arguments put forward in support of mega-event bids typically emphasize the public goods such as more jobs, economic development, new infrastructure and enhanced civic pride.

'Political attitudes' and 'voting patterns': Political scientists often study elections and under-lying voter attitudes and behaviour, including how political campaigns and specific messages affect the voter. When it comes to events, the most closely related approach has typically involved measures of resident or tourist perceptions of event impacts, and attitudes towards them. But that research has more of a sociological orientation than political science. More research is needed on how perceptions and attitudes translate into political action or voting patterns, and how interest groups lobby for and achieve their event-related goals. This is similar to stakeholder theory.

'International relations': Events often involve international relations, both as a reflection of trade, power and cultural exchange. Consider the importance of hosting a mega-event for national pride and the legitimacy of governments, the importance assigned to using events to foster trade and economic development, and the value of showcasing one's cultural and economic accomplishments in a global forum.

'Policy formulation': The ways in which event-related policies are formulated and implemented have not received much attention from researchers. Certainly we are all aware of how many tragedies at events gave rise to health and safety regulations. But what went into the decision of the Canadian government (and other nations) to ban tobacco sponsorship at events? Will the same happen to alcohol sponsorship? How did events lobby and why were they successful, or not? As the event management profession and industry become better established and more professional, it can be expected their lobbying efforts will increase and become more effective. But who sets and steers that agenda?

An interesting, events-related theme in policy-making is that of irrational decision-making. Elites, holding influence and power in society, tend to get what they want. It's a mutually reinforcing process! So when a mega-event is desired, or perhaps a subsidy for certain types of event, rational decision-making can get in the way. Accordingly, various spurious arguments about tourism impacts or infrastructure gains are used to make it seem like a rational decision. Those who use rational arguments to oppose such decisions are then branded as being unpatriotic, irresponsible or stupid. This is how power gets abused.

A kinder explanation is that emotions get the better of people. Consider how emotional a country can get when it is bidding for the Olympics against a rival country (does London versus Paris 2012 come to mind?). In a highly charged, emotional context, irrational decisions are more likely to be made. How can that be prevented or ameliorated? Should it be?

'Power' and 'resources': Much of politics can be construed as a struggle for power, and power means control of resources. When elections are held, the balance of power shifts: lobbyists have more or less influence, funds are re-allocated and new policies become possible. Political science deals with how power and the economy are interdependent, and in the events context this requires studying how various parties (political or otherwise) exert influence to get what they want.

In his examination of tourism and politics, Hall (1994) pointed out the negative side of using events to achieve political goals. Events can not only be used as an excuse for over-riding normal planning and consultation processes, but can also displace power-less groups – especially in the inner city – in the name of urban renewal and economic development. He rightly argued that mega-events are almost always sought after by the community's elite who stand to benefit the most, whereas ordinary residents are seldom consulted. Hall noted that proponents of the successful Sydney, Australia bid for the 2000 Summer Olympic Games regarded opponents as 'unpatriotic' or 'unAustralian' and that the public was consulted only by means of polls.

Sometimes we confuse power with dominant value systems, when in fact it is the dominance of a value or belief (say in the free market versus socialism) that gives power to certain groups and political parties. Is there any use in opposing a government's policy on events, such as whether or not to provide grants or tax relief, if in fact that policy reflects the country's dominant value system?

Research on the Political Science of Events

Both humanistic and scientific methodologies are employed in political studies. Political scientists use methods and techniques that relate to the kinds of inquiries sought: primary sources such as historical documents and official records, secondary sources such as scholarly journal articles, survey research, statistical analysis and model building.

Research by Hiller (2000a) provided a look at the politics of event bidding, namely the people and organizations backing Cape Town's campaign to win the Olympics. As observed by the Canadian Task Force on Federal Sport Policy (cited by Chernushenko, 1994: 57), community bids for sport events are usually promoted by influential community members which leads to intense pressure at political levels to give support. Events, given their image-making potential, present attractive opportunities for propagandizing and blatant political messages. At its worst, this can lead to manipulation or control over media coverage – either to hide elements or to highlight others. Event boycotts have occasionally been used as political tools, especially at the Olympics.

Hall (1992: 99) argued that 'Emphasis should be placed on the allocation of resources for events and the manner in which interests influence this process, particularly through the interaction of power, values, interests, place, and the processes of capital accumulation.'

Law

Governments at all levels pass a multitude of laws, each of which is enforceable by police or other formal action. Laws either forbid actions or mandate them. They govern how persons and organizations interact, and what happens in cases of violations and disputes. There is a vast legal system for law making and law enforcement, including layers of courts, the law profession and law enforcers. A central tenet of democratic societies is 'the rule of law' in which 'justice' is based on law and the courts rather than arbitrary decisions. This is all supposed to prevent abuses and protect 'fundamental rights', but of course all these concepts are value laden and change from one country to another (Figure 4.6).

Law	Nature and meanings: the event experience	Antecedents to attending events	Planning and producing events	Outcomes and the impacted	Processes and patterns
• The legal system, including legislators, courts and police • Specific laws and regulations	• Events as real and implicit contracts • Event experiences shaped by social/legal differences	• Perception of legal implications as a factor in the decision to travel or attend events	• Laws and regulations pertaining to event production • Legal considerations for event management	• Interpretations of justice • Legal recourse for loss or injury at events	• Changing laws and regulations, accountability

Figure 4.6   Law.

Events operate within political and legal systems that at once facilitate, constrain, and hold accountable the people and organizations producing them. What events can be held, and what activities allowed, is a legal matter. Every event producer understands the need for obeying laws, satisfying the regulatory agencies, involving the police in security matters, and obtaining the advice of lawyers when it comes to contracts, risk assessment, and many other technical matters. Event-producing organizations need to be legally sanctioned or incorporated. Taxes have to be paid and audits filed. One source is a book written and published by David Becker (2006) entitled the *Essential Legal Guide to Events*. Bear in mind that the law is different in every country.

Justice

'Distributive justice' is a principle that applies to economic development and impact assessment, raising the question of who benefits and who pays? 'Legal justice' is another concept altogether, and is tied closely to constitutions and the courts. If something goes wrong, can the aggrieved party find justice?

Legal Considerations Influencing Demand, Experiences and Meanings

Do people assess legal liabilities and risks when making decisions to attend events? They should, given all the things that can and do go wrong, often followed by police action or lawsuits. Because events exist within a legal environment, does this actually shape the experience or meanings attached to them? For example, attending a protest certainly carries with it some expectation of confrontation, possibly even civil disobedience. Going to a party and engaging in some form of elicit behaviour (drugs, drinking, sex) absolutely places the participant and others in a potentially dangerous situation. Even the most ordinary event experiences like attending a concert, convention or exhibition entail some form of risk, some degree of legal constraints on one's behaviour, and moral if not legal obligations in the case of emergencies. How do guests, consumers and participants feel about these issues?

Although advice is readily available on risk management and contracts for event management, little research has been undertaken on the legal side of events. There is a need to examine event organizations and the law, the marketing functions from a legal perspective and the event experience as impacted by all the stakeholders' perceptions of liability. It has to be asked if the fear of litigation is seriously altering the practice of event management and the range of event experiences available. Certainly it can be observed that many forms of organizational and individual risk taking are declining.

Chapter Summary

Philosophy was the first foundation discipline considered in this chapter. It has relevance to any discussion of aesthetics, as in event design, and ethics, which is important in event management. Of great interest is the potential for applying phenomenological methods and hermeneutics to gain a better understanding of the planned event experiences. Although it is not possible to advocate one all-embracing philosophy of events, a series of questions was asked that can help us when contemplating event policy and practice, and related societal values.

Religious studies is a social science, unlike theology which is based on faith and religious dogma. Because of the religious nature of many events and rituals, comparative religious studies has an important contribution to make in Event Studies. Religious and spiritual experience is also important as a motivator for attending certain events. The study of pilgrimage and related events is part of this discipline.

Within the events literature a huge reliance on economics is evident, but mostly for economic impact studies. Development theories are relevant here, with the observation that demonstrating general or long-term economic benefits of events is a difficult challenge. Other theories and methods from this discipline have unrealized potential to assist Event Studies, especially in the area of microeconomics – the economics of consumers, firms and organizations. Economics is relevant to consumer studies, and especially important is an understanding of supply and demand interactions, including the concepts of utility, price and income elasticity, latent and induced demand, willingness to pay and consumer surplus. Lastly, we looked at economic justifications for government intervention or subsidization in the event sector, including the powerful arguments of market failure, public goods and economic efficiency.

Management itself draws heavily from psychology and sociology, but contains many theories and concepts of utmost importance to Event Studies. First we have to distinguish between the management of governmental, not-for-profit and for-profit events, as well as the roles of events in destination (tourism) management. A number of theories of the firm are applicable, even though research in these areas has been slow to develop: resource and knowledge based, stakeholder, network and collaboration theory, and population ecology in particular are useful. Theories on institutionalization are directly related to the concepts of event sustainability, life cycles, competition, professionalization and bureaucratization.

Political science and law have so far made minor contributions to event studies, but they are important foundations nevertheless. Policy is one of the major themes in event studies, and it occurs with a political environment. Knowledge of ideology, government institutions, interest groups and elites, lobbying, power and law is essential to effective event management and policy formulation. Legal considerations can even affect the nature of planned events (risk avoidance) and event decisions and experiences (because of liability issues).

Study Questions

- Discuss phenomenology and how it has potential to help us learn more about the planned event experience and its meanings.
- What questions should be asked to develop a philosophy of planned events?
- In what ways do religions impact on planned events?
- What is pilgrimage, both in sacred and secular terms?
- What economic justifications are there for public intervention in the events sector?
- What is meant by economic demand for events?
- Describe several theories of the firm and show their application to private, not-for-profit and public-sector events.
- Use both network and stakeholder theory to develop competitive strategies for events.
- How does ideology shape event policy?
- What is power, and how does it affect decisions made about events?
- What is justice and how is it relevant to Event Studies?

Further Reading

Becker, D. (2006). *The Essential Legal Guide to Events: A Practical Handbook for Event Professionals and Their Advisers* (self published).
Scott, W. (2001). *Institutions and Organizations*. Thousand Oaks, CA: Sage.
Tribe, J. (2005). *The Economics of Recreation, Leisure and Tourism* (3rd edn). Oxford: Elsevier.

Chapter 5
Foundation Disciplines: Part Three

Learning Objectives

■ Understand the nature of, and contributions made to Event Studies by these foundation disciplines:
  - History
  - Human geography
  - Future studies.
■ Understand the importance of planned events throughout history, and how events give structure and meaning to history.
■ Be able to assess specific events in an historical or evolutionary context.
■ Know why many events are connected to specific resources and places and what that means for environmental and other impacts.
■ Be able to explain spatial and temporal patterns of planned events.
■ Learn methods of future scanning and scenario making, and how to apply them in strategic planning.

Introduction

Patterns and Processes is the dynamic element in our model of Event Studies (Figure 1.3). In this chapter the two foundation disciplines of history and geography are considered in depth, representing the temporal and spatial dimensions. Future Studies might be considered an extension of history, an element in strategic planning, or a field of study on its own, but it is treated separately in order to stress the need for future thinking. The other two dynamic processes shaping Event Studies are considered in separate chapters, namely policy and knowledge creation.

Event Studies requires an understanding of history and consideration of the future, and these cannot be separated from the spatial dimension. Whatever happens in the world of planned events occurs somewhere, and those places are often very important to begin with, or are given meaning by the events held there. Furthermore, spatial and temporal interactions are in themselves important, such as in the seasonal distribution of harvest festivals linked to natural resources and farming communities, the innovation and global spread of new events assisted by mass media, and the cumulative impacts of one or all events within an area.

History

Superficially history is about dates and chronologies, but historical facts are only the starting point. The American Historical Association puts it this way (www.historians.org):

> *History, then, provides the only extensive materials available to study the human condition. It also focuses attention on the complex processes of social change, including the factors that are causing change around us today. Here, at base, are the two related reasons many people become enthralled with the examination of the past and why our society requires and encourages the study of history as a major subject in the schools.*

According to the American Historical Association, the ability to assess evidence, and to assess conflicting interpretations are essential to what historians do. 'Experience in assessing past examples of change is vital to understanding change in society today' (online at www.historians.org). Because historians are usually researching a topic or theme, and often from a disciplinary perspective, it is common to speak of 'historical geography', 'historical sociology', etc. All of the disciplines we talk about in this book can be studied through the lens of historical fact-finding and interpretation (Figure 5.1).

Historiography

Who chronicles the evolution and determines the importance of events through history, and on what evidence? Historical method is often focused on finding and understanding

History	Nature and meanings; the event experience	Antecedents to attending events	Planning and producing events	Outcomes and the impacted	Processes and patterns
• Documentation and analysis of human evolution and historic events • Historiography evaluates historical evidence and interpretations	• Importance of events through history • Changes in meanings attached to events • Changes in how people experience events	• Historical patterns and trends in demand for, and consumption of events • Changes in why people attend and what they want from events	• Evolution and life cycle of events • Changes in the supply of events and event types • Changes in planning and designing events	• Historical evidence of impacts • Analysis of long-term impacts	• History of specific events and of event types • Evolution of planned events in different cultures • History reflected in, and commemorated through planned events

Figure 5.1 History.

documents, determining their veracity, comparing the information with other sources and interpreting the meanings. There are standard issues concerning the accuracy of documents or witness testimony, the perceptual abilities of observers, and the possibility of bias or outright lies. A search for the truth, or at least a consensus on what happened and why, is at the heart of much historical research. Many historians write about historical 'facts', whereas others are concerned with how history is researched and interpreted – these people are 'historiographers'.

In this sense we can speak of both the history of planned events and the historiography of writing about event history. Indeed, there has been much criticism about historical analysis. Postmodernists and critical theorists often argue that too much history has been written by and for elites, from a dominant positivistic perspective, often ignoring or devaluing minority groups, the exploited, or losers of wars. If we get history wrong, then our contemporary values and attitudes might also be wrong.

History through the Lens of Planned Events

Canada's Province of Alberta celebrated its centennial of confederation in 2005, and to commemorate this important year the Calgary Herald newspaper published Our Alberta: A Calgary Herald Magazine Series Celebrating Alberta's Centennial. It is noteworthy that Issue 3 of this series, distributed free to all subscribers, was called The Sporting Life. I think they hit on a big theme here, in that many people remember history through the lens of great sporting or other public events. It featured team rivalries, heroes, development of female sports, World Cup skiing accomplishments, the annual Calgary

Stampede, the success of Spruce Meadows (a private horse show-jumping venue of international status), and of course the Calgary Winter Olympics of 1988.

The Olympic mega-event forever changed the psyche and even the form of the city. In growing up, maturing into an economic superpower (all based on energy reserves), a mega-event was needed. Albertans will always remember how that one event made such a big difference. Why? 'For 16 days in February of 1988, Calgary was the centre of the universe. The Winter Olympics made the city a rock star in the world's eyes. And 17 years later the memories still seem fresh'. Of course statements like this, from the Herald (p. 18), represent self-image rather than a fair assessment of the world's true opinions. But it is clear that great events can make a huge difference.

It is amazing how many cities and countries feel this way, reflecting a universal quest to be acknowledged, accepted and liked. In Germany for the 2006 World Cup of Football, signs were posted along autobahns imploring Germans to be hospitable to their guests from all over the world. It seemed to work, as one widely acknowledged outcome of hosting the World Cup was a newfound appreciation (at least in the global media) of Germany's modern appeal, its traditional charms and the friendliness of its people.

A history of the world (or any corner or aspect of it) has to include major planned and spontaneous events. Wars might or might not be planned, but victory celebrations and remembrance commemorations certainly are. A simple listing of dates and events is one way that people remember the flow of history. Some of those events just happened, others were planned. Increasingly, and this is a personal view, planned events are more central to our recollection and interpretation of history and even geography. When I ask people around the world if they know anything about Calgary, about the only constant is knowledge that it hosted the Winter Olympics. The annual Stampede comes in a distant second.

Planned events now seem to occupy more space and time in the media, they enjoy a bigger piece of our attention and they seem to have more impact on how we perceive ourselves and our place in the world. I do not want to discount the significance of wars and natural disasters, but after a while – unless we were personally affected – they all seem to blur. But our memories of personal involvement in special events, of the big celebrations and shows we see on television, of the landmark meetings we went to, of the world getting together for 'The Games' or a Millennial party, those seem to endure.

There are good reasons why planned events mark and give meaning to history. First, I think we relate more to accomplishments and good times than to disasters and conflicts. Who really wants to remember death and destruction when it constantly repeats? We grow weary of it. Those desiring to keep alive the memory of dark parts of history have to go to great lengths to create historical places and events, even giving rise to what has been called 'dark tourism'.

And there is a diversity and creativity to planned events that signifies invention, rebirth, exploration and other great triumphs of the human spirit. They help us to transcend our personal lives, to become fulfilled. Ordinary news hardly ever does that, and when we do feel satisfaction from a news story, how often is a story derived from or about a planned event? Think of sports, the arts, education, trade – all require events to generate news.

Events and Ordinary Life

Lives in the millions go by unmarked by historians, but each individual, family and social group has its own myriad ways of marking or celebrating the little as well as the important occasions – the *rites de passage* much studied by cultural anthropologists. There are birthdays and anniversaries, weddings and funerals, reunions and periodic parties, first communions and *bar or bat mitzvahs*, graduations and recognitions, annual holiday celebrations (e.g., Christmas and Thanksgiving), Fathers' and Mothers' days, and so on. Think about the personal and family events in your life. Which ones are most memorable and which are most important in defining who you are and how you think about yourself? Now extend this mental exercise to the larger, public events you have attended.

From my own youth I fondly remember family outings to the circus (it was still a special event when it came to our small town), the little village and county fairs, the larger regional exhibitions in Ottawa and Kitchener, and the biggest of them all in Toronto, all in Ontario. Making a day-trip to the big city for the exhibition experience was something really special, associated with summer and holidays, family togetherness and treats.

Much has changed since then, including the explosion of sports and festivals, the heavy impact of the media and corporate sponsorship. The world was simpler then, but of course our recollections are always influenced by nostalgia.

Events and Society

Christmas, Thanksgiving or other religious holidays have the impressive consequence of getting entire populations to do very similar things by way of commemoration and celebration. In an historical context, these special times called holidays or the 'holiday season' do change, generally in response to evolving societal values, and perhaps in reaction to broader events shaping the times – like war or terrorism. In this sense, an entire population or country might change its traditions because of what else is happening in the world.

In some parts of the world, like China, Western holidays and celebrations including Christmas and Halloween are just catching on. Why? Is it the desire for new forms of celebration? Is there a fundamental human need for gift giving? Or is it the influence of the media and travel? The fact is, events and their social and cultural meanings are constantly shifting. Imitation is rampant, but there are also basic social and cultural reasons for the spread or demise of any type of special event.

Events and the Economy

There is no doubt whatsoever that the economic significance of planned events has grown dramatically in recent decades, so much so that scholars and critics are talking about the 'corporatization' of events, loss of authenticity, standardization and the 'festivalization' of cities. It has not all been a bad influence, of course, because so many resources have been provided to events of all kinds that they have flourished and become a mainstay of contemporary lifestyles.

With so much commercial and political–economic emphasis being placed on planned events, it is inevitable that their historical significance has increased. Many once-minor or regional/national sport events have become global media and touristic events, such as the football fever generated every 4 years by the World Cup. Do we not remember these events and who hosted them, visit the host communities because of their economic and touristic importance, then look forward to the next ones?

There is a natural tendency for people to assign extra importance to events that have become big, possess economic and media importance, receive the highest level of corporate sponsorship, generate the highest level of bidding and result in the most substantial tangible and economic impacts. These are all modern, global measures of importance and success, of uniqueness and noteworthiness. In effect, the economic significance of events has shaped our very definition of which events are truly special.

The History of Events, and Their Life Cycle

What are the earliest records of festivals and events? Why are the Olympics so well documented, and even the subject of research centres around the world, compared to other sport and cultural events? How have fairs and exhibitions evolved? Where and when was the first flash mob? These are all questions for historical research and historiography.

Planned events of all kinds have been an integral part of civilization for thousands of years, from political assemblies to sport competitions, feasts and revelry to religious celebrations. What explains the vast history of events? Some would suggest that people are simply gregarious, social creatures, but that in itself does not explain the economic and cultural importance attached to planned events, the formalization of related professions or creation of specialist venues. It could easily be argued that events are a fundamental and essential human experience, both rooted in culture and at the same time helping to define our civilizations.

The evolution and 'life cycle' of events is an important historical topic with management implications. Every consumer 'product', including events, has a life cycle. A life cycle is not fully predictable, nor is the model deterministic. Stages in the life cycle are not always clear, but events do have a birth, they grow and mature and many die or require rejuvenation. This temporal aspect of events, and factors shaping the life cycle, has been studied by several researchers (Getz and Frisby, 1988; Frisby and Getz, 1989; Getz, 1993a, 2000a; Walle, 1994).

Sofield and Li (1998) examined an 800-year-old festival in China from a historical perspective and showed how politics and tourism influenced its transformation in recent years. Despite the changes, the researchers believed it retained its cultural authenticity. Sofield and Sivan (2003) showed how Hong Kong's famous Dragon Boat Races had shifted from culture to sports tourism in its orientation, with tourism helping to preserve the tradition. For an account of the history of a category of event in its cultural context, see Jarvie (1991) on the Highland Games.

Beverland et al. (2001) compared the organization and evolution of several New Zealand wine festivals, concluding that all of them had changed in terms of organizational structure, programme, strategy or consumers, and indeed each stage had been marked by a crises. In fact that seems to be an emerging theme, that sustainable events learn and adapt from crises, and that they have to rejuvenate themselves to avoid decline. In the Management chapter more attention is given to sustainability and the institutionalization of events.

A History of Event Producers and Managers

Many people share my fascination with reading about events in ancient history. What's more, many of the forms and styles of planned events have continued uninterrupted through thousands of years! But there is one question apparently few have asked: Who planned and produced these ancient events? Were they revered and rich professionals? Did any historian record their stories? What can we learn from them?

The ancient Romans, although fond of their events, were contemptuous of slaves, prostitutes, actors and the procurers of gladiators. So perhaps the job of event producer was reviled, even while the rich sponsors were elevated in society by their largesse. Nevertheless they had a big job, and it must also have been dangerous. Consider the shows in which ferocious wild animals were turned lose on captives, or slaughtered; or the miniaturized sea battles requiring artificial lakes. Disasters were reported, such as crazed elephants rampaging through the crowd, and the collapse of temporary wooden seating. Standards were set for safety. And hooliganism was also known, with parochial rivalries among spectators resulting in riots; so much so that games had to be cancelled. It all sounds so familiar. (There are many websites devoted to ancient Roman and Greek games, such as www.roman-empire.net/society/soc-games.html.)

The Greatest Parade Ever?

What is amazing about the Grand Procession of Ptolemy II Philadelphus is not just its scale, but the familiarity of many of its elements to modern observers of parades and festivals. In the following extract is a description by the historian/travel writer Athanaeus. First he describes the great tent decorated with elaborate care. Then come details of the parade, full of religious symbolism and spectacle. The source is: *Ancient History Sourcebook*: www.fordham.edu/HALSALL/ancient/asbook.html.

Athanaeus (fl. c. 200 CE): The Great Spectacle and Procession of Ptolemy II Philadelphus, 285 BCE

History, Book V, Chapter 25: *'First I will describe the tent prepared inside the citadel, apart from the place provided to receive the soldiers, artisans, and foreigners. For it was wonderfully beautiful, and worth talking of. Its size was such that it could accommodate one hundred and thirty couches [for banqueters] arranged in a circle. The roof was upborne on wooden pillars fifty cubits high of which four were arranged to look like palm trees. On the outside of the pillars ran a portico, adorned with a peristyle on three sides with a vaulted roof. Here it was the feasters could sit down. The interior of this was surrounded with scarlet curtains; in the middle of the space, however, were suspended strange hides of beasts, strange both for their variegated color, and their remarkable size. The part which surrounded this portico in the open air was shaded by myrtle trees and laurels, and other suitable shrubs.*

And now to go on to the shows and processions exhibited; for they passed through the Stadium of the city. First of all there went the procession of Lucifer [the name given to the planet Venus] for the fete began at the time when that star first appears. Then came processions in honor of the several gods. . . .

The next-was a four-wheeled wagon fourteen cubits high and eight cubits wide; it was drawn by one hundred and eighty men. On it was an image of Dionysus – ten cubits high. He was pouring libations from a golden goblet, and had a purple tunic reaching to his feet. . . . After many other wagons came one twenty-five cubits long, and fifteen broad; and this was drawn by six hundred men. On this wagon was a sack, holding three thousand measures of wine, and consisting of leopards' skins sewn together. This sack allowed its liquor to escape, and it gradually flowed over the whole road.

[An endless array of similar wonders followed; also a vast number of palace servants displaying the golden vessels of the king; twenty-four chariots drawn by four elephants each; the royal menagerie – twelve chariots drawn by antelopes, fifteen by buffaloes, eight by pairs of ostriches, eight by zebras; also many mules, camels, etc., and twenty-four lions.]

After these came a procession of troops – both horsemen and footmen, all superbly armed and appointed. There were 57,600 infantry, and 23,200 cavalry. All these marched in the procession . . . all in their appointed armor . . .'

There is an apt expression in French: *'plus ça change, plus c 'est la même chose'* (or the more things change, the more they stay the same). It certainly appears to apply to the world of events. Their forms, and many of their meanings, have endured in most civilizations for thousands of years. Historical researchers should focus on the change process, and what exactly is different today.

Daniel Boorstin, 'Pseudo-events', and the Authenticity Debate

Historian Daniel Boorstin, in his book *The Image: A Guide to Pseudo-Events in America* (1961), opened a lasting debate about events and authenticity by claiming that life in America was full of 'pseudo-events'. They are staged, scripted and counterfeit – just like many celebrities and tourism products. According to Boorstin, a pseudo-event is ...

- Not spontaneous; it comes about because someone has planned or incited it.
- Planned primarily, but not always exclusively, for the purpose of being reported or reproduced, and its occurrence is arranged for the convenience of the reporting or reproducing media.
- Ambiguous in terms of its relation to the underlying reality of the situation; whether it is 'real' or not is less important than its newsworthiness and ability to gain favourable attention.
- Usually intended to be a self-fulfilling prophecy (in terms of public relations, if we produce an event to show that something is good, we expect that the claim will be accepted).

And why are they so popular? Boorstin suggested the pseudo-event is appealing because it is scripted and dramatic, includes a cast of interesting characters and produces iconic images such as impassioned crowds, hugging families or rainstorms of patriotic balloons. They are designed to be re-assuring, create the illusion that we who watch it are 'informed', and it leads to an endless number of other pseudo-events.

Boorstin particularly criticized public relations professionals, and they remain sensitive to the issue of manipulation through pseudo-events. Michael Turney wrote (online: www.nku.edu/~turney/):

> One of the most frequent and effective ways public relations practitioners control situations and the circumstances surrounding an organization's interactions with its publics is by conducting 'special events'. Instead of waiting for happenstance to provide a situation in which the organization and its publics encounter one another and which may or may not turn out positively, they orchestrate a situation that occurs when the organization wants it to and proceeds in ways that favour the organization.

Journalists are rightly concerned about pseudo-events, fearing they are being manipulated and that their reporting of a staged event actually makes a falsehood appear to be true. Judith Clarke write about this problem in the article 'How journalists judge the "reality" of an international "pseudo-event": a study of correspondents who covered the final withdrawal of Vietnamese troops from Cambodia in 1989' (in *Journalism*, Vol. 4, No. 1, 50–75 (2003). She said:

'As proxy information-gatherers for their audiences, journalists often cover "pseudo-events", whose purpose is to present to the world a version of reality set up by the organizers. These are usually people with links to wealth and power but they can also be out-groups trying to get their "real" news noticed. For reporters the challenge is whether to cover these events at face value or delve deeper to find the truth. This study examines through a questionnaire and content analysis how reporters who covered Vietnam's final withdrawal of troops from Cambodia in 1989, staged as a pseudo-event, dealt with the opposing interpretations by Vietnam, an international outcast, and its opponents, who said the pullout was a fake. The power of the pseudo-event was such that nearly all journalists accepted the Vietnamese version as it was shown to them but most also used their knowledge of the international situation as a reinforcement.

The sense that political conventions are no longer real events, but contrived, scripted performances, designed to create a marketable image of a candidate, is stronger now than ever, and has led networks and journalists to wonder cynically whether such events deserve coverage at all'.

Authenticity remains a hot topic in the tourism and events literature (also see Getz, 1998b for a discussion). More is said later in the book.

Human Geography

This social science discipline has concentrated on human–resource interactions, especially spatial and temporal patterns of human activity and including impacts on the environment. Human-to-human interactions are a related theme, encompassing social or economic reasons for meeting other people and how these are shaped by space and places (Shaw and Williams, 2004).

Geographic analysis can be linked directly to any of the other social sciences, and what is particularly relevant to the study of events can be described as economic/developmental, cultural/social, historical, political or behavioural geography. Geographical analysis can also be applied to almost any form of human endeavour or particular environment, so that we can also speak of urban and rural geography, or event geography (Figure 5.2). Links to physical geography, or the environmental sciences, are always present. And a feminist or welfarist/marxist perspective can be taken on geographic studies.

'Behavioural geography' draws mostly on psychology and focuses on the cognitive processes underlying spatial reasoning, decision-making and behaviour. Topics of relevance to events include 'wayfinding' (how people move around), the construction of 'cognitive maps' (our mental maps of places, like event sites), 'place attachment' (our emotional connections to communities), the development of attitudes about space and

Human geography	Nature and meanings; the event experience	Antecedents to attending events	Planning and producing events	Outcomes and the impacted	Processes and patterns
• Studies human–resource interactions, especially spatial and temporal patterns of human activity and including impacts on the environment	• Linking events to resources, culture and human activity (e.g., harvest festivals; seasonality factors)	• Demand linked to distance and accessibility • The influence of religion and culture across regions	• Event settings • Locational analysis	• Environmental impacts analysed spatially	• Spatial and temporal patterns (rural distribution; growth of events as part of urban renewal schemes)

Figure 5.2   Human geography.

place and decisions and behaviour based on imperfect knowledge of one's environs. There is clearly a close connection to 'environmental psychology'.

'Historical Geography' studies geographical patterns through time, such as the evolving distribution of events in a region. How people interact with their environment creates 'cultural landscapes', and this can include a variety of resource-based, place-specific events. 'Economic Geography' is the study of the location, distribution and spatial organization of economic activities. Questions asked might include: Do economic 'laws' determine resource use, settlement patterns or the distribution and evolution of events? What unique, local or national political and cultural forces shape event formation, sustainability and density? 'Development Geography' is a related field of inquiry, focusing on various factors shape economic and social development, or population and demographics.

'Welfare Geography' is also closely related. Why are some people disadvantaged, and what does this have to do with resource use, urban form or the distribution and nature of planned events? Welfare geographers tend to be 'critical' in their methodologies. 'Cultural Geography' looks at the relationships between environment and culture. For example, it is clear that cultures are shaped by the places in which they developed, featuring climate and resources and by trade and other external contacts, related to politics, accessibility and evolving communications. Cultural tourism is closely linked, especially in terms of assessing the distribution of cultural attractions or resources, consideration of cultural regions and place identity or distinctiveness.

Spatial and Temporal Patterns of Events

The spatial and temporal distribution of events is clearly a topic for geographers. Event distribution patterns are at least partially dependent on the natural resource base, such as those themed or derived from agricultural products or other primary economic activities like mining. But the pattern of events in the landscape has been changing dramatically in response to powerful forces. Specifically, the resource base of events has shifted away from natural resources and they are now created strategically.

Robert Janiskee's many contributions to the geography of events deserve special recognition. In a 1980 paper he examined the themes, locations, timing, programme of activities, reported attendance and benefits of rural festivals in South Carolina. His 1991 paper looked more carefully at festival history in the state, including when they were established, and their spatial distribution over time. Janiskee's (1994) paper documented how his 'Fest List' database was compiled from various published sources and interviews and presented analysis of growth in festival numbers. He saw clearly in graphical format an almost exponential growth rate, with exploding numbers of new events after 1970.

In a 1996 paper Janiskee examined the monthly and seasonal patterns of community festivals in the USA, making it clear that their numbers are relatively low in winter, late autumn and early spring. Although regional patterns are different, across the country a huge number occurs on the July 4th weekend. In the conclusions to this paper he raised the issue of saturation, and asked how many festivals can be held at any one time. It has been observed by other authors that growth in event numbers, and their concentration in certain areas or times of the year, could result in event failure (Jones, 1993; Richards, 1996).

Most contemporary festivals are held in summer or fair-weather months (also see Ryan et al., 1998, regarding New Zealand events), although it should be stressed that other types of events, like business meetings and conventions, peak in the Spring and Autumn and some sport events are most frequent in winter. Cultural factors and traditions help keep certain seasons dominant for specific types of events, but many are now being created specifically to overcome the traditional seasonality pattern of tourism. One study of event tourism seasonality was undertaken by Yoon et al. (2000) who examined the event market in Michigan. Wicks and Fesenmaier (1995) found summer to be the most popular for travelling to events in the US Midwest, with Fall being next more popular.

Event Tourism: The Geographical Perspective

Supply-demand interactions are fertile ground for event geographers. Analysis and forecasting of demand for a particular event or a region's events will in part depend on population distribution, competition and intervening opportunities. Along these lines, Bohlin (2000) used a traditional tool of geographers, the 'distance-decay function', to exam festival-related travel in Sweden. He found that attendance decreased with distance, although recurring and well-established events have greater 'drawing power'.

Getz (1997) illustrated several models of potential event tourism patterns in a region. One option is clustering events in service centres, as opposed to dispersing them over a large, rural area. These are related to the concept of 'attractiveness' and also have implications for the distribution of benefits and costs. Analysis of the zones of influence of events has been undertaken by Teigland (1996) specific to the Lillehammer (Norway) Winter Olympics, and this method has implications for event planning, especially regarding mega-events with multiple venues. The elements of these zones of influence are the gateways, venue locations, tourist flows, transport management and displacement of other activities.

Event Attractiveness

Arising from numerous event visitor studies it can be concluded that most events rely on local and regional (day-trip) visitors, not long-distance tourists. Even World's Fairs and Olympics must sell most of their tickets to residents. The concept of tourist 'attractiveness' must therefore be assessed for each event. How powerful an attraction is the event for various target segments? Who will travel and stay overnight, versus those who will only stay a few years then return home?

Lee and Crompton (2003) assessed the drawing power of three events located in Ocean City New Jersey. Three festivals in one city in one year (held in May, late September, and November to January) were compared in terms of the number of tourists attracted specifically because of the event, and the distances travelled (i.e., the 'market areas'). All three proved to be valuable in drawing tourists (41–55% of attendance) and generating economic benefits, although attendance was much higher at the September event.

Hierarchies of event places could be determined through analysis of existing events and event venues, leading to implications for place marketing. Better measurement of the spatial distribution of event tourist activities and spending will aid in forecasting event impacts, as will studies of 'time switching' and 'displacement'. Analysis of event patterns in time and space is essential to gaining a better understanding of event trends and potential competition. One technique deserving wider application was used by Verhoven et al. (1998). Their 'demand mapping' enabled them to examine patterns of travel to festivals.

Time Switching and Displacement

There is no doubt that people alter their travel plans because of events. For example, they are going to a certain destination for business or pleasure anyway, but decide to time their visit with an event because it provides additional value to the trip. This 'time switching' is an important limitation in estimating the economic impact of events, because the spending of time switchers cannot be attributed as a benefit of the event itself (Dwyer et al., 2000a, b). Switching is more likely to occur in major cities and resorts that have considerable drawing power all year round, as opposed to small towns and rural areas where an event might be the only reason for people to make the trip. Accordingly, economic and image-related impacts of events can be expected to be greater in smaller population centres.

Another theoretical and methodological concern when conducting impact evaluations is the matter of 'displacement'. Regular tourists can be displaced when events take up available accommodation, and it is therefore often counter-productive to hold major events in the peak tourist season. For example, Hultkrantz (1998) was able to demonstrate that the World Championship of Athletics held in Gothenburg, Sweden in 1995, had the effect of displacing as many expected tourists as were attracted by the event, resulting in no gain in tourist volumes. Of course, it is possible that event tourists generate greater economic impact owning to their spending patterns, and there is also the publicity value to consider.

Major events also motivate people to travel to one place as opposed to another, so that during the World's Fair (Expo) in Vancouver, Canada (1986) normal travel patterns were disrupted – Vancouver and British Columbia gained, but the rest of Canada lost traffic (Lee, 1987).

The spatial distribution of costs and benefits is of particular interest in event geography, and so too are issues of social equity. Two very specific geographic questions are those of defining the region for which economic benefits are to be estimated, and measuring the spatial distribution of spending by visitors.

Event Places

In terms of theory building, a crucial question is the extent to which certain types of events are resource dependent or rooted in specific environments. The matter of authenticity should be explored more from a geographic point of view, such as addressing the issue of how – for example – a food festival can both emerge from and reinforce a distinct sense of place. While economic and environmental impacts of events and event tourism have been explored by many, there is still a need for attention to the process by which events help shape and define urban environments, particularly in the context of urban renewal, mega-events and event venues. More attention should also be paid to explaining, rather than mapping, spatial and temporal variations in events. What are the relative contributions of resources, culture, policy and economics in accounting for patterns?

All events require a venue (often specific facilities, but sometimes a street or open space), people to organize and manage them, customers to pay and often sponsors to subsidize them. As communities and destinations become more competitive for tourism and investment, more economic resources are committed to events. So the nature and distribution of events is increasingly shaped by policy.

The study of event places has barely been addressed in the literature. Traditionally, many events have been associated with specific places that take on, at least temporarily, special cultural significance. Historically town squares and parks, even streets, have fulfilled this important civic function, but in recent decades the trend is to purpose-build festival and event places, including multi-purpose sport and arts complexes, festival squares and parks and waterfront facilities for community event programming. The result of these capital and social investments are special places that can be identified by their monuments, special-purpose buildings, attractive landscape and vistas and frequent ceremonial use. They definitely attract visitors who view them as must-see, urban icons. Several authors have reported on the roles of events in urban renewal projects (Hughes, 1993; Mules, 1993), and it can be concluded that event programming and creation of event places has become a necessary element in urban development.

What is the nature of an event place? Getz (2001) examined festival places, comparing a number in Europe and North America. A conceptual model was developed, but it's testing and elaboration will require collaboration from the fields of environmental psychology, urban design, arts, event management and sociology. The model focuses on the interdependence of elements of setting (location and design), management systems (including the programme) and people. An important issue for researchers is to examine the interactions of event places with tourists and residents.

The capacity of sites or communities to host events is an important topic in need of further research. While crowds often add to the appeal of events, how much is too much? One study (Wickham and Kerstetter, 2000) examined the relationship between place attachment and perceptions of crowding in an event setting. Abbott and Geddie (2000) argued that effective crowd management techniques can reduce management's legal liability. At the site level, attention is frequently given to the spatial component in estimating event attendance, such as through aerial mapping of crowds (Raybould et al., 2000) or spatial stratification in sampling (Denton and Furse, 1993).

Future Studies

Human fascination with the future is at least equal to our curiosity about the past. Visioning and goal setting is totally future oriented. When we talk about planning events we are actually seeking to shape the future. General research enables us to say more about probable future conditions, while marketing research gives us greater confidence that our plans will succeed. It is no wonder, then, that 'futurism' and 'future studies' have become so popular.

'Future studies' is not prophecy, as in predicting the future, nor is it science fiction in terms of letting one's imagination run wild. It is an interdisciplinary approach to gaining understanding of how today's conditions and trends will likely shape the future (in part, it is therefore impact forecasting), and how future conditions could be shaped by policies and actions taken (or not taken) today – as in how we need to reduce greenhouse emissions to avoid the worst effects of global warming. Trend analysis, forecasting, environmental and future scanning and scenario making are tools of future studies (Figure 5.3).

Future studies	Nature and meanings; the event experience	Antecedents to attending events	Planning and producing events	Outcomes and the impacted	Processes and patterns
• Future thinking (can we know or shape the future?) • Trend analysis • Environmental and future scanning • Forecasting and scenario making	• How we think about time affects our experiences and the meanings we attach to them	• How do people plan for future events? • Will virtual reality replace live event experiences?	• Environmental and future scanning applied to the event sector	• Predicting event impacts • Future scenarios (likely and desired future states)	• Changes in how we think about time and the future • What do we envisage about the future of events?

Figure 5.3 Future studies.

The Future is a Social Construct

The future is by definition unknown, and somewhat unpredictable. Even the ways in which we think about it, and the language we use, is a social construct. To some 'the future' is full of science fiction images, to others it is the great unknown, and for entrepreneurs it is opportunity.

Jason Ensor argued that our conception of time and modes of time keeping are culturally constructed, and therefore vary a great deal. 'Socio-temporal cues' exist in each society to help us keep track, and these cues are often annual events like national days and cultural–religious holidays. He also argued that time has become a commodity, with real value to companies and individuals, so that we have to save time, use time wisely, and keep track of billable minutes. We are always looking at clocks and counting down time to our next obligation. It is parcelled and rationed. 'Free time' is anything but free – it is extremely valuable.

We incorporate the future into our daily lives when we say things like: 'it's a good invest-ment' (i.e., I will be richer in a few years), or 'I will wait for the price to come down' (technological innovations are always expensive at first, then consumers see the price fall rapidly). Indeed, because technological progress is so fast, and most innovations have already been predicted (or pre-sold through exhibitions and TV programmes), we are no longer surprised by the next innovation – we are only surprised that it is not yet cheap to purchase! In other words, the future is already imagined and partially consumed.

The future is becoming an obsession, and this has direct policy implications. Politicians promise not just a better future, but actual deliverables. We begin to take for granted that it will get better, not worse, and that what has been promised will become reality. Jason Ensor argued that we should think about the future in ways that are critical and lead to more choices, rather than being constrained by current ideology or narrow thinking.

Mental Exercise

Imagine one aspect of event policy or of environmental conditions that affect you (say, financial support for festivals, or conditions affecting bidding on conferences, or ability to develop new event products) and then prepare a short list of:

1. *What you sincerely hope will happen.*
2. *What you fully expect to happen within 5 years.*
3. *What you will oppose, if it appears to be happening.*

Can you assign probabilities to these future occurrences? Can you assess the implications?

Trend Analysis and Extrapolation

A basic method is trend analysis and extrapolation, in order to demonstrate what will likely happen if current forces and trends continue. This is a useful starting point for discussions about the future. For example, I will argue that if current leisure and tourism trends continue it is probable that events will continue to grow in importance as tourist attractions and, more precisely, that sport tourism involving participants in marathons – already an obvious trend – will peak in popularity within 10 years. That, of course, com-bines extrapolation with a prediction based on general knowledge of leisure and tourism trends (i.e., that there is a typical growth and maturity process at work, based on both demand and supply factors).

A related issue is to separate fast-paced, but short-lived fads adopted by specific groups, from slow growth but persistent trends that effect whole societies. According to the article on 'trends' in Wikipedia there are three major types. 'Mega-trends' extend over many generations, consisting of complex interactions between many factors (e.g., major social trends such as the growth and globalization of event tourism). 'Trend babies' are possible new trends arising from innovations, projects, beliefs or actions that have the potential to grow and eventually go mainstream. Somebody has to identify these in the early stages, and they might get it wrong. 'Branching trends': Once a mega-trend is identified, many branching or inter-related trends can be detected and evaluated. For example, the whole event tourism trend has many niche-market trends spinning off, including marathon running, food and wine events, etc. One can then look at trends in the market segments for each type of event, such as gender based, linked to levels of involvement, or their destination choices.

Scenario Making

We can imagine the future in one of two ways, in the context of strategic planning. In the first we ask 'what might happen, and how can we prepare for it?' This approach includes the options of combating or opposing trends that lead to undesirable future states. It involves working backwards from a predicted or alternative future sate. In the second approach, ask 'how can we ensure the future that we desire?' This approach leads to strategies and actions intended to shape the future to our liking, such as policies and events that will achieve desired social or economic impacts.

All future scenarios begin with an understanding of history, current forces and conditions and trends. Scenarios emerge from understanding, not dreaming. The more you know about the world of events, the better you will be at scenario making and strategic planning.

Mental Exercise

Consider global trends that are shaping the world of planned events, then for one trend develop a scenario to describe both a desirable and undesirable future state and consider how to attain or prevent it from happening. This can be done at a local, regional or larger scale.

Delphi

The Delphi Method has traditionally been a technique aimed at building consensus about an opinion or future conditions. Multiple rounds of surveying are typically required, both to identify trends and possible future consequences, and to assign probabilities and consider implications. Because expert panels are usually recruited for Delphi, it is also a way to create new knowledge, or at least to synthesize the knowledge and opinions from many experts.

Ideally, through multiple rounds, the weight of evidence an opinion leads to a consensus or at least a dominant evaluation of what is likely to happen and its consequences.

Enduring minority views are also of interest, as they describe alternative scenarios that might have to be taken into account by planners.

Its use in the events sector has been limited, but Carlsen, Getz and Soutar (2001) employed Delphi to examine event evaluation practice and needs, while Weber and Ladkin (2004) used the expert panel to identify and assess trends affecting the convention industry.

Global Challenges for the Events Sector

'15 Global Challenges' have been defined and tracked since 1997 by The Millennium Project of the American Council for the United Nations University, in its State of the Future series of annual reports (see: www.acunu.org). The challenges were defined through a Delphi panel approach and are updated annually.

Are there 10 or 15 global challenges for the events sector? Here are my starting-point suggestions, each of which can be the subject of future and policy studies:

1. Terrorism threatens events more than most forms of business, leisure and tourism.
2. All events must become green and environmentally sustainable.
3. Events have to equally benefit residents as well as tourists.
4. Professionalism in event management must be globally implemented.
5. Event planning should be fully integrated with other forms of environmental, community, economic, tourism and leisure planning.
6. Governments at all levels should adopt comprehensive policies and support programmes for the event sector.
7. Events must be valued and evaluated equally in social, cultural, environmental and economic terms in order to be sustainable.
8. Event design, production and management education has to be embedded in Event Studies.
9. The event sector will continue to grow and diversify to the point where the supply of events in many areas threatens to exceed resources or demand.
10. New event types will continue to emerge, giving rise to unexpected challenges and opportunities for policy-makers, planners and managers.

In the spirit of Delphi, a group of expert panel participants could be asked to suggest new challenges (and opportunities could be added), the probabilities of certain consequences occurring within a specified time period and the importance or severity of each consequence. Through several rounds, a consensus or majority view would hopefully emerge. Minority or dissenting voices have to be respected and communicated.

Chapter Summary

The patterns and processes that provide a dynamic element to Event Studies include the spatial (geographic) and temporal (history and future studies), as well as knowledge creation and policy. These forces continuously interact, resulting in some obvious patterns and trends, and requiring serious study to detect hidden or emergent ones.

History is more than dates and chronologies, it is systematic exploration and analysis of the origins and evolution of events, their life cycles and possible future states. Without historical knowledge there can be no future studies, and no strategic planning. We should be particularly interested in the fact that many aspects of contemporary event design and programming were established hundreds and even thousands of years ago, yet we know little about who produced them.

Creative event ideas spread over time and space (innovation-diffusion was introduced earlier), as do policies and strategies such as those related to event tourism. Events themselves evolve, demonstrating a life cycle, with some failing and others becoming institutions. There are also globalization forces at work which result in a sense of 'placelessness' as some events can appear anywhere without authentic attachment to community or culture.

Taking a geographical approach, there is first the obvious seasonality of events and their distribution in both time and space. This leads to supply and demand interactions which affect opportunities to attend or participate in events, as well as encouraging event tourism. Place identity refers to the association of events with places, and the meaning that communities attach to events. These are largely social constructs that take time to evolve. Place marketing, using hallmark and iconic events, or the 'festivalization' of regions, derives from this temporal and spatial intersection. A final concern, one little studied, is the cumulative impacts of individual events, event types, or event-related strategies and policies. Researchers have seldom examined long-term changes attributed to events.

The 'future' is also a personal and social construct, with policy-makers trying to shape it, strategic planners hoping to anticipate it, and a lot of people worrying about it. Through careful analysis of forces and trends we can hope to gain a better picture of possible future states, and we can use tools like scenario making and Delphi panels to assist us. More thought has to be given to the future of events, event management and Event Studies. We get so wrapped up in today's fast-paced world that it is easy to lose site of the fact that we are collectively causing profound changes on society and the environment.

Study Questions

- Why have planned events become more important globally?
- Discuss Boorstin's notions of 'pseudo-events' and authenticity.
- What themes and issues are explored in 'event geography'?

- Define the 'attractiveness' of events in geographic terms. How can it be measured?
- Is the future just an extrapolation of current trends? Discuss.
- What research methods are used in Future Studies?

Further Reading

Boorstin, D. (1961). *The Image: A Guide to Pseudo-events in America*. New York: Harper and Row.

Janiskee, R. (1996). The temporal distribution of America's community festivals. *Festival Management and Event Tourism*, 3(3): 129–137.

Shaw, G., and Williams, A. (2004). *Tourism and Tourism Spaces*. London: Sage.

Glenn, J., and Gordon, T. (eds.). *Futures Research Methodology*, Version 2.0. AC/UNU Millennium Project Publications (CD format, no date).

Chapter 6
Closely Related Professional Fields

Learning Objectives

- Understand why and how events are important in closely related professional fields:
  - parks, recreation and leisure studies
  - tourism
  - hospitality
  - education and interpretation
  - communications, media and performance studies
  - arts and cultural management
  - cultural studies
  - sport management and sport studies
  - venue and assembly management
  - hospitality and hospitality studies
  - theatre studies.
- Know the contributions of these established fields to Event Studies and event management.
- Be able to apply concepts from Event Studies to benefit closely related professional fields.

Introduction

There are a number of closely related professional fields that involve events, contribute to, and can benefit from Event Studies. Although professionals in these fields might not call themselves 'event manager', the co-ordination, production or marketing of events is sometimes an important part of their work.

Professional fields tend to evolve along similar lines, generally starting with professional practice and over time developing related academic programs, their own lines of research and a degree of interdisciplinary theory and methodology. But while leisure studies are now widely accepted as an academic field, having grown out of parks and recreation administration, hospitality and tourism are much more associated with applied business studies. Why? It is partly that they are at a more immature stage in their academic evolution, and partly that tourism and hospitality are seen as more of an industry, and the academic programs are viewed as professional schools preparing students for industry careers and entrepreneurship. Yet social science foundations apply in all these fields, with different emphases, and each one has developed with varying degrees of interdisciplinarity.

Parks and Recreation Management: Leisure Studies (Figure 6.1)

Parks and Recreation Management

Recreation and park management professionals are responsible for the provision and management of parks, recreation facilities, and leisure programs and services. Their skill sets range from venue planning, management, and marketing to community development and therapeutic recreation programming. Commercial recreation requires knowledge of business management and tourism. Hospitality services are often integrated in leisure facilities, and events are both users of these facilities and elements in leisure programming. Parks and recreation facilities and services are found within all levels of government, numerous not-for-profit organizations, educational and religious institutions, private clubs, the military and private corporations.

The University of North Carolina, Greensboro offers a Bachelor of Science in Recreation and Parks Management (www.uncg.edu.rth):

> *The professional core curriculum and the programme concentrations in (1) Leisure Services Management, (2) Therapeutic Recreation, and (3) Commercial Recreation are based on the philosophy that leisure experiences*

	Nature and meanings: the event experience	Antecedents to attending events	Planning and producing events	Outcomes and the impacted	Processes and patterns
Parks management • Parks managed for recreation, aesthetics and environmental protection	• Communing with nature • The outdoor experience as therapy	• Parks are attractions and popular event settings • Outdoor events have a special appeal	• Planning for events as a park use • Site planning	• Impacts have to be evaluated across environmental, social and personal dimensions	• Changing demand and political support for public parks • Changes in resource availability and quality
Recreation administration • Public recreation • Therapeutic (special needs) recreation	• Events as fulfilling social and personal experiences • Well-being and health from recreation	• Recreation facilities are needed for certain types of events • The facility as an attraction	• Programming of recreation venues	• Impacts on the person and society	• Shifts in demand and political support for public recreation
Leisure studies • Theories of play and leisure • Intrinsic motivation • Leisure constraints	• Events yield leisure benefits • Serious leisure • Optimal arousal and flow • Lifestyle meanings	• Leisure motives for attending events • Leisure constraints and negotiation • Recreation specialization • Ego involvement • Commitment	• Implication of theory for design and planning of programs, venues and events	• How to measure the benefits of leisure (e.g., health, self-fulfilment, social integration) • Leisure careers	• Leisure trends, fads

Figure 6.1 Parks and recreation management; leisure studies

are essential to the growth and development of all human beings… The study of the recreation and park industries encompasses a broad range of events and activities related to camping, natural resources, outdoor activities, arts, amusement parks, therapy, sporting events, and community recreation programs.

Most towns and cities run sport facilities that host numerous events and parks that provide spaces for festivals and other public gatherings. Increasingly, they employ professional event managers to produce their own events or event co-ordinators to oversee the events strategy and portfolio. Many are also explicitly involved in event tourism.

Leisure Studies

Once it became accepted that the planning and management of parks and recreation services required professional training, it was not long until academics began to apply theory from foundation disciplines and to develop theory, especially within the social sciences. In many ways this evolution defines what is happening with event management and Event Studies. More importantly, we can probably learn the most from leisure studies when it comes to event-related motivation, experience and behaviour.

Much debate occurs over how to define leisure. It is often conceptualized as a component of lifestyle. To some it is activity, free time, meaningful and satisfying experience or combinations of these. Certainly we take it for granted that leisure is based on free time and free choice, so attending events for their 'intrinsic worth' is leisure (this is a social construction of both leisure and many types of event). When people attend events for 'extrinsic' reasons (i.e., compulsion, the requirements of work, of social obligation) that is not necessarily leisure; although we still want them to have a memorable and rewarding experience.

Neulinger's 'Leisure Paradigm' has been very influential. To Neulinger (1974), the defining criterion of leisure was 'perceived freedom'. That is, the individuals must believe they have choice in whatever they are doing and they want to do it for its own reward. Neulinger developed a model in the form of a diagram consisting of four cells labelled 'pure job' (constrained and extrinsically motivated), 'pure work' (constrained but intrinsically motivated), 'leisure job' (freely chosen but extrinsically motivated) and 'pure leisure' (intrinsically motivated and freely chosen).

We all recognize that various constraints always apply to our choices and actions, and that none of us are completely 'free' to do whatever we want, whenever we want. As well, there are often combinations of intrinsic and extrinsic motivation of work and pleasure. So it is more appropriate to think of free versus constrained as a continuum and intrinsic versus extrinsic motivation as not being diametrically opposed.

'Lifestyle' can be defined as a pattern of living, or as a set of values and actions reflecting personal preferences. There is no doubt that leisure and travel figure prominently in our lifestyle choices, to the point where we speak of the 'life of leisure' or say things like 'he is a globe trotter, a jet-setter'.

How do we define our lifestyles? By our material possessions, but also by reference to:

- where we live (coastal, mountain, suburban, urban) and what that means for recreation and event opportunities;
- what we do (hobbies, interests, travel – all connected to special-interest events);
- who we associate with (social networks, including events attended);

- our tastes and how we express them (art, music, food and wine and the related events we attend).

Shaw and Williams (2004) discussed new forms of tourist consumption, and this is quite relevant to Event Studies. They argued that 'Post-Fordist' (i.e., what follows mass tourism with its emphasis on standard products) tourists seek an 'accumulation of social and cultural capital' (p. 132). Shaw and Williams (2004: 130) believed that family life cycle and lifestyles are distinguishing variables '... across a range of new forms of tourism.' These new forms have symbolic meanings, and highly individualistic consumers expect product differentiations according to their personal needs. Informality and spontaneity also mark new forms of tourist consumption (p. 131), as does 'the employment of, and belief in, the use of all the senses for personal well-being.' Technology is increasingly integrated into the consumption process. Among certain lifestyle segments these trends have led to substantial increases in green and cultural tourism.

Play Theory

The concept of play is important to leisure theory and the practice of parks and recreation. Ellis (1973) summarized fourteen different interpretations or theories of play, many of which pertain to childhood behaviour and also relate to the animal kingdom, such as the burning of 'surplus energy' and 'preparation' for adult responsibilities. Modern theories of play stress 'arousal seeking' (the need for optimal arousal in work and leisure) and 'competence/effectance' (people feel better from demonstrating mastery or competence in activities).

From the classic work of Huizinga (1955: 13), play can be defined as '... free activity standing quite consciously outside "ordinary" life as being "not serious", but at the same time absorbing the player intensely and utterly.' It promotes the formation of social groupings. 'Playfulness' as a personality trait refers to having a sense of humour, being spontaneous and exhibiting joy. Playful people tend to be more creative.

Also keep in mind that people can play in complete isolation or in large, interactive groups. At the solitary end of this spectrum it might be thought of as fantasy, or mind-play, and at the other end many forms of events 'come into play'. We can easily connect play to leisure in general (although not all leisure is actually play) and the 'liminal/liminoid zone'.

Leisure Experience

Experience is a fundamental concept in leisure. According to Mannell and Kleiber (1997: 11) 'Success is based on structuring the leisure environment in such a way as to create or encourage predictably satisfying experiences ... it has become apparent that an understanding of the psychological or experiential nature of leisure must be developed.'

What a person perceives, feels, learns or remembers – in a word, his or her experience – is often inferred from behaviour. According to Mannell and Kleiber we have to examine experience through the interplay of internal psychological dispositions (e.g., perceptions, feelings, emotions, beliefs, attitudes, needs, personality characteristics) and situational influences that are part of an individual's social environment (e.g., other people, group norms, human artefacts and media).

To study leisure experiences, researchers have looked at what people are doing (the 'behavioural' or 'conative' dimension) moods, emotions and feelings (the 'affective' or evaluative components) and thoughts and images (the 'cognitive' component). Also related are studies on concentration, focus of attention and absorption, self-consciousness, self-awareness and ego-loss, sense of competence, sense of freedom, arousal, activation and relaxation, intensity and duration. More work has been done on emotions than on cognition.

'Optimal experiences' are states of high psychological involvement or absorption in activities or settings. For example, Maslow's (1968) notion of the 'peak experience' ('moments of highest happiness and fulfillment') and Csikszentmihalyi's (1975) 'flow' ('the best moments of people's lives') occur '. . . when a person's body or mind is stretched to its limits in a voluntary effort to accomplish something difficult and worthwhile' (1990: 3). Is this equivalent to the vernacular expression 'being in the zone'? Can it not apply equally to work or any other challenging or rewarding experience?

The 'quest' is a theme in the leisure and tourism literature. People are thought to search for authentic experiences (MacCannell, 1976); for 'centre' (Cohen, 1979); for meaning (Meyersohn, 1981) or for values (Przeclawski, 1985). Simultaneous 'seeking and escaping' are the drivers in Mannell and Iso-Ahola (1987) leisure and travel motivational model.

Rojek (1995) believed that leisure springs from the eternal desire to find pleasure. Such impulses are beyond rational control and not confined to specific times and places; they can occur chaotically, at work or at home. In this sense, leisure experiences are states of mind associated with pleasure. A related theory suggests that people are always likely to do things spontaneously for fun or diversion. These approaches to leisure experiences run counter to definitions of leisure as non-work or types of activity. Roberts (2006: 221) concluded that evidence suggest '. . . people seek and obtain not just one but many kinds of experience through their leisure – fun, company, relaxation, exhilaration and so on.'

Leisure Over One's Life (The Life-Stage Approach)
Overall, leisure participation decreases with age and we can assume (in the absence of any specific evidence) that this also applies in general to attending planned events as

part of leisure. There are bound to be exceptions however, and these will be worth studying. Do retired people suddenly attend more social events? How does the life cycle relate to the concepts of 'involvement', 'serious leisure' and 'travel careers'?

Leisure researchers have also noticed that people's interest in variety or change also varies over a lifetime with experimentalism (novelty seeking and trying things out) being strongest in youth. The social environment is changing rapidly as we mature and young people are flexible in adapting to changes. Iso-Ahola et al. (1994) found that '... the tendency to seek novelty through new leisure activities declines with advancing life stages, whereas the tendency to maintain stability through old and familiar activities increases with life stages.'

Leisure Careers and Leisure Socialization

Roberts (2006: 156) said 'The best predictor of any individual's future uses of leisure is the same person's last behaviour.' People are conservative and become more so as they age. We tend to stick to routines and we take fewer risks. It is therefore useful to longitudinally examine leisure careers, and this relates to other concepts like serious leisure, recreation specialization and involvement.

Early involvement in the arts, particularly within the family socialization context, explains life-long involvement with 'high culture' (Roberts, 2006: 157). It is unlikely that adults will show interest in opera or ballet if they were not socialized into these interests early in their lives. But early participation in sports does not necessarily lead to life-long sport careers. It is much easier for committed people to stay involved with sports than to restart after a lapse.

Leisure Benefits and Event Benefits

Central to the policy position that recreation and leisure are essential public services is the notion of 'benefits'. Certainly they exist in marketing terms, as consumers are obviously willing to pay for many tangible and experiential benefits, but are there benefits that justify public investment and subsidies? The same arguments apply in terms of events and social or cultural policy.

Benefits of events should be demonstrable in a 'triple bottom-line' manner (i.e., sustainability theory). However, over-emphasis on the economic benefits has possibly been counter-productive, and much more work needs to be done on demonstrating and effectively communicating the social, cultural and environmental benefits. To the degree that the benefit is primarily personal and hedonistic (fun) or personally financially rewarding, society generally favours no public support. Therefore, public-sector event policies depend on the ability of evaluators and researchers to first demonstrate societal benefits, and next to apply cost and benefit analysis to justify specific courses of action.

Event researchers have so far ignored most societal benefits outside narrow economic impact studies. Leisure researchers are well ahead in examining the following outcomes or benefits, and surely there are many event connections:

- fitness and health (stress reduction and fighting mental illness; healthy lifestyles/ workplaces);
- social (family bonding; friendships; active groups; voluntarism);
- community (integration and social harmony; fostering a sense of place; satisfaction with living environments);
- self-actualization (individual fulfilment; intellectual development; entrepreneurship);
- environmental benefits (environmentally responsible recreation; changing attitudes about global warming; saving endangered species).

What is it exactly about attending or participating in events, of various types, that helps create benefits? The following are the possibilities:

- 'Keeping active' (too much idle, undirected time leads to problems including delinquency and crime); active people are healthier and wiser.
- 'Psychological hedonism' (pleasure, relaxation, fun all contribute to psychological health and satisfaction with life; the healing power of laughter.
- 'Need-compensation theory': leisure pursuits or events can be selected to compensate for unmet needs in one's life; leisure can compensate for dissatisfaction with work or other social environments.
- 'Personal growth': leisure offers people a means to test themselves, develop skills, learn, fulfil their aspirations (the Maslow approach); the more people invest in their leisure the more they get out of it (serious leisure, involvement, commitment).
- 'Identity' and 'affirmation theory': self-awareness and development of self-image occur through leisure pursuits, especially in social settings (self-esteem and the esteem of others as basic human needs).

In leisure people are free to experiment and find out what settings and pursuits are best for them, to search for or affirm their self-image and identity. Certain activities, and events, have identity images associated with them. For example, golfers have been found to be more extroverted (Paluba and Neulinger, 1976) compared to bowlers and tennis players. Certain activities, and by implication events, are linked to our self-identity. Highly involved runners thought their activity said more about what kind of person they were than their job did.

Self-Determination Theory
Deci and Ryan (1985) proposed this theory to explain how intrinsic motivation works.

Intrinsically motivated behaviour occurs in the absence of any apparent external reward and when people have free choice. The activities, or events, are chosen out of interest in those events. The resulting experiences are optimally challenging and result in flow.

Intrinsically motivated behaviour is based on the innate psychological need for competence, relatedness (love and meaningful social connections) and self-determination.

Self-Construal

Self-construal refers to an individual's sense of self in relation to others (Markus and Kitayama, 1991). In collectivist cultures people tend to be more interdependent, whereas in more individualistic cultures tend to be more independent. Self-construal is believed to affect cognition, emotion and motivation.

Research Note

Walker, G., Deng, J., and Dieser, R. (2005). Culture, self-construal, and leisure theory and practice. Journal of Leisure Research, 37(1): 77–99.

Cultural differences must be taken into account when theorizing about intrinsic versus extrinsic motivation and the nature of free choice and leisure. Asian and other cultures with interdependent self-construals (i.e., people assign greater value to belonging and maintaining harmony, as opposed to individualism). Relatedness might be more important than autonomy and free choice, so that the basic assumption that leisure is based on free choice seems to be a 'western' construct. These cultural differences should be considered when designing events, in communicating their benefits, and when considering event impacts on individuals and communities. Benefits to persons and groups have to be evaluated separately. These authors note that Gabrenya and Hwang (1996) observed that in Chinese culture annual festivals and spectator sports facilitate social interaction outside normal social hierarchies and networks thereby releasing people from usual constraints on behaviour.

Leisure Constraints

Leisure researchers and theorists (e.g., Jackson et al., 1992) want to know why people participate, and what prevents them from doing what they want to do. Generic categories of constraints have been identified, including the intrapersonal (one's perceptions and attitudes), interpersonal (such as a lack of leisure partners) and structural (time, money, supply and accessibility). These are examined in more detail in Chapter 9.

Ego-Involvement

According to Havitz and Dimanche (1999: 123) involvement is '…an unobservable state of motivation, arousal or interest toward a recreational activity or associated product'. 'Involvement' is invoked by a stimulus or situation and has drive properties, that is it motivates related behaviour. Many researchers utilize the Zaichkowsky (1985) unidimensional 'Personal Involvement Inventory Scale', but Kyle and Chick (2002) said there is a general consensus that leisure involvement is best conceptualized as a multi-dimensional construct with the following dimensions being most important:

1. 'Attraction': perceived importance or interest in an activity or product, and the pleasure derived from doing or consuming it (e.g., running offers certain benefits, but what is the additional pleasure derived form participating in a marathon?).
2. 'Sign': unspoken elements that the activity or product consumption conveys about the person (such as the prestige associated with certain events).
3. 'Centrality' to lifestyle: referring to both social contexts and the role of the activity or product in the person's lifestyle (people who are highly involved in the arts will demonstrate quite different levels of interest in certain art events, and will look for different benefits from their attendance).

Laurent and Kapferer's (1985) 'Involvement Profile' is a 15-item, multi-dimensional scale that has been widely used and adapted. Brown et al. (2007) adapted it to wine tourism, and there is a great deal of scope for using this approach to explore the connections between any lifestyle dimension or leisure interest and related travel and event behaviour. One pertinent application of ego-involvement to Event Studies has been made by researchers examining runners. McGehee et al. (2003) determined that highly involved recreational runners travelled more on overnight trips to participate in events, compared to the medium-involved, using a uni-dimensional ego-involvement scale.

Recreation Specialization

This theory, or framework, was developed by Hobson Bryan who described specialization as '. . . a continuum of behaviour from the general to the particular, reflected by equipment and skills used in the sport, and activity setting preferences' (Bryan, 1977: 175). As experience in an activity increases, it is theorized that people will progress from more general to specialized behaviour and related patterns of consumption. Their identification with the activity will also change.

Characteristic styles of participation emerge, so that beginners can often be easily distinguished from the more experienced participants. The theory has been applied to many activities, and to comparison of participants in terms of their motivation, setting preferences, involvement, attitudes toward management and the use of information. It is clearly related to the concepts of ego-involvement, commitment and serious leisure.

Research Note

Burr, S., and Scott, D. (2004). Application of the recreational specialization framework to understanding visitors to the Great Salt Lake Bird Festival. Event Management, 9(1/2): 27–37.

A random visitor intercept and a mail-back survey were used, plus site visits to observe the festival. Specialization (in 'birding') of those attending this festival was measured in terms of their behaviour, commitment and level of skill. Only a small fraction were found to be highly specialized or serious about bird watching, and they were less satisfied with the event – which suggests the need for careful segmentation. Most visitors seemed to have an interest in birds, but they combined that interest with other leisure pursuits and enjoyed the general festival programming. To the organizers, this also helped them meet their aims of increasing awareness and improved conservation efforts. The authors suggested that specialization can be usefully applied to other types of events to increase understanding of motives and behaviour.

Commitment and Serious Leisure

'Commitment' is a social–psychological construct, used to explain consistent behaviour. In the context of leisure it has been defined by Kim et al. (1997: 323) as '... those personal and behavioural mechanisms that bind individuals to consistent patterns of leisure behaviour.' Those authors sought to explore commitment in terms of dedication, inner conviction, centrality, costs and social considerations. Becker (1960) used the term 'side bets' to describe what would be lost if an individual discontinued something he or she was committed to, such as loss of friendships, personal identity, investments of time and money, as well as consideration of the absence of alternatives.

Kim et al. (1997) determined that commitment (conceptualized as centrality to lifestyle) and social-psychological involvement scales were highly interrelated among a sample of birdwatchers, and that behavioural measures of involvement were more useful in predicting behaviour. According to these same researchers, involvement is likely an antecedent of commitment and might be at the root of 'serious leisure'.

Robert Stebbins' concept of 'serious leisure' (1982, 1992, 2001, 2006) appears to be closely related to commitment and involvement constructs. Serious leisure is (1992: 53) '... the steady pursuit of an amateur, hobbyist, or career volunteer activity that captivates its participants with its complexity and many challenges. It is profound, long-lasting, and invariably based on substantial skill, knowledge, or experience, if not on a combination of these three.' It is like pursuing a career, but without remuneration. Serious leisure participants '... typically become members of a vast social world, a complex mosaic of groups, events, networks, organizations, and social relationships.' The rewards of serious leisure include '... fulfilling one's human potential, expressing one's skills and knowledge, having cherished experiences, and developing a valued identity.'

According to Stebbins, characteristics of serious leisure include:

- Perseverance (learning to overcome constraints).
- Developing a career (includes stages of achievement or reward; may be assisted by experts; may include a progression of events leading towards the highest level of participation).
- Significant personal effort is required (acquiring knowledge and skills; travel).

- Durable benefits as outcomes (e.g., self-fulfilment, enhancement of self-concept, self-esteem; social identity).
- An ethos associated with the social world (common interests and intercommunications related to the 'social object' of interest to the group, such as sport, art, wine).
- Social identification with the activity (a subculture).

Mental Exercise

Do you have serious leisure interests? For example, does your interest in sport, the arts, food or hobbies lead to any or all of the characteristics mentioned above? What roles do planned events play in your resultant social world? Are their events that you want to attend because of your serious leisure? What about volunteering?

Research Methodologies and Methods in Leisure Studies

The North American approach to leisure studies field, in common with social–psychology in general, has been largely positivist and quantitative, but there has been growing interest in values, beliefs and the application of theory to practical social problems and policy issues (Mannell and Kleiber, 1997: 27). Leisure researchers have frequently used large-scale surveys, experiments, and time diaries to observe and measure leisure quantitatively and to develop or test theories. More qualitative and interpretive methods include participant observation and unstructured interviews, case studies and introspection.

Researchers can observe experience by having people tell them what is on their minds. A full understanding of behaviour can only be obtained when we know what it means to the person – which is phenomenology. 'Experiential Sampling' (Csikszentmihalyi and Csikszentmihalyi, 1988) is the related method used in leisure studies and we will re-visit it later in this book.

Tourism Management and Tourism Studies (Figure 6.2)

Tourism is often studied as an industry, alongside hospitality, with related educational programs stressing professional career preparation. But, like leisure and events, academics also want to study tourism as a social, cultural and economic phenomenon, and to consider all its potential impacts.

Tourism, like leisure, has a major stake in planned events and has evolved along similar lines from a management orientation to a full-fledged field of studies with its own advanced degrees. When defining tourism, scholars tend to separate the industry-oriented approach from the broader 'tourism studies' approach that relies on multi- and

Tourism studies • The study of travel and the touristic experience, and of the tourism industry	Nature and meanings: the event experience	Antecedents to attending events	Planning and producing events	Outcomes and the impacted	Processes and patterns
Event tourism • Travel related to planned events • Destination development and marketing through events	• The overall event travel experience • Tourism roles of events: attractions; place marketing; image creation; animators	• General travel demand affects event travel demand • Specific motivators for event tourism • Media coverage and media events influence demand • Increasing supply of tourist-oriented events	• Marketing for event tourists • Packaging • Events produced primarily for tourists or destination image enhancement • Destination event portfolios	• Event tourism impacts • Economic impacts and EIA's • Cost and benefit evaluations	• Event tourism trends (e.g., changing demand for long- or short-haul event trips)

Figure 6.2   Tourism management and tourism studies.

interdisciplinarity. There has also been an ongoing debate about whether tourism is, can be or should be a discipline (see Leiper, 1981; Stear, 1981; Jafari, 1987; Tribe, 1997; Rojek and Urry, 1997; Echtner and Jamal, 1998; Hall, 2005).

Jafari (1987) and Leiper (1981) argued that a multi-disciplinary approach was an impediment to tourism education, and that what is needed is an interdisciplinary approach that integrates concepts from other disciplines and fields. Tribe (1997), on the other hand, recommended that there is nothing to be gained by disciplinary status, and that tourism studies does not qualify. Rojek and Urry (1997) asked where does tourism begin and leisure studies end?

Hall (2005: 6) listed the disciplinary traditions contributing to the study of tourism and a very similar approach has been taken in this book on Event Studies. A major difference is Hall's emphasis on transport studies, as his 2005 book sought to place tourism within 'the social science of mobility'. Hall's graphical representation of his approach (p. 5), called 'The Disciplinary Spaces of Tourism', shows the fields and disciplines in an outer ring, a middle ring consisting of 'multi-disciplinary approaches', and an inner zone identified as 'interdisciplinary approaches to tourism and the emerging field of Tourism

Studies.' Certainly this reflects a widespread academic belief that a field of studies deserves or requires its own concepts and methods (i.e., interdisciplinarity).

The group ATLAS (Association for Tourism and Leisure Education) has assembled a Tourism Body of Knowledge (see Hall, 2005, p. 10) that constitutes a minimum curriculum for undergraduate students. This BOK contains many themes found in Event Studies, although it treats events mainly as a type of product or attraction.

Leisure and tourism studies clearly overlap if one views tourism as a social phenomenon taking place within leisure, and they overlap at the business and management level because numerous enterprises exist to deliver recreational/travel experiences. Events can be viewed as a sub-set of this leisure/tourism interdependence, but neither leisure nor tourism studies deals centrally with the planning, design, experience and management of events. Rather, in tourism and leisure events are treated as attractions, activities or aspects of some larger tourism/leisure construct, such as business travel, pilgrimage or serious leisure.

Event Tourism: The Destination Perspective

As with any niche market, or special-interest travel segment, we can define 'event tourism' from two perspectives – the consumer's and the destination's. First we look at event tourism as a destination strategy to develop and market events for their specific tourism and economic benefits. The five main roles played by events in tourism are discussed below.

In a study of Canadian Destination Marketing Organizations, Getz et al. (1998) discovered that events were the only 'product' that tourism agencies became involved with in terms of development or ownership. Events were singled out because the industry needed them in off-peak seasons, new ones could be created for minimal cost and the direct involvement of DMOs ensured that events met tourism goals.

Events as Attractions

Although many tourism organizations stress international tourism, there is no doubt that most festivals and events are dependent on local and regional audiences. But whether events are true tourist attractions (i.e., motivating overnight or non-local travel), or a reason for visitors already in an area to stay longer, they can have tourism value. Events can also have the effect of keeping people and their money at home, rather than travelling outside the region.

Event 'drawing power' or 'attractiveness' can be measured by how many tourists will be attracted, and how far or frequently they will travel. Important goals are to use events to overcome the seasonality problem, and to spread demand geographically throughout a country or region. Destinations often classify events according to their drawing power, scale or tourism potential. Bos (1994) reported on classification in the Netherlands, and the Economic Planning Group and Lord Cultural Resources (1992) developed a system for the Canadian Province of Ontario. Often these are intended to assist in funding decisions.

Resources for event tourism consist of more than just events. An inventory of resources has to include organizations capable of producing events, companies that sponsor them, agencies to assist, all possible resources (human, financial, natural, political) and themes. One issue to consider is that cultural and environmental 'resources' are often in the public domain and anyone can 'exploit' them without compensation or regard to impacts. The 'law of the commons' applies here, as a community and its resources could become damaged by too many events, too much event tourism or by poorly managed events. This is a strong argument for public policy and regulation of events, encompassing the principles of resource stewardship and sustainability.

The goal should not be to maximize event tourism volumes, but to develop a manageable and balanced portfolio of events that meet multiple goals and generate many benefits (see Chapter 12 for details). An emphasis on event tourist quality, that is attracting high-yield, dedicated event tourists, is preferred. Strategies employed in event tourism have not generally been evaluated for effectiveness. They include bidding on events (see Emery, 2001; Getz, 2004), starting new events for tourism purposes, using events in theme years, cultivating and improving many local and regional events, developing one or more events into 'hallmark' status and hosting the occasional mega-event.

Events as Animators

Resorts, museums, historic districts, heritage sites, archaeological sites, markets and shopping centres, sports stadia, convention centres and theme parks all develop programs of special events. Built attractions and facilities have everywhere realized the advantages of 'animation' – the process of programming interpretive features and/or special events which make the place come alive with sensory stimulation and appealing atmosphere.

The potential benefits of animation through events are of major importance to facility and attraction managers:

- To attract people who might otherwise not make a visit because they perceive the facility or attraction itself to be uninteresting.
- To encourage repeat visits by people who might otherwise think that one visit is enough.
- To attract publicity for the site or facility, including the highlighting of historical events associated with the site.

- To encourage longer stays and greater spending.
- To target groups for special functions.

Kelly (1985: 281) described the Six Flags philosophy on events at their theme parks: 'Special events are employed to attract local repeat trade'. The events are mostly entertainment in nature, and this element, combined with new rides and site amenities, is designed to help extend the life cycle of the product. Baxter (2001) looked at how waterparks employed entertainment and special events, finding that some of them view it as a way to increase attendance and revenues while others want to increase consumer awareness among target segments and reinforce branding.

Events and Place Marketing: Co-Branding

Kotler et al. (1993) in their book *Marketing Places*, identified the value of events in enhancing the image of communities and in attracting tourists. They demonstrated how places compete for investments, quality people and tourists, all in pursuit of more liveable and prosperous communities. 'Place marketing' provides a framework within which events and event tourism find multiple roles, as image-makers, quality of life enhancers and tourist attractions. More traditional approaches to economic development stressed industrialization, provision of physical rather than cultural infrastructure and downplayed the economic value of tourism.

'Co-branding' between events and destinations is one strategy gaining popularity (Brown et al., 2001; Chalip and Costa, 2006). Jago et al. (2002, 2003) believed there was substantial potential for events to be used in destination branding but that neither event nor destination managers do a good job in harnessing that potential. The intent is to reinforce the destination's brand with compatible events, a transferral of positive images, with a classic case being surfing competitions in Surfer's Paradise. Because most destinations contain an array of events of all kinds, largely beyond control, it might be wise to focus on one or a few well-imaged 'hallmark events' to achieve place marketing and branding goals.

Events as Image-Makers

It is apparent that major events can have the effect of shaping an image of the host community or country, leading to its favourable perception as a potential travel destination. With global media attention focused on the host city, even for a relatively short duration, the publicity value is enormous, and some destinations will use this fact alone to justify great expenditures on attracting events. For example, Wang and Gitelson (1988:5) observed that the annual Spoleto Festival in Charleston, South Carolina does not appear to be economically justifiable, '. . . but the city holds it every year to maintain a desirable image.' Cameron (1989) noted the role of festivals and events, and cultural tourism in general, in altering the image of the Lehigh Valley in Pennsylvania.

Longitudinal studies of the impact of hosting the 1988 Winter Olympic Games on Calgary (Ritchie and Smith, 1991) showed how a definite positive image boost grew, peaked and started to decline afterwards, so there is a life cycle to image enhancement related to one-time events. But additional gains in tourism infrastructure and the legacy of enhanced tourism marketing and organization can potentially sustain the effect.

What happens when negative publicity strikes a destination? To a degree, bad news events can be managed: both to minimize the negative impact and to fight back. Ahmed (1991) argued that negative images can be turned into positive ones by organizing festivals and commemorations of the event, although this is restricted mostly to natural disasters and entails the risk of stirring up unhappy or controversial memories.

Hede and Jago (2005) placed the discussion in the context of theory about planned and reasoned action (Ajzen and Fishbein, 1973; Fishbein and Azjen, 1975; Fishbein, 1980; Ajzen, 1985, 1991) in which positive perceptions created by the publicity surrounding events (or viewing the events, reading about them, etc.) leads to positive attitudes, intentions to travel there, and to eventual travel.

This theory, or belief, underlies a great deal of destination promotion. Hudson et al, (2004), however, in conceptualizing (with a graphic model) the process in which events might influence travel choices, concluded that there were many intervening factors separating perception from travel behaviour, and that watching events – especially sport events – might lead to travel elsewhere to participate in the sport. Indeed, many sport-event broadcasts do not provide much in the way of destination imagery or information.

Research Note

Chalip, L., Green, B. C., and Hill, B. (2003). Effects of sport event media on destination image and intention to visit. Journal of Sport Management, 17(3): 214–234.

Using experimental methodology, this research examined the affects of exposure to eight media conditions surrounding a sport event (Indy car race) on destination image (namely the Gold Coast, Australia). The event telecast, event advertising, and destination advertising each affected different dimensions of destination imagery. Destination image was significantly related to intention to visit the host destination, showing that events can potentially influence subsequent travel decisions. The newness of messages to the American audience had a greater impact than the same messages had among New Zealanders who already had been exposed to the Gold Coast as a destination. Results confirm what is known about the transference between a sponsor's image and the sponsored event's image. Hosting an event is therefore an exercise in co-branding. Also, the authors concluded that if dimensions of destination image that are affected by an event are not those that drive destination choice, there will be no resultant affect on travel. Images surrounding an event could also negatively impact on travel to the host area.

The somewhat limited research on media impacts suggests that enhanced image is difficult to obtain, let alone prove (Mossberg, 2000). A study by Boo and Busser (2006) concluded that the festival under study did not contribute to a positive destination image among participants. Indeed, it appeared to have a negative impact owing to poor marketing and quality. The researchers pointed out the necessity for further research on the imputed connections between events and image enhancement. Hede (2005), however, concluded that Australians who viewed telecasts of the Athens 2004 Olympics did change their overall attitude toward Greece as a destination. Ritchie et al. (2006) concluded that media broadcast of events helped change images of Canberra, and they recommended that events be part of any promotional strategy for national capitals.

Events as Catalysts

Mega-events, such as World's Fairs and Olympics, have been supported by host governments in large part because of their role as catalysts in major redevelopment schemes. The Knoxville World's Fair was conceived as a catalyst for urban renewal through image enhancement and physical redevelopment, and left a legacy of infrastructure, a convention centre, private investments, a better tax base and new jobs for the Tennessee city (Mendell et al., 1983). Dungan (1984) gave a number of examples of the indirect and direct physical legacies of major events. Atlanta's 1996 Summer Olympic Games generated two billion dollars in construction projects in Georgia, including sport facilities, an urban park in central Atlanta, housing improvements and educational facilities (Mihalik, 1994).

Major events tend to attract investment into the hospitality sector, especially hotels and restaurants. Sometimes these additions have been brought forward in time, while others represent new infrastructure related to expected longer-term increases in demand. Sport events generally lead to new or improved facilities which can be used to attract events in the future, and improvements to convention or arts centres can have a similar effect. In this way a community can use the event to realize a 'quantum leap' in its tourism development, accelerating growth or jumping into a higher competitive category.

'Leveraging' events is a related concept. The idea is to exploit or 'leverage' events for broader business benefits, through enhancing event tourist spending at the event and elsewhere in the destination, and through building new relationships (Faulkner et al., 2000). The 'legacy' of events is also part of the 'catalyst' role, to the extent it is planned. Ritchie (2000) deduced ten lessons from two winter Olympics for getting the most out of the investment in the long term. See Chapter 11 on Outcomes for more discussion on these topics.

The Cultural Event Tourist

Many event tourists are 'cultural tourists' – that is, they are seeking cultural experiences – while other events certainly can be designed to deliver cultural experiences. The

Travel Industry Association of America, together with the Smithsonian Magazine (2003), reported on The Historic/Cultural Traveller. They found ever-increasing demand, with 81% of Americans who had travelled in the past year considered to be 'historic/cultural', based on their interests and activities. For 30%, their choice of destination was influenced by a specific cultural event or activity.

Although there are many definitions of cultural tourism in the literature, McKercher and du Cros (2002: 3) said it can be approached from four perspectives: 'tourism derived' (a form of special interest travel; a product); 'motivational' (what travellers are looking for, including visits to the arts, monuments, festivals); 'experiential' (an emphasis on cultural learning; the quest for understanding and self-fulfilment) and 'operational' (related to the purpose of the study, as in this case to examine festivals as a form of cultural tourism). They also postulated (p. 16) seven possible relationships between tourism and cultural heritage assets, ranging from 'full cooperation' to 'full conflict', and this provides a framework for investigating the marketing and tourism orientation of cultural festivals. The in-between categories include 'working relationships', 'peaceful co-existence', 'parallel existence/blissful ignorance', 'mild annoyance' and 'nascent conflict'.

In terms of planning and developing cultural tourism, McKercher and du Cros (p. 186) employed a 'Market Appeal-Robusticity' matrix which bases tourism potential on an evaluation of the asset's (in our context, planned events) market appeal and its ability to cope with visitors '... or to be modified in a way that does not compromise its values'. Different strategies are therefore required for festivals that have strong touristic appeal but are not robust, compared to those with little appeal but substantial robusticity. Although criteria were suggested for tangible heritage assets (p. 191), little has been said about events – especially regarding their robustness/adaptability versus cultural significance and authenticity. In other words, is it possible and legitimate to turn any or all cultural festivals into tourist attractions?

Ideally, many events should attract a segment that McKercher and du Cros (2002: 148) called the 'purposeful cultural tourist' who wants a deep cultural experience and has been motivated to travel to a destination by its cultural attractions. However, the event organizer must also prepare for visitors with lesser need for cultural experiences, including those who are not really attracted by culture at all (in other words, they are seeking other benefits such as fun, social opportunities, or are motivated by escapism).

Research Note

McKercher, B., Mei, W., and Tse, T. (2006). Are short duration festivals tourist attractions? Journal of Sustainable Tourism, 14(1): 55–66.

These researchers profiled attendees at three Hong Kong festivals with a view to determining their roles in attracting tourists to the territory. McKercher and du Cros' (2002) cultural tourist classification system was employed, distinguishing between the 'serendipitous cultural tourist', the 'purposeful', 'sightseeing', 'casual' and 'incidental' types. Visitors were largely ignorant of both the existence and meaning of the festivals. They drew mainly from the small pool of long-haul, long-stay, first-time visitors. Only about 25% of respondents indicated the festivals had any impact on their decision to visit Hong Kong or extend their stay. However, the festivals did contribute to the exoticness of Hong Kong, its cultural uniqueness, and this 'marker' can be more important than their actual power in attracting tourists. The authors recommended that local festivals be promoted before visitors arrive so that the stay can be planned to include them, as each one can be a full day's commitment. Bundling festivals, so that there is something on all year, is another approach and would require close cooperation between event organizers and the DMO.

Hospitality Management and Hospitality Studies (Figure 6.3)

This professional field is focused on hotels, resorts and food and beverage services (e.g., catering, restaurants and bars) and often encompasses elements of the travel and tourism industry. Some diploma and degree programs specialize in clubs, business and industry dining, leisure services, campus dining, convention facilities, transportation, theme parks, state and national park operations and casino operations. Increasingly convention and event management is included within hospitality curricula. Frequently hospitality and tourism programs are integrated within business schools, and in some cases with sport and leisure as well.

Hospitality management • Hotel, resort, restaurant management; service provision; gastronomy; events as 'functions'	Nature and meanings: the event experience	Antecedents to attending events	Planning and producing events	Outcomes and the impacted	Processes and patterns
Hospitality studies • Studies host–guest interactions and interdependencies • The nature of hospitality and service	• Receiving hospitality at events (being a guest) • Corporate hospitality as a unique event experience	• Service quality as a determinant of future demand • Growth in demand for corporate and private events as as professional services	• Service quality • Atmospherics • Technical considerations (lighting, sound, safety, health)	• Business impacts • Client and guest satisfaction	• The competitive environment for events is dynamic • Rising expectations for quality

Figure 6.3 Hospitality management and hospitality studies.

At San Francisco State University (www.sfu.edu/hm) hospitality is located within the College of Business:

> *The interdisciplinary program provides an academically sound business foundation with core hospitality management courses and specialized classes in each concentration. This curriculum prepares highly professional and marketable specialists to manage complex and diverse hospitality organizations.*

Hotel, club, convention centre and restaurant managers are responsible for the events or 'functions' markets in their properties, while many resorts specialize in festivals and sport events suited to their recreational amenities and beautiful settings. The most common 'functions' held in hotels, restaurants and other hospitality venues are:

- weddings with banquets;
- private parties (graduations, *bar and bat mitzvahs*);
- meetings and conventions;
- consumer and trade shows;
- entertainment events;
- corporate functions like product launches.

For hospitality establishments to enter the conventions or exhibitions market they must have special-purpose facilities, equipment and services above and beyond the usual catering competencies. An important trend is the use of unique, non-traditional venues for meetings and conventions, such as museums, historic houses or even zoos.

Most hospitality programs are applied in nature, usually requiring hands-on training and job experience. At the university level there is increasing emphasis on hospitality studies, or the academic bases for a professional career in hospitality. This foundation has to include general business management, services management and marketing, the special management challenges of hospitality venues and events or functions – often tied to catering.

As its core phenomenon, hospitality studies deals with formal, usually commercialized, host–guest interaction and interdependence. To be a 'host' in this context entails legal and social responsibilities, and requires an understanding of service provision both as a business, a technical skill, and a fundamental aspect of human nature.

Education and Interpretation

(Figure 6.4)

Education and informal learning are embodied in many types of planned events, notably meetings and conventions, but little attention has been paid to the educational

	Nature and meanings: the event experience	Antecedents to attending events	Planning and producing events	Outcomes and the impacted	Processes and patterns
Education • What is knowledge? • Didactics (teaching) • Learning styles	• Events as learning experiences	• The influence of education levels on demand • Desire for learning as a motive to attend events	• Programming and design for learning (e.g., seminars, speakers, clinics)	• What participants learn (i.e., measures of educational effectiveness)	• Rising education levels affect motives and demands
Interpretation • Theories and practice of interpretation in various settings (e.g., heritage sites, museums, events)	• Interpretation through events • Interpretation of the meanings of events	• Availability of interpretation as it affects demand	• Programming with interpretation (styles of interpretation)	• Measuring the effectiveness of interpretation	• Growing demand for profound experiences leads to greater need for interpre-tation

Figure 6.4 Education and interpretation.

roles of events in general. A study by Gitelson et al. (1995) was a rare look at the educational objectives of an event and related effectiveness.

Sponsors and social marketers are very concerned with how to best get across their messages to event audiences. We also need to be concerned with how events themselves can be interpreted, for example to explain symbolic and culturally significant elements to visitors, and to engage visitors more through learning opportunities at events. The event designer and programmer therefore has to draw upon the education and interpretation fields, including their understanding and use of cognitive psychology and learning styles.

Learning Theory

'Learning' is a process requiring the active involvement of the learner – knowledge cannot simply be transferred to people by teachers or any other means. 'Experience' is often said to be the best teacher, and certainly graduates are fond of saying they learned more in the first week of employment than they did in their entire academic career (teachers dispute this). In addition to basic knowledge, the learning process can be focused on physical or problem-solving skills, or shaping one's values and attitudes. Teachers generally stress that their job is to enable students to become life-long learners – to learn how to learn.

'Bloom's Taxonomy' (1956: 201–207) divides the learning process into a six-level hierarchy, where knowledge is the lowest order of cognition and evaluation the highest:

- 'Knowledge' is the memory of previously learnt materials, such as facts, terms, basic concepts and answers.
- 'Comprehension' is the understanding of facts and ideas by organization, comparison, translation, interpretation and description.
- 'Application' is the use of new knowledge to solve problems.
- 'Analysis' is the examination and division of information into parts by identifying motives or causes. A person can analyze by making inferences and finding evidence to support generalizations.
- 'Synthesis' is the compilation of information in a new way by combining elements into patterns or proposing alternative solutions.
- 'Evaluation' is the presentation and defence of opinions by making judgements about information, validity of ideas or quality of work based on a set of criteria.

How do people learn? The four main styles of learning can be adapted to meetings, conventions and other educational events as follows (they are not mutually exclusive and some people learn best by one style or several combined):

- 'Visual' (learn by seeing): use movies, graphics, performances.
- 'Verbal/auditory' (learn by hearing); use speakers, discussants, panels, tapes.
- 'Reading/writing' (learn by processing text): use readings and printed material; have attendees write things, make notes.
- 'Kinesthetic' or 'experiential': involve people in creating or discussing; take field trips; get people to participate in events; run experiments; combine observation with reflection and discussion/writing.

Meeting Professionals International (MPI, 2003: 62), in their Planning Guide, advised members they must know how adults learn. They discussed how learning can be influenced by a number of event-related facets including emotional stimulation, socializing, setting and conference programme. 'Tools of the trade' for meeting planners to foster learning experiences include case studies, lectures, discussions, poster sessions, demonstrations, participatory workshops and 'experiential learning' (i.e., learn through doing).

Hilliard (2006: 46) noted that '... education is the most consistent function of associations' but there has been little research devoted to how adult learning principles should be applied at conventions. Hilliard therefore discussed how meeting planners can better achieve their goal of educating association members. Common challenges include an over-emphasis on content, rather than delivery, and a one-way flow of information rather than creation of an interactive learning environment.

Interpretation

It can mean language interpretation, or the interpretation of signs and symbols (i.e., semiotics), but we are interested here in the forms of education or other communications designed to reveal meanings and relationships. Interpreters work for parks, heritage sites, zoos, museums, galleries, aquariums, theme parks and tour companies with the purpose of making certain their visitors truly understand what is being displayed, observed or otherwise experienced. The National Association for Interpretation (www.interpnet.com) is international in its membership and proclaims that '... interpretation is a communication process that forges emotional and intellectual connections between the interests of the audience and the meanings inherent in the resource'.

With regard to parks and heritage interpretation, Freeman Tilden (1957) is considered to have hade the greatest influence. His six Principles of Interpretation are widely used:

1. Any interpretation that does not somehow relate what is being displayed or described to something within the personality or experience of the visitor will be sterile.
2. Information, as such, is not interpretation. Interpretation is revelation based upon information. But they are entirely different things. However, all interpretation includes information.
3. Interpretation is an art, which combines many arts, whether the materials presented are scientific, historical or architectural. Any art is in some degree teachable.
4. The chief aim of interpretation is not instruction, but provocation.
5. Interpretation should aim to present a whole rather than a part and must address itself to the whole man rather than any phase.
6. Interpretation addressed to children (say, up to the age of 12 years) should not be a dilution of the presentation to adults, but should follow a fundamentally different approach. To be at its best, it will require a separate programme.

Bramwell and Lane (1993) have argued that interpretation is a cornerstone of sustainable tourism, but they identified a number of related issues or pitfalls. One concern is that interpretation can alter the meaning of cultural assets, such as by emphasizing economic roles. Deciding on what to interpret for visitors is an issue, as only a few themes or stories can be told, and this can be a political or even divisive process. Should only the unusual or spectacular be interpreted? There is also a danger of aiming interpretation only at the educated elite, while ignoring the needs of mass tourism.

Thematic Interpretation

Based on cognitive psychology, 'thematic interpretation' is based on a key premise: that people remember themes far easier than they remember facts. If event designers tap into universal belief systems they can more easily communicate with audiences, and audiences both need and want meaningful experiences as opposed to simple entertainment. Thematic interpretation aims to create visitor experiences that have lasting impact, translating into higher levels of satisfaction, positive word of mouth, sales and repeat visits. It is best described as strategic communication.

Prof. Sam Ham of the University of Idaho is most closely associated with developing and applying thematic interpretation within parks, heritage and tourism. Dr. Ham, Anna Housego and Betty Weiler together authored the Tasmanian Thematic Interpretation Planning Manual (May 2005: available online at www.tourismtasmania.com), as part of that Australian state's innovative Experience Strategy. We can adapt their planning process to events, so let's start with their definition and explanation of theme:

> *'A theme is a take-home message; it's the moral of the story or main conclusion a visitor takes away ...' (p. 3).*
> *'A theme is a whole idea ... is the way you express the essence of the message you and others in your organisation want to impart to visitors; it is not necessarily the set of words you would use in direct communication to visitors. when a moral to the story really matters to the visitor then it touches them in lots of ways, and that's when it really sticks' (p. 13).*

If an event theme is thought of merely in terms of decoration or entertainment, which is appropriate at many events then interpretation is not really required. But at cultural celebrations, religious ceremonies, arts festivals and many other planned events, we want the visitor to be emotionally and cognitively affected; we want a memorable, even transforming experience. While event guests and customers might not remember all the activities or information provided, they should be provoked into reflection and involvement by the main theme so they can make their own meanings from, and about the event, the place and the time they spent there. Using both tangibles and intangible elements (such as symbols and emotional engagement) in interpretation makes for more powerful theming.

Ideally, the theme and various interpretive media (or tools) are targeted to various audiences depending on their levels of interest, extent and nature of their participation, and how managers want to influence them, thereby requiring a fairly sophisticated research and evaluation process. Higher levels of effectiveness can probably be achieved through greater investment in planning and research. Evaluation of results will have to include measures of actual behaviour at the event and afterwards, questions about more intangible emotional and cognitive outcomes, and effects on other people through word of mouth.

Interpretation Tools

Interpretation of, and at, events can include the following tools. They can be thought of as different 'media', each with their own application depending on audiences and situations.

- Guides who interpret the setting, performances, food and beverages, as to their cultural significance.
- Signage: not just directional, but explanatory; impressive entry statements.

- Printed information: programs and souvenir material.
- Websites (informing and preparing potential visitors; before and after augmentation of the event experience).
- School-oriented programs, integrating events with the academic curriculum.
- Audio–visual presentations (slide shows, videos, sound).
- Interactive Displays: hands-on exhibits, computer simulations, talking robots.
- 'Live interpretation': including performances and storytelling.
- Direct involvement by guests or experiential learning (learn by doing).

Recall these tools when reading about event experience design. In the research note below, by Philip Xie, it is shown that festival-goers really want interpretation.

Research Note

Xie, P. (2004). Visitors' perceptions of authenticity at a rural heritage festival: a case study. Event Management, 8(3): 151–160.

Xie concluded that most visitors to a rural heritage festival in Ohio enjoyed their experience, but were confused by the programming because of a lack of interpretation. The majority did not have the depth of experience to understand the more complex aspects of traditional culture on display, so they were mostly recreational rather than cultural in their orientation. Xie argued that authenticity was to some extent 'existential,' that is in the minds of the attendees rather than an aspect of the programme itself. Visitors wanted detailed interpretation of local heritage, and Xie concluded by recommending that event organizers should provide a clear heritage theme, add tour guides, integrate cultural values, and make interpretation as historically accurate as possible. Identifying and involving important players who can authenticate heritage resources is desirable. The shorter the visit, and the more structured the programme, he suggested, the more likely it will be that visitors do not get a sincere contact with local heritage.

Communications, Media and Performance Studies (Figure 6.5)

Communications Studies

Communications' can be defined as the exchange of meanings between people through a common system of symbols, such as – and especially – language. Jaworski and Pritchard (2005: 2) said communication '... refers to the practices, processes and mediums by which meanings are provided and understood in a cultural context.'

This field covers a wide range of topics and issues, particularly speech and rhetoric, intercultural communication, information theory, public relations, propaganda and mass communications technology. It is often considered to include broadcasting, media and performance studies. Events can be considered as communication tools or artefacts,

	Nature and meanings: the event experience	Antecedents to attending events	Planning and producing events	Outcomes and the impacted	Processes and patterns
Communication studies • Theories of information; symbols and semiotics; discourse • Problems and methods in communications	• Events as symbols and communications tools	• Symbolic representations of events can encourage 'consumption'	• Communication effectiveness • Branding • Interpretation • Edutainment	• Evaluation of marketing effectiveness resulting in changes in attitude or behaviour	• Technological and media trends (TV coverage, virtual reality, Internet)
Media studies • Studies the nature and influences of mass media on individuals and society • Media content and representations • The audience • New media	• Homogenization of events through mass media effects • Virtual experiences	• Effects of advertising on decision-making	• Events designed for media audiences, both mass and segmented	• Global audiences • Displacement of indigenous forms of communications/events	• Trends in mass media affecting the event sector
Performance studies • The study and uses of performances, including planned events	• Events as expressions of sub- and counter-cultures • Create your own event experience	• Desire for alternative experiences	• Actors and audience merge	• Personal and group identities	• Values and attitudes toward performance styles

Figure 6.5 Communications, media and performance studies.

both from the point of view of event marketing (i.e., sponsors' messages at events) and as a means to interpret culture. Elsewhere we have examined interpretation as a form of communication and education.

'Information theory', at its most basic, is concerned with the communication process between a 'sender' (e.g., the event or some element of it) and a 'receiver' (a person or a broader audience). Masterman and Wood (2006: 4) described how the event organizer tries to convey 'messages' through specific 'media', and these messages are 'encoded' through selection of certain images, words or symbols. The target audience might fail to get the messages owing to environmental 'noise' (i.e., all the competing stimuli and messages) or might incorrectly 'decode' (i.e., misinterpret) the messages because of ambiguity, social or cultural biases. Unless this process is monitored and evaluated, the senders could be wasting their efforts.

There are many communications and information issues: is the message clear, accurate and compelling? Does the receiver get the intended message, and act upon it in accordance with the sender's intent? Are there cultural differences that affect the communication process? Are certain channels or media more effective? These issues have obvious event marketing implications.

Communications can also be ritualistic, as with events that hold meanings such as pilgrimage and *rites de passage*. Information has to be communicated in certain ways, and perhaps only the initiated understand the true meaning. Events, in this context, can hold both superficial appeal as entertainment and deeper cultural meanings for participants.

Discourse

'Discourse' on any subject, such as a political process for determining support for cultural festivals, involves two-way or multi-stakeholder communications with the aim of ensuring mutual understanding. It is a rule-based process in which arguments are evaluated for their validity, and it facilitates shared decision-making or consensus building. Stating one's opinion is not discourse, nor is propaganda and advertising. Argument without rules is not discourse. Allowing statements to be made that cannot be verified as to fact or source violates the principles of discourse.

Conflicting views exist on discourse, including those of Foucault (1972) and Habermas (1973). Foucault, the French philosopher, saw discourse as a system of ideas or knowledge, with its own vocabulary (such as the way academics speak to each other). This can result in the power to monopolize communications and debate and to enforce particular points of view. For example, if only certain people can speak the language of Event Studies, their 'discourse' will dominate. It is far better that everyone be able to participate.

To Jaworski and Pritchard (2005: 1), discourse is ' a semiotic system': textual-linguistic, visual or any other 'system of signification'. Discourse can mean conversation and language use, whereas 'critical discourse' examines cultural/social practice and processes including politics, values, norms, ideologies (p. 4). 'Social lives are constructed in and through language/discourse...' (p. 5).

Mental Exercise

In what sense are events communications tools, or a form of discourse?

Find examples of the following:

- *Events as interpretive tools, as when aspects of culture are interpreted to visitors?*
- *Events as symbolism (nationalism, pride, etc.?)*
- *Events as reflections of dominant values and power elites (are they open to interpretation and debate?)*

Media Studies

Media Studies covers the nature and effects of mass media upon individuals and society, as well as analyzing actual media content and representations. The pioneer scholar in media studies, Marshall McLuhan, wrote in his book *Understanding Media* (1964) 'the medium is the message', which is probably one of the most misunderstood popular phrases of all times. Mark Federman of the McLuhan Programme in Culture and Technology at the University of Toronto explains it this way on their website (www. mcluhan.utoronto):

> *McLuhan tells us that a 'message' is 'the change of scale or pace or pattern' that a new invention or innovation 'introduces into human affairs.' Note that it is not the content or use of the innovation, but the change in inter-personal dynamics that the innovation brings with it . . . McLuhan always thought of a medium in the sense of a growing medium, like the fertile potting soil into which a seed is planted, or the agar in a Petri dish. In other words, a medium – this extension of our body or senses or mind – is anything from which a change emerges. And since some sort of change emerges from everything we conceive or create, all of our inventions, innovations, ideas and ideals are McLuhan media.*

> *Thus we have the meaning of 'the medium is the message.' We can know the nature and characteristics of anything we conceive or create (medium) by virtue of the changes – often unnoticed and non-obvious changes – that they effect (message).*

My own interpretation of McLuhan's dictum is that planned events are not merely communications tools, but are media for change. And we will understand events only by examining those changes, intended or otherwise.

The study of the effects and techniques of advertising forms a cornerstone of media studies. 'Critical Media Theory' looks at how the corporate ownership of media production and distribution affects society, and this can be applied to the events world by examining how sponsorship and media coverage can convert a local production into a global event, or how mega-events have been converted into advertising platforms and instruments of cultural influence.

Tom McPhail's (2006) theory of 'electronic colonialism' has gained international recognition. He argued that mass media over time will impact upon more and more individuals, primarily using the English language, resulting in greater similarities. Indigenous films and artefacts become marginalized by high-quality and mass-produced media. Perhaps this can be called the Hollywood effect.

Mental Exercise

Examine planned events as communications media, from a corporate and a cultural perspective; link to interpretation, sponsorship/corporate ownership, events as counter-culture; authenticity. Consider the use of various media within events.

Performance Studies

Performances, including planned events, are studied from multiple perspectives in terms of their contribution to society. Wikipedia defined it this way:

> This field of study engages performance as both an object of study and as something to be experienced, practiced, enacted. Events are more than their face value. A sporting event, a ceremony, a protest are all performances in their own right. Events have specific actors, costumes, settings and audiences. Within these performances are more minute performances of self: of gender, of societal role(s), of age, of disposition(s). Examining events as performance provides insight into how we perform ourselves and our lives.

According to John Deighton (1992), consumers and events/performances interact in the following ways:

- People attend performances (passive spectators).
- People participate in performance (active roles).
- consumers 'perform' with products (they buy goods that have symbolic meaning and use them with others, to impress them for example, which becomes a performance (see Goffman's 1959 book *The Representation of Self in Everyday Life*).
- Products 'perform' for consumers: this is a metaphorical use of the term, as performance here means meeting technical specifications; but the marketer uses the analogy of theatrical or event performance to help sell the product (e.g., car ads that feature speed, glamour, etc., in a way that clearly suggests that buying the car will positively impact on your lifestyle).

Deighton also assessed how people assign meaning to their experiences. Photography is often a record of the good aspects of the trip or event, not the bad. When the photos are viewed at a later date, especially when shared, they are a record of the good times experienced. Given the imperfections of human memory, it is possible that we remember our remembrances (through photos and stories) more than the real experience. Telling stories – a 'narrative' – is the other common way that people assign meaning to experiences. This leads to several research methods, including asking people to construct a narrative, or analysing what people are saying on blogs. These narratives are 'social constructions' and can be heavily influenced by cultural/social conventions and interactions with fellow event-goers. They can also be quite unique, with different meanings assigned to exactly the same tangible experience.

When it comes to evaluating the quality of performance, Deighton argued that they must be considered in a different light from other goods and services. The event-goer might very well ascribe satisfaction to his or her participation or mood, or to others in the audience, rather than to the event organizers or performers. As well, surprise must be considered – people's expectations can be met and exceeded through good marketing and event design, but surprising people introduces a whole new set of factors. Is the audience delighted with the surprise or angered?

As a consequence of temporality, people asked to evaluate satisfaction levels or quality during an event are likely to consider benefits that have not yet accrued to them, such as how they anticipate they will feel when it is over. Even when it is officially over, there is the possibility that event-goers need a lot of time to really come to a conclusion about how the event affected them, and what it means – if anything – in their lives. A good event designer also has the opportunity to educate the audience during the event, so that their evaluations at the beginning, mid-way and end might be quite different. For example, if the audience are not familiar with a particular form of interpretation, art or contest, they will need time and instruction before they can pass any judgement about the event's quality and their own satisfaction with it.

Deighton analysed performance failures related to the intention behind the performance.

Expectations are a big issue. If the audience feels deceived in any way, such as the performance was quite different from what was advertised, the quality of the performance becomes rather irrelevant to them. The skill level of performers might be judged incompetent (lip-syncing rather than live singing; rigged outcomes rather than unpredictable). A lack of originality can lead to the failure of performance; if it is highly predictable there will be no surprise. In thrill events (races) the audience might conclude that risks were minimal or were manipulated. Finally, if the audience is not brought into a festive event, if it lacks involvement, the organizers are likely to be blamed.

Deighton concluded that a 'show frame' rather than a 'skill frame' should be created for certain performances so that audience expectations are not disappointed as, for example, when athletes at all-star games or exhibition matches do not put everything into the contest. In the 'festive frame' organizers have to involve the audience and a certain amount of spontaneity should result. In a 'thrill frame' the risks have to be perceived to be real. Many implications for marketing and communications follow from this conclusion. As in the SERVQUAL model, consumer expectations directly impact on their evaluation of satisfaction and quality.

Performance (or 'live') Art
Performance art consists of the impermanent actions of an individual or a group at a particular place and in a particular time, which of course also defines an 'event'. Presumably there has to be an audience, for can there be art without appreciation? Busking can be viewed as performance art. Take away the audience and you have a flash mob, with the immediate and short-lived experience for participants overriding any concern for art.

Installation Art
Sometimes artists are commissioned by governments or companies to enliven a space, get media attention or realize tourism and place marketing aims. The installation artist can use a variety of media, and the installation is always temporary. The idea is to

modify a space in terms of our tangible experience or concept of it. Most art installations are indoors, often in galleries. When they are outdoors they can attract a lot of attention, like a planned event but without a programme.

Arts and Cultural Management

(Figure 6.6)

Superficially, arts and cultural management (or administration) is the application of management, including business practices and theory, to the operation of arts and cultural organizations and their work. It gets more complex, however, when we hear that many people in the arts or cultural sectors do not think that what they do is a business, or that normal management functions like marketing should not apply. Why? Because what they do requires 'artistic integrity' that should not be diluted or commercialized by business methods – that audience development and accessibility are more important than pricing for profit, or that cultural tourism erodes authenticity.

Arts and cultural management	Nature and meanings: the event experience	Antecedents to attending events	Planning and producing events	Outcomes and the impacted	Processes and patterns
• Management of arts and cultural organizations • Community building through the arts and culture	• Events as artistic and cultural expression • Fostering appreciation and interpretation of arts and culture	• Audience building efforts generate demand for events	• Management of arts and culture organizations that programme venues and produce events • Volunteerism at events • Partnerships for the arts/culture	• Evaluating satisfaction with venues and performances • Cultural impacts on society	• Changing cultural norms • Elitist perspectives on what is important • The distribution of venues, events and organizations

Figure 6.6 Arts and cultural management.

Nevertheless, numerous arts and cultural administration programs have been created. As an example, Columbia University (*www.tc.columbia.edu*) offers an Arts Administration programme that:

> '...*reflects the conviction that the management of cultural institutions and arts organizations requires strategic planning, artistic creativity and social commitment. The arts managers capable of responding to the challenges and responsibilities of the arts must possess integrated management and financial skills, knowledge of the artistic process in which they are involved and sensitivity to the dynamics and educational needs of the communities they serve.*'

Degree programs in arts administration present one means of getting professionally involved with events, especially arts festivals and events held in art and cultural venues, such as theatres, concert halls, museums and galleries. This is also a pathway into community outreach to foster art and cultural appreciation. In these programmes business management is applied to governmental and not-for-profit organizations that produce or commission events. Community building is covered, including outreach programs, fundraising, volunteerism and partnership building, all of which is useful to the event manager. Perhaps more importantly, the student will get an appreciation of the importance and roles of arts and culture in community life.

Cultural Studies (Figure 6.7)

The meanings and practice of everyday life are the subjects of cultural studies, a field that draws from anthropology, sociology and theory about all the forms of art and communications. Cultural practices comprise the ways people do particular things (such as watching television or eating out) in a given culture. Researchers examine how art, or popular activities like watching television, relate to matters of power, ideology, race, social class or gender. There can be a heavy Marxist bent to cultural studies, or a more neutral attempt to understand mass culture and how consumers attach meanings to forms of cultural expression. Hermeneutics is therefore employed to study the various 'texts' of cultural productions or artefacts.

Cultural Studies	Nature and meanings: the event experience	Antecedents to attending events	Planning and producing events	Outcomes and the impacted	Processes and patterns
• Critical study of popular culture and ordinary life	• The appeal of art and entertainment events • Importance and nature of cultural performances • High and popular culture • Cultural policy	• Cultural capital • Extrinsic motives to attend events	• Linking the event sector to power and politics, gender and inequality	• The distribution of costs and benefits	• Culture is dynamic • Cross-cultural comparisons and interactions

Figure 6.7   Cultural studies.

Sport Management and Sport Studies (Figure 6.8)

Sport management focuses on sport organizations, such as professional clubs and public facilities, with specific interests in sport marketing, human resources, finance, organizational structure, organizational behaviour, ethics, information technology, policy development and communications (North American Society for Sport Management; www.nassm.com). NASSM's *Journal of Sport Management* carries articles on sport events and sport tourism which are of particular interest to Event Studies.

	Nature and meanings: the event experience	Antecedents to attending events	Planning and producing events	Outcomes and the impacted	Processes and patterns
Sport management • Management of sport organizations, venues and events **Sport studies** • Sport psychology, sociology, history, geography	• Sport is both big business and public good • Sport for health, fitness and mastery • Sport as a social phenomenon • Sport as entertainment	• Unique motives for competing in or spectating at sport events • Demand for sport tourism	• Sport venue mangers produce and host events • Competitions produced by leagues and clubs • Sport events bid on as part of sport tourism • Social structures, patterns and organizations engaged in sport	• Sport tourism impacts • Personal well-being and social benefits of participation in sport events	• Sport trends, fads (e.g., the diffusion of new sports) • Sport development policy • Sport history • Sport geography (patterns of sport and sport events)

Figure 6.8 Sport management and sport studies.

Sports by nature involve competitions, both regularly scheduled and one-time, so the co-ordination, production or marketing of events is usually an essential part of the job. This generally applies in athletics departments of educational institutions, international sport federations, professional sport clubs and leagues, sport facility and fitness club management, recreational sports (for parks and recreation departments or associations), sports commissions (city-based agencies active in event tourism development) and sport marketing firms. Graham et al. (1995) in their book *The Ultimate Guide to Sport Event Management and Marketing*, described this sector in detail, including types of careers and specific sport-event issues. In the book *Profiles of Sport Industry Professionals* by Robinson et al. (2001), many contributors described their career paths and jobs, many of which involve events.

Sport Studies

'Sport Psychology' is primarily concerned with the athlete, but the sport fan is also studied. Why does 'hooliganism' plague football, and why do fans celebrate to excess? Are there differences in motives between male and female fans and sport tourists? 'Sport Sociology' relates more to Event Studies in that it focuses on groups and organizations engaged in sport, including those that produce and consume events. Studies of particular interest include sport subcultures, sport politics and national identity, sport and the media, violence, and sport influenced by gender, class, race or ethnicity. 'Sport Anthropologists' are interested in the cultural importance of sport and cultural differences reflected in sport.

Research Note

Daniels, M., and Norman, W. (2005). Motivations of equestrian tourists: an analysis of the Colonial Cup races. Journal of Sport Tourism, 10(3): 201–210.

These researchers adopted the Sport Fan Motivation Scale of Wann (1995) to test on fans who had travelled to a horse-racing event. The scale includes eight common motives, both intrinsic and extrinsic in nature: escape; eustress (stress evoked by any positive emotions or events, and in this context considered to be positive stimulation); aesthetic appreciation of sport; self-esteem; group affiliation; family; entertainment; and gaming. Results showed there were no gender differences in terms of motivation. The equestrian event was perceived to be a highly social activity, especially with those who did not highly 'identify' (a concept similar to ego involvement) with the sport. Their top-three motivations were 'entertainment', 'group affiliation' and 'family'. Event those who most identified with the sport gave 'entertainment' as their highest motive, but it was followed by aesthetics and eustress.

'Sport Economics' covers the economics of sport organizations, teams and events. Although sport-for-all and amateur athletics are often publicly supported to encourage healthy pursuits and socialization, subsidies for professional sport venues and teams have been quite controversial. Similarly, the bidding on and construction of facilities for sport events (i.e., sport tourism) almost always generates debates on costs and benefits.

'Sport History' includes the history of events and venues, with a great deal of attention having been paid to the Olympics. 'Sport Geographers' examine the spatial distribution of sport events and where athletes come from. The diffusion of new sports and of sport events combines the spatial and temporal dimensions.

'Sport Tourism' has emerged as a sub-field, particular because it has become major element in destination competitiveness. The following research note is an example of the growing body of research pertaining to sport tourism.

Research Note

Chalip, L., and McGuirty, J. (2004). Bundling sport events with the host destination. Journal of Sport Tourism, 9(3): 267–282.

These researchers examined 'bundling' for runners, specifically how these athletes could be attracted through augmentations such as other activities and attractions. Bundling can include event elements (including educational and celebratory, external cultural events, tours and visits to attractions, and shopping. A sample of 277 adult runners at events in Sydney and Melbourne were asked to consider bundling options for possible participation in the Gold Coast Marathon. Cluster analysis was used to develop four segments that differed in terms of their bundling choices. 'Dedicated runners' were older and only interested in official marathon parties, not the destination. The other segments had varying degrees of interest in destination bundling. 'Running tourists' were younger and less 'involved' with the sport, so they were less attracted by opportunities to celebrate with other runners. 'Rather, for these runners, the event represents an opportunity to combine running with a holiday at the host destination.' (p. 278).

Venue, Club and Assembly Management (Figure 6.9)

Events are often held in single or general-purpose arenas, convention centres, stadia or theatres, all of which can belong to the International Association of Assembly Managers (www.IAAM.org). When you own or manage a venue, events are at the top of mind: they are sometimes clients who pay to use the facility and sometimes they are bid on or created to fill gaps. Hotels, clubs, restaurants and many other facilities with function spaces are also in this business.

Venue, club and assembly management	Nature and meanings: the event experience	Antecedents to attending events	Planning and producing events	Outcomes and the impacted	Processes and patterns
• Design and management of event settings	• Club membership generates expectations and participation • Experience is shaped by the venue and its management	• Some venues are attractions in their own right • Big events usually require big arenas	• Venues produce and host events • Policy and regulations affecting venues and clubs	• Private versus public access to venues and events • Small, private events versus large, public events	• Venue technologies and design • Popularity of types of clubs • Locational patterns (supply and demand factors)

Figure 6.9   Venue, club and assembly management.

Clubs are usually private, owned by members or based on paid membership, and often closely tied to sports (e.g., golf or yacht clubs), fitness and health. Not-for-profit associations, including ethnic groups, often run clubs with facilities. The magazine

Club Management is aimed at professional club managers, and their association is Club Managers Association of America (www.cmaa.org). Entertainment and catered events are common at clubs. Their 'events directors' might have responsibility for booking entertainment, arranging caterers or hiring decorators.

Research Note

Preda, P., and Watts, T. (2003). Improving the efficiency of sporting venues through capacity management: the Case of the Sydney (Australia) Cricket Ground Trust. Event Management, 8(2): 83–89.

Idle capacity and bottlenecks were examined with a view to improving this sport venue's efficiency. Each stage of the service process for patrons was timed and studied, with ticketing and entrances receiving the most attention. An efficiency table was constructed, using specific performance categories, which showed management where improvements could be made.

Event visitor management, including demand, flow, capacity, queuing and service, has also been discussed by Yeoman et al. (2004).

Theatre Studies (Figure 6.10)

Theatre studies are liberal arts programs that typically encompass acting, production, technical aspects of theatre and the history of theatre. This programme description is from Canada's Acadia University *(www.acadiau.ca):*

The[theatre studies] program provides practical classes in acting, speech and voice, movement, children's theatre, and stage production, and also courses in theatre history, dramatic theory and criticism, film, Canadian film and drama, and women in theatre. The program includes a 'technical component' in its acting courses, so that all students are required to learn something of the complex activity which goes on behind the scenes and makes theatre productions possible.

Theatre Studies at Duke University, North Carolina (www.duke.edu/web/ theaterstudies) is described this way:

Combining respect for history with immersion in contemporary issues, and intellectual engagement with creative expression, the Department of Theater Studies offers students opportunities to study and practice theater. The faculty view theater as a form of human expression, shaped by social, economic, technological, personal, and artistic forces. As such, the study and practice of theater are valuable components of a liberal arts education.

Theatrical productions are events. While they are typically produced as the regular business of theatrical companies, in regular seasons or programs, they are also produced in festivals. And plays or other theatrical productions can certainly be viewed as special

Theatre studies	Nature and meanings: the event experience	Antecedents to attending events	Planning and producing events	Outcomes and the impacted	Processes and patterns
• Professional preparation for theatrical productions • Drama • Acting • History and types of theatre	• Professional theatre applied to events • Events as entertainment or social commentary • Cultural meanings	• Cultural traditions shape demand for theatre • Demand shaped by opportunity (supply) • Unique theatrical productions motivate travel	• Creativity • Scripted performances • Setting design (staging)	• Personal versus societal benefits • Theatre as a business	• Arts and cultural policy • Changing societal values

Figure 6.10 Theatre studies.

events from the perspective of the audience. More importantly, the very concepts of theatre and performance, steeped in tradition and culturally distinctive, lie at the foundation of event design. And theatre is relevant to all forms of event, from sports (especially 'professional' wrestling, which hopefully everyone recognizes as being staged), to meetings (the 'drama' of debate and the 'staging' of presentations) to festivals ('rites and rituals performed' for the audience, and including the audience) to trade shows (replete with entertainment and 'showmanship').

Scripting Events

The metaphor of events as theatre is good only to a point. First, theatres are production houses (business or not-for-profit) that create programmes of scheduled events. Second, while many event producers have a theatrical background, only certain types of planned events can be fully staged and scripted.

Pine and Gilmore used the framework of Richard Schechner from the book *Performance Theory* (1988). The base is 'drama', which can be any form of story or strategy. Drama depicts the theme of the performance, and can be expressed through different media. For a conference, the drama is the collective mission and discourse of those in attendance; for a gala banquet it can be an historical theme. The 'script' tells performers what to do, and it can include precise instructions or general directions. A script can incorporate elements of surprise or improvisation.

Theatre, in this framework, is the event itself – the performers implementing their script. Staff members, even volunteers at events are performers in this theatre because they have such an important role to play in creating the desired experience. Accordingly, everyone has to have a script. What Pine and Gilmore wanted to stress is that work, in the workplace, should also be thought of as theatre. And of course if the theatre is interactive, involving the audience by way of activity and mental/emotional immersion, the experience will be that much more unique and memorable. Finally, Schechner defined 'performance' as being dependent on having an audience. Performances are perceived or simply enjoyed. An interaction has to occur, but the 'audience' does not necessarily have to appreciate that they are part of a performance or being influenced by a script.

Forms of Theatre (Figure 6.11)

Schechner also differentiated between four basic forms of theatres, each embodying varying degrees of being scripted in combination with stable or dynamic performance. The first is 'improvisation' (or 'improv'), a form of theatre in which the script is very flexible and the outcomes unpredictable. It is most used for comedy, but also seems to describe many flash-mob events. Improvisation actually requires preparation and many skills to be effective as theatre or to be used in a special event. Audiences should quickly appreciate that they are part of an experiment and the journey they are taking with the performers is going nowhere in particular, or inevitably will result in surprises. At a minimum, 'improv' events need a premise or a scenario, a starting point or concept. They offer great scope for audience involvement.

Street theatre • Dynamic performance • Stable script	Improv theatre • Dynamic script • Stable performance
Platform theatre • Stable performance • Stable script	Matching theatre • Dynamic script • Dynamic performance

Figure 6.11 Schechner's (1988) four forms of theatre.

In stark contrast to the 'improv' is the 'platform' theatre that we associate with plays and musicals. The performance is generally fully scripted (memorized and rehearsed) and the performers clearly separated from the audience. In these types of event the guest is seldom motivated to attend twice, unless the excellence and subtleties of the show encourage a desire for deeper understanding; unless it is so enjoyable that experiencing it again is more enjoyable!

'Matching theatre' is edited like a film or television show. Someone has to put it together to create a coherent whole. The audience can be asked to move about a venue, as in some murder mystery performances, trying to form a mental picture of everything that is happening, despite discontinuities in both space and time.

'Street theatre', otherwise known as performances by buskers, or travelling minstrels, can be informal and highly individualistic or packaged within festivals. The entertainers have to put on a show, first drawing the audience then engaging them sufficiently to secure a voluntary financial reward. Ordinary space has to serve as a stage, and in some cases can be incorporated into the act, becoming really unique, temporary event settings. Their script has to be relatively stable, after all they are jugglers, or fire-eaters, or singers or clowns. But each performance is also going to be a unique blend of audience–performer interactions, setting (imagine the street noise) and programme (they have to posses an adaptable repertoire in terms of specific acts, and be able to alter their sequence, timing, etc.).

Chapter Summary

Closely related professional fields were discussed as to their links with and contributions to Event Studies. These fields all involve events to some extent, so Event Studies, as it develops, can feed back important concepts to them. Note how each field has to draw upon foundation disciplines for theory and methodology, and how the ways in which they apply theory suggests possibilities and direct applications for Event Studies.

Leisure Studies is very important, particularly in terms of its application of social psychology to the understanding of play, leisure experiences, needs and motives, benefits, constraints, and the related concepts of serious leisure, commitment, involvement and recreation specialization. While those theories pertain mostly to intrinsically motivated event behaviour (i.e., freely attending events for personal benefits), there are also profound implications for designing event settings and experiences, such as the concepts of 'peak experience' and 'flow' as they pertain to our model of what happens in the 'Liminal/Liminoid Zone'.

Tourism has great relevance to Event Studies both in understanding the destination approach to developing and marketing event tourism and to segmenting the event tourist. Many events are specifically part of cultural tourism, while equal attention has to be given to sport, business and other travel markets. Each of the five main economic and tourism roles of events has been given considerable attention in the research literature.

Hospitality, and closely related venue management, focuses on the providers of venues and services for events. Host–guest interactions, and what it means to provide hospitality, are the key concepts of value to event management.

Education contributes learning theory which is critical in meetings, conventions, scientific congresses and symposia. Principles and methods of interpretation are vital in shaping planned event experiences and giving them meanings. Communications, media and performance studies are inter-related. We need 'information theory' for event marketing and for understanding why events are 'media' for change in society. Performance studies specifically relate to theatre studies and all planned events draw from these two fields. There is a strong thread of symbolic 'interactionism' in performances. In theatre studies the importance of different forms of theatre, staging and scripting are emphasized, with clear applications to planned events. Cultural Studies should be read in conjunction with cultural anthropology, sociology and media studies. Scholars in cultural studies take a critical perspective on popular culture which includes many forms of event.

Sport events are of central interest in sport management and sport tourism has become global big business. In terms of sport studies, sport sociologists, psychologists, historians and economists all make a contribution to knowledge about sport organizations, sport events, athletes and fans.

Study Questions

- Distinguish between intrinsic and extrinsic motivations as they apply to events.
- Discuss the relevance of serious leisure, recreation specialization, involvement and commitment to Event Studies.
- In what ways can all planned events be considered part of cultural tourism?
- How can events contribute to destination image enhancement?
- Why exactly are venue managers and hospitality professionals involved with planned events? What can their field contribute to Event Studies?
- How can learning theories be applied to events?
- Discuss the meaning and applications of thematic interpretation.
- Show how to apply information theory to the study of events and for event marketing.
- What are the fundamental principles of performance? Link performance to social interaction theory.
- Distinguish between cultural management and cultural studies.
- Apply Schechner's four forms of theatre to other forms of planned events.
- In terms of experiences, are all planned events similar to theatre?

Further Reading

Gibson, H. (ed.) (2006a). *Sport Tourism: Concepts and Theories*. London: Routledge.
Masterman, G., and Wood, E. (2006). *Innovative Marketing Communications: Strategies for the Events Industry*. Oxford: Butterworth-Heinemann.
McPhail, T. (2006). *Global Communication: Theories, Stakeholders, and Trends* (2nd edn.). Blackwell Publishers.
Schechner, R. (1988). *Performance Theory*. New York: Routledge.
Schechner, R. (2002). *Performance Studies: An Introduction*. New York: Routledge.

Concert: Edmonton Folk Festival
Themes: the event experience; entertainment; staging; logistics; leisure constraints; crowd management
Photo Credit: Travel Alberta

Competitor, Dragon Boat Races
Themes: challenge; intrinsic motivation; participant event
Photo Credit: Tourism Calgary

Festival at the Bay, Glenelg (Adelaide, South Australia)
Themes: celebration; time out of time; special/public place; community building;
the street as event setting; festivalization of cities
Photo Credit: Steve Brown

Winter Olympic Venue, Calgary
Themes: legacy; politics; mega events and urban form; cultural and national identity
Photo Credit: Tourism Calgary

Gothenburg Sweden 'Varvet' (Half Marathon)
Themes: participation sport event; involvement;
event careers; sub-cultures; linear-nodal setting
Photo Credit: Henrik Sandsjö

Winter Olympics, Turino
Themes: mega event; ritual; symbolism; spectacle;
event tourism; image making and place marketing;
economic impacts; globalization
Photo Credit: © Brian Bahr/Getty Images

Multicultural Carnival, Adelaide
Themes: ritual; cross-cultural comparison; celebration; authenticity ; animation of places
Photo Credit: Steve Brown

The Calgary Exhibition and Stampede
Themes: Institutions; intrinsic motivations to attend; site planning principles; perceptions
of crowding; behavioural settings; risk management; hallmark event
Photo Credit: Travel Alberta

German National Garden Show
Themes: experiential learning; edutainment; aesthetics; interpretation; behavioural cues; target marketing
Photo Credit: Ulrich Wünsch

International Rotary Convention
Themes: assembly venues; business events; bidding on events; event tourism
Photo Credit: Queensland Events Corporation

Special Events Show
Themes: designing the setting; theming; setting affordances; sensory stimulation; social experiences; entertainment
Photo Credit: Ulrich Wünsch

European Athletics Championships, 2006 (Ullevi Stadium, Gothenburg, Sweden)
Themes: investment; sport tourism; fan motivation; social experiences
Photo Credit: Leif Gustafsson

TransRockies Challenge
Themes: participant event; media; environmental impacts; stakeholders and the political market square; risk and safety
Photo Credit: TransRockies Inc./Dan Hudson

Frankfurt International Motor Show
Themes: Commerce; meeting and learning; communication; extrinsic motivation; site design and circulation; sponsorship; branding
Photo Credit: Ulrich Wünsch

Concert in Leeds, England
Themes: Staging; logistics; concerts; suppliers; human resources
Photo Credit: Simon Bell, UK, Centre for Events Management

Chapter 7
The Event Experience and Meanings

Learning Objectives

- Be able to define and explain the planned event experience in its cognitive, affective and conative dimensions.
- Understand the concepts of liminal and liminoid in the context of cultural anthropology and as applied to event experiences, with specific reference to rites and rituals.
- Learn the meaning of 'communitas' and its importance in event experiences.
- Know how event experiences can be different for customers/guests, spectators or participants, volunteers, organizers/staff and other stakeholders.
- Be able to explain the experiences associated with planned event types, and the meanings attached to those experiences by individuals and societies.
- Learn why some experiences are memorable or transforming.
- Understand the scope for, and limitations related to designing event experiences.

Defining 'Experience'

This chapter concerns the core phenomenon of Event Studies – planned event experiences – and meanings attached to them. If we cannot clearly articulate what the event experience is, then how can it be planned or designed? If we do not understand what it means to people, then how can it be important?

Our starting point is a definitional discussion, noting different meanings of 'experience' and how it can be used as both a noun and a verb. We recall the interpretation of 'leisure experiences' then add a discussion of the 'experience economy' and how the corporate world has been developing 'experiential marketing'. Then a model of the planned event experience is presented, derived from anthropology, leisure and tourism studies. The notion of 'liminal' and 'liminoid' experiences, and the creation of special places and times are central to the model.

Specific types or forms of events are revisited, looking at the experiential dimensions associated with each, and how people might describe them. Each stakeholder group is also examined, from customers to volunteers, in order to demonstrate substantial differences in event experiences and how they are obtained. Meanings attached to event experiences are examined from the perspectives of individuals, society, culture and the corporate world.

'Experience' Defined Generically

In normal conversation people might use the term 'experience' in several ways, either as a noun or a verb. In each of the immediately following examples 'experience' is used as a noun. I constructed these statements to illustrate key points, so a little commentary is attached to each.

> *'I had an intellectually stimulating **experience** at the meeting.'*
> This statement describes the experience both in terms of cognition (i.e., learning) and affect (attitude or emotion).

> *'The marathon was a challenging and exhausting **experience**, but I was exhilarated by my success!'*
> The runner describes her/his experience in terms of:
> (a) physicality (exhausting), which is the conative or behavioural dimension of experience;
> (b) feelings about it (exhilaration is an emotional state);
> (c) 'challenging', in this context, can relate either to the physical experience (he/she had to push themselves extra hard to complete the race) or to a post-event assessment of meaning, in which case the runner might be saying he/she felt a sense of accomplishment or mastery in the achievement of personal goals.

*'I am a person with lots of event **experience**.'*
That is, I have been to many events and learned a lot about them; there has been an accumulation of knowledge or skill.

*'The **experience** of attending my first World's Fair was a highlight of my life and I will never forget it!'*
The person is talking about being at the event, involving direct observation and a stream of consciousness; there is also profound, transforming meaning attached.

We also use 'to experience' (the verb) in different ways. Here are event-related examples:

*'As an event manager I have **experienced** (i.e., lived through) many near disasters'.*
This a simple statement about something that happened, not a value judgement, emotional reaction or inference of meaning.

*'I want to **experience** the excitement of a Rolling Stones concert!'*
This use of the verb is loaded with emotion or feelings, and it refers to the knowing and feeling that comes only through direct participation, or 'being there'.

*'You have to get **experienced** in many tasks at real events before you can become a competent manager.'*
Here it means to undergo a change, an accumulation of transformative experiences, becoming more knowledgeable and skilled.

Referring back to these examples, note that the 'conative' dimension of experience describes actual behaviour, the things people do including physical activity. To be more precise, in cognitive psychology this is the component of attitude that involves actual behaviour.

The 'cognitive' dimension of experience refers to awareness, perception, memory, learning, judgement and understanding or making sense of the experience. This is likely to be dominant in meetings, conferences, scientific forums and some business and trade event where education or sharing ideas and knowledge are the main goal.

The 'affective' dimension of experience concerns feelings and emotions, preferences and values. Describing experiences as fun or giving pleasure reflect emotions, while many social aspects of experience reflect values – including being with friends and family, and a sense of sharing and belonging to a wider community.

How people describe event experiences as they occur, and talk about them afterwards, remains in large part a mystery and therefore must be of considerable interest to event researchers and producers. It is certainly possible that events satisfy those in attendance at one level, but at the same time fail to achieve the organizers' intended experiences (such as learning, cultural appreciation, social integration, increased brand identity). It is also quite possible that events are determined to be successful in terms of desired outcomes (e.g., money earned, attendance, brand recognition), but the experiences of guests are unsatisfactory, even negative.

'Leisure Experience' (Intrinsic Motivation and Freedom of Choice)

Mannell and Kleiber (1997) discussed leisure experiences using the concept of 'immediate conscious experience' (or stream of consciousness) which, to understand it, requires the monitoring of real-time behaviour. To be 'leisure', the experience should be accompanied by a sense of freedom, and of competence and control. We want to know the following about immediate conscious experience at events:

- Anatomy of the experience (What happened to you? Intensity, duration.).
- Moods, emotions, feelings (self-evaluation of the experience); intensity, relaxation, arousal, activation (bored/excited; energetic/tired; active/passive; alert/drowsy).
- Involvement: perceived duration; narrow focus of attention; ego-loss.
- Cognitive components (ideas, beliefs, thoughts, images/imagination, meanings attached).
- Sense of competence/control.
- Sense of freedom.

We will return to this approach when talking about experiential sampling, the phenomenological method used to study experiences.

The 'Experience Economy'

One of the most profound trends in the world of events has been the corporate sector's embracing of the desirability of using the concept of 'experiences' for purposes of marketing and branding. This has occurred because of the readily observed rise of demand for experiences rather than products, and the power of events and other 'experiences' to emotionally connect with consumers, while traditional methods of marketing have declined in impact. All of these have given rise to what some are calling the 'experience economy' and a host of 'creative industries'. Mossberg (2006: 51) explained the trend this way: 'The growth of these industries can be explained by new consumption patterns, new technology and the need for meetings, caring, entertainment and delight.'

Consequently, there has been an explosion of literature on the 'experience economy' and 'experiential marketing'. Pine and Gilmore in their influential book The *Experience Economy* (1999: 3) claimed that '. . . companies stage an experience whenever they engage customers, connecting with them in a personal, memorable way.' When the customer becomes part of the interplay (i.e., a co-performer) the experience becomes individualized. Four 'realms' of experience were suggested, derived from two inter-secting dimensions.

The horizontal dimension in their model is a simple active/passive dichotomy, reflect-ing the activity level of the customer or event-goer. The vertical dimension is much more interesting, reflecting the connection between customer and event. People are 'absorbed' in the experience when the performance occupies our attention and is brought into our minds. 'Immersion' is when the person is physically or virtually 'into' the experience.

Pine and Gilmore (p. 31) quoted the Oxford English Dictionary to define 'entertainment' as 'the action of occupying a person's attention agreeably; amusement'. They sug-gested that it is one of the oldest forms of experience. In 'esthetic' experiences (p. 35) '. . . individuals immerse themselves in an event or environment but themselves have little or no effect on it, leaving the environment (but not themselves) essentially untouched.' Thus, 'passive participation' in the Pine and Gilmore model equates with entertainment or a esthetic experiences, while 'active participation' equates with edu-cation and escapism.

Education, to Pine and Gilmore (and many educators), should be interactive, with the onus on the learner to become involved and on the educator to facilitate it. Mental engagement is probably more difficult to realize than physical engagement, as in out-door pursuits and recreation. Hence, physical engagement is often used to promote the mental side. As well, making education fun, as in 'edutainment', is an effective approach.

'Escapist' experiences require much greater immersion than either educational or entertainment experiences, according to Pine and Gilmore (p. 33). 'Rather than playing the passive role of couch potato, watching others act, the individual becomes an actor, able to affect the actual performance.' This approach is counter to most theatre or concert events as entertainment, and most closely resembles the festival, party or flash mob which all depend on interactivity.

Theorists will see in the four-realm model of Pine and Gilmore the basic 'seeking-escaping' motivators identified by Iso-Ahola that apply to all leisure and travel, as confirmed in many studies of the motivations of event-goers. It is a very useful model in stimulating thought about the nature of designed experiences, but it is short on mak-ing explicit the theoretical underpinnings.

Pine and Gilmore on Designing Experiences

The Experience Economy provides details on how to create experiences, and their guide-lines resonate well with event professionals. Of course they were originally aiming their process mostly at retailers. The first job is to establish the 'theme' of the experience, including the scripting of a 'participative story' to unify all the elements (p. 48).

Themes should alter the guests' sense of time, place and reality. Themes are made tangible and memorable through 'positive cues' that leave lasting impressions, notably high-quality customer service, design elements, the entertainment, food and beverages and various other sensory stimulations. Remember how smell triggers memories! Negative cues must be eliminated. Guests should be given, or be able to purchase memorabilia of their experience.

Surprise is a big element in the Pine and Gilmore approach, by which they mean 'staging the unexpected' (p. 96). Surprise has to be built on customer satisfaction (basically, delivering what was promised) and eliminating customer 'sacrifice' (i.e., the difference between what they expect and what they perceive they received, often a deficit). Surprise can mean departing from the script, or including seemingly bizarre elements into it. Surprise can come from juxtaposition of contrasting elements of style, out-of-context performance or display, humour and even fright. It will often require a pre-formulation of guest expectations. And it can be risky!

Taking the theatrical analogy further, Pine and Gilmore discussed the various roles and actors required for a theatrical production, all of which are directly pertinent in the events business. There are producers who financially back the event, and directors who are in charge of the actual production. 'Dramaturgs' act as interpreters of the theme or story, and in the events business they might be consultants from various backgrounds as diverse as theatre, education/interpretation, sport or commerce. Scriptwriters have to prepare the written script or other forms of directions for performers. In dance they are choreographers. In sport they are coaches, and in athletics they are trainers. Singers require song writers and voice trainers.

A host of technicians make essential services happen, while set designers make the setting work visually. In the events world, set designers and technicians can be the same, as in making a spectacle from fireworks and lasers, creating intriguing sound and light effects, or decorating tables. Chefs have to both cook and create interesting, tasteful delights. Flower and balloon arrangers stress esthetics, but must know what will work in various circumstances. Good set designers know about environmental psychology, whether or not they have studied it formally. Prop managers, costume designers, stage crews and casting companies are also needed.

The final topic covered in *The Experience Economy* is 'transformation'. Pine and Gilmore argued that events are 'produced experiences', but transformations occur within the guest or customer. Many event designers seek to facilitate or guide such transformations, specifying outcomes in terms of health and well-being, learning, self-actualization and happiness. These arise from meaningful experiences and may be cumulative. 'When you customize an experience you change the individual' (p. 165).

If an event is merely intended to inform or sell, entertain or amuse, achieving transformations will not be a goal of the designer. Increasingly, however, events are planned explicitly for this purpose. Companies want employees to become committed and achieve their full potential, so their corporate functions are intended to transform attitudes and behaviour. Governments and cause-related organizations want the public to not only give money, but also to become healthier, wiser, more involved citizens.

Tourism Experiences

Ooi (2005: 53) identified six approaches to identifying and studying tourism experiences. The first derives from cognitive psychology and relates to leisure theory. Preconceived ideas, expectations and perceptions affect how tourists consume, evaluate and experience tourism 'products'. The second approach reflects a great deal of tourism literature, all based on the assumption that travel generates positive experiences; tourism is a means to an end, resulting in learning, happiness and nice memories. In the third approach (again from leisure studies) researchers concentrate on state of mind and the depth of engagement, or 'flow' and 'optimal experiences'.

The 'phenomenological' approach is fourth, for example, as proposed by Li (2000) to describe the immediacy of personal touristic experiences through rich, reflexive and intimate data. In the fifth approach Urry's (1990, 1995, 2002) concept of the 'tourist gaze' is employed, focusing on how travellers notice differences from their own environment and daily life. But because the visitor lacks local knowledge, their experience is a reflection of their own background. In the sixth approach, the theatrical analogy is used, as by Pine and Gilmore in *The Experience Economy* (1999), arguing that 'engaging experiences' depend on the degree to which tourists interact with the 'product'.

Ooi (2005: 54) also suggested that tourist experiences are enriched or shaped by 'mediators', including guides, DMOs and the information available. These help to catch the attention of travellers and even to manage their experiences. Ooi said 'Tourism mediators craft tourism experiences by controlling and directing tourists' attention (p. 55).'

People can only pay attention to one thing at a time, and we are easily overwhelmed by too much information or stimuli. When attention shifts, our experience is altered; individuals are both drawn to different stimuli, and react differently to the same stimuli.

Event Experiences According to O'Sullivan and Spangler

O'Sullivan and Spangler (1998: 5) in their book *Experience Marketing: Strategies for the New Millennium* stated that in the 'experience economy' there are three types of actor. 'Infusers' are manufacturers who infuse their products with experiences for marketability. 'Enhancers' are service providers who use experiences to heighten satisfaction levels, to differentiate from competitors. And 'experience makers' are service providers who create experiences as the core of their business. To O'Sullivan and Spangler (p. 3) event experiences involve the following:

- Participation and involvement in the consumption.
- The state of being physically, mentally, socially spiritually, or emotionally engaged.
- A change in knowledge, skill, memory or emotion.
- The conscious perception of having intentionally encountered, gone to or lived through an activity or event; and . . .
- An effort directed at addressing a psychological or internal need.

They also identified five 'parameters' of experience (p. 23):

1. Stages: Events or feeling that occur prior to, during and after.
2. The actual experience: Factors or variables that influence participation and shape outcomes.
3. Needs being addressed.
4. Roles of the participant and other people involved (personality, expectations, behaviour) in shaping outcomes.
5. Roles of and relationships with the provider of the experience (ability and willingness to customize the experience, control it).

O'Sullivan and Spangler ask a lot of pertinent questions about the event experience. To what extent is the experience real versus virtual, customized or mass produced, unique or commonplace? Is it focused on people, an attraction, a facility, equipment or performance? Does the event experience consist of concrete or disconnected episodes? Is the guest, customer, participant or spectator facilitated or self-directed? Does the event create a temporary or transforming change, result in pleasure or preservation? What is the level of authenticity?

The 'Guaranteed' and Safe Experience

How do we explain the popularity of theme parks and entertainment events – including cultural productions? One answer is that they provide 'guaranteed' and safe experiences. Their predictability, combined with perceived personal security, assures the customer that they will get what they expect, even though their expectations are limited.

By contrast, travel and many event experiences are somewhat unpredictable, with plenty of risks.

If people are willing to sacrifice spontaneity, cultural authenticity and surprise for the safe and mundane, that is their business. The more highly 'involved' traveller, plus the many novelty seekers of the world, will certainly continue to seek out special experiences. To the extent that the mass market fails to provide certain event experiences, that is probably good for those who are specialists and dedicated event tourists.

The Wow! Factor

Event designers strive hard to impress the visitor. Citrine (1995) held that the 'wow factor' is a guiding principle for event designers. Visitors, he said, should be 'dazzled' when they arrive and leave. Is this the same as saying event designers seek to create really special, emotionally engaging and memorable experiences?

Much of what goes into 'wow!' is art and spectacle – a visual impression. Sound and smell can also be combined with décor, lighting and other programmic elements of style, so 'wow!' can be a complete sensory reaction. Clearly this can be designed. But can you have a 'wow!' experience in terms of learning, cultural authenticity or perhaps physical mastery? That's a little more difficult to conceptualize, let alone to design or programme.

Considerably exceeding expectations, and building in elements of surprise, could achieve the 'wow!' reaction. So too could disappointment and failure, giving rise to the wrong kind of 'wow!' (as in, that really stunk!).

Mental Exercise

In the foregoing and following discussion, pay attention to the various theories of experience, including leisure and spectacle, and try to determine what exactly constitutes 'wow!' Is it testable in theoretical terms, or merely a buzzword?

A Model of the Planned Event Experience

The ethnographer and folklorist Arnold van Gennep, author of *The Rites of Passage* in 1909, suggested that rituals consisted of stages: a 'pre-liminal' phase (the separation from normality), a 'liminal' phase (the transition into another realm of being) and a 'post-liminal' phase (reincorporation into everyday life). Much later, anthropologist Victor

Turner (1969) described the detached state of being associated with ritual as 'liminality'. In this state one was in 'limbo', an ambiguous state characterized by humility, seclusion, tests, sexual ambiguity and 'communitas'.

Applied to the event experience in general, we can say that 'communitas' applies to that temporary state in which people are together, removed from ordinary life, so they have something very specific in common. Their experience should be unstructured, relative to the outside world, and egalitarian (everyone accepted as being equal). 'Communitas' experienced at events is always transient, whereas sub-cultures, affinity groups and the highly 'involved' might seek this social state on a permanent basis. Event organizers, even in the case of designing personal rites of passage like the *bar mitzvah* or a wedding, cannot guarantee this sense of belonging and sharing.

'Liminoid' is a term Victor Turner used to describe the same state of transitional being, but in 'profane' rather than 'sacred' terms, so that it applies to carnivals and secular festivals. 'Communitas' in carnivals has more to do with emphasizing the notion of separation, loss of identity and social status and role reversals. In this state people are more relaxed, uninhibited and open to new ideas.

Jafar Jafari's model of 'tourist culture' (1987) is based on this socio-anthropological theory concerning 'liminality' (from van Gennep and Turner) and Falassi's notion of festivity as a time that is out of ordinary time. To Jafari, the separation from home establishes 'tourist culture' which is quite different from one's normal culture. This transient state of being applies to the entire trip, and just like the event experience, it enables (but does not guarantee) the creation of 'communitas' among fellow travellers.

In support of this theory, Ryan (2002: 3) called tourism a 'liminoid' phenomenon, saying that travel is a personal experience, occurring outside normal social processes but given meaning by them, and is 'profane' (i.e., not 'sacred') in the sense of involving role reversal, fun and idiosyncratic behaviour.

The 'Liminal/Liminoid' Zone and 'Communitas'

At the core of our model (Figure 7.1) is a distinct experiential or zone called 'liminal/liminoid'. It is a zone that must be delineated in both spatial and temporal terms. This is a 'special place' because of programming and how it is designed, all in preparation for the guests, viewers or participants. Designers can make it special through décor, entertainment, activity and sensory stimulations of all kinds, and they should use Falassi's 'valorization' concept to make event-goers aware that they are entering a space/time that has been set aside for their special purposes.

Meaning is conveyed through opening ceremonies, symbolism such as banners or logos and the theme. Some event experiences can be called 'sacred' (religious, spiritual) and

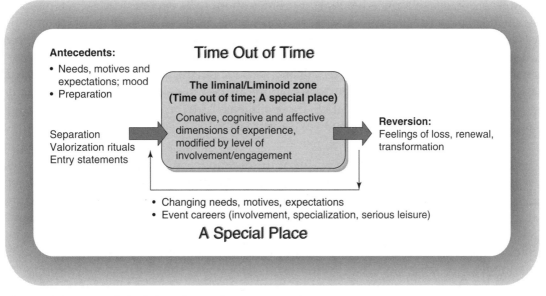

Figure 7.1 A model of the planned event experience.

others 'profane' (fun, escapist). However, it should always be a 'time out of time', to use Falassi's terminology – that is, it should be perceived to be outside the normal, beyond routine, unique. To the extent possible, all those involved with the event should experience the belonging and sharing that defines 'communitas'.

Research supports the existence and importance of 'communitas' at events. Hannam and Halewood (2006), in a study of participants in Viking festivals, concluded that group identity was fostered, even to the point of establishing a 'neo-tribal' community. Green and Chalip's study of women athletes determined that the event was a celebration of sub-cultural values. See also the research note by Fairley and Gammon (2006), a bit later, which deals with sport fan communities. This is a key theme running through event-related research.

It is easy to think of this special place as an event venue, like an arena, theatre or convention centre. But it can also be a temporary event space, or a whole community. The question of scale is important, because as we move from venue to large public space to entire community, we have a much more complex and difficult job of design and programming. Nevertheless, many communities manage to make themselves festive throughout, or at least at important entrances and meeting places, during the time of special events.

Before we get to the event there is preparation and anticipation. Most people go to an event having some expectations of the experience to be obtained (or partially self-created), or at least some foreknowledge that an event is about to be experienced. Much research has been conducted on motivation to attend events, especially festivals, and it mostly confirms the 'seeking-escaping' theory, suggesting that people clearly anticipate that an event is going to be out of the ordinary. I suppose you could stumble upon an event and be surprised, but even so there will be a sense of having left somewhere and arrived at some special place. Even where expectations are completely absent, that is the event-goer never gave it any thought at all, there still has to be the 'entering into' events that marks a transition from ordinary to extraordinary.

Csikszentmihalyi's theory of 'flow' fits into this model. It suggests that people seek 'optimal arousal', leading to 'flow' experiences which can be characterized by deep involvement, intense concentration, lack of self-consciousness and transcendence of self. These are intrinsically rewarding experiences. To the extent that designers can facilitate 'flow', event-goers can be expected to report exhilaration (from fantasizing or total immersion in music or activity), a sense of accomplishment (athletic achievement, mastery of a skill, intellectual stimulation) or transformation (through an intense emotional or spiritual process). How to foster a high level of involvement is the real challenge, and events that provide mere entertainment will find this illusive.

'Liminality' is not strictly dependent on the type of event or venue. This space/time exists in the minds of the attendees and participants, not within the programme or venue themselves. It can therefore be entered through the pathways of 'fantasy' (the heart of many theme parties), a willing suspension of the ordinary to play a role (as in carnival), engagement in new ideas and processes (such as discourse, clinical learning, team projects), participation with others (like celebration) or any kind of higher-than-usual level of involvement.

In the case of 'flash mobs' and other events at the fringe it is the participants who, according to some unwritten script or external prodding, largely make their own experiences. They are temporarily using (or 'liberating') a space for their purposes, perhaps making a social or political statement in doing so, but quickly returning it to the ordinary.

'Reversion' to normal life should be accompanied by a sense of change, going from the special to the ordinary. There might be a feeling of accomplishment, renewal, transformation, relief or loss. It is important to feel something at the end, otherwise what was special or memorable about the experience? I often feel a sense of loss at the end of conferences, not necessarily because the stimulating programme is over, but because of separation from friends and colleagues. It is the loss of 'communitas', and it leads to the drive-to-attend future events. Anyone who is highly 'involved', or emotionally moved by events will experience this loss. It gives meaning to the event and to our ordinary lives.

To the extent that people enjoy events, or at least derive some benefits from attending, they might very well develop an event career. Similar to Pearce's 'travel career', we learn from events and perhaps desire more of the same (the loyal festival-goer), or we crave the uniqueness, even surprises that come from many different types of event (the cultural event tourist), or we want ever-increasing challenge (the amateur, competitive athlete).

Research Note

Fairley, S., and Gammon, S. (2006). Something lived, something learned: nostalgia's expanding role in sport tourism. In: H. Gibson (ed.), Sport Tourism: Concepts and Theories, pp. 50–65. London: Routledge.

Fairley and Gammon suggested that for many sport fans there is a nostalgic desire to re-enter the liminoid space they associate with events and with the group experience of travelling to events. This space involves a strong sense of community or shared subcultural identity, and resembles the carnival in its acceptance of abandoning social norms. There is also the appeal of escape from everyday life. Nostalgia, in this context, fuels a career of event-related travel, and it relates to volunteers at events as well.

Tom O'Dell (2005: 133) argued that we must not over-emphasize the disjuncture from ordinary life when we consider 'liminal' or 'liminoid' experiences. His point is that touristic and event experiences can only be special or exceptional when considered in light of one's ordinary life and experiences. He said, 'To a large extent people learn the ropes of 'experiencing' through their daily consumption patterns. Also, we need to develop competencies for experiencing, and this is embodied in the concepts of serious leisure, specialization and self-efficacy'.

What Makes an Event Experience Memorable?

Drawing on cognitive psychology, three levels of experience have been distinguished: from Hover and van Mierlo (2006), adapted from a model by Gool and Wijngaarden (2005):

1. *'Basal experience'*: An emotional reaction to a stimulus, but with insufficient impact to stay long in one's memory.
2. *'Memorable experiences'*: The emotion can be recalled at a later date.
3. *'Transforming experiences'*: These result in durable changes on an attitudinal or behavioural level.

To be truly memorable also requires more than the 'wow!' factor, there has to be substance in additional to surprise or sensory stimulation. And intense stimulation and highly emotional, memorable experiences do not necessarily transform the individual. Often experiences merely reinforce existing values and attitudes and do not challenge us, or present the opportunity for learning and growth.

Generic and Specific Types of Planned Event Experiences

Recall the earlier discussion of how our planned event typology (Figure 2.1) is based on event forms, which are social constructs, and not on unique experiential components. Not only it is difficult to describe experiences, but also any event can conceivably engender many different experiences. The following discussion is an attempt to show that there are both generic and specific experiences associated with types of event, but this is not the same as formulating an experiential typology of events.

Generic Event Experiences

'Generic experiences' are those which can occur at any event, and therefore have more to do with the individual's state of mind and particular circumstances than with the event theme, programme or setting. I am convinced that many people attend events for generic personal benefits such as entertainment and simple diversion (we can call this 'escapism') and 'having fun' is probably how most people would describe the experience. Meanings attached to these experiences would not normally be profound. We cannot expect them to be memorable or transforming, but that is possible.

Anything can be 'entertaining', as entertainment is a point of view, or reaction to something. The event might be solemn and sacred, but some people do not get the point. Sports can be violent, but to some this is 'fun'. Similarly, anything can be 'relaxing', 'novel', 'stimulating' or 'enjoyable'. These and many other terms cannot be used as descriptors for specific event experiences because they are both ambiguous and generic.

More important are the generic social motivations and benefits associated with leisure and travel in general, which apply to intrinsically motivated event experiences – especially to have quality time with friends and family, and to enjoy that sense of belonging and sharing we call 'communitas'. Social experiences can occur whenever and wherever people get together, but planned events definitely facilitate them. Indeed, social and cultural groups create events specifically for this purpose, or find that certain events are good at facilitating it.

Research Note

Nicholson, R., and Pearce, D. (2001). Why do people attend events: a comparative analysis of visitor motivations at four South Island Events. Journal of Travel Research, 39(4): 449–460.

The authors studied motivations to attend four quite different events in New Zealand: an air show, award ceremony, wildfood festival, and a wine, food and music festival. They concluded that multiple motivations were the norm, and that while socialization was common to them all, it varied in its nature. Event-specific reasons were tied to the novelty or uniqueness of each event. In practical terms, they advised that event organizers cannot rely on demand patterns observed at other events.

Specific Event Experiences

In this section we examine the kinds of experiences that can and should be associated with certain types of planned events.

Cultural Celebrations

Cultural experiences in general are all about seeking knowledge, learning and understanding something new, and appreciating some aspects of culture – both the travellers and that of the destination. The cultural tourist or cultural event-goer wants to engage emotionally and cognitively with places, people and dimensions of lifestyle, including tangible things like historic sites, cultural performances, food and beverages, or meeting real people, and with intangible aspects including the symbolism of art and architecture. Simply sightseeing, or enjoying entertainment or spectacle, does not constitute a cultural experience.

Celebrations and commemorations in general reflect and foster belonging and sharing among a family, social group, community or nation. Values come to the fore, and a clear sense of place is usually present. The event's theme suggests what is to be celebrated, although in many cases it is the community itself that is the object of celebrations. In all cultural events we should be concerned with the notion of 'authenticity' and what that means in experiential terms. A detailed discussion of authenticity follows, in the section on meanings.

Festivals and Carnivals

Festivals and carnivals, as discussed previously, are to be joyous experiences. But they can range from solemn and sacred festivals to profane carnivals marked by wild revelry. Role playing and inversion are found in many carnivals, including masquerading. They usually embody rituals and symbolism that act as cues in suggesting the appropriate mood and emotions. These experience domains have been studied in depth by sociologists and anthropologists, such as Turner and Falassi.

Many so-called 'festivals', however, seem to provide little more than packaged entertainment and a party atmosphere, leaving it up to the audience and others involved to create their own, deeper experiences – if possible. Thematic interpretation can help communicate what is culturally significant about events, including their setting (the place), symbolic elements and historic context.

Religious and Spiritual Experiences

Sacred and spiritual experiences are not necessarily the same, as 'sacred' generally refers to established religious dogma (e.g., the Holy Scriptures are sacred, communion is a sacred rite). Spiritual experiences could be non-religious in nature, consisting of feelings of transcendence (e.g., 'I felt completely removed from, even raised above the worries of daily life') or self-discovery ('I was on a different plain of existence where I felt connected to every thing and every one'). Timothy and Olsen (2006: 271) argued that there are significant differences between being religious and being spiritual. Spiritual refers to personal belief, a search for meaning in one's life, and so any tourist could have a spiritual experience in a sacred place or alongside religious pilgrims.

Rapture, ecstasy, transcendence, revelation are terms used in conjunction with intense religious or spiritual experiences. Is this what is supposed to happen at a church service or during a Papal tour? Can these experiences be designed or facilitated at religious events? Certainly there is often the intent to do so, as when a preacher calls upon people in the congregation to come forward to repent. There is also a special dimension of 'communitas' in religious events, as highlighted by the rite of 'communion'.

Reisinger (2006) saw possibilities for spiritual experiences being incorporated into, or modifying many common forms of tourism, from nature tours to attending farm shows and harvest festivals, food and wine tastings to spa visits. While often associated with visits to scared places, spiritual experiences are also realized through meditation, exploring and performing rituals. In this sense the search for meaning in life can propel, almost invisibly, many leisure and travel activities.

Pilgrimage

Pilgrimage is a quest, a journey and the experience of a sacred place. For many it is a duty. The entire pilgrimage can be conceptualized as a special event in a person's life, a rite of passage and a transforming experience, but there are often well-defined events associated with religious pilgrimages. Pilgrimage occurs in stages, as in Turner's model. To prepare for the Hajj in Mecca, Muslims are to put their earthly affairs in order and become spiritually prepared. The event itself involves a number of rituals including those of purification, praise, repentance and sacrifice. Upon completion of the Hajj, one becomes '*Hajji*' and gains special status, making it a transforming process, at least in symbolic terms.

Singh (2006: 232) said that Hindu pilgrims '. . . enjoy sacred journeys as an earthly adventure from one place to another that entails the combined effects of a spiritual quest and physical hardship'. But could that not also describe the experience of a long-distance runner? Certainly the key elements that make religious quests and experiences different from other spiritual or emotionally uplifting experiences are participation in specified rituals or ceremonies that have deep meaning to the devoted and faithful. The place itself is crucial, but unlike a secular event venue, the meaning of sacred places is permanent, traditional and sanctioned by official religious bodies.

Virtual and Secular Pilgrimage

Only Muslims can experience the Hajj in person, but others may visit websites that provide a simulacrum of what it is like to be a pilgrim. Of course it is questionable if this is really pilgrimage, or if it is some kind of entertainment. Many tourism scholars now speak of secular pilgrimages, such as a golfer's pilgrimage to St Andrews in Scotland (the generally recognized birthplace of the game) or a wine lover's pilgrimage to the regions in which favourite wines are produced. Gammon (2004) wrote (p. 40): pilgrimage '. . . will include a journey of some kind to a place (or places) which holds personal and/or collective meaning to the "pilgrim"'. The experience might provoke 'awe and wonderment', whether at a sport shrine or a holy event.

Within special interest groups, or sub-cultures, certain events have prestige and become must-see, must-do 'icons'. For example, marathon runners strive to qualify for the Boston Marathon, making participation in that event almost like a pilgrimage. Does this apply to music concerts or other types of events? Could consumer researchers identify an 'evoked set' of events that people just have to attend because of their symbolic value?

Political and State Events

Many political and state events will have a high degree of formality, pomp and ceremony attached to them. Terms like stately, regal or dignified might be used to describe the mood. What you will experience at such events can vary greatly, depending on why you attended (to protest, participate or report on?), what access you have to the VIPs, and how you interact with security. For the politicians in attendance there should be dialogue, negotiation and public displays of diplomacy.

Arts and Entertainment Experiences (Including the Aesthetic)

By labelling entertainment an 'industry', society has created a social construct that depicts many forms of planned events (especially concerts, award shows and sports, but even festivals and art exhibitions) as entertainment. Events, for many, have become legitimate outlets for consumerism where we spend our time and money oblivious to, or unwanting of, any deeper experience or meaning than short-lived amusement. This, of course, is a dangerous thing for anyone concerned about the arts, cultural authenticity or social values.

'Aesthetic judgement' concerns art and beauty, but is value laden and relative. What one person finds attractive, another might describe as boring or disgusting. An aesthetic experience, however, is one in which we find something to be pleasing to our senses. It can be the aesthetic appreciation of paintings, food, fashion or music. Hence it is intensely personal, which leads to the expression 'you can't please everyone'. Designers take note: aesthetic experiences are valued, and they motivate a great deal of travel and consumption, but you cannot guarantee satisfaction. For most appreciators of fine art, food, music or whatever, it is the exploration and sense of discovery that matter most.

Limited research has been reported on art exhibitions, but Axelson and Arcodia (2004) argued that they should be viewed in the context of special event motivation and experience. A review of the literature suggested that people attend art galleries for reasons of learning, social interaction, status and novelty.

Smith (2006) discussed the rise of 'new leisure tourism', linking it the increasing blurring of work and leisure, and to 'de-differentiation' or the breakdown of boundaries between previously distinct activities. New leisure tourists are engaging in escapism, looking for fresh experiences, wanting fun and high-quality entertainment. Novelty seeking is a key aspect of this trend, leading Urry (2002) to say that people are becoming insatiable for their quest for novelty because reality never matches their expectations.

Youthful, hard-working consumers, brought up on music videos and computer entertainment, seem to have a very limited attention span and are constantly seeking stimulation. Smith (2006: 224) concluded that new leisure tourists are not interested in culture, but want playful, event fantastical experiences. Contrived, simulated, even obviously fake settings can provide this. Interactivity is desired, but in a technological sense. Fascination with celebrities is part of this new experiential realm. Industry has responded (in the spirit of the 'experience economy') with theming, overtly catering to hedonism, celebrity endorsements and what is being called 'shoppertainment'.

Mental Exercise

Find examples of edutainment and shoppertainment on the internet. Describe the range of experiences being suggested or facilitated and analyse them in the context of environmental and cognitive psychology. Are they leisure? Intrinsically motivated experiences?

Competitive Sport/Recreation Event Experiences (for Athletes)

It has to be more than just winning! Although competitive sports superficially involve games played by persons or teams with the intent of winning, that in itself does not constitute the entire experience or meaning. Many people compete for very personal reasons such as to gain fitness and mastery, while others compete for social reasons – to be part of a group and to enjoy a social event.

Bouchet et al. (2004) reviewed the literature on sport tourist experiences and concluded there are four theoretical streams evident. From a 'behavioural theory' perspective, group activities and interactions are the focus. For example, Green and Chalip (1998) found that strong sub-cultural meanings were attached by participants to a women's sport event (see the research note). From cognitive psychology comes attention to needs, motives, values and risk taking. A third approach combined the psychological and the behavioural roles of travelers, and the fourth is the experiential model.

Bouchet et al. (2004) advanced their own approach to analysing the sport tourist experience, encompassing considerations of self-worth (perceived risk, optimal stimulation, variety and novelty seeking), spatial variables, or the place (including functional components and a post-modernist view of how visitors create their own experiences and living space) and interpersonal variables (new relationships, and 'communitas').

What particularly distinguishes competitive sport experiences from any other event experiences is the structure (venues, rules, team versus single play, etc.), all of which are specific to each sport. Either this structure appeals to a person or it does not, and the diversity of sport gives rise to an almost infinite variety of experiential possibilities. Some are less combative than others; some require brute strength, others demand finesse and artistry. Sport is both highly personal (what the athlete accomplishes on their own) and social (the team, the community of athletes, the whole event organization).

The Sport Spectator and Sport Fan Experience

In the report Travellers Who Attend Sport Events (Travel Industry Association of America, 1999), it was documented that sport event tourism is a major social and economic phenomenon, and that 84% of the American adults who had travelled for sport reasons had been spectators. Many of these were parents or grandparents going to watch children play in competitions. In other words there is a huge family market within sport event tourism. Only 16% travelled to participate, and some of them also spectated.

Gibson (1998; 2006) found in her research that the 'active sport tourist' was mostly a male with college education, and higher income. This segment, she concluded, will likely continue to travel for participation in their favourite sports well into retirement.

Attending a sport event can be motivated by a desire for entertainment and spectacle (i.e., simple diversion), the desire for emotional stimulation, or having a social outing. Being a sport spectator is a role we can all play, and most spectators know that it is generally more interesting (certainly more emotionally exciting) to be at a live event as opposed to watching on TV. Being a sport 'fan', however, is something quite a bit more engaging.

Wann (1995) and Wann et al. (1999) developed a 'sport fan motivation scale' which covers both intrinsic and extrinsic motivation. It consists of eight common reasons for watching sport, and these can also be conceptualized as desired experiences: escape, *'eustress'* (i.e., stress evoked by emotions or events, here considered to be positive stimulation), aesthetics (appreciation of the beauty of sports), self-esteem, group affiliation, family, entertainment and economic (e.g., betting). Chen (2006) provided a review of the literature on sport fans, in a paper devoted to a phenomenological study of event sport fans' behaviour, experiences and values (it is also profiled in a Research Note on phenomenological method in Chapter 13).

Studies of sport fans have taken psychological and social–psychological approaches (see, for example, Smith and Mackie, 2000; Wann, 1997). Specific attention has been given to 'affect and emotion' (Dietz-Uhler and Murrell, 1999; Wann et al., 2002; Madrigal, 2003) motives (Trail and James, 2001; James and Ridinger, 2002), 'identification' (Laverie and Arnett, 2000), gender differences (Dietz-Uhler et al., 2000; James and Ridinger, 2002), factors influencing fan behaviour (End et al., 2003), and loyalty (Mahony et al., 1999, 2000; Tapp, 2004). Some fans can be considered to be engaging in 'serious leisure' (Gibson et al., 2003). It has even been determined that highly 'committed' sport fans spend more in destinations than casual fans.

Chen concluded that most studies suggest that personally relevant values (from needs and the benefits sought), and 'identifications' (such as social identity) most explain why fans become highly involved and committed to teams (see also Wann and Branscombe, 1993; Madrigal, 1995; Bristow and Sebastion, 2001). Chen's (2006) study determined that 'personal balance' and 'socialization' were the essential parts of the experiences being sought, and these were obtained through volunteering, being at events, travel with other fans and the team, 'pilgrimages' to places with special meanings, and non-related social and touristic activities in destinations.

Theory of Spectacle

John MacAloon (1984) has also contributed to understanding of the event experience from an anthropological base. Regarding the Olympic Games, he argued that of the genres of cultural performance (p. 242), 'spectacle' and 'games' appeared first, then festival and ritual. Spectacles are things to be seen, with both visual sensory and symbolic codes. Spectacles must be grand, dramatic or huge. There is no spectacle without actors and audience, or performers and spectators. Spectators must be excited by the spectacle, or otherwise emotionally moved. The Olympics, said MacAloon (p. 245), '. . . must be seen, and seen in person, to be believed.' Host cities are transformed, animated. The scale and intensity of the overall experience cannot be captured on television.

Ritual is a duty, but spectacle is by choice. Outsiders, or uninformed audiences, might mistake ritual for spectacle or not care about the cultural meanings embedded. While 'festival' requires a certain style of celebratory mood, and internal 'special observances', spectacle does not. MacAloon was suspicious of spectacles, as they tend to be 'tasteless' and become a 'moral cacophony'.

Although the Olympic Games proclaim to be a festival, MacAloon (p. 250) said festival and spectacle are in opposition. Nevertheless, both share one feature – they erect frames of cultural performances around a variety of genres; they both make '. . . differentiated forms of symbolic action into new wholes by means of a common spatio-temporal location, expressive theme, affective style, ideological intention, or social function.'

In this way the Olympics embodies ritual organized around the classic rites of passage (i.e., opening and closing ceremonies) which introduce liminality, intensification (i.e., victory and medal awards), closure and reaggregation. Further using the concepts of van Gennep and Turner, MacAloon (p. 253) noted that at the Olympic Games '. . . the assembled thousands and the space that they occupied are released into an extra-ordinary expression of spontaneous communitas.'

MacAloon concluded (p. 268) by saying that spectacle has destructive effects on ritual, festival and games. These genres of cultural performance bring people together, a 'communitas', whereas spectacle is just about watching. On the other hand, in societies favouring individualism, spectacle can act to bring people into a festival or ritualistic environment that they would otherwise be suspicious of.

Exhibition Experiences

A study by Jung (2005) on exhibition attendee perceptions of service quality gave some insight on desired experiences, namely the importance assigned to the number of exhibitors, quality of goods and services exhibited and the seminars, conferences and other events that were part of it. These are all product quality items that reflect the learning and marketing content of the event.

Convention and Meeting Experiences

It is probably assumed that people attend conferences and meetings for extrinsic reasons, because it is part of their business or job description, so very little pertinent research has been done. Certainly event marketers need to know more about how to attract and satisfy their clientele, while in Event Studies we want to know if these experiences are categorically different from those at other events.

Oppermann and Chon (1997) discussed the decision process, constraints, and both extrinsic and intrinsic motivations for convention attendance by members of associations. They observed both push and pull factors, and noted that many people were annual attendees. Professional goals and the opportunity for networking are key extrinsic motivators, with people assessing the value that a particular event would provide them. A lot of choice exists, so intervening opportunities, locational factors and destination image play a role. Davidson (2003) discussed the benefits to destinations and convention-goers in adding pleasure to their business trips. A convention might represent a rare or once-in-a-lifetime opportunity to visit an attractive area. Spouses and other family members often want to come along.

Rittichainuwat et al. (2001) determined that attendees at a hospitality educator/ researcher conference were motivated primarily by self-enhancement, business and association activities, and sightseeing. The work of Severt et al. below, reveals that different types of conference and meeting will be associated with different motivators and experiential dimensions.

Research Note

Severt, D., Wang, Y., Chen, P., and Breiter, D. (2007). Examining the motivation, perceived performance, and behavioural intentions of convention attendees: evidence from a regional conference. Tourism Management, 28(2): 399–408.

The researchers studied motivations, satisfaction and behavioural intentions of a group of small business owners and managers attending a regional-level conference with exhibition produced by a national trade association. An intercept sampling method spread over 2 days of the 4-day conference yielded 155 useable questionnaires. Respondents were about equally male and female, and some 24% were repeaters at this periodic conference. Their most important motivations for attending, in order, were: education; educational information at exhibits; reasonable travel time to the event; networking opportunities; and business activities. Four of these five are clearly experiential in nature, while accessibility is a facilitating/constraining factor. Attendees were very satisfied with the educational component, ranking it highest. Those most satisfied with education were the most satisfied overall, and the most likely to both return and tell others to attend the conference.

The Centre for Exhibition Research (CEIR, 2003) said their research confirms that face-to-face interaction is vital in marketing, and this will ensure the continuance of live events. Indeed, it appears that although business events are the first to be cancelled in times of troubles (terrorism, pandemics, natural disasters), they bounce back very quickly and continue to grow in number. There really is no 'virtual event' that can simulate symbolic interaction, socializing or having fun while doing business. People love to travel and meet, and always will.

The Experiences of Different Stakeholders

Figure 7.2 lists many event stakeholders, from guest and customer to the media and general public, each of which can have quite different experiences from the same event. The event experience is always at least partially dependent on the expectations and attitudes of those involved, and on one's willingness to enter into the spirit of the occasion. As well, different stakeholders will be directly or indirectly affected (on-site versus off-site) and dependent on their roles (organizers, volunteers, etc.). Accordingly, we need more understanding of the expectations people bring to events, and how they describe their experiences.

Most of the experiences shown in the figure are, of course, attainable by many of the stakeholders in many event settings. What I have tried to do is identify those that could be different or special, for each stakeholder – not their full range of potential experiences.

Groups having event experiences	Sub-categories	Unique or especially important experiential dimensions
Paying customers	• Sport spectators • Concert audience • Exhibition and conference attendees • Festival tourists	• Escaping, being entertained • Belonging and sharing • Authentic cultural experience • Emotionally involved and loyal fans (also nostalgia) • Socializing and communitas • Learning and seeking self-actualization
Guests	• Persons invited to a private event • The public at free events • Guests of sponsors	• Socializing, networking • Being part of a community or family • Sub-cultural identity • Being treated as honoured guests, VIPs
Participants	• Athletes at competitions • Performers in arts competitions	• Challenge and mastery • Communitas and sub-cultural expression
Media audience	• Remote TV viewers, radio listeners, webcast participants	• A virtual entertainment experience shaped by the media
Performers	• The entertainers at events • Buskers, street performers • Professional athletes	• Professional competence, mastery • Self-esteem • Ancillary enjoyment of the event
Producers and organizers	• Owners • Directors • Managers	• Might be similar to staff and volunteers • Need to be responsive and reflective
Very important people (invited VIPs)	• Politicians • Celebrities • The Olympic 'family' • Investors	• Doing their duty • Protocol shapes their experience as 'performers' • Being treated with honour and respect • Gaining self-esteem • Ancillary enjoyment of the event
Officials	• Referees, timekeepers, stewards, etc.	• Professional conduct and responsibility define their involvement
Regulators	• Police, fire, health inspectors, etc.	• Professional conduct and responsibility define their involvement

Figure 7.2   The experiences of different stakeholders.   (*continued*)

Groups having event experiences	Sub-categories	Unique or especially important experiential dimensions
Sponsors and grant givers	• With their own hospitality component • Or, as VIPs	• Business success, networking • Providers of hospitality to their own guests (the event is still the attraction) • Or, same as VIPs
Suppliers and vendors	• External suppliers • Or, on-site vendors	• Contractual relationships define their involvement • Ancillary enjoyment of the event
Volunteers	• Board members (may be workers or VIPs at the event) • Unpaid workers at the event	• The 'cast', part of the experience for others • Enjoyment of the event • Communitas among volunteers • Self-fulfilment
Paid staff	• Paid workers at the event • Security staff, after hours	• Paid employment defines their experience • Ancillary enjoyment of the event
The media	• Official (as sponsors) • Unofficial media	• Might want a VIP experience • Professional competence
The public	• Indirectly experiences the event (overspill effects or vicarious experiences)	• The public's experience can range from 'psychic benefits' to being inconvenienced or harmed

Figure 7.2 *(continued)*

Paying Customers

Many events charge admission and attract paying customers who will expect delivery of the promised product or experience, to a high standard. They are entitled to complain if they do not get their perceived money's worth. Marketers might be content with determining satisfaction levels, as that is the simplest measure of experiential effectiveness in a commercial context. 'Fans' might have other experiences on their mind, including loyalty, communitas and nostalgia (see Fairley, 2003 on nostalgia). Cultural tourists might stress belonging and sharing, an authentic cultural experience, and a learning experience.

Satisfaction levels do not provide much insight to the event experience. Deeper inquiry can reveal how memorable the event was, its meaning to the customer (especially in terms of personal and social constructs) and whether or not the customer had a transforming experience in any way. These phenomenological measures could be potentially valuable for improving the event.

Guests

This term, 'guests', implies that the event-goer is there because he or she is wanted. They will expect to be treated like a personal guest, with hospitality being a key service quality. Guests expect to be greeted and honoured by their hosts. While guests at private parties know they were invited, which shapes their expectations about hospitality and possibly about service levels, making paying customers feel like guests is a real challenge. The guest 'experience' will inevitably include a strong social component, because they are part of an invited group. 'Communitas' is often presupposed in this context, with all guests having an existing affiliation, but it also might have to be facilitated when strangers are in the mix. The use of esoteric rituals and symbols known only to 'insiders' is one form of bonding that designers can use.

Participants

This group consists of the athletes in sports or recreational events, dancers in dance festivals, pianists in music competitions, and to a degree the delegates attending conventions. The event is all about them; it does not exist without their participation. They are likely to feel that the event is for their benefit and its organizers should respect their needs and wishes. Participants also might feel a personal responsibility for the success of the event, but that is contingent on factors such as who owns or sponsors it.

To understanding participants' experiences requires knowledge of their motives, expectations, activities, emotions and cognitive processes in the specific context of the event. The full range of planned event experiences can apply, but participants are typically looking for mastery through meeting challenges, learning opportunities and sub-cultural identity or communitas.

Media Audience

Presumably most 'virtual' experiences of planned events, especially TV coverage of sports and concerts, award ceremonies and spectacles, would be described as entertainment. A key question for Event Studies researchers is whether or not media experiences can be the same as live experiences in terms of emotional engagement and cognition? Can they be as memorable or transforming? We will have to rely on media studies for answers. The research note by Chalip et al. (2003) sheds some light on the potential impacts of media coverage of events on destination image. With the ascendancy of webcasts there is a need for researchers to examine interactive media experiences.

Performers

This group consists of paid entertainers or athletes, all part of the show that customers want to experience. They have quite different motives for being at the event, and gaining a sense of professional accomplishment has to be important. If their experience is bad it can negatively impact on the overall event quality and customer satisfaction. Producers generally know how to treat professionals with dignity and respect, and to look after their tangible and emotional needs. If the opportunity arises, some performers can also get to enjoy parts of the event themselves.

Producers/Organizers

Sometimes the producers/organizers are also involved, working alongside other volunteers; in other events they are completely detached from the experiences they are seeking to create and therefore need to be responsive, and reflective on what they are doing and the feedback they are getting.

VIPs

Whether they are politicians, royalty or celebrities, being a Very Important Person by definition means that event organizers will be giving them special treatment, honour, respect and a lot of security, with protocol often determining what can and cannot be done. Their experience cannot possibly be the same as other guests or customers, and indeed they might become part of the spectacle, temporarily becoming performers. Despite these considerations it might be possible to segregate VIPs enough that they can enjoy part of the event.

Officials

Professional conduct and specific responsibilities govern the event experiences of referees, stewards, timekeepers and other officials. They might be almost invisible, or play an important and highly visible role in the event. Their experiences will perhaps include off-duty enjoyment of part of the event, otherwise their main concerns are purely technical.

Regulators

They attend events to supervise and ensure compliance, but also have to be made comfortable, kept safe, and have their basic technical and human needs looked after. Professional conduct defines their roles, but might they not take a little time to actually enjoy the event? Perhaps some of them deserve to have VIP status.

Sponsors and Grant Givers

Unless they see themselves as regulators, these 'facilitating' stakeholders should be given VIP treatment at events. Corporate sponsors often want specific hospitality services for themselves and their guests, even to the point of having private and exclusive areas and mini-events. Business has to be done, and that is an experience realm that does not have to be divorced from having fun.

In addition to enjoying the event, which might be of secondary importance, facilitators also have a vested interest in its success and might therefore play the role of supervisors or evaluators. Some might want status as producers or owners. Needless to say, their overall, multidimensional experience has to be made satisfactory.

Suppliers and Vendors

Often these contracted service and goods providers are brought into the event as sponsors as well, giving them a vested interest in its success. They might also find time to enjoy the event. Yet they have specific, professional functions to complete which have to be supervised and evaluated by event management. That means there is a risk of 'split personality' when it comes to the event experiences of contracted suppliers.

Volunteers

To the extent that they interact with other people at the event, they are both helping to create, and sharing in the experiences. Volunteers should have a unique perspective on the overall experience and how others are enjoying the event. They have to be satisfied or they will not continue to volunteer. Johnston, Twynam and Farrell (2000) found that sport involvement led directly to volunteering at sport events, which suggests that they want an experience related to that sport, such as contact with its stars.

Saleh and Wood (1998) found some unique motives held by volunteers at a multicultural festival (namely sharing their culture and maintaining cultural links). Elstad (1997) studied student volunteers at the Winter Olympic Games in Lillehammer, Norway and determined that satisfaction with their experience related most strongly to expanding personal networks, being part of the event atmosphere, and achieving job-related competence. In another study, Elstad (2003) found the top reasons for event volunteers to quit were workload, lack or appreciation, and poor organization, all of which suggest experiential implications.

In the research notes below, additional insights are provided on event volunteer experiences.

Research Note

Ralston, R., Lumsdon, L., and Downward, P. (2005). The third force in events tourism: volunteers at the XVII Commonwealth Games. Journal of Sustainable Tourism, 13(5): 504–519.

The authors reviewed the literature on event volunteers, covering motivation, profiles, and satisfaction studies and theory. Their own research in Manchester employed focus groups and a survey of Commonwealth Games volunteers. Results on why they volunteered clearly pertain to the experiences they sought, including: excitement, uniqueness (the chance of a lifetime), meeting interesting people, and being part of a team. Meanings attached to the experience included: supporting sport, doing something useful for the community, helping the city, region and country, and using their skills. The authors concluded that large-scale sport event volunteerism can build future capacity through creation of a committed volunteer force, and is therefore an important element in sustainable tourism. However, policy initiatives are needed to recognize its importance and provide the necessary volunteer planning and management.

There is more on volunteer motives and experiences in the human resources section of Chapter 10.

Paid Staff

Most paid staff will be able to have some direct experience of the event, if only when off-duty, but some, like overnight security, will not. Because they are all paid for specific duties they have to be supervised and evaluated, with event enjoyment being an ancillary goal, and (ideally) secondary to the experience of professional accomplishment. There can be overlap, of course, between the roles and experiences of volunteers, paid staff and performers. This will depend on the extent to which these groups are part of the show (as 'cast members') and how dependent guests/customers are on each group for their experiences.

The Media

Hopefully most media people attending the event are official sponsors, in which case they require technical support and VIP status. But there are also likely to be unofficial media whose access to the event might be restricted. Conflicts could occur between the two groups of media, between media and VIPs or performers, and between media and organizers/staff. Media relations have become a major task at events and cannot be left to chance. If they have a bad personal or professional experience the event's image could consequently take a negative hit.

The Public at Large

There might be spillover effects from events, such as noise, light, traffic, smell, crowds and bad behaviour, all of which can cause bad feelings among neighbours and the wider community. Media like to focus on all these issues. The public at large, even those not attending and not interested, can nevertheless gain 'psychic benefits' from their vicarious experience of events, such as increased community pride and perceptions of economic and other impacts.

Meanings Attached to Planned Event Experiences

Event experiences can mean as little to us as fleeting entertainment (not important and not memorable), to profoundly transforming. To a community or society events can have simple commercial meaning (as part of the 'entertainment industry') or they can be significant economic and place marketing forces. From a cultural perspective events can be reinforcing or threatening. From an economic and tourism point of view events are products to sell, and they must generate tangible as well as image benefits. And to corporations that sponsor or produce events, they have importance in terms of marketing, branding and corporate responsibility.

Meanings attached to planned events are at once anticipatory (as in, 'we are going to the festival to celebrate our heritage'), evolving (e.g., 'the event itself was responsible for changing everyone's attitudes towards the arts') and reflective (such as, 'looking back, it was clearly an event with great economic and political impact'). Historians, and critical researchers, help to attach meanings to events. So do political ideologies and the interactions of all the stakeholders involved. Meanings that are political and societal might not impress the individual, who is, after all, able to formulate personal interpretations and meanings for any event. But, if events have little or no meaning of importance to people, they will not attend. If events lack social, cultural and economic meaning, who will support them?

Personal Meanings

The meanings that individuals attach to event experiences are 'personal constructs', which can be defined as a level of cognitive significance that represents how we understand the world around us. In effect, we construct reality in our minds to explain experiences.

'Personal Construct Theory' posits that people attribute meanings to their experiences, and each person therefore has different experiences. Epting and Neimeyer (1984: 2) said these personal constructs '. . . serve not only as interpretation of past events but as hypotheses about events yet to be encountered.' Botterill and Crompton (1996) used personal construct theory to examine leisure/tourist experiences and concluded that emotional states are integral to 'optimal experiences' as defined by interviewees.

At one level, we can say that personal meanings relate directly to personal needs, the motives expressed for attending events, and the anticipated benefits to be obtained through the planned event experience. Ask yourself, how do you give meaning to your life through work, leisure and family? Where do events fit into that meaning system?

The rites of passage that mark our lives are bound to be memorable, and full of personal meaning, helping to define who we are. But most of them, like birthdays, anniversaries, weddings and graduations, are also social occasions, with substantial meaning to families and other social networks.

Experience marketers have also realized that they must engage consumers in events that hold meaning for them. Diller et al. in their book *Making Meaning* (2006: 3) concluded:

> *Our own work in the field has led us to the conviction that for companies to achieve enduring competitive advantage through experience design, their innovations cannot be based simply on novelty. Increasingly, they*

must address their customers' essential human need for meaning. To do this, companies must first under-
stand the role that meaning plays in people's lives, how products and services can evoke meaning, and then
how to identify the core meanings they should target with their own offerings. For companies facing both
globalization and the end of the mass market, 'making meaning' is one of very few strategies that will work.

The personal benefits and meanings can include any of the following, derived from earlier discussions as well as the contribution of Diller et al. (2006: 320):

- Communitas (as a result of belonging and sharing, from reaffirmation of roots or of connections and values).
- Esteem: validation of oneself in the opinions of others, self-worth, prestige and reputation (such as may be realized through competitive or intellectual accomplishments).
- Learning, enlightenment (e.g., from new cultural experiences or a connoisseur's appreciation of food, art or music.
- Self-discovery, self-actualization, understanding, wonder.
- Transformation (in religious terms, or of personality or character; or in motivation).
- Redemption and atonement (from failure or sins).
- Mastery (from skills, physical triumph).
- Accomplishment or success (from business, trade, commerce, networking, creativity, artistic expression).
- Creativity or innovation (making a lasting contribution)
- Fulfilment of responsibility (professionalism, or as a dedicated sport fan, or from getting involved as a volunteer).
- Health and well-being (through physical activity, learning).
- Security (living without fear).
- Duty (military or civic) fulfilled, patriotism and loyalty to a cause.
- Truth, honesty, integrity (a meaning given to relationships and to one's own behaviour).
- Beauty or aesthetic appreciation.
- Freedom (acting without constraint, intrinsically rewarding pursuits.
- Harmony (with nature or others) and oneness (belonging, unity).
- Justice (fairness and equality, democratic expression).

People might not be able to articulate the meanings they assign to event experiences; they might not think of meanings at all. You could ask them what benefits they expected and derived from the experience, and that comes close. They can be asked to respond to a list of statements or adjectives about the event to see if they found it memorable, transforming or meaningful in terms of the above-mentioned dimensions. People want to give meaning to their experiences and to their lives in general, but expressing those meanings requires deep thought and a good vocabulary! This is a real challenge for researchers and theorists.

Social Meanings

These are meanings given to events by social groups, communities and society as a whole. Individuals are affected by these meanings, but are also able to make their own interpretations of events. Event types or forms, as previously discussed, are to a large extent 'social constructs', with collectively assigned and generally recognized meanings. Abrahams (1987) noted that the way we frame or attach meaning to experiences is embedded in social and cultural order.

Our most poplar religious holidays and civic celebrations have generally accepted meanings. For many people the sacred might have given way to the profane for holidays like Christmas, nevertheless society as a whole recognizes and needs the social and personal benefits of these holidays despite some differences in meanings attached to them.

Forms of event, like festival and sport competition, are expected to conform to widely held expectations regarding where and when they are held, who attends, accepted and expected behaviours, and even their programmic elements. Going beyond the norms, as innovative event designers are want to do, risks alienating or at least mystifying elements of the potential audience. If the changes are accepted, perhaps over a long period of time, then they are added to the social constructs we hold. We can call this process the making of tradition, or the establishment of social norms and conformity.

Social and Political Constructs

Roche (2000: 7; see also Roche, 2006) saw events, like the global Millennium celebrations, acting as '. . . important elements in the orientation of national societies to inter-national or global society.' Indeed, many countries have used mega-events to gain legitimacy and prestige, draw attention to their accomplishments, foster trade and tourism, or to help open their countries to global influences. This is much more than place marketing – it is more like national identity building. And Whitson and Macintosh (1996: 279) said countries and cities compete for mega-sport events to demonstrate their 'modernity and economic dynamism'.

Russell (2004) examined the political meanings attached to the National Eisteddfod of Wales, which has a tradition dating back to 1176. She found this annual competition of music and poetry is simultaneously an arena for performing arts, a forum for preserving the Welsh language, a tourist attraction, a trade fair and a platform for political acts of Welsh significance. 'As an arts and cultural festival . . . the Eisteddfod also delivers the wider range of economic and socio-linguistic benefits which embrace the interests of the Wales Tourist Board, the Arts Council of Wales, the Welsh Language Board, local authorities and others'.

Sense of Community and Sense of Place

Derrett (2004: 48) discussed how communities share their culture through festivals and events, and how the interdependencies of residents, place and visitors help establish a valued sense of community and place. 'They celebrate a sense of place through organizing inclusive activities in specific safe environments. They provide a vehicle for communities to host visitors and share such activities as representations of communally agreed values, interests and aspirations, Thirdly, they are the outward manifestation of the identity of the community and provide a distinctive identifier of place and people.' On the other hand, 'commodification' or 'festivalization' of culture is a threat.

Cultural Meanings

Quinn (2000: 264) concluded that 'If at the heart of every festival are a place and a place-based community actively reproducing its shared values and belief systems, there is an important sense in which these cultural meanings are intentionally produced to be read by the outside world.' A related challenge stems from the fact that meanings are easily and often contested, based on different values and belief systems within the same community. So while the festival is a 'text' on culture, to be interpreted, it is often an ambiguous one.

Sport As Cultural Expression

'Games and sports, like religious rituals and festivals, can be interpreted as reflections of broader social relationships and cultural ideals' (Mitler et al., 2004: 348). To Geertz (1993) they are models of culture depicting key values and ideals, such as fair play or friendly competition. Sport can also have more sinister or controversial significance, reflecting or encouraging aggression and dominance of one group over another, or territoriality and cultural imperialism. Many people see elements of a national culture in their sports, and in the emphasis they place on sports. We should be asking, does policy regarding sport reflect or shape culture?

> **Mental Exercise**
>
> *The Olympics is an event that everyone can relate to at some level, because of its global media coverage. How do you feel about the Olympic Games? Are they celebrations of youth and amateurism, or do they signify commercialization, corruption and waste? How was your interpretation of meaning affected by your education, cultural heritage, event experiences or other factors?*

Cultural Authenticity

There has been a lot of debate about what an 'authentic' experience or event really is, and if it is even desired or understood by tourists or event-goers. We are speaking here of cultural authenticity, which is really the cultural meaning attached to an event.

Boorstin's famous (1961) description of 'pseudo-events' was really a commentary on mass tourism, as he believed that culture was being commodified and that many events were created to cater to tourists' expectations. This belief contrasts with those of MacCannell (1973) and others who believed that people sought out authentic cultural experiences because they lived shallow or uninteresting lives. Cohen (1979) argued that different types of tourists required different experiences, which hold different meanings, all of which are mediated by culture. He distinguished two major streams: those searching for authenticity (or on a spiritual quest) called 'modern pilgrimage' and those seeking pleasure.

Wang (1999) identified three types of authenticity. 'Object-related authenticity' pertains to the true nature of the event as a cultural expression. In this context, event producers have to ensure that their performances, design features and other programmic elements are genuine reflections of the culture being displayed. But who is to judge this? 'constructive authenticity' is projected onto the event in terms of images, expectations, preferences and beliefs. Visitors might be fooled, and they might not care if the event is not a true cultural expression. Event producers have considerable scope for entertaining people, but should they be concerned about meanings attached by visitors? Does the event producer have an obligation (moral, or in terms of marketing) to ensure that the event is not misperceived?

To Wang 'existential authenticity' occurs because whatever the nature of the event (authentic in cultural terms, or not), event consumers might have their own, meaningful experiences which they interpret as being authentic. The theory is that authentic experiences enable discovery of one's true self. This presents a real challenge for the event producers, as they must acknowledge that their programme is (merely?) a setting or background for desired, highly individualized experiences.

In a variation, Timothy and Boyd (2006) discussed 'relative authenticity', saying authenticity is a subjective notion varying from person to person, depending on our social conditioning. Meaning is not derived from the event, in this interpretation, but from the interaction of event and visitor-created meanings.

The conclusion we are left with is that 'cultural authenticity' is a theoretically difficult concept. My own belief is that when it comes to determining what is authentic or not, only the cultural groups being represented, or doing the performance, are qualified to judge. Within cultures there often rages a debate about whether modern performances are authentic and justifiable, but surely outsiders cannot be expected to decide.

There is a completely different approach to 'authentic' experiences, one that has wider application. Consider this: are sport events authentic? Not in cultural terms, but as events deserving of trust and belief in them? Despite the occasional scandal arising from gambling or bad refereeing, sports are generally considered to be authentic because the outcome is unpredictable, the players give their best, and talent plus hard work is rewarded. Many other forms of entertainment are widely thought to be contrived and unbelievable. Even the so-called television 'reality shows' appear to be nothing more than stylized, scripted theatre. More research on event–consumer beliefs and on mass media experiences related to 'authenticity' is warranted.

Contested Culture, Stakeholders and Legitimacy

Will all stakeholders in a community agree on core values and what is to be celebrated? In fact, culture and its representations are often contested. To examine this issue, Crespi-Vallbona and Richards (2007) interviewed many stakeholders in Catalonia, finding there were common issues surrounding festivals in that region. Cultural identity was the strongest and most common theme, reflecting this region's long struggle to establish a national identity. This was a binding factor, even though differences in meanings were evident. Nevertheless, the researchers observed tension between the local and global perspectives on events, and there was concern for preserving cultural integrity when events were also expected to serve political, economic and social goals. Differences in meanings attached to festivals are related to claims to power, legitimacy and urgency by the various stakeholders involved in the policy process.

Economic Meanings

To a large extent we have already defined the economic meanings attached to events by looking at event tourism and the roles of attraction, catalyst, animator, image maker and place marketer. These meanings are shaped by politicians and industry, rather than the general public or travellers themselves. Many events are also considered to be part of the 'entertainment or culture industries', or perhaps the 'creative industries', and these represent economic meanings. Within the context of 'popular culture', using the term 'industry' is likely to imply commercialization and mass consumption.

Although many events are within the realm of arts and culture, they do have to be managed as businesses. This introduces a tension between the values of arts/culture on one hand, and the potential for hard-nosed management or commercialization on the other. Ideally the economic and arts/cultural meanings can be brought into balance.

Sports as 'big business' is a recurring theme. For example, Rozin (2000) described Indianapolis as a 'classic case' of how sports can generate a civic turnaround. Sports Business Market Research Inc. (2000: 167) observed that in the 1980s and 1990s American cities '. . . put heavy emphasis on sports, entertainment and tourism as a source of revenue for the cities.' Gratton and Kokolakakis (1997) believed that in the UK sports events had become the main platform for economic regeneration in many cities.

Corporate Meanings

Berridge (2006) observed that 'The discipline of events is expanding significantly from its cultural and celebratory origins and the role of events in business is changing as its effectiveness in 'brand marketing' is more clearly understood and the levels of investment increase as a result.'

Within the corporate world it is now fashionable to think of a brand in terms of relationships, with 'live communications' or 'event experiences' building and sustaining these relationships between company and customer. In this context planned events are brand-building tools, and the experiences have to be evaluated in terms of how they meet corporate marketing aims. There is growing competition to attract and 'engage' customers this way, so events will tend to have a short life-cycle. Something new will always be needed.

When companies practice corporate responsibility their participation in events takes on new meanings. To the extent that corporations show commitment to the community and the environment out of altruism or necessity, events can be expressions of that commitment. Contemporary consumers and lobby groups expect companies to behave responsibility and that should lead to something of a reversal in the trend towards viewing participation in events as just marketing. In this context it seems reasonable to suggest that 'authenticity' and commercialism are incompatible. What do you think?

Chapter Summary

The planned event experience, and meanings attached to it, is the core phenomenon of Event Studies. This chapter first explored the meaning of 'experience', including how it is conceptualized in leisure theory and within the context of the 'experience economy'. To develop a model of the planned event experience also required drawing upon anthropological theory, particularly to employ the notions of 'liminal', 'liminoid' and 'communitas'. In this model, planned event experiences are conceptualized as being a time out of time, within a special place.

People entering this 'valorized zone' come with needs and expectations, willingly enter the event setting to experience something different and rewarding, and engage with the event programme and other people in terms of behaviour, emotions and cognitive processes. The more involved or engaged the person is, the more they are likely to get out of the experience and the more memorable it will be. Event-goers might even experience 'flow' or 'optimal arousal', which in terms of leisure theory are states of mind that transcend time and place. Upon departure and reversion to normal life there should be a sense of loss, or perhaps renewal and transformation, depending on how profound the experience was. People are changed by their experiences, so future expectations are altered and perhaps an event career is developed.

Persons, groups, societies and corporations all assign meanings to events. We used the concepts of 'personal construct' and 'social construct' to examine how meanings are formed, and what events might mean. Just as the event producer or designer cannot guarantee that intended experiences will be obtained by people attending events, it is also impossible to predict exactly what meanings will be attached to the experiences. However, 'social constructs' emerge which suggest to people what certain forms of planned events are supposed to embody by way of experiences, and what they should mean in terms of social, cultural and economic values. 'Cultural authenticity' as explored in some detail because of its importance in understanding cultural meanings, and the theoretical difficulty of applying the concept.

Different event stakeholders will have different motives, experiences and meanings, so producers have to understand how, for example, paying customers are different from invited guests or VIPs. A summary table was provided for all the stakeholder groups to suggest the ways in which their experiences will vary.

Some event experiences and meanings are generic, while others are associated with specific forms or types of event. All events can aspire to provide generic benefits like entertainment, social interaction, learning and 'communitas'. The 'theory of spectacle' provides a warning however, that by stressing larger than life, visual stimulation, we can impede or overshadow other desired experiences and meanings. In this chapter we also reviewed cultural celebrations, including festivals, carnivals, religious events and pilgrimages, as to specific experiences and meanings associated with them. This was also done for sports (both participation and spectator), political and state events, arts and entertainment, and meetings and conventions.

The mental exercise that follows is intended to help readers relate to this chapter's topics at a very personal level.

Mental Exercise

When exploring your own experiences at an event, ask yourself these questions:

1. *What is happening around you, and to you? What are you doing? how are the environment, programme/ management systems and other people affecting you? (this is the tangible, 'life being lived' layer of experience; you have to perceive it with your senses, you have to be there; other people are having this same experience in a general sense, but there are many variations possible); you can evaluate this layer of experience both in technical terms (the decorations, the service quality, the food, the entertainment) and in personal terms (I do not like the setting, it is a low-quality event, not much is happening).*
2. *How do you feel about what is happening to you and what you are doing? Are you having fun? Is your mood changing? What are you learning? (this is the 'affect' layer of experience, and it is very personal – everyone has a different experience at this level); you can evaluate your reaction to the event (I am bored, happy, exhilarated, excited, feeling challenged, learning a lot; you can try to guess what others are feeling, but it is better to ask!).*

3. *What does it all mean to you? Is this a cultural experience in terms of its symbolism and your personal identity with the performances? Is this a memorable aesthetic experience (art, music, etc.), never to be forgotten? Do you think you will be changed by this experience? (again, this is a completely personal layer of experience, yet it can be shared with others – the extent to which the meanings are shared defines culture or sub-culture, belonging and sharing); in terms of evaluation, you have to assess both the longer-term meaning of the event to you in personal terms (it changed me!) and in relation to others (I made new friends because we all shared a common experience; there was a sense of community).*

Study Questions

- What are the behavioural (conative), emotional, (affective) and mental (cognitive) dimensions of 'experience'?
- What do intrinsic and extrinsic motivations have to do with event experiences?
- Why are corporations so interested in event experiences, within the context of the 'experience economy'?
- Describe the model of planned event experiences, and specifically define 'liminal' and 'liminoid' in this context, drawing on anthropological theory.
- Discuss the concept of 'communitas' as it applies to event experiences, including why it can be a 'generic' event experience.
- How do the concepts of 'optimal arousal' and 'flow' relate to the planned event experience?
- In what ways can event experiences be 'memorable' and 'transforming'?
- What is the 'theory of spectacle' and how does it apply to event experiences?
- Give examples of how different types of planned events can facilitate both 'generic' and 'event-specific' experiences.
- Show how different stakeholders experience events in different ways, related to their motives and functions.
- Use the concepts of 'personal construct' and 'social construct' to explain various meanings attached to events.
- What is meant by 'cultural authenticity' and why is it important in Event Studies?

Further Reading

Diller, S., Shedroff, N., and Rhea, D. (2006). *Making Meaning.* (Pearson) Upper Saddle River, NJ: New Riders.

Gibson, H. (ed.) (2006). *Sport Tourism: Concepts and Theories.* London: Routledge.

MacAloon, J. (1984). Olympic Games and the theory of spectacle in modern societies. In: J. MacAloon (ed.), *Rite, Drama, Festival, Spectacle: Rehearsals towards a Theory of Cultural Performance,* pp. 241–280. Philadelphia: Institute for the Study of Human Issues.

Pine, B., and Gilmore, J. (1999). *The Experience Economy: Work Is Theatre and Every Business a Stage.* Boston: Harvard Business School Press.

Timothy, D., and Olsen, D. (eds). (2006). *Tourism, Religion and Spiritual Journeys.* London: Routledge.

Chapter 8
Event Design

Learning Objectives

- Know the meaning of design and how it is applied to planned events.
- Be able to apply principles of psychology, sociology and other disciplines to event design.
- Understand how to use various design tools in terms of the event:
  - setting (site and venue) and atmosphere
  - theme and programme (including performers, participants and programmic elements of style)
  - services (service quality; staff and volunteers as 'the cast')
  - consumables (gastronomy; gifts).

What Is Event Design?

'Design' is neither pure science nor art; it is both a technical and creative act. The chapter starts with definitions of design and the meaning of Event Design, addressing the basic question of whether or not planned event experiences can be designed, and if so, how. When it comes to the tools of event design, we can draw on a number of principles from psychology, environmental psychology and social psychology in particular. The opinions of a number of event designers are also presented, in order to ground the discussion in real-world professional practice.

Because creativity is an integral part of design, we look at its meaning and tools that have been used to foster creativity or innovation. This takes us into the arts, but surprisingly also draws from science and engineering. Detailed discussions are presented on the event setting (the site, venue and atmosphere), the programme, including elements of style, and services that have to be managed for quality and experiential impact.

Definitions

Nathan Shedroff (2001) wrote *Experience Design* and co-authored *Making Meaning: How Successful Businesses Deliver Meaningful Customer Experiences* (Diller, Shedroff and Rhea, 2006). This definition of design is taken from his website (www.nathan.com).

> *Design is a set of fields for problem solving that uses user-centric approaches to understand user needs (as well as business, economic, environmental, social, and other requirements) to create successful solutions that solve real problems. Design is often used as a process to create real change within a system or market. Too often, Design is defined only as visual problem solving or communication because of the predominance of graphic designers.*

Shedroff distinguishes several fields of design applications including 'environmental design' for structures or settings, and 'experience design'. Experience, to Shedroff, is:

> *The sensation of interaction with a product, service, or event, through all of our senses, over time, and on both physical and cognitive levels. The boundaries of an experience can be expansive and include the sensorial, the symbolic, the temporal, and the meaningful.*

Steve Brown is an event designer in Adelaide, South Australia. To him event design requires an audience orientation . . .

> *Event Design is the creation, conceptual development and design of an event to maximise the positive and meaningful impact for the event's audience and/or participants.*

Brown and James (2004: 59) argued that 'Design is essential to an event's success because it leads to improvement of the event on every level.' The 'core values' of the event provide the starting point: Why is it held, and for whom? What is its substance and intended outcomes? They discussed five design principles for events that are incorporated into the ensuing discussion: 'scale, shape, focus, timing and build.' Also emphasized is the need for creativity and uniqueness in event design, as generic events offering the same benefits are unlikely to endure. This can be accomplished, in part, by incorporating the rituals and symbols of the host community.

Julia Silvers (2004: 5), in her book Professional Event Coordination, expressed it this way:

> *Remember that you are packaging and managing an experience. This means that you must envision that experience, from start to finish, from the guest's point of view.*

Graham Berridge, A UK event professional and lecturer, has written a book devoted to the subject. In Event Design (2006) he discusses the field of 'experience design' at length, saying it is in its infancy. Unfortunately, the term is being used to describe the design of everything from websites (digital media) to storytelling, theme parks and corporate 'brand events'. He argued that the purpose is to create desired perceptions, cognition and behaviour. Building and maintaining relationships is at the core, and stimulating emotional connections through engagement is the vehicle.

Berridge also advocated 'experience engineering' through the application of design principles to all aspects of event planning and production. This requires event managers and other key stakeholders to engage in conscious experiential design, marketing and delivery. He employed the theatre metaphor to suggest that both the stage (setting) and performance (the entire experience) must be designed.

We often associate 'design' with fashion, aesthetics or visual graphics. Events do require aesthetic design, particularly to create the right atmosphere, but there is much more to it. Think more about industrial design, with its emphasis on problem solving. A chair has to be designed for efficiency and comfort, plus be pleasing to the eye. An event, both its tangible setting (the site and venue), the atmosphere (with sensory stimulations of all kinds) and its programme (together these are the 'experiential components') also have to be designed, both with the producer's goals in mind and the needs, preferences and desires of the audience or customers. If design is separated from goals and real-world needs, we are left with art for its own sake.

Can Experiences Be Designed?

Go back to the previous chapter and re-read the definitions of 'experience', look again at how meanings are attached to experiences, and think about that long list of stakeholders (much more than guests or the audience) who are experientially influenced by planned events. It is possible to get people involved, have them do specific things, and receive desired stimuli, but it is not possible to guarantee or predict what individuals actually 'experience' cognitively and emotionally as an outcome. Nor can the event designer know for a certainty what meanings will be attached to those event experiences, or whether they will have any transforming impact.

It is true that 'experienced' event producers build up an understanding of what seems to work well to make people happy, or at least to say that they are satisfied. And 'practice does make perfect' when it comes to both getting the design elements right (i.e., technically perfect, and in keeping with the designer's vision), and also in avoiding mistakes. In these ways the designer's experience and intuition go a long way to improving event experiences. But whatever the design process, there has to be research and feedback from the stakeholders leading to improvement, otherwise the designer is guilty of either taking a 'product orientation' (here is what I offer, its good for you), or creating art for its own sake (with no problem being solved).

An experience is so highly personal that it cannot be planned, designed, or even promised to event goers. The purpose of any event is to suggest what experiences might be had (through theming and interpretation), facilitate positive experiences (through design of setting, programme, services and consumables), and to enable everyone concerned, as much as possible, to realize their goals. On the other hand, design and management also seeks to constrain undesired experiences, including aggression, violence and over-stimulation.

Design and Creativity

A simple definition of 'creativity' is that it is the mental process of generating new ideas or concepts. It can be equated with invention and innovation, as in the engineering and entrepreneurial contexts. Creativity not found only in the arts – creativity is a fundamental part of all human endeavour. Where does it come from, and can it be taught? It does appear that some people are more naturally creative than others, perhaps benefiting from unique mental processes or their upbringing. We sometimes say that creative people show 'genius' because their ideas or their art just seems to be so novel or fresh.

With whole 'industries' now devoted to creativity and knowledge formation, it is becoming more and more unlikely that individuals will spontaneously generate truly original ideas or non-derivative art. So another approach to creativity becomes more important, and that is to actively search for, discuss and refine new associations between facts and concepts. That is one of the aims of this book – to encourage students, researchers and policy makers to put things together in new ways. You not only need a lot of information as the starting point, you need some advice on how to proceed.

Richard Florida's concept of 'the creative class' is relevant here.

R. Florida (2002). The Rise of the Creative Class: And How It's Transforming Work, Leisure, Community and Everyday Life. New York: Basic Books.

According to Florida, creativity is becoming a driving force in American economic life, and a key source of competitive advantage. Some cities flourish because of their creative class, and Florida argued that creative-class workers choose cities for their tolerant environments and diverse populations, as well as good jobs. The event sector has to be part of this creativity, and is therefore deserving of attention by both cultural and economic policy makers. 'Creative capital' has value, and it has to be attracted, even though the people displaying the most creative capital might otherwise be viewed as eccentric, at best, or just plain weird. Tolerance, technology and talent go together.

Creativity can certainly be taught, at least to a degree. If the social environment is supportive, more people will become artists and inventors. If the learning environment is oriented in such a way, students at all levels can learn to be more creative. Hopefully this book accomplishes something of that nature by encouraging readers to make new associations between ideas, see new problems and opportunities that emerge from a discussion of existing ones, and think up research that can lead to new knowledge. Merely spending a few minutes on the suggested 'mental exercises' will get the creative juices flowing.

Nickerson (1999) summarized the various creativity-boosting techniques proposed by industry and academics, in the book *Handbook of Creativity* (R. Sternberg, editor). Many come under the general heading of providing motivation and a supportive environment, while others are techniques or tools. Also see Wiersma and Strolberg's (2003) *Exceptional Events: Concept to Completion*, for tips on event creativity.

What Elements of Planned Events Can be Designed?

Given that event experiences cannot themselves be designed, only suggested, constrained and facilitated, what is the scope of event design? The EMBOK model (Figure 1.1) lists the following under design: catering, content, entertainment, environment, production, programme and theme. Lynn Van der Wagen's book (2004: 26) lists event elements that are 'designed':

- Theme (appealing to all the senses).
- Layout (creative use of the venue).
- Décor (reflects the theme; requires quality suppliers).

- Technical requirements.
- Staging (in the theatrical sense).
- Entertainment (programming, and the talent).
- Catering (and quality service).

The following four general categories of event design elements emerge from the preceding discussion, and will be examined in greater detail in the ensuing sections of this chapter.

- *Setting*: The site and venue as to layout and décor; the creation of a pleasant and appropriate ambience or atmosphere through various expressions of the theme including technical elements and sensory stimulation (lighting, sound, smells, touching, colours, flowers, art); access, flow and crowd management measures including information and signage; facilitated interactivity (which is in part a 'setting affordance').
- *Theme and programme design*: The theme (what is being celebrated, or other integrative themes); activities people engage in (including interactions and spontaneous action); the scripted program people observe; entertainment; interpretation; emotional stimulation and all the other programmic elements of style.
- *Services*: To the extent that service quality is blueprinted, this is a design process; there is creativity in establishing the 'servicescape' and how service encounters occur; technical skill is required for hidden management systems including security, health and safety measures; staff and volunteers are 'cast members' helping to create experiences.
- *Consumables*: Gastronomy is both technical (i.e., food and beverage preparation) and creative (i.e., the aesthetics of 'taste' and visual presentation); gifts (to the extent that people take things home with them) are also subject to design.

Designing the Setting

Philip Pearce in the book *Tourist Behaviour: Themes and Conceptual Schemas* (2005) conceptualized tourist space from an experiential perspective. Pearce labelled three intersecting circles as: (1) activities available on-site for visitors; (2) the physical or cultural setting or resource and (3) the meanings and understandings brought to or influenced by or negotiated at the site.

At the core of Pearce's approach (p. 136) is the notion that a setting likely to promote positive on-site experiences should offer '… clear conceptions of what the place is about, the activities available are understood and accessible, and the physical elements that constitute the setting are distinctive and aesthetically pleasing.' Emphasis should be placed on understanding the guests, their expectations and involvement, and how they are transformed.

Generic Event Settings

Event settings, first of all, are places that have to be defined as 'special' for the duration of the 'time out of time' that constitutes a planned event. The main initial considerations are location (e.g., centrality and accessibility), site characteristics (Is it suitable for the event?), and the social-cultural context (Has it historic and cultural meaning?). Infrastructure and management systems then have to be developed or modified, including basic services, theme and programme, amenities and guest services, security and controls. Both site planning and aesthetic design are important.

Settings and management systems will interact with the people dimension (staff, volunteers, participants, performers, other guests and customers) in shaping the event experiences. There are unlimited ways to combine setting, management and people, yielding great opportunities for creative event design. However, each setting poses its own challenges and opportunities, some of which are identified in the ensuing discussion of generic event settings. By 'generic', I mean all events will fit into one or more of them because they are defined by function.

Assembly
Conventions, concerts, festivals and spectator sports – any event bringing together large numbers of people – require settings that provide for sitting, viewing and listening. The event manager can often rent 'assembly' venues that have their own management systems, including convention centres, hotel ballrooms, exposition halls, concert halls, auditoria and arenas.

Major design challenges include the fact that many venues are either halls or arenas with no inherent aesthetics, or require substantial modification on technical or creative grounds to suit the event. This negative factor might be compensated adequately by the presence of staff and systems to facilitate events. Opportunities for using unique and even strange venues abound. Meeting planners seek out venues in special places with inspiring or provocative features.

Advice on meeting and convention venue design can be found in Meeting Professionals International (2003) *Meetings and Conventions: A Planning Guide*. Party design is covered by Bailey (2002), and Lena Malouf's (2002) *Parties and Special Events: Planning and Design*.

Procession
Parades, flotillas, cavalcades marches and other similar events are linear, mobile forms of entertainment, spectacle or ritual with special design and management requirements. The audience might be standing, seated or moving along with the procession. The most common linear setting, however, is a street with a static audience along the

route. Some processions pass through seating areas and even stadia, where they take on the form of theatre.

Logistics for such events are challenging, such as getting everyone in a parade or race mobilized for proper sequencing, the likelihood of causing traffic disruption and congestion, and the fact that most streets are unsuited for spectating. Gregson (1992) gave advice on using sidewalks, streets and buildings to stage events, noting that architects generally fail to take account of seasonal changes and the needs of public gatherings. Also refer to IFEA's publication Parades (2000).

Linear-Nodal

Many sport events involve races or other linear forms of activity, including long-distance running and auto racing, which combine procession with nodes of activity. Usually the audience congregates at the nodes, such as start, finish and transition points. The event designer will often have to provide live video feeds from the linear portions to the places where fans congregate. Service points for athletes and vehicles are also needed.

Open Space

Frequently events make use of parks, plazas and closed-off streets. Free movement is a feature of these settings, but they usually also contain sub-areas for assembly, procession and exhibition/sales. European cities seemed to have the advantage in terms of beautiful, culturally significant squares for events, while North American cities tend to have more space, such as waterfronts and natural parks to use for large public gatherings (Getz, 2001). Environmental concerns are important in parks, while potential damage to buildings is a concern in urban plazas.

Exhibition/Sales

Purpose-built exhibition and convention centres are the best suited for trade and consumer shows, although any event can incorporate areas for food and beverage or other merchandise sales and demonstrations. These settings are designed to entice entry and circulation, browsing and sales. Sometimes the audience merely views the exhibits, at others sales are made. Since the purpose of these events is usually commerce, a number of principles from environmental psychology have to be applied to the design in order to ensure that interpersonal contacts are facilitated. Good circulation is necessary, but it is also desirable to have people linger and talk. See *The Art of the Show* (Morrow, 1997) for details on exhibition design.

Events as Theatre

Theatre is one form of planned event, but as already discussed it is also a metaphor for performances and events of all kinds. Certainly there is ample scope for the event designer to draw upon theatrical productions to enhance event settings and experiences.

'Experience Design' according to Haahti and Komppula (2006) draws heavily on 'dramaturgy', which is part of theatre and performance studies. They provide examples in which high-contact, high-involvement tourists co-create experiences with professional 'stagers' of facilitators. Ideas for 'manuscripts' and 'staged experiences' have to be generated with the needs and expectations of guests in mind, embodying myths, stories and history from the place or event. 'This enables the creation of a place and a space for being together and the development of a group identity in experiencing' (p. 103). In this approach, the 'stage' is whatever venue the experience takes place in, but it has to be appropriate to the design.

Staging

This is the most fundamental theatrical concept, based on the fact that plays and many other performances are usually produced in a specific (assembly) venue with a stage and an audience. 'Staging' or 'stagecraft' applies to both the layout of this type of setting and to what is done on the stage (or within the entire performance space, whatever it is) to facilitate the performance and enhance the audience's experience. The basic components are:

- scenery and other artistic design elements, including curtains;
- lighting and related special effects (e.g., lasers);
- sound systems, musicians, orchestras;
- props (short for 'theatrical properties') such as furnishings and hand-held items;
- costumes and makeup;
- direction, and other management or control systems.

Brown and James (2004) discussed five specific theatrical applications to events. Scale, shape and focus apply to the setting, whereas timing and build come under the heading of scripting or programming.

Scale: It is important to matching the scale of the event or activity to the venue, in part to ensure the audience can see and understand what is happening. This principle will affect decisions on whether to stress the visual over the aural, and three-dimensional over two-dimensional. The audience needs enclosure, but does not want to feel restricted.

Shape: Drawing from environmental psychology, knowledge of how an audience relates to and moves within an environment, is essential. Removing visual and tangible clutter or distractions, and keeping things simple and legible are important design principles for event settings.

Focus: The use of blocking techniques from theatre and film direction ensures that the audience concentrates on what the designer/programmer wants them to focus on. Consider how lighting, colour, movement and shape affect people (this draws on both cognitive and environmental psychology).

Sensory Stimulation at Events

There is both art and science in the following specific design elements. Environmental psychology provides the theoretical foundation for researchers who want to know to what extent these variables can affect the event experience.

Light

Experiments have shown that lower levels result in greater interpersonal intimacy and quieter or reduced conversation. So event designers reduce lighting just before the curtain rises or the speakers take the stage in order to quiet the audience. On the other hand, soft lighting during a banquet will likely encourage conversation. Lighting also impacts on functionality. If the event purpose is to discuss important topics, dim lighting will be counter-productive. If it requires audience attention on a stage or person, then dim ambient lights plus a spotlight are effective. Light shows, often including lasers, provide a lot of mental stimulation and generate emotional arousal.

Too much light stimulation can be counter-productive if the audience is expected to calm down immediately afterwards. Light stimulation generates a lot of brain activity that is difficult to turn off, hence you are wise to avoid watching television before sleep time, and do not want to have a strobe-light effect just before listening to a speaker.

Colour

People have colour preferences, and colours affect mood. Colour can be manipulated through lighting or other design features. Perceived spaciousness can be influenced by colours and lighting, helping to reduce feelings of crowding. 'Colour theory' relates to how specific media affect color appearance (i.e., the effects of context on color appearance) whereas 'colour psychology' considers the effects of colours on feelings and behaviour (e.g., Will a pink room really calm prisoners and a red room increase tension? Does blue make people feel calm and cool?). 'Colour symbolism' is culturally defined, as in whether red suggests heat, anger or danger.

Sound

Loud noise is universally shunned, as it both physically hurts and gets in the way of desired conversations or other interactions. Quiet, ambient music has been found to be relaxing, although many people are rather sick of the elevator music we are too-often subjected to.

Aesthetics

Art, colour, light, and decoration, all have aesthetic effects. We either like some art and designs or we do not. Aesthetic stimulation might lead to conversation, intellectual appreciation, quiet contemplation, or be ignored. Aesthetic design elements might also hold symbolic meaning, and this can be manipulated by event designers. For example, certain colours, design features (like expensive art) and shapes or patterns are associated with political ideologies, royalty, life-styles, social class, or other potentially unifying or controversial themes. Being in a pleasant setting can also impact on people's willingness to help each other, but it might prove to be a distraction of serious business discussion is required.

Smell

Food-service professionals know that their best advertisement is often the smell of cooking. I walked into a newly renovated shopping centre recently and on either side of the entrance was a coffee shop and a cinnamon-bun dealer. The smells were strategically intended to get consumers in the mood for shopping. If we are hungry, the right smells can invoke salivation. The wrong smells can make people physically ill. Indeed, the military has experimented with smell as a weapon!

Over-Stimulation or Complexity

The well-known phenomenon of 'museum fatigue' has to be understood by event designers. Whatever is on display, or in learning situations, people only devote so much attention before becoming mentally fatigued. In a museum, visitors eventually start passing by many exhibits without stopping or even looking, because they have already absorbed enough. The same kind of mental fatigue can result in conventioneers skipping sessions, students falling asleep in class (boredom might also be a factor there), or visitors to art exhibits merely glancing at outstanding works of art. Event designers can plan their setting to focus attention quickly on the primary exhibits or other features, to reach visitors prior to fatigue setting in. Lecturers can hit the highlights first, then go on to the mundane details.

Attraction Gradients

When designing for pedestrian flow, ask what is in the event or its design that will most attract people? Exhibition planners know that the best sites are right at the entrance, facing those entering the hall. After that, there is a gradient of desirable locations based on visitor movements (often towards the centre, to the exits, the food or the washrooms), although the movement can be influenced by both overall design and individual exhibit design.

Taste

While this is obviously the critical factor in dining experiences, and at food festivals, taste can be manipulated in other event environments to stimulate emotional and behavioural responses.

Touch

Exhibit designers understand that involvement with displays is better than mere visual stimulation. Getting people to touch and try is one key step towards learning, or buying. Harvey et al. (1998) discovered they could more than double the time visitors spent at exhibits by making them interactive and multisensory, along with better lighting and easier-to-read lettering. Visitors felt more immersed in the overall museum experience.

Preferences

The Kaplan (1987) model helps predict people's preferences for various types of environment:

- *Coherence*: The scene is organized, everything hangs together.
- *Legibility*: We can categorize or understand the setting, everything is clear to us.
- *Complexity*: A measure of the number and variety of elements in the setting.
- *Mystery*: Hidden information is present and we are drawn into the setting to learn more.

Too much complexity or mystery, however, can be a bad thing. Too much mystery can be incompatible with legibility, and can become frightening. If the event designer provides light and dark contrasts, the viewer might be drawn in, whereas too dark a room can be scary and might discourage entry. Also, consider an empty room versus one in which people are present. Are we normally inclined to enter a space in which no other people are present? What appeals to people for meetings, trade shows and learning seminars might be quite different from settings for sports, public celebrations and private parties.

Cognitive Mapping and Wayfinding

We know that coherence and legibility are important when it comes to environmental preferences, so how do we translate that into event design, and how does it impact on event experiences? Bateson (1989) said that 'legibility' is crucial in all 'servicescapes', because customers arrive with expectations of how the site will function. These are, of course, social constructs, such as the notion that festival sites should always have a main stage and a food/beverage area.

Kevin Lynch (1960) provided the classic approach to cognitive mapping in cities, with implications for event settings. His key principles should be applied to event site planning so that people can easily understand the layout and efficiently navigate within it. The larger, more complex the site, the more important it is to strive for coherence and legibility. Lynch stressed the following features for wayfaring:

- *Nodes*: Activity places (provide a central stage and entertainment area within a park; arrange the venue to have multiple, easily located focal points).
- *Paths*: Routes people follow (direction and flow within an event venue has to be controlled; use signs and edges).

- *Landmarks*: Shapes, signs or symbols that everyone can see and refer to (e.g., every World's Fair builds a monument, usually in the centre).
- *Districts*: Neighbourhoods, shopping centres and other themed areas (group compatible activities together).
- *Edges*: Perceptual or real barriers between districts (people should recognize where they are in relation to other districts).

Lynch also found age and gender differences in how people wayfare, and probably there are many cultural differences as well. This suggests a research project for application to a variety of event sites.

Barker's (1968) behaviour settings can be adapted to fit different circumstances and goals. The three generic means of control pertain to:

- Access (who gets in, or under what schedule).
- Design capacity (i.e., the numbers allowed; consider peak and average attendance).
- Flow (time spent on site; turnover rates).

It is necessary to also consider accessibility for persons with physical and other disabilities or special needs (see Fleck, 1996). Darcy and Harris (2003) showed how to do an accessibility plan for events which provides for all needs.

Traffic management in and around events presents serious challenges, and practical advice is available from a number of sources. The UK National Outdoor Events Association has a manual on traffic (see www.noea.org.uk), and from New South Wales, Australia there is Traffic Management for Special Events (www.rta.nsw.gov.au).

The Affective Quality of Places

A model by Russell and Lanius (1984), called 'adaptation level and the affective appraisal of environments' seems very applicable to events. The basic premise is that emotional reactions to environments can be described in words along two continua: from pleasant to unpleasant, from arousing to sleepy. Forty descriptors were developed through research, falling into the four quadrants:

1. Highly arousing and highly pleasant (e.g., exciting, exhilarating, interesting).
2. Highly arousing and unpleasant (e.g., distressing, frenzied, tense, hectic).
3. Unarousing and unpleasant (e.g., dull, dreary, unstimulating).
4. Unarousing but pleasant (e.g., serene, tranquil, peaceful, restful).

Is quadrant 1 close to the 'wow!' factor desired by many event designers? Note that the descriptors are not specifically experiences, only reactions to stimuli.

Russell and Lanius determined through experimentation that the same stimulus (they used photographs) can generate widely different affective appraisals. In other words, setting designers cannot be certain their work will elicit the intended emotional response. One major reason is that people adapt to the environment and particular stimuli, so they react differently the next time.

Arousal: Interpersonal and environmental stimuli cause responses, both physiological and psychological, triggering behavioural responses. Sometimes event designers want to increase arousal, as in fostering celebration or revelry, and at other times they decrease stimulation in order to foster reverence or attentiveness. People have a limited capacity for dealing with a lot of stimulation and can become overstimulated. When this happens it can trigger a response such as withdrawal or anxiety, and it will usually result in a filtering of stimuli to focus on the necessary or desirable inputs. Another strategy frequently employed by people is to attempt to eliminate or adjust the stimulus, such as by screening information, turning down noise and light levels, or engaging in conversation in order to mask an annoying or boring speaker.

Optimal Stimulation: People have their own ways of finding optimal arousal levels, and this can be accomplished through escaping or seeking of stimulation. This is at the core of leisure and travel theory, based on the notion that motivation or need for leisure and travel is a result of simultaneously seeking and escaping. Continuous exposure to simulation can result in 'adaptation', such as people in cities adapting to higher levels of noise or crowding.

Behaviour Constraints: Loss of perceived control is the first step in the behavioural constraints model. It leads to discomfort and 'reactance' – that is, we try to regain control. Even the anticipation of loss of control, or another threat, can trigger reactance. If people are constantly told they cannot do something a possible consequence is 'learned helplessness'. People are likely to give up trying to make changes after a while, and that can apply to any consumer of any product or service.

Environmental Stress: What causes us stress? Certainly when things feel out of control, beyond out ability to cope, we feel stress. But environmental factors can also cause stress, such as event settings or programmes that generate sensory overload, overcrowding, nasty surprises, bad behaviour on the part of other guests, or poorly managed environmental systems leading to bad air. Fear causes stress, and a lack of knowledge about what is happening can generate fear.

Personal Space

What is the difference between intimacy, personal distance, social distance, and public distance? We want intimacy with lovers and family, but not strangers. We tolerate crowds, even seek them out, when a certain atmosphere is desired. At meetings, we might feel uncomfortable if the seats are too close.

Hall (1966) identified the four spatial zones, with 'intimate distance' being 0 to 1.5 feet (touching and feeling distance, with lots of contact and various sensory exchanges). 'Personal distance' is 1.5 to 4 feet (mostly verbal and visual contacts; contacts with friends and regular acquaintances). 'Social distance' is 4 to 12 feet (impersonal and businesslike eye and voice contacts, no touching, normal voice levels). Fourthly, 'public distance' is over 12 feet (formality, as in students' relationship to a lecturer in a classroom; the need exists for technical assistance or raising one's voice).

Environmental psychologists have studied personal space in various settings, using laboratory experiments and simulations or field methods. For event researchers, field observations and tests will yield the best results. Remember that cultural factors are likely to be important, and that age and gender have to be considered.

'Personal space' can be used by event designers to help achieve goals. For example, it is well known and easily observed that communication effectiveness diminishes with distance from the speaker. That is why classrooms are designed as amphitheatres and not long halls. There have been studies of optimal spacing in learning environments, for professional interaction, and for facilitating group processes. 'Sociopetal' distance brings people together, such as the circular or opposite layout of chairs in one's living room, while 'sociofugal' spacing diminishes interaction (e.g., rows of chairs).

A related concept is 'territoriality', which refers to a tendency for similar groups to stick together and apart from other groups. Within- and between-group interactions are easy to observe in most social settings, such as the little cliques that form at parties. If you want people to join in, leave an obvious opening, as in a crescent, but if you feel exclusionary, form a tight little knot with everyone facing inwards. Another form of territoriality occurs when people protect space for themselves or their group, like reserving seats or claiming tables at a banquet. Is this a good or bad thing?

Crowding

'Density' is an objective measure of how many people there are in a given area, but 'crowding' is how people feel about the situation. Studies have shown that in wilderness settings even the sight of a few other canoeists is crowding. Although a potential problem at events, people often expect crowds and they can even add to our enjoyment (Lee et al., 1997; Wickham and Kerstetter, 2000; Mowen et al., 2003).

Some of our reactions to the presence of others is related to the size of the group and our personal space – that is 'social density' (Bell et al., 2001: 296), whereas some of it depend on how much space there is – that is 'spatial density'. It is the difference between too many people to interact with, versus not enough space. Freedom to move, perceived control and risks can also be factors. For example, what would happen in a panic – can we escape? Certainly the context also influences our judgment of what is crowding. Researchers have found that males and females are equally affected by high social density, but males suffer more from high spatial density. Friends and social support mitigate stress or anxiety caused by crowding. Evidence linking crowding with aggression or other anti-social behaviour is not clear, especially within event settings.

Bell et al. (2001: 315) compared various theoretical models pertaining to crowding. Critical causes of crowding (not of density, but the resultant feeling) have been attributed to excessive social contact and social stimulation, reduced freedom (e.g., to move about), scarcity of resources (bathrooms?), violations of personal space, unwanted contacts (groping?), interference with desired behaviour, and lack of privacy. Possible coping mechanisms to crowding include withdrawal, attempts to reduce stimulation/arousal, escape, aggressive behaviour, territoriality and other attempts to maintain freedom, control or privacy. Some of these coping mechanisms might be desirable even if the crowding is considered to be, overall, unavoidable or fun. Cutting across most of these models is the notion of perceived control. If we believe we can take control of the situation, the negative impacts will be diminished.

Freedman's (1975) 'density-intensity model' appears to have great relevance to events, although it has been controversial. His model suggests that density intensifies reactions that would otherwise occur given the particular situation, so that high density heightens the importance of other people and magnifies our reactions to them. High density therefore intensifies the pleasantness of positive situations (e.g., a party or celebration) and intensifies the negativity of situations we would rather avoid. Accordingly, your expectations, desires and mood upon entering an event setting will directly impact on your reaction to density – whether or not you feel crowded. Mowen et al. (2003) found that crowding at events is more likely to be a positive factor at the entertainment stage, and negative at food and beverage outlets; it varies by zone and activity.

Stressors

'Stressors' at events can lead to problems. These include: excessive waiting; over crowding; excessive sensory stimulation; overwhelming security, regulation or threats; fencing that prevents escape (people feel trapped), and other restrictions on movement.

Berlonghi (1990: 73) concluded that panic at events is likely to stem from real or perceived threats, and he discussed eight crowd characteristics to help managers or security identify crowd problems and security threats.

Freedman (1975) also experimented with 'contagion', which is the rapid spread of emotions or behaviour through a group or crowd. This phenomenon obviously has a direct bearing on events, as in some cases we want to foster positive contagion (especially celebration and humour) and in others it is very bad (fear and fighting).

Crowd Management and Crowd Control

'Crowd management' has to be integrated throughout the design process and management systems. The purpose is to both prevent problems and facilitate good experiences. 'Crowd control', on the other hand, involves security and other measures that only become necessary when there is a problem and should be handled by experts (Rutley, n.d.).

Setting a firm site capacity (or 'design capacity'), in terms of the number of people invited or permitted, is one way to prevent over crowding and related problems. Similarly, managers can try to regulate the flow and turnover of patrons. Other capacity and crowd management techniques include advance and group ticketing (to avoid bottlenecks), physical barriers and activity spacing, information provision, and the management of queues (Mowen et al., 2003). See also Ammon and Fried (1998) for advice on event crowd management.

Theme and Programme Design

A 'theme' is a unifying idea or concept which gives meaning to the event, or is the object of celebration or commemoration. It can be a visual or sensory theme, in the realms of decorators and chefs, an activity theme (styles of sport, play, recreation) a fantasy theme (usually combining décor and entertainment), an emotional theme (such as a celebration of something of value), or it can be intellectual in nature (such as the conference topic or workshop problem).

Recalling our earlier discussion of 'thematic interpretation', the theme should be stimulating and provocative, embodying tangible and intangible elements. Memorable themes tap into universal belief systems and should provide the take-home message, the moral of the story. Many entertainment or decoration themes do not do that, nor is it necessarily appropriate at concerts, parties and other social gatherings. Whatever goes into the event programme, from sensory stimulation to entertainment and spectacle, should ideally reflect and reinforce the theme.

Programme Planning

A programme is the scheduled or 'scripted' activities for the audience and other participants. A concert programme can be quite simple, consisting of the order of artists or musical pieces. A festival programme might be complex, involving multiple days and venues with numerous activities and performances. Sport events have scheduled times for competitions and award ceremonies. Meetings and conventions typically operate with tight agendas to make sure the programme of speakers, plenary and breakout sessions, meals, coffee breaks and social events keeps to the schedule.

Programme 'portfolios' consist of all the different activities and services provided at events. They have to meet multiple objectives, appeal to diverse audiences, and ideally be sustainable. To evaluate feasibility, desirability and continuance requires measures that reflect underlying goals and values. For example, commercial events have to monitor economic demand and profits, while public festivals might be focused on fulfilling social aims, like awareness building or providing cultural opportunities to specific groups in the community. Other possible values and measures include image, tradition, stakeholder desires, market potential and share, growth potential.

The 'programme planning process' usually starts with an evaluation of existing programming and/or new idea generation. It is generally wise to test ideas, although for planned events this can be difficult. At a basic level focus groups can be held to test programme ideas with potential patrons or with stakeholder groups, and at a more costly level mini-events can be held to see if the concept is feasible and satisfies target segments.

'Life-cycle' considerations are important. Some programmes and services can be slated for a short life expectancy, including planned termination, while others can be allowed to run a full course through growth, maturity, and decline. If sales and profits are the primary measure of success, a programme or service will have to be terminated or 'rejuvenated' through re-investment and re-positioning when profit margins shrink. Community-service and goodwill programmes do not have to be terminated because of cost and revenue considerations, but their ongoing effectiveness has to be demonstrated.

Sustaining traditional programmic elements, while innovating regularly to test new ones, is a model followed by many events including the Calgary Stampede (see Getz, 1993b, 1997). At some point, changes to programming can be so substantial as to constitute repositioning of the entire event.

Scripting and Choreography

In most forms of theatrical performance the 'script' is followed to the letter. How appropriate this is at other events is a matter of style and intent. In some respects a schedule of activities, or the event programme, is a script. Specific elements of an event can be scripted while the overall 'performance' is improvized or merely themed.

'Choreography', borrowed from dance, is an alternative approach for events. Here, characters and interactions are suggested through notations, but the actual behaviour of 'performers' is somewhat creative and unpredictable.

Timing and Build

'Timing', or scheduling, has to consider the audience's attention span and responses to stimuli, keeping in mind that '… event time is different from real time and audiences respond differently to it.' In general, Brown and James (2004: 61) recommended programming 'tightly' and accurately to maintain 'flow' and contact with the audience.

'Build' is the use of time and programming, including ebbs and peaks of intensity, to maximize impact on the audience. There is a skill in using limited resources to achieve great emotional or intellectual stimulation.

Programmic Elements of Style

'Style' means a characteristic way of doing things (to create a unique event), excellence of artistic expression (a measure of product or programme quality), or fashion (which always changes). We can say that designers have their own style, and that all events are stylistically different. Recall our earlier discussions of aesthetics and beauty, because style is largely subjective and therefore subject to widely different interpretations.

Each 'programmic element of style' has a creative and a technical component. Elements can be combined in unlimited combinations to design a unique event programme. Generally the elements have to be designed in concert with the setting and implemented through physical development and all the management systems.

Some programmic elements of style are 'hallmarks' of particular types of event. That is, the event form requires it by definition, or as a social construct this element is closely associated with it. For example, business and trade events like fairs and trade shows involve commerce by nature. Festivals are celebrations so they have to incorporate belonging and sharing, emotional stimulation, rituals and symbolism. Sports and recreation must involve games or competition. But standing alone, one element of style looks bare and will generate a rather narrow range of experiences. Sports are packaged as festivals for a good reason, to expand their appeal and generate additional benefits. Business events are serious, but they almost always base part of their appeal on social and touristic opportunities.

One way to specify programmic elements of style is to list the actions a programmer or designer can include, or the activities that participants and guests are to engage in. These are the main activity elements subject to design, but keep in mind that each one can have varying cognitive and affective outcomes:

- Teach (interpret, inform; engage people in discourse or problem solving).
- Play and compete (games; mental and physical activity).
- Amuse (use of humour and surprise).
- Entertain (including spectacle, performances).
- Engage in rites and rituals (including symbolism and protocol; cultural authenticity must be considered).
- Exhibit (art; goods and services for marketing purposes).
- Buy, sell, trade (commerce).
- Mix and mingle (socializing, partying, group discussion).
- Sensory stimulation (sight, sound, touch, taste, hearing).
- Hospitality (welcoming, guiding, services, satisfying basic needs such as eating, drinking, resting, toilets).

We have already examined the main programmic elements that constitute sensory stimulation, so here we need to add a list of ways to stimulate emotions. Just about any combination of activities and sensory stimulation can provoke emotional and cognitive responses, but these elements are tried and true in the context of politics, patriotism, religion and affinity groups:

- Ritual and symbolism that reflects or suggests cultural and social identity; the display of scared or respected artifacts.
- Direct verbal appeals to loyalty, pride, community or faith (i.e., preaching and propaganda).
- Celebrity endorsements and the charisma of speakers, especially from recognized leaders.
- Selected information and interpretation (as social marketing and propaganda).

For event designers and programmers there can be a fine line between emotional or cognitive stimulation and exploitation, between facilitating a powerful, transforming experience and provoking a negative, even violent response. 'Playing with emotions' should always be undertaken with the benefit of research and evaluation, and this has often, sadly, been ignored.

Programme (or 'Product') Quality

Getz and Carlsen (2006: 146) discussed the main dimensions of event quality. Quality begins with the organization: its mandate and vision, philosophy and customer orientation; competence of its staff and volunteers; its governance, and effectiveness of its management. Programme (or product) quality is experiential and subject to qualitative evaluation by all the stakeholders. Customers evaluate quality by expressing their level of satisfaction with the event overall, or with the quality of what is being presented to them in the form of sport competition, the musical performance, the speakers at a convention, art at an exhibit, food at a banquet, etc. Product quality can also be assessed through benchmarking against other events, the opinions of expert judges, or through experiential research.

Love and Crompton (1996) tested the hypothesis, based on the works of Herzberg (1966) that some event elements are 'dissatisfiers' which can undermine the visitor experience, while others are 'satisfiers' which provide benefits. 'Dissatisfiers' are like Herzberg's 'maintenance' factors – they must be provided to expected levels of quality, but in themselves do not satisfy visitors. The researchers argued that most of the physical factors at events, such as parking, rest rooms and information, are dissatisfiers, while ambiance, fantasy, excitement, relaxation, escape and social involvement are satisfiers. High-quality events must meet expectations in both categories, but they are non-compensatory in that a single or small number of attributes can determine perception of overall quality. Tentative support for this model was confirmed, and the researchers believed that certain attributes were perceived to be of so poor or high quality that visitors disregarded or discounted other attributes in giving their overall appraisal.

Baker and Crompton (2000) determined that generic and entertainment features of an event are more likely to generate increased satisfaction and motivate return visits or positive word-of-mouth recommendations. Saleh and Ryan (1993) found that quality of the music program is the most important service factor in attracting people to jazz festivals. Overall satisfaction levels affected the intention for repeat visits. Similarly, Thrane (2002) explored the link between satisfaction and future intentions of festival-goers. The most important conclusion from his study in Norway was that event managers must try to improve program quality (in this case music) AND be concerned with other factors that shape overall satisfaction.

Ryan and Lockyer (2002) studied satisfaction levels of participants in the South Pacific Masters games in New Zealand – a friendly, multi-sport event for older athletes. The results showed that sport event managers need to pay particular attention to improving items of high importance but low satisfaction. In this sample the prime motivators – seeking challenge and fun – were found to be satisfied by the event. A factor analysis was also used to identify five components of importance to participants, namely: social (social events plus meeting people); registration (good communications); challenge; after-event communication; and that the competition is both fun and serious.

Service Design and Quality

Researchers have demonstrated that event satisfaction is primarily dependent on the core elements of the programme, whether this is music or sport competition, and that is exactly what theme and programme design seeks to accomplish. In this context, the setting, service delivery, and consumables are supporting factors. An exception is for food and beverage events where consumables are the core, or commerce events where people purchase tangible products. Nevertheless, service delivery is important, as bad service easily displeases people. It is a design process because good service is both technical (e.g., no errors made, everything is done on time) and creative/qualitative (staff are friendly and helpful; staff as part of the experience).

There is a huge body of literature on service marketing, quality, and delivery, especially for the tourism and hospitality sectors (see, e.g., Prideaux et al., 2006). Applied to event design, the basic principle is that all management systems as well as staff and volunteer actions, directly affect the customer's perceptions of quality and therefore their level of satisfaction with the event experience.

Drummond and Anderson (2004) discussed the meaning of quality and how service management impacts on events. They explained what has to be done to create a satisfying 'service experience' before, during and after the event. They argued that service enables the guest or customer to more fully enjoy the product or experience. Wicks and Fesenmaier (1993) studied differences between visitors and vendors in their perceptions of service quality at an event. A comparison of alternative approaches to evaluating event quality was undertaken by Crompton and Love (1995).

Service Blueprinting and Service Mapping

'Blueprinting' is a tool with value in all the services, but its application to planned events has been minimal (see Getz et al., 2001). The idea is to create a chart or 'blueprint' based on the flow of intended visitor activities and experiences, and to show how the experiences are facilitated by the setting (or 'servicescape'), all the management systems, and human contacts. The service 'map' is a diagnostic or evaluation tool which can precede blueprinting, or test its effectiveness. Let's look at the key elements in blueprinting.

Customer Actions

The blueprint anticipates the flow of customer actions, starting with approach to the site and ending with departure. If there are many activity options or venues it will be necessary to have multiple blueprints, some in great deal and one for the overall process. Although the blueprint specifies actions in settings, it should consider the intended customer or guest experience. For example, 'viewing art in gallery' can be expanded into 'the guest will enjoy a quiet, aesthetic experience, aided by interactive information about the artists and their displays'. This experiential elaboration will greatly assist in planning the 'physical evidence' and staff–guest interactions.

When doing a service mapping exercise, as evaluation, multiple observers (engaged in direct and participant observation) will be needed to plot the actual flow and activities of guests and to summarize the experiential dimensions.

Tangible Evidence of Product and Service Quality

Above the customer-actions flow chart, the blueprint specifies all the physical evidence of quality, such as entertainment, the competition, exhibits, facilities, signs, equipment and audio-visual effects. Include the hygiene factors like toilets and soap, water and comfort stations. Anticipate everything the guest will need or desire and specify the quality standards. In the case of evaluations, describe gaps and flaws in tangible evidence, such as crowding, unanticipated behaviour, safety and health hazards, obvious customer confusion, inadequate signage or direction. Describe programme or product quality as experienced by observers.

'Hygiene factors' have been found to be extremely important at events, not in motivating people to attend or affecting their assessment of overall program quality, but in terms of causing dissatisfaction (these include security, cleanliness, comfort). Event quality can also be assessed by reference to its impacts, through measuring the attainment of positive goals and avoidance or amelioration of negative outcomes.

Visible Staff Contacts

For each customer action, or experience setting, the blueprint has to specify staff or volunteer support that will, or could involve staff–guest interaction. These also define potential 'critical incidents' where service failure could occur. This line, under the flow chart, also quantifies human resource needs, in terms of staffing levels, duties, and necessary training.

Viewed as 'cast members', staff and volunteers have both technical roles to play in delivering essential services, and an experiential role to play in facilitating desired experiences. Their appearance and demeanour are important to theming as well as service. In terms of service marketing theory (i.e., SERVQUAL, developed by Parasuraman et al., 1988), staff and volunteers have to exhibit 'responsiveness' (willingness to help; promptness), 'assurance' (knowledge and courtesy; convey trust and inspire confidence), 'empathy' (caring; providing individual service), and 'reliability' (ability and dependability).

Invisible Management Processes

The usual practice is to draw a line under the 'visible staff contacts' and in this bottom space on the blueprint to indicate the management systems that have to be in place to support the entire service process (which, at events, inevitably means the programme as well). In evaluations, the observers can work backwards from obvious failures or problems to determine what was missing or flawed in these hidden systems (e.g., police should have regulated the approach road).

Experience Factor Model

Ralston et al. (2006) developed an 'experience factor model' for event design which combines experiential and service quality elements. The 'experience factors' consist of themed experiences, targeted impressions, reducing negative cues, engaging multiple senses, providing a mix in memorabilia, customizing to the individual, getting into and staying in character and performing to appropriate form. The service factors are those of SERVQUAL: tangibles, reliability, responsiveness, empathy, assurance, recovery, competence, courtesy, security, access/welcome and communications.

Their model can be used as a diagnostic tool, using a type of SWOT analysis, which includes independent assessment of critical incidents, to assess an event's or attraction's 'experience quotient' and 'service quotient'. Service quality has to be high in order to achieve a high 'experience quotient' (i.e., to achieve memorable and transforming experiences), so the model encompasses an 'experience threshold'. This zone separates displeasure from enjoyment.

Design of Gastronomy and Other Consumables

At many events the food and beverage service is incidental to the main theme and programme, but at others it is experientially paramount. This is true at food and wine festivals, gala dinners, and other events that stress cultural authenticity. Tellstrom et al. (2006: 130) stressed that 'Food and meals are a central field in the communication of culture'.

In terms of quality and design, this is the realm of the chef and banquet manager, who are in turn dependent on suppliers for quality. Eating at many events is nothing more than a basic service, but it should be an experience. Lashley et al. (2004) defined the dimensions of this eating experience: the occasion; the company one dines with; atmosphere; food; service, and setting.

Gustafsson et al. (2006) noted that the meal product consists of visual effect, taste/expectation compliance, reflection of style, and standard of service. They said (p. 89) '. . . the whole product process requires both craftsmanship, science and aesthetical/ethical knowledge in order to produce good meals and result in the optimum experience for the guest/diner . . .'. All the senses have to be stimulated, '. . . and in harmony to create agreement that it was a good meal experience . . .' (p. 90).

Gift-giving is also important at some events, including those in which sponsors provide samples to take home, or when employers reward their staff. In these cases the tangibles are a key part of the event experience, so their inherent (or perceived) quality, and how they are presented, are critical. To marketers, each gift is a branding exercise – sponsors want guests to go away with favourable and enduring perceptions of their brand. To employers rewarding staff, the symbolic value of the gift is usually more important.

Chapter Summary

Although experiences can neither be designed nor guaranteed, event producers and designers must do their best to specify intended experiences, and to anticipate the motives, needs and desired experiences of all the stakeholders. Design is both a technical and creative process to meet goals and solve problems. While some authors and event professionals take a holistic view of design, applying it to the entire planning and production process, this chapter has stressed four elements of the planned event that are clearly the realm of designers. The interactions of setting design with theme and programme, service quality, and provision of consumables have direct bearing on experiences.

The first design realm is the setting, with foundation theory coming from environmental psychology, and design principles potentially being adapted from theatre. Certainly there are some elements in every planned event that are 'theatrical', as in scripted, staged, or choreographed. Technical considerations like sound and light also have psychological impact, so we have to understand cognitive psychology and how settings are changed by various sensory stimulations. Concern for aesthetics or taste takes us back to a discussion of philosophy. Knowledge of aesthetic and setting preferences helps the event designer, while site planning that creates coherence and legibility will be much appreciated by all in attendance. Thinking back to the model of planned event experiences, the designer has to have a clear vision of how the intended experiences are to be suggested and facilitated.

The theme, in cognitive terms, should be a powerful interpretive tool to achieve memorable and transforming events. The theme, purely in design or programmic terms, provides a way to integrate all design elements and perhaps achieve the desired 'wow!' effect. Many programmic 'elements of style' can be utilized by designers to create unique events, including specific activities for guests (e.g., games, commerce, mingling, learning opportunities), sensory and emotional stimulation. Event programmes can be scheduled and scripted, but what the programme designer is actually doing is creating the 'product' that people come to experience. Their experience of this 'product' is the key factor in shaping satisfaction levels.

Program or product quality was examined, stressing the importance of knowing what motivates people to attend events. Satisfaction is generally linked to the core programme and experiential elements of an event, whether it is competition, education or music, or the more experiential elements including atmosphere, socialization and relaxation. Service elements are potential dissatisfiers that can spoil the experience, but research has shown that product quality is still more important in explaining overall satisfaction.

Service quality and management are also design processes, particularly because the people-component (staff and volunteers) both facilitates the customer's experience and, as the 'cast', can be part of the experience. Service 'blueprinting' and evaluative 'mapping' are primary design tools for designing and improving the total event experience.

The chapter concluded with a brief discussion of 'consumables' as design elements. Food and beverages should be designed as experiences and not simply offered for sale as commodities. The experiential dimensions of meals were examined, and these provide guidance to event designers who want to create unique, cultural experiences. Gifts also have to be designed, as they both represent the quality of the event and have a symbolic connection with sponsors and their brands.

Study Questions

- Define 'design' and discuss its importance in Event Studies.
- Do you believe experiences can be designed? How?
- Explain the necessity to base event setting design on theory from cognitive and environmental psychology. Give specific applications.
- In what ways can the event designer adapt principles from theatre?
- Give examples of how coherence and legibility can be achieved in event site planning.
- Do people have preferences for event settings? Are these 'social constructs'?
- Discuss how 'crowding' is more than just the number of people at an event.
- What are the main tools in crowd management and crowd control?
- Illustrate how various 'programmic elements of style' can be used for learning, sensory and emotional stimulation.

• What is program and service quality, and how can they be measured or evaluated?
• Describe 'service blueprinting' as an event design tool, including reference to 'the cast'.

Further Reading

Graham Berridge (2007). *Event Design*. Oxford: Butterworth Heinemann.

International Festivals and Events Association (IFEA) (2000). *Parades*. Port Angeles, WA: IFEA Publications.

Meeting Professionals International (2003). *Meetings and Conventions: A Planning Guide*. Mississauga: MPI.

Prideaux, B., Moscardo, G., and Laws, E. (eds.) (2006). *Managing Tourism and Hospitality Services: Theory and International Applications*. Wallingford: CABI.

Wiersma, B., and Strolberg, K. (2003). *Exceptional Events: Concept to Completion* (2nd edn). Weirmar, Texas: Culinary and Hospitality Industry Publications Services.

Further Reading

Chapter 9

Antecedents and Choices

Learning Objectives

- Understand the relationships between personal antecedents and event attendance (or participation), the barriers and constraints, decision-making, post-experience evaluation and future decisions.
- Know how intrinsic and extrinsic motivation leads to participation in, and travel to attend events.
- Understand specific constraints influencing the decision to attend events, and how people negotiate through barriers to achieve their goals.
- Know why some people do not attend events.
- Learn how different stakeholders make decisions about attending events, including guest/consumers/participants, organizers and volunteers, sponsors and suppliers.

What Are Antecedents?

Why do you attend an event? Surely there are myriad reasons, depending on your own needs and motives, the circumstances and the types of events that you can choose from. Event-related behaviour is complex and probably ever-changing, but there are theoretical fundamentals that will help us understand the process and apply this knowledge to all planned events.

'Antecedents' are all those influences that shape interest in, demand for, choices, and actual event attendance or participation. We start with needs, which are closely linked to intrinsic (self directed) and extrinsic (from outside) motives. A discussion of demand takes us from social-psychology to economics, then we draw upon consumer research to explore decision-making. Leisure theory provides a solid base for examining barriers and constraints, and how people overcome or negotiate through them to achieve their goals.

To start the discussion, a conceptual model of the main factors shaping participation/attendance at planned events is presented in Figure 9.1. Numerous models and frameworks are available from consumer research in general and, more specifically, tourism

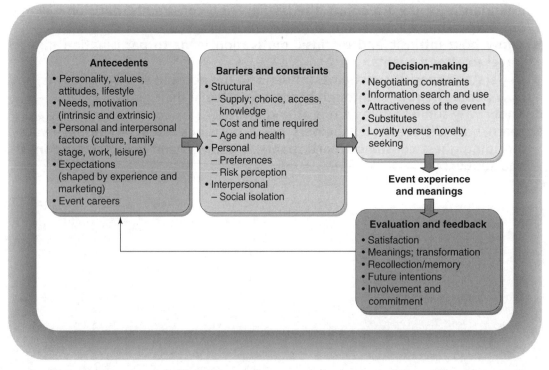

Figure 9.1   A framework for studying the antecedents and decision-making process for attending planned events.

(see overviews in Ryan, 2002; Crouch et al., 2004; Decrop, 2006) and leisure (see Walker and Virden, 2005; Hinch et al., 2006). The rest of the chapter reflects the main elements of the model, with sections on barriers and constraints, decision-making, evaluation and feedback.

Although this framework is designed as a process, it is not predictive. It shows all the main factors we need to understand, and suggests how they interconnect, but it is not possible to forecast that any particular set of antecedents will result in certain decisions, or that certain experiences lead to predictable future behaviour.

Personality

Personality, values, attitudes and lifestyle preferences are the psychological factors that lie at the foundation of human behaviour. Individuals will show a propensity for certain behaviour as a result of these factors, but that does not necessarily mean they will act, or act consistently on them.

'Personality types' were previously explored, noting that some people have a higher propensity to seek novelty or take risks. Some people, in the terminology of Stanley Plog (1987), are more 'adventuresome' than others, leading them to seek out unique leisure and travel experiences. Others have a greater need for consistency and therefore a higher tolerance of boredom.

According to the theory of 'personality-environment congruence', 'extroverted' risk takers will be happy at raucous concerts, but probably shy 'introverts' will not. Events often cater to certain personality types without the organizers being aware of it. Another theory of potential relevance is that of 'optimal challenge', which suggest that in event programming the matching of challenges with participants' skills will likely produce the desired 'flow' experience. This is more critical for sport events that attract competitors at different levels, for educational events where people want to learn different things, and for recreational events where there are certain risks involved. Csikszentmihalyi (1975, 1990) concluded that boredom results when challenges are too low, and anxiety stems from challenges that are too great.

Values

Values are subjective reactions to, and assessments about the world. They are deeply held, and in behavioural terms they imply a conscious assessment of the desirability of alternative behaviours, including what is right and wrong. Values are shaped by experience, religious or political affiliations, general social and cultural influences and perhaps by personality. Do you value freedom of choice? Having decisions made for you by government? Environmental responsibility? How are your personal values different from the important people in your life? And have you any values that shape your interest in, or event-related behaviour?

Research Note

Green, B. C., and Chalip, L. (1998). Sport tourism as the celebration of subculture. Annals of Tourism Research, 25(2): 275–291.

Green and Chalip (1998), determined that participants in the Key West Women's Flag Football Tournament sought (beyond the usual mastery and competency motives in sport participation) the opportunity to get together to celebrate their subculture (i.e., to meet affiliation needs). The place of the event could be much less important than the nature of the event, especially the opportunities provided for both formal and informal socializing and celebration. The overall event package, they recommended, should be designed to appeal to particular sub-culture values.

Attitudes

Allport (1937) provided the classic definition of attitude as a ' learned predisposition to respond to an object or class of objects in a consistently favourable or unfavourable way.'

Attitudes are theorized to contain 'conative' (action and behavioural intention), 'affective' (evaluation and affect, or emotion) and 'cognitive' (perception and belief) components. Note that this trilogy is also used, in a slightly different way, to describe the dimensions of 'experience'.

Within the context of the 'theory of planned behaviour' (Ajzen, 1991), researchers have examined attitudes towards leisure participation. Many other factors influence actual behaviour, but measuring attitudes can be a good predictor if the attitude is linked to specific behaviour, such as 'how do you feel about attending a rock concert/cultural festival/art exhibition in the next 12 months?' As opposed to general behaviour (such as 'how do you feel about attending special events?'). What are the influences shaping attitudes towards planned events? Some combination of personal, social and cultural factors lie at the base of beliefs and predispositions.

Lifestyle

'Lifestyles', as unique patterns of thinking and behaving, arise from personality, values and attitudes. Some researchers refer to these, together, as 'psychographics'. According to Decrop (2006: 11), lifestyles reflect the 'self concept' of people. Although seldom explored in the context of planned events, as opposed to leisure and travel in general, there must be lifestyles that predispose or facilitate participation in events. Examples could be dedicated marathon runners whose 'lifestyles' are built around training and travelling to events, or the 'lifestyles' of food and wine connoisseurs which predispose them to attend certain festivals and exhibitions.

Needs

According to Maslow (1954, 1968) 'needs' are both physiological (what we need to live and be safe) and socially learned (what we need to belong and be happy). The following four were said to be 'deficit' needs, and people instinctively seek to meet them. In times of stress regression can occur, but people are said to move from the lower to the higher order needs in a developmental process:

- Physiological: survival needs, including water, food and shelter.
- Safety and security needs: stability, order, protection, structure.
- Love and belonging needs: social needs, a wish for affection and to show affection, a sense of community.
- Esteem needs: hierarchical, with the lower order consisting of respect of others, status and recognition; higher order – self-respect, competence independence, achievement and mastery.

Others have argued that there are additional needs, and that the hierarchical nature of Maslow's theory is unsupportable. However controversial, Maslow's hierarchy of needs have been tremendously influential, and are referenced again in our discussion of volunteer motivation.

Self Actualization and Peak Experiences

Maslow's hierarchy is often shown as a pyramid with self-actualization at the top. Maslow believed that certain people, only 2% of the population, could be called 'self-actualized', and they have many more 'peak experiences' than others. A 'peak experience' is available to all, and self-actualization is 'growth motivation', or a process of seeking.

'Peak experiences' were described as sudden feelings of intense happiness and well-being. They are nonreligious, quasi-mystical, or mystical in nature, and possibly accompanied by awareness of 'ultimate truth' and the unity of all things. Also accompanying peak experiences is a heightened sense of control over the body and emotions, and a wider sense of awareness. The experience fills the individual with wonder and awe.

Maslow described 'peak experiences' as self-validating, self-justifying moments with their own intrinsic value; never negative, unpleasant or evil; disoriented in time and space (which sounds like the liminal/liminoid zone of Turner, as well as Csikszentmihalyi's 'flow') and accompanied by a loss of fear, anxiety, doubts and inhibitions. Critics argue that anybody, whether good or evil, could have one of these peak experiences, so it has no moral basis. Others find it unscientific and untestable.

'Benefits' are what people believe they will obtain from consumption or participation, and these are generally expressed in terms related to need fulfilment. For example, of all the benefits provided by leisure services and sport, improved health has to be near the top of the list. People 'want' many things or experiences, but that is not necessarily the same as needing them. Only the individual can decide when a want becomes a need, although society often makes judgements as to what is a basic need. Often potential substitution comes into play, because many needs and wants can be met through different means.

Do People Need Events?

I think the answer is absolutely yes. People might not respond to questions by saying they need to attend a party or cultural celebration, but they do need the socializing, relaxation or escapism that events offer. People need to discover, learn and fulfil their aesthetic ambitions, and attending events provides these benefits. Companies have to market and do business, so they need exhibitions and consumer shows. Associations have to meet. Humans need to recreate, leading to sport events. Events of all kinds have been successful because they meet so many fundamental personal, social, cultural and economic needs.

One question that gets at the heart of the issue is this: If all festivals were removed, would people create new ones? If sports events were cancelled, would there be high demand to bring them back? If conferences ceased because of terrorism, how long would it be before companies and associations found alternative ways to get their people together? Clearly, there is demand for events, and history has demonstrated that this growing level of demand reflects underlying, fundamental needs. Individual events may be substitutable, and people have lots of choices, but events do meet basic human needs.

Motivation and Motives

'Personality traits' have a rather permanent influence on behaviour, whereas 'motivation' is dynamic, it can and does change. 'Motivation' refers to the process by which people are driven to act in a certain way (Decrop, 2006: 9). Iso-Ahola (1980, 1983) took a more comprehensive approach in saying that motivations are internal factors that arouse, direct and integrate behaviour. Another way to look at 'motivation' is to think of a need or 'disequilibrium' which is accompanied by an expectation that action will reduce it. If the expectation is met, satisfaction results. The experience of or failure to attain satisfaction influences future behaviour (i.e., there is a feedback mechanism).

'Motives', by contrast, are specific reasons for doing something, and they have to follow from underlying needs and motivation. For example, people who are 'highly involved' in a sport or lifestyle pursuit (like running) have a strong 'motivation' to attend events where their specific needs can be satisfied. But their 'motives' for deciding to attend a specific event might include consideration of who else is attending, the entertainment opportunities and the attractiveness of the location.

It is common in the tourism literature to use the terms 'push factors' or 'drivers' and 'pull factors' or 'attraction/attractiveness' to cover travel motivation. When we speak of the interaction of push and pull factors, Iso-Ahola's (1980, 1983; Mannell and Iso-Ahola, 1987) 'seeking and escaping' model comes to the fore. Seeking and escaping motivation simultaneously influences our decisions because we are both seeking to find personal and interpersonal rewards and hoping to escape aspects of personal and interpersonal environments that bother us. Both seeking and escaping are forms of intrinsic motivation, or what we want to do for its own sake.

In escaping our everyday environment we seek change and novelty, especially new experiences. Under or 'over-arousal' gives rise to this need for escape, but of course we also have to seek out something to alter our arousal levels – hence the need for 'optimal arousal' at events. Have a look at travel and entertainment marketing to the importance of 'escapism' in motivating consumer choices.

When it comes to 'seeking' motives, personal satisfaction or rewards can be obtained through relaxation, exploration, learning, aesthetic experiences, meeting challenges or mastery (a sense of competence). Interpersonal rewards can include social contacts and connectedness (belonging and sharing).

The Travel Career Trajectory

Philip Pearce based this model on Maslow's needs hierarchy, adapting it to travel and tourism. It has obvious relevance for studying event tourism, but also appears to be a good starting point for conducting research on personal event antecedents, experiences and outcomes in general. The key concept is that through experiences one's motivation and satisfaction will tend to shift from basic 'relaxation' to 'stimulation/novelty', to 'relationship', to 'self esteem and development' and ultimately to personal 'fulfilment'.

In other words, our experiences transform us, so that we become more motivated to seek fulfilment of the higher-order needs through travel and participation in events.

The term 'careers' implies 'serious leisure' as theorized by Stebbins. What we want to look for, and researchers have so far only scratched the surface in this context, are people who for reasons of their 'involvement' or 'commitment' not only attend many events, but demonstrate a progress or pattern of event participation and attendance that stems from their increasing experience and shifting motivation. For example, early results from a study of mountain bikers (Getz and McConnell, 2006) suggest that these amateur athletes compete in many events, and in several sports, all looking for challenge and accomplishment. There is a sense of community with other event participants that provides motivation. Novelty seeking is evident in their selection of events. Attractive destinations and well-organized events go together in appealing to the highly involved mountain biker.

Much more research is needed along these lines. What are the short-term and ultimate goals of highly involved event participants? Do some 'iconic' events compel them forwards, training harder, searching for better performance? How do they combine their interest in running, or art, or any other pursuit with more general leisure and travel preferences? How can event designers maximize the desired experiences of the 'highly involved' as well those for whom the event is only of general interest?

Motivational Research in the Event Sector

Motivational studies have been frequent in the events literature (e.g., Mohr et al., 1993; Uysal et al., 1993; Leibold and van Zyl, 1994; Backman et al., 1995; Scott, 1996; Nogawa et al., 1996; Crompton and McKay, 1997; Oppermann and Chon, 1997; Formica and Murrmann, 1998; Formica and Uysal, 1998; Green and Chalip, 1998; Raybould, 1998; Pitts, 1999; Ngamsom and Beck, 2000; Nicholson and Pearce, 2001; McGehee et al., 2003; Xiao and Smith, 2004; Ryan and Trauer, 2005; Funk and Brunn, 2006) including review articles by Lee et al. (2004), Gibson's (2004) review of sport tourism motivation, and a review by Li and Petrick (2006).

Li and Petrick (2006) reviewed the literature on festival and event motivation studies and drew a number of important conclusions. They found that most such studies were theoretically grounded in, and gave support to the 'seeking-escaping' motivation theory, and the similar push/pull model (Crompton, 1979; Dann, 1977, 1981). There is as yet, however, no agreement on whether motivations are common across all types of events. A study of events in New Zealand by Nicholson and Pearce (2001) found a more complex and diverse range of motives by employing the open-ended question 'Why did you come to this event?', and they concluded that event-specific factors were important.

The Xiao and Smith's (2004) study of residents' attitudes towards Oktoberfest in Kitchener-Waterloo, revealed the following perceptions of the event which suggest likely motivations for attending or, in this case, recommending the event to others: entertainment/fun; cultural experience; socialization and vitalizing the local economy.

Li and Petrick's review related to sports resulted in several important conclusions. First, a general motivation scale for attending sport events has been developed and widely applied. Second, studying potential attendees adds to our understanding (as opposed to surveys of actual attendees) and third, travel and event motivation might be different – a finding of significance for sport tourism.

Research Note

Ryan, C., and Trauer, B. (2005). Sport tourist behaviour: the example of the Masters Games. In: J. Higham (ed.), Sport Tourism Destinations: Issues, Opportunities and Analysis. Oxford: Elsevier.

These authors studied a major participant-based, multi-sport event, for which they believe location is a secondary consideration to the sport tourists. Masters Games attract a large core of sport 'enthusiasts' who invest heavily in their athletic pursuits – including travel – and also those who only participate at the local level. Ryan and Trauer talked about a 'career' that leads from local to international competitions (p. 179): 'It can be hypothesized that participants form a degree of involvement with games participation that in part is a confirmation of self-identity as an exponent of a particular sport.' The highly involved participants who are willing to travel may be critical for the success of events.

Ryan and Trauer argued (p. 181) that pleasure in sporting leisure can be derived from the activity itself, the 'subsequent sense of well-being and achievement, and camaraderie derived from sharing the experience with others.' Their model of 'the nature of participation in Masters Games' incorporates four types of competitors:

1. *'The games enthusiast': highly involved, motivated by both intrinsic rewards (a sense of well being) and social interaction; challenge is important but they might also be interested in fun runs.*
2. *'The serious competitor': highly involved, motivated by a wish to compete successfully.*
3. *'The novice/dabbler': less involved, motivated by fitness or play; might be beginning a competitive career.*
4. *'The spectator': high interest in sport but low involvement, therefore spectators perhaps can be motivated to participate.*

Ryan and Trauer also consider Csikszentmiahlyi's theory of 'flow' to apply, in the sense that 'serous competitors' need to have their competence challenged and might be disappointed if the competition is not at a high level.

The above research note clearly demonstrates how involvement influences event behaviour, although the researchers looked at only one type of event experience. In the following study a running event was examined, and it is one of the few cross-cultural studies of event motivation.

Research Note

Funk, D., and Bruun, T. (2007). The role of socio-psychological and culture-education motives in marketing international sport tourism: A cross-cultural perspective. Tourism Management, 28(3): 805–819.

The authors conducted a survey among international runners at the 2005 Gold Coast (Australia) Marathon. Several well-tested scales were used: Personal Involvement Inventory, Strength of Motivation Scale, Attitude Towards Australia, Knowledge-Learning Scale, Cultural Experience Scale and Cultural Learning Inventory. 'The study found that participants, regardless of cultural background, had a positive attitude towards Australia, a high level of running involvement, and a strong desire to participate in organized running events.' (p. 10). Running was the primary travel motive, but Japanese runners in particular also wanted to learn about Australian and Australian culture (leisure activities, music and art, and lifestyle). The authors concluded that little is actually known about how sport tourists actually gain cultural experiences in the destination.

When it comes to other types of events, research has been very limited. For example, Lee and Back (2005) concluded in a review article that more attention has to be given to association-member decision processes regarding attendance at conventions: their meeting participation behaviour had been largely overlooked, with researchers more concerned about economic impacts and locational decisions for meetings.

We should expect that motivations to attend meetings and business-related events will be quite different from leisure motivation, specifically that extrinsic motives will often dominate. These extrinsic motives range from being required to attend (lack of choice), to seeking a rewards for attending (learning something useful, developing a personal or business network), all the way to a mix of extrinsic and intrinsic rewards (i.e., combining business and pleasure).

Personal and Interpersonal Factors

Sport, entertainment and business events are an integral part of many cultures. A person's cultural background can have a profound influence on their perceptions of need for, or their interest in certain types of planned events. In some societies individuals are encouraged to think in terms of hedonistic consumption, leading to event 'consumption', but in others the collective will or religious/political doctrine generates a quite different pattern of socially acceptable behaviour.

There are many common reasons for attending cultural celebrations, including entertainment, spectacle and social, but we also need to focus on the cultural antecedents. For traditional events, people are expected to participate and even organize them because of the cultural norms existing in their communities.

How much does social obligation impact on attendance and participation in cultural celebrations? Some take on the status of institutions, thereby attracting volunteers who gain prestige or social standing. Buying tickets to some arts festivals might be considered the thing to do if one is in the higher social classes, while travelling to the annual Wagnerian opera festival in Bayreuth, Germany might be considered both a pilgrimage and a chance to meet the European elite.

Lifestyle is in part a social construct, dependent on others as reference points and participants. Peers are an especially important element in events that have sub-cultural dimensions, including cultural celebrations and sports.

Expectations

Needs and motives give rise to expectations that certain behaviours will yield desired benefits, and this is the essence of the 'theory of planned behaviour'. Expectations are also shaped by communications (advertising and image-making) on the part of events, and particularly by word-of-mouth recommendations or expressed opinions from valued reference groups.

The 'travel career trajectory' is also applicable, as the more experience one has with events (either particular events or events in general), the more it will affect expectations. For example, marathoners will build up specific expectations of what the event should offer by way of challenge, services to runners and the nature of their own experience. The greater the involvement in, or commitment to a particular pursuit, the more it will shape expectations and future participation.

In SERVQUAL, expectations are measured against post-experience satisfaction, revealing specific perceived gaps in quality. However, many researchers do not think it is necessary to measure expectations in order to gain a valid evaluation of customer satisfaction.

Barriers and Constraints

All the antecedents we have considered act together to shape a person's desire and propensity for certain event experiences, but there are often constraints on our actions, especially time and money, and specific barriers to overcome. The next section deals with 'leisure constraint theory' applied to events. There is no comparable theory for extrinsically motivated event participation, but it is probable that a mix of intrinsic and extrinsic motivation applies to many business-event decisions.

Leisure Constraints Theory

Why do some people not participate in events? This question is vital in marketing, but there are also important theoretical considerations that get to the nature of motivation, benefits and the nature of the event experience. In Event Studies the challenge is to not only identify constraints on attendance but to examine how people overcome constraints to attend, and how that knowledge might affect both event planning and marketing. In the context of 'serious leisure' or frequent event participation by 'high-involvement' types, we should be studying how constraints are 'negotiated' over a lifetime.

The leisure researchers Crawford et al. (1991) identified three general categories of constraints to participation: 'structural', 'personal' and 'interpersonal'. They are not necessarily hierarchical, and might be interactive. Let's examine each of these in turn.

Structural Constraints

The first and foremost of these is accessibility, which stems from the location and timing of events of all kinds – they are simply not always available, convenient or known by all potential participants. All aspects of supply analysis come into play here, as does marketing and communication. For example, it has long been observed that there is a huge gap between tourists' interest in attending cultural events in other countries and actual participation. Why? Because they have imperfect knowledge of what's available, and are most likely to be in an area when the events are not held. This is also why we are so interested in the 'dedicated event tourist' who travels specifically because of events.

Time and cost are always structural constraints. On the one hand we need to identify who is left out of the arts, or sports, or any other type of event because they are unable to afford it or cannot make the necessary time. On the other hand, 'not enough time or money' are convenient excuses, and might often mean the person does not assign any priority to a given opportunity. The first is a constraint issue, the second pertains more to preferences.

Age and health are obvious factors to consider. In youth we cannot get about on our own, and until we have income we cannot do what we want. With advancing age and declining health (or at least specific health problems) interest and participation in many leisure and work-related events will likely decline. For events, there is a need to combine both life cycle and work/career evolutionary approaches.

Personal Constraints

These are individual psychological conditions, including personality and moods, that hold us back from participating. Some people are pre-disposed to social activities, others to introversion. Sometimes we want to mix, at other times we need to be left alone. This category is similar to our earlier discussion of personality, values, attitudes and lifestyle.

Risk perception, and tolerance for risk, enters into many leisure and travel decisions. Do we want to have a thrill if it means assuming personal risks, or can we afford to spend time and money on an event that might not satisfy us? How preferences are first formed for events or event experiences has not been researched, but for ongoing participation there are explanations within the concepts of 'serious leisure', 'recreation specialization', 'commitment' and 'involvement'.

Interpersonal Constraints

These constraints arise within social contexts, taking into account the influence of others. This might take the form of letting significant others make decisions for us, being influenced by peer pressure (e.g., fear of ridicule) or being subjected to discrimination. Social isolation is often a limitation, especially for certain types of events – after all, who wants to go to a party or celebration alone? On the other hand, events are often great places to meet people.

A lot of research has documented gender differences in travel, leisure and sport, but little of this has been applied to events. Also, more research on why people do not attend events is necessary, such as in the research note below.

Research Note

Miller, L., Jago, L., and Deery, M. (2004). Profiling the special event nonattendee: an initial investigation. Event Management, 8(3): 141–150.

A representative telephone interview sample of residents of Melbourne, Australia, was undertaken to examine why some people did not attend festivals or other special events in the city. Theoretical underpinning of the research came from leisure constraint research. Results highlighted that older age explained a lot of non-interest in events, and especially older widows were not going to events. Being single or having younger children at home was positively associated with attending events. Full-time employment resulted in greater participation than part-time work. The fact that demographic variables explained attendance seems to be in contradiction to findings of festival-motivation research, but there are theoretical differences between motivation and attendance/ non-attendance.

Specific identified barriers included health, lack of time, perceptions of crowding and accessibility concerns, while a general lack of interest was the biggest reason given. The authors suggested that future research try to determine if a lack of interest in events is absolute, related to life-stage, or a result of situational constraints. Finally, it is worth noting that only 13% of respondents had NOT attended an event in the past 5 years.

Constraint Negotiation

Because constraints almost always exist, how do people who do participate or attend events overcome them? 'Negotiation' of constraints is the individual process of finding ways to do what we want to do. If we really want to attend a concert, how do we get the money, make the time, find someone to go with, book the tickets, etc.?

Jackson et al. (1992) discussed generic strategies for negotiating constraints. 'Cognitive' strategies are the internal, psychological ways we deal with constraints. For example, the theory of 'cognitive dissonance' can be applied by suggesting that if we cannot attend a concert because of high costs we will devalue the artist or type of music and do something else that we perceive to provide equal benefits. In this sense, when people say they do not like certain types of event, they might mean they cannot afford them. We all want to feel good about the choices we make, even if they were influenced by constraints.

'Behavioural' strategies include better time management, learning new skills, earning more money or modifying our routines in order to do what we want to do. Some people turn leisure into work, or vice versa. For 'serious leisure' one generally has to acquire knowledge to get the most out of the experience, and this applies to many volunteers at events. In order to think of oneself as an expert or connoisseur, say for the purpose of getting the most from a wine festival, advanced wine knowledge is essential. Similarly, to really be satisfied with your performance at the next Masters Games or X Games, you need to advance your skills through training and competition. To even compete in many sport events you have to qualify through lower-level competitions.

'Time management' is something we all try to improve, particularly in an age when a majority of people complain about time pressures, or lack of time to get active. 'Multi-tasking' (or 'pluriactivity') is the norm for most students, working people and home-makers. Mannell and Zuzanek (1991) reported that even retired seniors felt that a lack of time was a serious leisure constraint.

Setting priorities is the key. Generally, when respondents to a survey say they did not do something because of time or money constraints, they are probably truthful in a general sense. But this common response might very well be hiding a conscious or sub-conscious prioritization, so they really mean 'attending the event is not high enough on my current list of priorities to justify making the effort or paying the price.' So the researcher will have to dig deeper.

It seems paradoxical, but the most constrained people sometimes are the most active! How do they manage to engage in preferred leisure pursuits when others give up? The fact is that many people find innovative ways to overcome or negotiate through constraints (see Hinch et al., 2006, for a discussion and references).

The concepts of 'ego-involvement' and 'serious leisure' are very relevant here (see the discussion by Jones and Green, 2006) because those committed to certain leisure pursuits (e.g., long-distance running has been studied by McGehee et al., 2003) are more likely to overcome constraints, to persevere, in order to develop a 'career' of participation. 'Careers', in this context, include stages of achievement or reward, so that progress can be measured by the participant. This certainly seems to apply in amateur athletics where participation in the sport inevitably involves travel to events, and the setting of performance and destination goals.

Events for participation sports tend to generate 'travel careers', simply because there is a hierarchy of events in terms of prestige, desirability or qualification. For example, marathoners want to get into the top races, especially Boston. Most sports allow for and encourage competition at local, regional, national and international levels. This career-formation process definitely applies to other types of event, but the phenomenon has not yet been studied.

What about exhibitions and conferences? Is it not true that within every trade, profession or scientific field there is a geographical hierarchy of events as well as globally prestigious events? Experience with minor, local events, might lead to future participation at a higher level, involving greater commitment of time and money.

Thought Experiment

In order to attend an event or do something else you really wanted to, what have you changed or sacrificed? Is the benefit you get from an experience equal to what you sacrificed in order to be able to do it? What if there was no sacrifice or change required, what was the value of the experience in that case? (Did your parents ever tell that something is worth having only if you must work or make a sacrifice in order to get it? In the world of consumerism, is it not an adage that if it's 'free' it isn't worth doing or having?)

Setting Affordances

Pertinent to Event Studies, 'setting affordances' are those objective characteristics of the venue or setting that make certain actions and behaviours possible. For example, an attractive, spacious function room presents many social possibilities to dinner guests, but without wheelchair accessibility some people cannot enter. 'Affordance' is also a concept rooted in cognition and environmental psychology, placing the emphasis on 'perceived affordances'. Regardless of the venue manager's or event producer's intentions, people's perception of what is possible and what is a barrier, can differ greatly.

Decision-Making

Negotiation of constraints is both a background antecedent and a key part of specific decision-making processes. Then it is necessary to study how people search for and use information, especially because events are very time-sensitive opportunities. As well, in the context of economic 'demand' for events, we have to consider their 'attractiveness', the possibility of substitute experiences (including competition) and whether or not people are loyal to certain events.

Information Search and Use

An important consideration is whether the decision is 'routine' or 'unique'. For some sport events and concert series a consumer can buy season's tickets, or multi-day passes, thereby necessitating one big purchase decision – but there will still be a decision required for attending each and every game. Loyal festival fans can also return year after year, in which case most of the same variables enter into the decision. When decision-making becomes 'routine', the person does not need a lot of information (or perceives this to be true), takes less time and already has a predisposition.

Most event opportunities are likely to be 'unique' decision-making episodes, especially when a purchase decision is required. In these cases the consumer needs lots of information and might take a lot of time obtaining it. Part of the appeal of modern Internet marketing is that the time component can be reduced substantially, and research has found that Internet shoppers tend to use only a few sites, thereby limiting their time expenditure. The risk factor also has to be considered because every new decision to attend or participate in an event poses risks such as wasted time and money, bad experiences, and health and safety concerns.

The ensuing research note again deals with involvement and its links to participation in events, including constraints and loyalty, but also specifically addresses information needs.

Research Note

McGehee, N., Yoon, Y., and Cardenas, D. (2003). Involvement and travel for recreational runners in North Carolina. Journal of Sport Management, 17(3): 305–324.

These researchers determined that highly involved recreational runners travelled more on overnight trips to participate in events, compared to the medium-involved, using a uni-dimensional ego involvement scale. This confirmed the well-established proposition that greater involvement results in higher levels of participation, and for runners this means participation in competitive events. Although they found that runners did not attend all the races they would have liked, owing to a number of constraints such as family obligations, they did not examine race characteristics or destination choices. Interestingly, highly involved runners also participated in more races in their own communities.

An important implication drawn by the researchers from the general literature is that highly involved people seek and process information differently, particularly leading to brand loyalty. The authors recommended that race organizers provide to the highly involved as much information as possible about the race and race location; information on travel-related amenities must be combined with race information. Once attracted, the authors suggested that highly involved recreational runners could become repeat visitors, assuming they had a good, overall race and destination experience.

Demand

'Demand' is often equated with how many people will come to an event, or pay for it. More correctly, in economic terms, it is a function of the relationship between price and the quantity 'demanded' for an event in particular circumstances. For each price the demand relationship tells the quantity the buyers want to buy at that corresponding price.

Consider other related factors. Usually price is a monetary cost, as in how much an admission ticket costs, but you might also want to put a value on the consumer's time and energy expended, especially if travel is involved. What about 'free' events? For these it is common to measure demand in terms of attendance, but organizers have to be cautious about interpreting this. Many people might not pay anything for an event that is currently free. Research on 'willingness to pay' is then required.

Attractiveness of the Event

A related concept is 'attractiveness'. This means the 'drawing power' or 'pull' of an event, both its general appeal (generic benefits) and its targeted benefits for specific needs and interests. In the context of economic 'demand', attractiveness could be equated with 'market potential' and measured by 'penetration rates'. That is, within a given market area, how many purchases can be expected, expressed as a percentage of the population? (If half the people come twice, that is considered to be 100%.) Different market areas also have to be considered, such as local, regional, national and international zones.

As an example of 'attractiveness' or 'drawing power', note how Runners' World Magazine ranked the top ten marathons (see: www.runnersworld.co.uk), all of which are in world-class cities: London, Chicago, Berlin, New York, Boston, Stockholm, Paris, Honolulu, Amsterdam and Rotterdam. What were the criteria? They favoured the point of view of ordinary, not elite runners, and scored them according to beauty, atmosphere and speed. In describing the top ten they mentioned the following attractiveness factors:

- A festive or party atmosphere; entertainment along the route; fireworks.
- The route (historic sites; flat and fast or highly challenging; interesting things like views, crossing bridges).
- Well-organized.
- Size (number of participants – either many and crowded or few and intimate; number of spectators).
- Age and prestige (especially Boston).
- Exclusivity (qualifying times required).
- Climate (mild, sunny).

Substitution

Just about every leisure and travel pursuit can be substituted. We do not absolutely need to go to a specific destination or participate in a specific event and, (this is assuming free choice) there are always alternative ways to meet our leisure needs. Thinking again of the theory of 'cognitive dissonance', we can easily convince ourselves that one form of music appreciation, or sport, or hobby is as good as another, even if we were influenced by constraints.

If extrinsic motivations to attend an event apply, substitution takes on a different meaning. We might be able to learn what we need to know from different trade shows, or meet the necessary contacts at different conventions, but these choices are less common than in the leisure realm. Many event attendees go to specific events because it is the only one, or the best one to satisfy their purposes.

The theory of 'leisure substitution' suggests that if a person cannot do one thing, he or she will chose another that provides similar psychological experiences, satisfactions and benefits (Brunson and Shelby, 1993). This appears to be very true for primarily social experiences where the activity, setting or event is of secondary concern. Events offering 'targeted benefits' for highly involved persons are less substitutable than those offering only 'generic benefits'.

Decision to Attend or Participate

Wanting to attend, even planning to, is quite different from going to an event. At some point commitment is made, perhaps money spent on travel or tickets, but something might still intervene to prevent attendance. Researchers therefore seek to discover the links between levels of awareness, interest in attending, forming a specific intention to go and actual attendance.

How are decisions made to attend or travel to events, and what factors are considered? Consider all the context and choices we have to understand:

(a) 'Consumers' decide to spend money on a concert ticket or sport event (Go alone or with others? Which day and hour, if there are choices? Is overnight travel necessary or desirable? What seat, depending on availability? How much can I afford to/want to pay?).
(b) 'Guests' decide whether or not to accept an invitation to a party, wedding or company function (What's in it for me? Who else is going? Who will be offended if I do not go? What will I wear? Was it fun last time?).
(c) 'Volunteers' decide if they will be part of the community festival (Can anyone take my place? Will I be rewarded? How much time is required? Am I skilled enough?).

Decision-making occurs in stages, with feedback called 'post-purchase evaluation'. There is an awareness and opinion-forming stage, which might be combined with information gathering (even if its no more than asking for someone's advice), during which the consumer forms an intent, rejects the opportunity or waffles indecisively.

Loyalty versus Novelty Seeking

Loyalty in the events sector is a tricky concept – it is not at all similar to being loyal to a car brand or a favourite restaurant. For one thing, except for professional sports and regular theatrical productions, most events are unique opportunities. Numerous event-related decisions are never exactly repeated. As well, it is known that many people engage in novelty seeking in travel and leisure, generally preferring something new each time a decision is made.

But event loyalty does exist in some forms, as indicated by the earlier research note which showed how highly involved runners could become loyal to events. Loyalty to periodic conferences exists, both because of the business or professional advantages and the enjoyment of socializing with friends who always meet there. Many people do go to the same festivals year after year, especially those that have become traditions in their home communities. Hypothetically, event loyalty is likely to result from obtaining specific benefits, especially those related to special interests. Loyalty might also be a lifestyle factor stemming from events that fit one's work-life and social calendar.

Post-experience Evaluation and Feedback

Satisfaction, Meanings and Transformation

Was the event experience as expected? Was it merely satisfactory or in some way exceptional, even surprisingly pleasant? Presumably people who have disappointing event experiences are less likely to become loyal or to develop an event career. However, novelty seekers might very well seek out new events regardless of the quality of a given event, simply because they get easily bored or constantly need new experiences. By contrast, do loyal event-goers necessarily have a low level of need for novelty?

If events are memorable, assigned profound personal and social meanings, or somehow transform the individual, then surely this will encourage loyalty or development of an event career? That is a hypothesis to be tested. The 'event careerist' might be constantly engaged in evaluation and planning for new events. One leads to another, until some point of diminishing returns is reached (i.e., 'satiation') or certain constraints (perhaps health) become insurmountable.

Creating memorable, transforming event experiences is the goal of many event producers, and if people really do enjoy and recollect events they are more likely to return or seek out comparable experiences. As noted by Gibson (2005), below, nostalgia can be an important motivator.

Research Note

Gibson, H. (2005). Understanding sport tourism experiences. In: J. Higham (ed.), Sport Tourism Destinations: Issues, Opportunities and Analysis. Oxford: Elsevier.

According to Gibson, in this review, some research evidence suggests that sport tourism fans and participants value ritual and nostalgia. As sport tourists enter the 'liminoid' space/time (based on Turner's theory of ritual process) formed by an event or trip, they are able to put aside normal behaviour and enjoy a new, often social experience, free from norms and values that govern everyday work and home life. Competition-related rituals, shared with a like-minded group of peers, define these experiences and give rise to considerable nostalgia about those experiences. The event itself can be merely a facilitator of these shared, valued memories. Repeat sport tourism behaviour might often be motivated by attempts to re-create past, shared experiences. Gibson also referred to involvement and specialization theories to help explain motivation and travel behaviour.

Future Intentions

Intentions can be measured, and in the context of the 'theory of planned behaviour' a specific intent to attend an event is a very good measure of demand. In fact, it is commonly used in attendance forecasting for major events, following the logic that within specific markets (geographically, or otherwise segmented) awareness has to build, then interest and finally clear intent to travel or make the purchase.

This brings us full circle in the model, stressing that antecedents include the influence of previous experience. What is not shown are the affects of other kinds of experience on event-related behaviour. Also, broader forces are at work, including a person's experiences with entertainment, sport or business in general. At what point do events become part of the opportunities people are willing to consider? How is a festival substitutable with all other forms of entertainment? There is so much to study!

Chapter Summary

In this chapter a model was illustrated to shape discussion of all the main factors considered in order to understand decisions and choices leading to event attendance. This is partly the realm of psychology and consumer research, but also the economics of supply and demand, and of cultural and social forces. The discussion started with personal factors, specifically personality, values, attitudes and lifestyle. Then needs, motivations and motives were examined, including the travel career trajectory and how it can help explain event-related behaviour.

'Intrinsic' motivation is at the heart of leisure theory, and can be applied to many events, but there is a need for more research and theory on 'extrinsic' motivation in the event sector. An argument was made that people, and society, 'need' planned events. Some of the motivational research that has been done on events was summarized. Many researchers have looked at festivals, confirming the 'seeking-escaping' theory of leisure and travel motivation. Sport motives have been examined frequently, but not related to event careers. Motives for attending other types of events have been studied much less.

'Leisure constraint theory' was discussed at length, noting the different types of barriers and constraints acting against event attendance, but also considering how people can negotiate through constraints. This is vital in decision-making and exercising choices. Other factors of importance include information seeking, event 'attractiveness' and 'substitution'.

Completing the model are considerations of satisfaction, meanings and recollection of events, all of which might lead to loyalty (versus the competing force of novelty seeking) or help develop travel and event careers. The concepts of ego involvement, commitment, serious leisure and recreation specialization all apply here. 'Nostalgia' can also have an important influence on future behaviour.

The antecedents and choices framework is not a predictive model, as there are too many variables involved to know how individuals or groups will act under different circumstances. However, continued research on event-related demand and behaviour will add greatly to our understanding, and to our ability to make reasonable forecasts.

Study Questions

- Explain how 'personality', 'values', 'attitudes' and 'lifestyle' relate to interest in, and demand for event experiences.
- What are basic human 'needs', and how do they link to 'motivation'?
- Explain the 'travel career trajectory' and show how it can be adapted to understanding the antecedents to attending planned events.
- How important are 'seeking' versus 'escaping' motivations in explaining event attendance? What have researchers found that confirms or rejects this theory when applied to events?
- Who needs planned events? Why?
- How are 'expectations' formed? Consider post-event evaluation.
- Explain 'leisure constraint theory' and how it applies to events. Differentiate between the main types of 'constraints', and give event-specific examples.
- Use the concepts of 'serious leisure', 'commitment', 'ego involvement' and 'recreation specialization' to help explain how people develop event careers and negotiate constraints.
- What is 'demand' for events? How are 'attractiveness' and 'substitution' related to demand?
- What factors help explain the differences between 'loyalty' and 'novelty seeking' with regard to event behaviour? Where does 'nostalgia' fit in?

Further Reading

Decrop, A. (2006). *Vacation Decision Making*. Wallingford: CABI.

Gibson, H. (ed.) (2006). *Sport Tourism: Concepts and Theories*. London: Routledge.

Jackson, E. (ed.) (2005). *Constraints to Leisure. State College*. PA: Venture Publishing.

Li, R., and Petrick, J. (2006). A review of festival and event motivation studies. *Event Management*, 9(4): 239–245.

Pearce, P. (2005). *Tourist Behaviour: Themes and Conceptual Schemas*. Clevedon: Channel View.

Chapter 10

Management of Events

Learning Objectives

- Be able to use foundation theories and methods in studying the following event management functions:
  - Leadership (including organizational culture).
  - Organizational and inter-organizational behaviour (including organizational structure, co-ordination and stakeholder management).
  - Planning (strategic, project, business) and decision-making.
  - Operations and logistics (including service quality management).
  - Human resources (including volunteer management).
  - Financial management and control (including sponsorship).
  - Marketing and communications.
  - Risk, health and safety.
  - Research, evaluation and information systems.

This is not a chapter on how to plan and manage events, but on what we need to know to study the management of events. Management is a broad field, encompassing business, not-for-profit and public administration. Management research for events has been spotty, and although many important topics receive substantial attention, there are outstanding knowledge gaps.

A very positive trend has been the expansion of event-specific management texts, most of which are cited in this chapter. Students and practitioners now have both overview books covering all of event management and event tourism, and function-specific books for details. Some are written by practitioners, and some by academics, so they vary in the balance of theory and practical applications.

Most of the management functions are discussed in this chapter, however programming and design have already been covered. There is no correct place to start, as all the management functions are crucial, but I have elected to start with leadership, including a discussion of event founders and organizational culture. For each management function a figure is provided to summarize major themes or topics covered, an indication of the disciplinary foundations for theory and methods, and unique issues or applications for events.

Leadership, Founders and Organizational Culture

A 'leader' is someone who provides direction, or examples that others follow. Leadership is the pivotal role of managers (Mintzberg, 1994) and of boards of directors. Of course, in many small organizations and informal events everyone chips in as needed, in which case leadership is somewhat of a collective process (Figure 10.1).

Leadership, founders, organizational culture	Foundations	Unique issues or applications for events
• Leadership roles and styles • Power • Organizational culture • Entrepreneurship • Intrapreneurship	• Psychology (personality) • Sociology and anthropology (culture; social groups) • Economics (theories of the firm)	• Are event founders and leaders unique? • Balancing creativity with managerial competence • Business and social entrepreneurship

Figure 10.1 Leadership, founders and organizational culture.

Leadership in events requires the setting of a vision, developing strategies and goals, and inspiring everyone to work together towards those goals. Oakley and Krug (1991) believed that creative leaders empower their workers, but also take responsibility for all the decisions made by workers; they focus on goals and results, are both current and future oriented.

Group leadership, where no-one dominates and all decisions are taken democratically, is an alternative approach, but difficult to implement – especially in projects where rapid decision-making is necessary. Events typically require both artistic and management leadership. An over-emphasis on business might stifle artistic innovation, whereas an over-emphasis on creativity might compromise the event's financial viability.

Leadership ability is essential for owners and founders of events, but leadership skills come to the fore, and have to be learned, as workers become supervisors and progress to managers. Technical skills and hands-on operations have to give way to people-skills such as motivating and problem solving. At the highest management levels, conceptual knowledge (theory) is needed, as well as the ability to formulate vision, goals and strategies, alongside research and evaluation skills.

'Power' and leadership go together. Owners typically have the legal power to compel obedience, just as in the military. Boards of Directors can use legal power to enforce their policies. Managers often have 'legitimate' power (Mintzberg, 1983) by virtue of their position to direct or coerce the actions of subordinates. Other sources of power identified by Mintzberg include 'reward power' (the ability to bestow or withhold tangible and intangible rewards), 'expert power' (people follow because of superior knowledge or ability), 'information power' (obtained through control of vital information) and 'referent power' (stemming from loyalty and admiration).

Leadership Styles and Roles

Boella (1992) discussed generic leadership styles, many of which are found but have not been studied within the events context. They include charismatic, autocratic, democratic, bureaucratic, inspirational, artistic, technocratic, entrepreneurial and visionary. While some managers seek to lead through a vision and setting a good example, others merely give orders. What is most effective in any given event setting is difficult to say, and deserves serious research. Van der Wagen (2006: 152) argued that leadership for events must be more flexible than in a typical business setting, sometimes being autocratic, as in a crisis, and at other times collaborative and appreciative.

Leadership Roles

For the Sydney Summer Olympic Games of 2000 a graphical leadership model was developed which placed the various leadership roles in a circle to emphasize the need for a non-liner approach (see Van der Wagen, 2006). The three most important roles were thought to be 'energizing', 'appreciating' and 'managing time and stress' (this latter one is not usually considered in management texts). The more usual roles of planning, co-ordinating, controlling, directing, decision-making and informing were also included. 'Energising' (p. 151 in Van der Wagen, 2006) was thought to be essential in celebrations, to create and sustain the right atmosphere for guests, staff and volunteers. The longer the time-frame, the more difficult it is to keep everyone's energy levels high.

Can Leaders be Trained?

Goldblatt (2004) suggested that event leaders need to have the qualities of integrity, confidence, persistence, collaboration, problem solving, communication skills and vision. Locke (1991) identified personality traits found in successful leaders, but many people reject the notion that leaders (or entrepreneurs) are born, or that certain traits lead to success.

Van der Wagen (2006: 222) describes an approach to event leadership training that includes imparting knowledge about the event, the organization, the workforce/ volunteers and their tasks. Potential leaders also engage in self-analysis of their own attributes and potential strengths or deficiencies. Specific advice from experienced event leaders can help to develop decision-making ability and lead to desirable behaviour.

The Event Founder as Leader

How do events get started? Somebody, or a group, has to take the initiative, and this leadership can continue well into the lifespan of the event and its organization. One of the leadership styles is entrepreneurial, and we need to explore this in more detail because of its importance in both business and the other management environments.

Entrepreneurs (Social and Private)

The term 'entrepreneur' is not easy to define, and there are two major schools of thought about entrepreneurship: that it is a personally trait held by rather unique persons; or that it is one or more actions that can be observed and measured. Furthermore, entrepreneurship can apply to personal business ventures or to social situations.

The 'personality trait theory' suggests that entrepreneurs are born, not made. Some people are compelled (or have an inborn propensity) to create businesses or events, seek out opportunities that others ignore (especially in terms of finding a niche in the marketplace), pull together resources (often through personal networking), take personal risks and (but not necessarily) create personal wealth. Innovation or creativity is often thought to be inherent in entrepreneurs, and this is certainly evident among those who establish festivals and other events.

Being one's own boss, or wanting to take a hands-on approach to work, is also a personality trait clearly associated with people who start up new businesses or events.

Entrepreneurs are not discouraged by failures, and often bounce back from a failure to try again. 'Serial entrepreneurs' keep starting new ventures in a rather restless fashion which leads some observers to think of them as socially dysfunctional or psychologically disturbed.

If the motivations driving entrepreneurs are mostly personal, or connected to family values and goals, it is clearly within the realm of business and microeconomics. But there is little doubt that 'social entrepreneurs' are very active in the arts, leading to establishment of many not-for-profit festivals and events. A 'social entrepreneur' might also work within governmental or not-for-profit organizations to create profits (or profitable events) to be used for social projects. Cause-related events can be created this way.

'New venture' creation is the starting point for discussing entrepreneurship as observable activity. Starting up an event could be motivated by the desire for profit, or social good. Risks are inherent in this process, especially when it comes to acquiring and spending one's own and other people's money. Reputations are also at stake. The entrepreneur's personal network can be vital at this start-up stage and in the subsequent years when vital support and resources have to be sustained through effective stakeholder management.

Intrapreneurship
Within organizations 'intrapreneurship' can be a valuable process, but it usually has to be fostered. Can a whole organization, or a group within, really behave as if they were private entrepreneurs? The object would be to encourage innovation in particular, hopefully leading to higher profits or other forms of corporate effectiveness. In this context it is possible to establish new events, or bid on them, within a government or tourist agency. Another application would be within an event production company that wants to stay ahead of the competition, or within a large corporation that sponsors or produces its own events.

Often it is necessary to set up specific intrapreneurial units to achieve these corporate goals, and such units need leadership. By nature, persons attracted to government and corporate employment might be lacking in those entrepreneurial traits necessary for innovation. Or at least they might lack experience in new venture creation. In such cases there is a serious risk of creating a culture clash!

Organizational Culture

Culture in general is based on shared beliefs, values, practices or attitudes, and it is a concept of importance to companies and other organizations. Schein (1985) defined organizational culture as:

> *A pattern of shared basic assumptions that the group learned as it solved its problems of external adaptation and internal integration, that has worked well enough to be considered valid and, therefore, to be taught to new members as the correct way you perceive, think, and feel in relation to those problems.*

In a strong cultural context everyone works together towards common goals because they share the vision and underlying values of the organization. This is where event founders have the greatest influence, in establishing the 'core values', but this unity of purpose can fade with time. In other organizations, recruitment, indoctrination and compulsory conformity to norms ensures that values are preserved, but at the cost of individual choice and expression. In both situations, if everyone thinks the same way – called 'groupthink' – there is a serious risk that innovation will be stifled.

According to Schein an observer can assess organizational culture by first identifying superficial but 'tangible attributes' such as facilities, rewards, dress and interactions.

The 'professed culture' of an organization is reflected in its mission statements, codes of conduct, public statements and the expressed values and attitudes of members. At the third and deepest level are an organization's 'tacit or unseen assumptions'. They can be unspoken rules, guiding behaviour and decisions in a taken-for-granted manner. The researcher or member might have to spend a lot of time within an organization to come to any conclusion about its deepest cultural values.

Hofstede (1980) demonstrated that there are national and regional cultural groupings that affect the behaviour of organizations. These five characteristics of culture can be influential in all organizations:

- 'Power distance' – the degree to which a society expects that some individuals wield larger amounts of power than others.
- 'Uncertainty avoidance' reflects the extent to which a society accepts uncertainty and risk; this is associated with entrepreneurship.
- 'Individualism versus collectivism' refers to the extent to which people are expected to act on their own versus being a loyal group member.
- 'Masculinity versus femininity' – male values supposedly include competitiveness, assertiveness, ambition and the accumulation of wealth and material possessions.
- 'Long versus short-term orientation' – describes the importance attached to the future (fostering stewardship and sustainable development) versus immediate profit or gratification.

There is no doubt that organizations evolve in terms of their culture, and this affects other management functions in profound ways. Getz (1993a) observed that festival organizations exhibited life-cycle dynamics, and that festival founders did shape their culture. Several festivals in Calgary were seen to have experienced cultural crises, such as changes in strategic direction which occurred when founders were replaced by newcomers.

O'Toole and Mikolaitis (2002) emphasized the importance of understanding culture when producing corporate events. Such events have to 'fit' in terms of company values, goals, politics and style. But despite the importance of culture within mainstream management theory and practice, there have few event-related studies published that even mention the concept.

Strategic Event Creation and Public Policy

Perhaps the most significant aspect of modern planned events is their elevation from the private, community and institutional domains to a formal incorporation into the public policy domain. Events of all kinds are being created, and bid on, to meet diverse, strategic goals of society. This has several important implications related to leadership, culture and management. First, those who plan and produce events are often dealing with a single client but are held accountable to very wide group of stakeholders. This fact also applies to many events produced for corporations and non-profit societies.

Resources utilized by events are often heavily competed for, by groups with many legitimate and appealing claims about their cultural, social, economic or environmental benefits. Therefore, the allocation of public resources (including subsidies) to events generally requires their organizers and producers to explicitly justify their public benefits.

Those who produce events that are at least partially in the public domain have a far greater planning, control and evaluation challenge than those who produce small, private events. Professionalism and the credentialing of event managers are increasingly demanded by funding agencies because of the need for open, public accountability and for liability reasons. Finally, the sustainability of periodic events is of public interest and directly linked to specific policies on funding, regulations, subsidies, facility development, etc.

The following research note from Quinn illustrates aspects of festival leadership, politics, culture and evolution.

Research Note

Quinn, B. (2006). Problematising 'festival tourism': arts festivals and sustainable development in Ireland.' Journal of Sustainable Tourism, 14(3): 288–306.

Qualitative and longitudinal research was conducted on the Wexford Festival Opera and Galway Arts Festival through archival research, interviews, resident and visitor questionnaires. In terms of their management, Quinn found that festivals tend to 'emerge as bottom-up enterprises, small in size, local in scale and initially, heavily dependent on dedicated volunteers.' Wexford's emerged from the city's social and economic elite, but they were careful to involve a broad section of the community. 'Politicians lobbied for resources, business people sought financial support from local businesses and the church leaders praised the festival in their Sunday sermons' (p. 296). Festival relationships with the Arts Council of Ireland, state tourism agency, national media and commercial sponsors 'have all placed increasing pressure on the festival organisations to view the arts through economic lenses'(p. 297). Tourism has been especially important for Wexford in terms of paying audiences and protection from arts critics. Being a successful tourist attraction makes both Wexford and Galway festivals worthy of state support and corporate sponsorship (i.e., committed stakeholders).

Organizational and Inter-organizational Behaviour

Organizations are social groups, and therefore sociology and social-psychology have made substantial theoretical contributions to our understanding of how they function and change. Microeconomics is also relevant, pertaining especially to how firms acquire and utilize resources. In the research literature little attention has been paid to event organizations, although some progress has been made in examining events in the context of collaboration and stakeholder management, and regarding human resources and especially volunteers (Figure 10.2).

Organizational & inter-organizational behaviour	Foundations	Unique event issues or applications
• Ownership • Governance • Organizational structures • Open-system diagnostics • Organizational quality • Evolutionary stages • Bureaucratization • Institutionalization • The learning organization • Inter-organizational relationships (stakeholders)	• Sociology and social psychology (social groups and networks) • Economics (theories of the firm)	• How are public, for-profit and not-for-profit events different? • Governance and management challenges facing the volunteer event organization • Special challenges facing one-time and pulsating events

Figure 10.2 Organizational and inter-organizational behaviour.

Ownership, Governance and Organizational Structure

There are three generic ownership, or legal models found in the events world: (1) private, for-profit companies that produce events; (2) government agencies (such as parks and recreation, sport or arts and culture) that produce or facilitate events and (3) the large not-for-profit sector that includes clubs, charities and event-specific organizations like festival societies.

There has been no research published on the relative advantages or problems associated with these ownership types, or the business models they follow to provide their 'products' and 'services'. One important question to be addressed is whether or not they are substitutable. For example, in China and other countries local authorities are the dominant producers of festivals and other events. Can they create private or not-for-profit organizations to take over from the public sector? Clearly legal and cultural constraints exists, especially in societies without a strong volunteering or entrepreneurial tradition. And how is a festival or event different, better, or more sustainable if it is produced by one of these forms of organization? From a tourism or economic development perspective, is it better to work with public-sector events or the other types?

'Governance' is a big issue. In for-profit companies there are owners and employees, so the question of who runs the business is generally clear. In government agencies there can be a confusing and stifling bureaucracy to deal with. Within not-for-profit societies, the relationships between boards of directors and professional staff have to be sorted out. Who sits on the board is a major issue, especially with regard to the pros and cons of involving key stakeholders. In all-volunteer events, governance and coordination present special challenges, and the organizations can be faced with dissenting opinions within or take-over attempts by organized, external interest groups.

This entire area of organizational structure and coordination (both internal and external) has largely been untouched by event researchers, although plenty of advice is available through professional associations and books written by experts. It ties closely to other topics covered in this chapter, including decision-making and planning. The second level of concern is organizational structure, which has a direct bearing on stakeholder relationships, internal coordination and control. A number of typical structures are illustrated and discussed in Getz (2005), including single and multi-organizational structures. Festivals are often produced by clubs, internally, and by stand-alone not-for-profit societies, but it is also common to find different organizations cooperating to produce events. As well, sport events are frequently produced through formal links between governing bodies and local organizing committees.

Open-System Theory

No organization can exist independent of its environment, indeed it has to be 'open' to obtain resources. Its impacts (especially for events) are also felt by the community and environment, giving rise to many stakeholder claims. There is a 'general environment' in which global forces have to be considered through environmental and future scanning, and a 'community context' which includes most event stakeholders and the origin of most 'inputs' (information, support and resources). The 'internal environment' is the organization that produces the event, and all its management systems.

In this conceptualization, the event (its theme, programme, facilitated experiences) is a 'transforming process' intended to achieve specific desired outcomes. There can also be unintended 'outcomes' and 'externalities' like pollution that are not normally accounted for by the event organizers. However, multiple stakeholders will evaluate the event and its organization, and this process is labelled 'external evaluation'. The 'internal evaluation' process is the task of managers or owners who have to determine if they are meeting their goals (i.e., their effectiveness) and how efficiently they are utilizing their resources. Evaluation and feedback should influence future decision-making through strategic planning.

'Open-system diagnostics' involves using this model to identify problems and to improve both efficiency and effectiveness. 'Effectiveness' means the degree to which goals are obtained or the organization fulfils its mandate. Use of the model helps in identifying how the mandate and goals are externally driven by various stakeholders and environmental forces, and how transforming processes are directed towards achieving those goals. Evaluation systems have to be directed towards identifying goal attainment, although the 'goal-free evaluation' approach sometimes has benefits. 'Efficiency' refers to how well resources are used to generate the desired outcomes. The model suggests ways to improve the flow and use of resources, to cut costs (such as heavy administration costs) and to evaluate outcomes achieved in terms of resources required (i.e., measures of costs and benefits).

Organizational Quality

Any discussion of event programme or service quality has to include the 'quality' of the organization producing the event. The people producing events have to demonstrate professionalism and competency, trustworthiness and reliability. One trend is to require or encourage event companies and suppliers to adhere to ISO 9000 or similar standards (see International Standards Organization), as implemented by the Western Australia Events Industry Association (Carlsen, 2000). The British Standards Institute (2006) standards for 'Sustainable Event Management' fall into this category as they lay out procedures for event organizations to follow in pursuit of a 'triple-bottom-line' approach to sustainability.

Policy on organizational quality is a direct reflection of culture and vision. It will have to cover organizational philosophy, ensure proper documentation in all the management systems, effectively engage all staff and volunteers, and take into account all outcomes. Bowdin and Church (2000) argued that quality programmes cost money, but the investment is quickly recovered by reducing waste and eliminating failures. Over time the costs of auditing and evaluation decline.

Evolution, Bureaucratization and Institutionalization

Organizations have to be created, as in the establishment of a legal corporation or not-for-profit society, or they evolve from informal organization. For example, many professionally managed festivals and events have evolved from club-produced events.

Once established there can be an evolution towards greater 'formality', emergence of leadership and increasing 'professionalization' (in terms of hiring professional staff and professional conduct) and 'bureaucratization' including formal committee systems and strategic planning (Katz, 1981).

Frisby and Getz (1989) modelled this hypothetical evolution for festivals, noting that at each evolutionary stage there was a risk of having to return to the previous stage owing to failure or loss of resources. They also suggested that in cities, with larger populations and presumably more resources to draw on, festivals were more likely to professionalize.

Richards and Ryan (2004) adapted the Frisby and Getz's (1989) model by suggesting three axes: (1) 'informal/grassroots resource base', (2) 'organizational age' and (3) 'organized public and private sector involvement'. They argued (p. 96) that '... being a grassroots event does not preclude the adoption of a formal or professional approach to event organization.' Professionalism, they said, can be externally imposed on an event organization.

In Schein's (1985) conceptualization of the evolution of organizational culture various crises are likely to occur as the organization evolves, linked to leadership changes and value conflicts, particularly as sub-cultures emerge. Richards and Ryan (2004), through their historical assessment of the evolution of the Aotearoa Traditional Maori Performing Arts Festival in New Zealand, agreed that various crises will accompany event maturation. In their case study the issues or crises stemmed from the need to achieve financial stability, addressing the festival's cultural orientation and significance, gender issues, the increasing roles of media and sponsors, the representations of groups and regions, and tensions between competitive and performative orientations.

Why do some events, like the Calgary Stampede (profiled in Getz, 1993b, 1997, 2005), become permanent institutions in their communities? Can all events aspire to this status, and should they? One meaning of the word 'institution' is that of '... constraints or rules that induce stability in human interaction' (Voss, 2001). These arise because societies face recurrent problems, so that when we call an organization an 'institution' we are saying that it exists to deal with a fundamental – or at least important – social need (including cultural and economic needs). Since not all people can be directly involved in creating institutions, a set of actors or stakeholders, has to decide – or establish through repeated interactions or interdependencies – the rules or the organizations to deal with major social problems. Stability in these institutions has direct benefit to the stakeholders, or society as a whole, and should ideally generate increased efficiency in resource use.

The study of institutions is very well established. Selznick (1957) distinguished between institutions as tools to accomplish specific tasks and institutions to which people formed commitments. Emile Durkheim (1978) argued that sociological analysis should discover the causes, mechanisms and effects of institutions on societal life. Essentially, institutions regularize social life, and may foster cooperation and increase efficiency. Applicable to many festivals, it can also be said that institutions are like 'public goods' in that all members of society may benefit from them, whether or not they contribute to their establishment and upkeep. Coleman (1988, 1990) believed that institutions are part of what is often called 'social capital'. An anthropological perspective (Sahlins, 1976) suggests that cultural institutions mainly serve symbolic purposes.

Another way of looking at institutions is through the lens of evolutionary game theory. Young (1998) showed that certain institutions arise as equilibria in games played by members of a population of agents who recurrently interact. This ties institutional theory directly to stakeholder and network theory. As well, since powerful agents or special interest groups might create and support institutions, there is a need to take a political science and welfarist approach to their study.

A central focus of the 'old' study of institutions is the evolving relationship between an organization and its environment, which of course includes all its stakeholder interactions. 'New institutionalism', according to Heimer (2001), is an outcome of organizational sociology. It focuses on the process (symbolic reasons are emphasized) by which a practice or structure is diffused, becomes a prerequisite for legitimacy (among key stakeholders), is taken for granted and expected.

By definition, therefore, an event that becomes an 'institution' exists with a specific mandate or purpose, is permanent, and fulfils an important social role or solves social problems. A community cannot do without its institutions, and when threatened they will receive strong support; if they disappear, another will have to be created to carry on their function. Very few events fit these criteria, yet recent research involving a survey of festivals in Sweden suggests that many festival managers actually believe their event to be an 'institution' (Andersson and Getz, 2007). Their research also provides insight on the process by which this might occur, with a key element being transition from an internal to an external orientation. Relationships with stakeholders will probably increase in number and complexity, and the most important of them can be internalized (i.e., given a directorship).

It appears that increasing dependency on committed stakeholders is a large part of becoming an institution. In other words, independence might have to be sacrificed for sustainability. The Stampede reflects his evolution, with the City of Calgary owning the land, having a permanent representative on the Stampede board, and assisting the Stampede in its ongoing development plans. Richards and Ryan (2004: 115) also concluded that the history of the Aotearoa Traditional Maori Performing Arts Festival '... illustrates that cultural festivals mirror many different dynamics and are places of discourse between different paradigms of traditional and evolving culture, between minority and majority groupings, between a need for independence and a dependency, usually on public authorities that might in other circumstances be seen as part of the majority-dominated structures.'

Another way to look at this institutionalization process is to think of what it means to become a 'hallmark event'. If the destination and event are co-branding, their images mutually reinforcing, this suggests institutional status.

The Learning Organization

How do organizations 'learn' and retain memory? Senge (1990: 3) said the 'learning organization' is one in which '… people continuously expand their capacity to create the results they truly desire, where new and expansive patterns of thinking are nurtured, where collective aspiration is set free, and where people are continually learning to learn together.' (Also see, Senge et al., 1994.) In part this is a reflection of organizational culture, and in part it can be facilitated through constant research, evaluation and reflection. The open-system model is a good starting point for structuring the learning process.

'Benchmarking' against other events is another way by which managers learn. To a degree, studying other events is both inevitable and good, but it can and does result in copying and standardization. Proper benchmarking looks at the ways successful organizations do things, in other words their processes or 'best practices'. Getz (1998a) studied the searching and sharing practices of festival organizers and classified them as being 'inward- or outward-looking organizations'. Searching was either formal or informal in nature, and varied a lot in terms of space (local through international), substance (comparisons with similar festivals versus all events) and theoretical (education) versus experiential (learning through visits and conversations).

One-Time versus Permanent Event Organizations

There are big differences between permanent event organizations, such as festival societies that produce annual events, and one-time organizations that have to be decommissioned when the event is over. Little attention has been paid to the one-time event organization from a theoretical or even a comparative perspective. Typically established for major sport events or world's fairs, the one-time event organization has to engage in project planning and apply a project management organizational model.

One of the unique aspects of permanent event organizations is their 'pulsating' nature (Hanlon and Cuskelly, 2002). They need a permanent, small core of volunteers and professionals, but must be able to substantially expand their staff and volunteer force to produce the event. This is examined later in the Human Resources section.

Inter-organizational Behaviour

The need for resources involves organizations with individuals (like customers) and other organizations. Theories of resource dependency, population ecology, collaboration, network and stakeholder theory (see Chapter 4) are powerful when trying to explain external relationships. Another look at stakeholder theory is warranted here, as some pertinent research has been completed regarding events.

Stakeholder Management

The article by Getz et al. (2007) described and classified external festival stakeholders based on case studies from Sweden and Calgary. Figure 10.3 shows the resulting conceptualization.

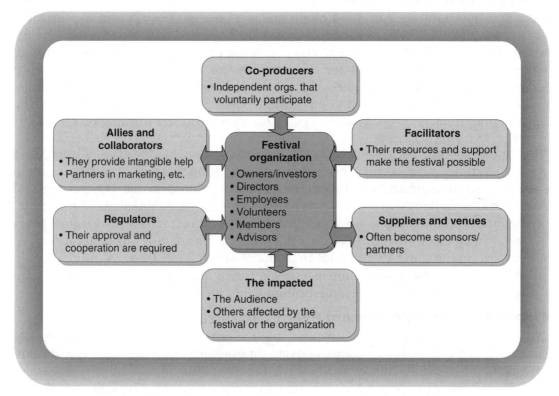

Figure 10.3   Major stakeholder types and roles in festival networks (*Source*: Getz, Andersson and Larson, 2007).

The various categories are not mutually exclusive, and indeed the research showed clearly that some stakeholders have multiple roles. For example, city government is often simultaneously a 'facilitator' (giving grants and other resources), 'co-producer' (sharing staff and venues), 'owner/controller' (being on the board of directors) and 'regulator', which can make its event-related policies confusing or contradictory.

'Suppliers and venues' are often brought into the festival organization as sponsors, as this is generally recognized as being a good strategy for reducing dependency and costs.

'Allies and collaborators' might include marketing partnerships with tourism or the collaborative work of professional and affinity groups. How these stakeholders wield power and negotiate the goals and strategies of the event can be referred to as a 'political market square' (Larson and Wikstrom, 2001; Larson, 2002).

Planning and Decision-Making

Planning is a future-oriented process in which organizations set goals and put in place actions to attain them. It is always political, with groups in society or within organizations competing for influence or resources. Although planning by nature should be a rational process, it is clear that decisions in the events sector are often made in an irrational manner (e.g., see Armstrong, 1985; Butler and Grigg, 1987; Bramwell, 1997) (Figure 10.4).

Planning and decision-making	Foundations	Unique event issues or applications
• Rationality versus irrationality • Heuristics • Incrementalism • Advocacy • Feasibility • Project planning • Strategic planning • Business planning	• Psychology (cognition and environmental) • Sociology (social groups and networks) • Mathematics and engineering (systems modelling)	• Events are projects • The need for event producers to think strategically, and to manage the organization like a business • High likelihood of organizational crises

Figure 10.4   Planning and decision-making.

Decision-Making

Are leaders and managers 'rational' when it comes to making decisions? Surely the whole emphasis on planning and research is intended to produce rational decisions that achieve goals, yet Bramwell (1997) concluded that for mega events there was little evidence of a rigorous application of the full planning cycle as advocated in planning texts.

Laybourn (2004) explored theory on decision-making and applied it to the events sector. She found that the generic literature supports the contention that decision-makers are not naturally rational! They tend to use simplifying short-cuts called 'heuristics'. In particular, potential negative impacts are commonly underestimated, which has serious implications for risk assessment and management at events. When people stand to gain from a decision they tend to be more cautious than when they stand to take a loss. And of course everyone notices when something goes wrong, whereas competency and success might be ignored.

Current decisions are strongly influenced by previous decisions, especially when a lot of money has been invested, leading to 'entrapment'. There is a natural tendency to want to recover 'sunk costs' (i.e., money already spent) and maximize return on investments made. This can help explain why risky decisions are made, and the frequent pursuit of losing courses of action, despite obvious and compelling arguments to the contrary. There are always costs of withdrawal to consider, but perhaps more important is 'losing face'.

Laybourn also emphasized that decision-making is affected by personality, perceptions, emotions and moods, social factors, experience, the cost of information, time constraints and gender. There are many constraints on perfect knowledge and perfect judgement, so people should be trained in effective decision-making. A variety of techniques can be used to aid decision-making, including the 'decision tree', or mathematical modelling as found in operations research and management science. But do event planners and managers use them?

Planning Theory

'Rational Planning' is always future oriented, involving a vision, the setting of goals, consideration of alternative courses of action and their potential consequences, the formulation and implementation of strategies and actions to realize goals, and continuous evaluation and feedback in order to improve the system. It is a process, continuously evolving and hopefully learning from past mistakes. Planning is always political, especially when public agencies or public money are involved, but even within organizations 'politics' (i.e., the resolution of competing claims and goals) is always a factor.

Not everyone believes in or practices rational planning (for general reviews of planning theory and practice see Mandelbaum et al. 1996; Sandercock, 1998; Campbell and Fainstein, 2003). 'Muddling through', and 'incrementalism', are alternative approaches to managing organizations and events, although few professionals would admit to being 'muddlers'. 'Incrementalism', that is developing or progressing slowly, in measured steps, is a defensible approach when uncertainty or complexity is high. It does not attempt to be comprehensive, but attacks problems and policy issues with precision instruments rather than broad strategies. It is also closely connected to the notion of a 'political market square' in which decisions are made through bargaining and the exercise of power among all the stakeholders, rather than by professional planners or technocrats. 'Collaborative' or 'consensus-building processes' are similarly intended to involve all parties and points of view, but with the emphasis on formal issue identification and conflict resolution. It is arguable, however, whether rational planning or incrementalism is more democratic or effective.

'Advocacy' is another approach to planning, policy and decision-making that might have relevance to the events sector. Advocacy is based on the premise that disadvantaged and marginalized groups in society are normally left out of planning and policy-making and therefore their interests must be represented by others. To the degree that citizen involvement or 'community-based planning' works, advocacy should not be needed, but that is a seldom-achieved ideal.

Project Planning

Rooted in engineering, where project planning is a vital skill, and in logistics (which has to be mastered in the military), project planning is applicable to all events – even those produced by permanent organizations which also do strategic planning. The basic nature of events is that they are defined by time (a limited duration) and their schedule is announced and usually fixed well in advance. This necessitates getting all the planning and preparations done according to a fixed and often tight schedule. According to O'Toole (2000) many event projects fail, or overrun their budget and schedule, and perhaps this is due to poor planning or control systems.

'Feasibility studies' should ideally precede, or at least accompany project planning. In a rational planning process we do not commit to an event until we know it is affordable, desirable, environmentally sound, marketable and manageable. All too often, however, events are bid on and planned without full feasibility studies or cost and benefit forecasts, generally arising from corporate and political influences rather than public input.

Project planning and management for events is covered in the book *Corporate Event Project Management* by O'Toole and Mikolaitis (2002). Specific tools are employed in project planning, including project scoping, work breakdown and task analysis, costing, risk analysis, and scheduling and controlling with critical paths. Management of time is critical, and often time pressures lead to modifications or political actions to get the job done. A full life-cycle approach is recommended, including how to wind up the event and deal with the legacy.

Business Planning

Ample advice is available on how to prepare and use a business plan, as well as reasons for doing it (see Getz, 2005). Unfortunately, the business plan is often overlooked or done only for show. It is a convenient and useful way to summarize the event concept, its feasibility in financial and marketing terms, and its management. At the core of every business plan is a believable budget with costs fully estimated and revenues realistically forecast.

It is the budget, or financial feasibility, that sinks many events. 'Costs' are viewed as commitments and the money is spent in preparation for the event. However, 'revenue' forecasts contain a lot of wishful thinking or just plain guesswork. So money gets spent but projected income does not materialize, resulting in shortfalls, debt and ultimately failure. Cashflow projections and management are also vital components in business plans. Many events have to spend up front, but earn most of their revenue only at the time of the event through sales – or even afterwards when grants come in.

Strategic Planning

Although there is no real evidence to support the claim that strategic planning results in better events or more sustainable organizations, it seems inconceivable that event producers would not want to have a vision, set goals, and make strategies for the long term. One-time events also need goals and a plan, and if the planning period is measured in years it will have strategic elements built in.

What separates strategic planning from project planning, in theory, is first of all the principle of 'adaptability'. A project usually has a fixed goal, an event with known form, timing and programme – like a sport competition or exhibition. But permanent events and their organizations have to adapt to changes in their environment, their goals are changeable and the events evolve. Being a 'learning organization' improves adaptability. Strong external stakeholder relationships help to ensure permanence and diverse inputs. The mandate or mission of the organization needs to be periodically reviewed, leading to a re-assessment of goals and strategies.

'Strategy' is the second main difference, in the sense that a project has a single outcome (the event) whereas strategy to implement goals or fulfil a mandate can evolve and be multi-dimensional. Perhaps goals can be achieved by changing the event, terminating or replacing it. A 'strategy' is defined as an integrated set of policies, programmes and actions intended to fulfil the organization's mandate, realize its vision and achieve its goals.

In contrast to rationally planned strategies, 'emergent strategy' just happens as a consequence of the many decisions taken or untaken, and is often only realized in hindsight. For example, a manager might say 'it was not until years later that I could identify our strategy as one of accommodating and integrating key stakeholders, bringing them in as partners; it just seemed the right way to develop'.

A lot of research has to accompany the process of strategic planning, including 'environmental and future scanning' (forces and trends), 'situation analysis' (where we are, our current situation), stakeholder input and issues identification, and market and consumer research (including strengths, weaknesses opportunities and threats relative to competitors). Specific outputs in the process typically include a vision statement, goals, strategies, action or implementation plan (actions, costs, schedule and responsibilities defined), and a marketing/communications plan.

Operations and Logistics

'Operations' refers to all those systems that must be in place and the actions that have to be taken to produce the event. Clearly these have to be planned well in advance, unless you are doing a 'flash mob'. Operations can also be thought of as the day-to-day decisions and actions within the event organization or company, as opposed to strategic and business-level actions (Figure 10.5).

Operations and logistics	Foundations	Unique issues and challenges for events
• Transforming processes • Customer, supplier-oriented and communication systems • Procurement • Supply chain management • Critical path analysis • Queuing theory • Risk assessment and management • Security • Environmental management systems	• Engineering and mathematics (systems modelling) • Social psychology (crowd behaviour; perceptions of risk; behavioural controls) • Environmental sciences (reduce, reuse, recycle) • Environmental psychology (design for crowds and security)	• Complex and risky event settings and programmes • Crowd emotions and behaviour • Lack of experience for one-time events • Peak demand periods and simultaneous entry or exit from venues • The perishability of event capacity • The need to be 'green'

Figure 10.5   Operations and logistics.

Operations and logistics generally apply to three sub-systems, namely:

1. Customer-oriented (traffic, queuing, ticketing, information, essential services, comfort and safety, crew management).
2. Supplier-oriented (utilities, infrastructure, technical services, security systems).
3. Communications (equipment, procedures, accreditation, hosting the media, scheduling).

My own model of events operations planning (from Getz, 2005: 114) starts with a variety of factors that can influence the event, namely programming, theming, experiential goals, management (budget, etc.), site and venue, and any other constraints. From these considerations comes specific goals and detailed plans for the venue or setting, food and beverages, technical support, and service quality.

The book *Management of Event Operations* by Tum et al. (2006) provides a more comprehensive event operations model. Its main components are the analysis stage (environmental scanning and situational analysis), the operations planning process, both strategic and detailed, implementation and delivery, and performance evaluation. The basic theory and methods come from 'operations management' and from project planning and management.

Tum et al., use the concept of 'transforming processes' (as in our open systems management model) to describe operations. Resources and other inputs are converted into the desired outputs, namely the event or other services and products. Operations in this context are influenced by four major event characteristics:

1. Size and volume of output (How many guests? How many transactions?).
2. Complexity and variety of services/products offered to the consumer (size of the site, complexity of the programme).
3. Uncertainty (of attendance, costs, time, technical requirements).
4. Interactions (extent and nature of contacts between guests and staff).

Logistics

The basic idea of 'logistics' is to move people, goods and equipment (even money and tickets) to the right place at the right time. The event producer could take the approach of trying to schedule it all to perfection, as in 'just-in-time delivery', or simply get everything and everyone together at one place at one time and then try to sort it out. Obviously, this latter approach could prove chaotic.

The most fascinating job of event logistics I ever observed was a military-organized ANZAC day parade in Adelaide. Assembling and dispatching the many and varied parade groups, in batches, was a masterful work of precision. The starting point was a large square into which four or five wide streets flowed, thereby providing organizers with the means to stagger the assembly and start-up of units; they flowed together like a choreographed dance routine.

People Movement

There has to be a plan for traffic and parking, including policing and security. Site planning takes into account accessibility, flow and emergency evacuation. Queuing and service provision efficiency are related issues. Some event production companies also engage in 'destination management', which in terms of logistics involves greeting and transporting arriving guests/participants, getting them from place to place, and even providing tours and entertainment. Registration and ticketing are key elements, as these often cause bottlenecks; its best to do it in advance, electronically. Security can be a nightmare if everybody has to be searched, and preventing a crowd-rush to the stage is always necessary.

Queuing Theory

For many events, especially meetings and sport competitions, everyone arrives and leaves at roughly the same time, often resulting in traffic congestion and long line-ups. To the extent that arrivals and departures can be staggered, congestion can be reduced. 'Batch' arrivals and departures can be utilized to ease the problem, such as by assembling guests at various external points and then bringing them to the venue in groups. Reservation systems, specifying times and places for guests, is an alternation solution.

How to manage people in queues or line-ups is another management challenge. Theme parks have become skilled at both the psychological and physical management of queues, including offering people the option of paying extra to avoid them! Tum et al. (2006: 210) provided a queuing formula that can help event managers. It considers the rate of arrivals and average service time (e.g., how fast are people arriving and how long does it take to get them through the gates?). The resultant measure of 'customer intensity' shows the probability of queuing and queue lengthening.

Critical Path Analysis

Critical Path Analysis (CPA) is the best way to schedule complex projects and event programmes. It starts with the work breakdown and task analysis, involves staffing and costing estimates, and works backwards from the event date or programme start time to demonstrate the fastest possible path to getting the necessary tasks accomplished. Detailed examples are provided in Tum et al. (2006) and Getz (2005).

Procurement and Supply Chain Management

Many goods and services (including information) have to be purchased or sub-contracted, which is 'procurement'. The 'supply chain' refers to how needed information, goods and services flow through the event system, corresponding to the inputs, transforming processes and outputs in the open-systems model. For events, a failure in the supply chain could mean cancellation, programme reduction or quality problems.

Supply chains should be managed to achieve a number of objectives:

• Maximize efficiency (no waste or time delays; getting only what was ordered).
• Ensure quality (through setting standards and inspections).
• Minimize costs (e.g., through competitive bidding).
• Bring suppliers into the event as sponsors or partners.
• Ensure security (theft protection) and safety.
• Benefit the host community (source locally).
• Ensure a green event, by requiring all suppliers to conform to environmental management standards.

A key decision for any organization is that of outsourcing versus internal supply. It might look attractive to avoid external supply costs by doing it yourself, but that strategy entails many potential costs and risks. Tum et al. (2006: 123) provided an illustration of the 'chain of decisions and decision points' associated with supply chain management. Clearly the process requires a technical knowledge of the event's needs as well as how to work with suppliers.

Capacity Management

How much is needed: of food, water, tents, car parking, staff? Being able to forecast attendance and other needs is critical to supply management. It is a very high-risk strategy to allow unlimited access to an event and then try to match supplies to the actual demand. The safer alternative is to establish a 'design capacity', then restrict attendance to numbers that can be accommodated (with reference to both physical capacity and desired level of service quality). Modularization of an event can be used to combine these strategies: set design capacities for critical elements (such as concerts) and allow open attendance at others (e.g., parades).

How long does it take to sell tickets, get people through security, for customers to buy food or use the toilets? Efficiency studies are often needed to identify bottlenecks and management solutions. Capacity can often be increased, and wait times reduced, by either physical re-design, changes in staffing, or the addition or deletion of certain services within the site or venue. See the previous research note by Preda and Watts (2003).

One of the severe challenges facing many event producers is the fact that if tickets are not sold (for concerts, dinners, etc.), the lost revenue cannot be made up later. In technical terms, this kind of capacity cannot be stored, it is 'perishable'. That is why the practice of revenue or yield management is required.

Marketing and Communications

Although the practice of marketing is often reduced to, or confused with advertising and sales, it is best described as the management of the interface (or 'exchange relationships' between an organization and its stakeholders, in pursuit of achieving the organization's goals. Communications are a key element in this ongoing process. Marketing requires research to gain understanding of customer's and other stakeholders' needs, motives and choices, the effectiveness of communications, and the influences of price and supply. Its theoretical foundations lie mainly in psychology and economics.

Customers are not the only group that requires relationship management – that task starts internally with staff and volunteers and extends externally through 'facilitators' and 'regulators'. The essence of 'exchange relationships' is that the organization offers something of value that others are willing to buy or support; it has to be a voluntary and mutually beneficial process. In our case, events are offered as an experience for consumers to buy or guests to enjoy, a product to be delivered to clients or a marketing tool for corporations (Figure 10.6).

Marketing and communications	Foundations	Unique issues and challenges for events
• Marketing concept • Customer orientation • Marketing mix • Relationship marketing • Demand forecasting • Segmentation • Marketing strategies • Target marketing • Positioning and branding • Communications mix • Product life cycle	• Psychology (perceptions, attitude formation, involvement, communications, motivations, decision-making) • Economics (demand and pricing; competition) • Social-psychology (group influences on consumer decisions) • Anthropology (the planned event experience)	• Many event producers are product oriented • Marketing the one-time event (e.g., demand forecasting is problematic) • The need for multiple target markets for many events • Events are experiences, not consumable products • One-time events have to be pre-sold (little time for recovery) • Co-branding and marketing augmentation through sponsorship • Create a tourism orientation

Figure 10.6   Marketing and communications.

The Marketing Concept: Customer versus Product Orientation

The classic 'marketing' concept embodies the principle of 'customer orientation', which means the organization develops events that are in demand by clearly defined customers or clients. In contrast, a product orientation is often found in the events sector, particularly in the arts, where the event is presented as a work of art that has value on its own, regardless of economic demand or support. Art event producers do not necessarily have to sell their concepts to paying customers, but they do have to 'sell' to public grant-giving agencies and corporate sponsors.

We should modify the classic marketing concept in at least two important ways. The first is to argue that the customer is not always right, and event producers should not merely provide the entertainment and spectacle that will generate the highest profit. Customers do need to be educated, and many will be happy to have their tastes modified, their minds stimulated, their emotions uplifted. And even if customers are happy to pay for unsafe or environmentally destructive events, that is not an adequate reason to provide them. A second modification is to note that many events exist in the realm of public policy or social services, and do not need to respond only to market forces. But they do need to practice marketing in the form of relationship management.

Mayfield and Crompton (1995) studied the marketing orientation of festivals in Texas, revealing substantial differences. Interestingly, older events tended to have less of a marketing orientation, perhaps reflecting complacency or lack of professionalism compared to younger organizations. A related study was completed by Mehmetoglu and Ellingsen (2005), with the conclusion that there were multiple reasons why none of the small Norwegian festivals in their sample demonstrated a full marketing orientation.

The Marketing Mix

The 'marketing mix' consists of the elements that can be managed to build and sustain those essential stakeholder relationships. I prefer the '8-P's approach of Alastair Morrison (1995), but have grouped them into 'experiential' and 'facilitating elements'. The 'product' is in fact the event experience, and I believe marketers have to learn a lot more about experiential marketing through research and theory building. There have been a lot of naïve opinions expressed about how retail, brand and entertainment 'experiences' can change people and make companies successful.

The other marketing mix elements that directly affect the experience are 'place' (site, venue or setting), 'programming' (including the theme) and 'people' (interactions among staff, volunteers, guests, participants). Facilitating components consist of 'partnerships', 'promotions' (i.e., communications), 'packaging' including distribution and 'price'. Partnerships refer to all the external stakeholder relationships that have to be managed. Packaging, especially in the context of event tourism, can sometimes be thought of as a 'product'. That is because the tourist often prefers to buy travel, accommodation, and events all at once. Distribution is the process of communicating with customers and selling the products, including by means of the Internet, in-person sales and packages sold through agents. Finally, 'price' is a facilitating component because it determines who can, or wants to make the purchase. Price can also affect the experience in the sense that perceived value for money impacts on a consumer's overall satisfaction.

The Communications Mix (Integrated Marketing Communications)

Masterman and Wood (2006) in the book *Innovative Marketing Communications: Strategies for the Events Industry* deal with not only the traditional 'communications mix' by which the event reaches its targets, but also examine how events are used as communications tools. They emphasize 'Integrated Marketing Communications' (IMC), which has been advanced in response to perceived failures of mass media, new media options and demands from clients for demonstrating the return on investment from marketing efforts. IMC is highly targeted (both customer and multi-stakeholder oriented), combines all the communications tools for consistency and synergy, and stresses relationship and branding goals.

Research, Evaluation and Information Management for Event Marketing

Wood (2004) outlined the main marketing information needs for events, starting with setting event objectives. Research and information are also needed in the context of environmental scanning, customer analysis (including segmentation and targeting, satisfaction and expectations), competitor analysis and positioning, tactical marketing decisions, impacts and strategic planning. The main research and data collection tools of event marketers include surveys, interviews, focus groups and observation. Attendance counts (or estimates) and evaluation of marketing effectiveness are important tasks.

Wood (p. 152) graphically illustrated and discussed a comprehensive marketing information management system for events organizations. It covers both internal and external data sources, stakeholder information files (customers and others) and the various applications of research and analysis.

Segmentation and Target Marketing

This is one topic in event management that has received a lot of research attention, and segmentation is often tied to motivation studies. For example, see Taylor and Shanka (2002) who profiled wine festival attendees, and Oakes (2003) who segmented visitors to music festivals. Basic variables used in market segmentation for events start with simple geography (market areas), demographics (age and gender) and socio-economics (income and class), and can proceed to more challenging variables including benefits sought (generic versus specific), consumption patterns (what people buy, how and where) and visitation patterns (repeat visits, loyalty, seasonality). Psychographics is the most complex approach, dealing with lifestyles and values – as illustrated in the following research note:

Research Note

Hede, A., Jago, L., and Deery, M. (2004). Segmentation of special event attendees using personal values: relationships with satisfaction and behavioural intentions. Journal of Quality Assurance in Hospitality and Tourism, 5(2/3/4): 33–55. Also published in Hospitality, Tourism, and Lifestyle Concepts: Implications for Quality Management and Customer Satisfaction, 2004. M. Thyne and E. Laws (eds.), Binghamton New York: Haworth.

Lifestyle segmentation identifies similar groups based on attitudes, opinions and interests and is therefore as application of psychographics. Personal values are at the root of attitudes and much behaviour. In this study, patrons of a musical theatre show were surveyed over a 10-month period. The sample was mostly married, working females. Factor analysis of results from the value scale revealed three personal value domains: 'extrinsic' (to have a sense of belonging; to be well respected; to be in warm relationships and to have security); 'hedonistic' (to have fun and enjoyment; to have excitement), and 'achievement-based' (to be self-fulfilled, and to have a sense of accomplishment). Then exploratory hierarchical cluster analysis was used for segmentation purposes.

Prentice and Anderson (2003) segmented visitors to the Edinburgh Festival on the basis of 'tourism styles', which is similar to a benefits-sought approach. Seven clusters of 'consumption style' were identified, reflecting different interest levels in international or Scottish performing arts, and in the historic city.

Positioning, Branding and Co-branding

Although branding is a huge marketing topic, and has been studied in the context of event tourism and destinations, little work has been published on branding specific events. The following research note provides a single case.

Research Note

Oldberding, D., and Jisha, J. (2005). 'The flying pig': Building brand equity in a major urban marathon. Sport Marketing Quarterly, 14: 191–196.

Oldberding and Jisha reported on how this marathon, established in 1999, became a 'must-run' event, first attracting 6000 participants and growing to 12,000 by 2004 (counting marathon runners and walkers, relay racers and walkers, 5-mile, 5 K, 10 K and 'piglet' categories). The organizers specifically wanted to create distinct positioning, with a brand that would appeal to the target segment. Organizers (the Cincinnati Marathon Inc.) recognized the potential for a niche-market event that focused on the new marathoners – first-timers, and older runners who were less interested in their times.

Mossberg and Getz (2006) used case studies to examine a number of concepts and issues involving festival branding. One of the standard approaches is to use a city's name, often in conjunction with specification of the festival genre, as in Calgary Children's' Festival. Another common approach, at least in North America, is co-branding with a corporate sponsor including the selling of title rights (e.g., 'TD Canada Trust Calgary International Jazz Festival'). One conclusion of the Mossberg and Getz (2006) study was that festival managers were not fully applying branding theory to their events.

Resources and Financial Management

Very little research has been conducted on events as businesses, or from a business management perspective, so their comparative financial operations are little understood. Perhaps this is because so many events are in the public domain and not subject to normal business management principles, or because not-for-profit event organizations somehow believe they do not have to operate like a business. The basic facts, however, are that all events have to secure, manage and account for their resources, and that financial problems are the main source of business and event failure (Figure 10.7).

Resources and financial management	Foundation theories and concepts	Event-specific issues and applications
• Resources and dependency • Business models • Pricing theory and strategies • Revenue or yield management • Return on investment • Financial risk • Controls and accountability • Valuation (what's an event worth?) • Sponsorship	• Economics (theories of the firm; supply and demand; pricing; valuation) • Political science (policy to support events) • Sociology (social networks)	• Huge capital costs for mega events • Making money from 'free' events • Events as public services (subsidies; break-even; underwriting financial losses) • Cashflow problems arise because revenue is earned only at or after the event • Multiple sources of financing are needed • Multi-stakeholder perspectives on success and ROI • Sponsorship as co-branding

Figure 10.7 Financing, financial management and control systems.

Sponsorship and Other Sources of Revenue

Purely as a business venture, events would have to sell products (i.e., merchandise) and services (i.e., admission fees for entertainment) that are in demand in order to generate sufficient revenue to survive, or sufficient profit to justify investment. But many other resources are actually relied upon, including grants and subsidies from public authorities, sponsorship revenue and in-kind support from private sponsors, and fund raising through many activities. For-profit event firms might have a more difficult time getting grants, but might actually have an advantage in obtaining commercial partners.

Sponsorship has received the greatest amount of attention from practitioners and researchers, undoubtedly as a reflection of its global importance in the events sector. It can best be defined in economic and marketing terms as an exchange relationship involving payments made to events by external organizations (these can and do include public agencies) or persons, for specific benefits provided by the events. Discussion and advice on event sponsorship can be found in Skinner and Rukavina's book (2003) *Event Sponsorship*, and in Getz (2005). The International Events Group (IEG) specializes in seminars and publications on event sponsorship, including a legal guide to sponsorship. Most event associations have publications and hold seminars on sponsorship.

Catherwood and van Kirk (1992) commented on the growth of corporate sponsorship after the commercial success of the Los Angeles Olympic Games. Crompton (1993, 1995) reviewed reasons for sponsorship growth, and examined criteria used by corporations when deciding on what events to sponsor. Weppler and McCarville (1995) did research on how corporate decisions on event sponsorship were actually made.

Two studies, by Wicks (1995) and by Mount and Niro (1995) examined event sponsorship in small communities. In this environment decisions are often made on the basis of community goodwill and civic duty. Perhaps the same thing occurs at the community level or among distinct social and cultural groups.

There are numerous issues and risks associated with corporate sponsorship. Events have to worry about 'goal displacement', with the interests of commercial sponsors possibly taking over. Dependency on one or a few sponsors is potentially a problem. Sponsors face risks from 'ambush marketers' and a loss of goodwill if the event goes bad for them. Indeed, it is a form of co-branding that impacts on both parties.

Some research on the effectiveness of event sponsorship has been done. Kerstetter and Gitelson (1995) and Coughlan and Mules (2002) tested sponsorship recall among event patrons, revealing that it is not easy to obtain positive results. The mainstream marketing literature has many more studies on effectiveness, benefits and risks – mostly from the sponsors' points of view. Sponsorship has to be researched and understood from many perspectives. It relates to stakeholder management, strategic planning, organizational culture and its evolution, risk management, financial controls, marketing and communications, legal issues and branding. There remains a need for research aimed at improving our understanding of the multi-dimensional effects of sponsorship in the events world.

Resources and Dependency

Theories of the firm were examined in Chapter 4, demonstrating the importance of having a competitive advantage in securing resources and other forms of capital. While it might appear to be desirable in all circumstance to avoid resource dependency (and instead become financially self-sufficient), dependency on committed stakeholders might actually be a wise strategy to pursue, if permanent institutional status is desirable. Researchers are just beginning to look at resource acquisition and management strategies for events.

The Event as a Business Venture

Very little research has been done on events as business ventures, so our knowledge of microeconomics in the events sector is limited. The key question has to be: How effective are events at generating revenues and profits? Wanhill (2006) is one of only a few researchers to have examined event finances. Pricing theory and related marketing strategies are relevant here.

Research Note

Wanhill, S. (2006). *Some economics of staging festivals: the case of opera festivals. Tourism, Culture and Communication, 6(2): 137–149.*

Wanhill examined how a Finnish opera festival secured resources and sustained itself financially. Its pricing reflects its charitable status and public service aims, and its capacity is fixed, so that rising costs cannot be matched by revenue from ticket sales. However, the government of Finland subsidizes the organization as a way to support opera and cultural tourism. The researcher recommended a revenue management model to improve decision-making, specifically to asses pricing strategies.

The study by Andersson and Getz (2006) on a single festival's costs and revenue management, and related issues, showed that strong stakeholders (particularly entertainment booking agents) could inflict higher costs on an event, while the event organizers had the potential to keep costs under control from weak stakeholders (i.e., where choices were available). A related issue is the fact that so many events are produced in the public (governmental) sector and by not-for-profit societies. To some extent they are isolated from market forces, or the normal laws of supply and demand. Government subsidies can support events, for the 'public good', that could not survive on their own. Not-for-profit organizations can sometimes continue to produce events even when in chronic debt because stakeholders, including sponsors, value what they do or trust them.

Revenue or Yield Management

McMahon-Beattie and Yeoman (2004) discussed revenue management for events. Similar to 'yield management' as practised by hotels and airlines, this financial management approach is suitable for events with a fixed and 'perishable' capacity (i.e., only so many tickets to sell, but if unsold the capacity is wasted), and predictable demand fluctuations (by day, week, hour). Using historical data on demand fluctuations, or forecasts, revenue managers adjust prices or make special offers to entice customers in what would otherwise be low-demand periods. This can affect programming and staffing as well.

Seasons' tickets, multi-entry passes, discounts for seniors or other groups, and various other pricing and promotion tactics have to be integrated with revenue management. So far no-one has reported research on the application or effectiveness of such techniques at events.

Return on Investment

For owners and other private-sector investors, return on investment (ROI) is a simple calculation of profit realized from investment. But ROI has different meanings to other event stakeholders. Tourism officials generally measure their return on investment from events as total economic impact for the destination (which generally leads to exaggerations). In social or cultural policy fields ROI is not usually used, but it could be measured by reference to specific outcomes like changes in awareness and attitude or behaviour.

Controls and Accountability

Raj (2004) examined the human, or behavioural aspects of financial management for events. This approach covers not only professionalism but also internal relationships and morale. It was stressed that 'budgeting' is not just financial planning, it is also designed to influence human behaviour and goal setting.

Human Resources and Volunteer Management

Human Resources management for planned events includes the normal considerations of staffing common to all forms of organization, plus several unique challenges. There is the special importance of volunteers and external suppliers or contractors, and unique characteristics of events in terms of how they are governed; the need for project planning and management, and their fluctuating need for workers are special considerations. Lyn van der Wagen (2006: preface) in the book *Human Resource Management for Events: Managing the Event Workforce*, emphasized 'There is no more challenging environment for human resource management than the event business.' She shows how the challenges stem from a combination of the importance people assign to events, the nature of project planning and management, numerous stakeholders to consider and the risks associated with every aspect of event production.

Events have unique human resource needs and challenges, especially because of their usual reliance on volunteers. 'Pulsating' event organizations have to manage resources quite differently from permanently staffed organizations. Planned event experiences are also often dependent on staff and volunteers for providing service quality as well as being part of the performance. Sometimes a lack of professionalism is an issue, especially where leadership and organization are informal (Figure 10.8).

Human resources and volunteer management	Foundations	Unique event issues and applications
• Motivation (discipline and rewards; burn-out and rust-out) • Locus of control (supervision; team work) • Induction or indoctrination • Training and professional development • Careers • Risk management (health and safety)	• Psychology (needs, motivation, cognition, learning) • Sociology (social groups) • Anthropology (culture) • Education (training)	• Pulsating events need periodic, large-scale infusions of workers • Heavy reliance on volunteers, both in governance and operations • Staff and volunteers as 'cast' members (part of the experience)

Figure 10.8 Human resources and volunteer management.

Human Resource Planning

Getz (2005) and Van der Wagen (2006) both provided detailed Human Resource planning models. Van der Wagen's approach starts with the event's purpose and strategic plan, and integrates Human Resource within project planning and across all the functional areas – from accreditation to workforce planning. Key steps include: an Human Resource strategic plan; work breakdown structure; assessment of labour needs forecast versus supply assessment (considering paid staff, volunteers and contractors); risk assessment; Human Resource operational plan and budget; recruitment and selection; training; staffing logistics; performance management; recognition and reward system, and post-event evaluation.

Hanlon and Stewart (2006) conducted a study of staffing for a major sport event organization, raising the question of what strategies are best. A mix of full-time, outsourced, seasonal and volunteer personnel might be involved. A complex structural arrangement can exist, numbers fluctuate, and everyone is on a defined-term contract. Temporary work teams are one solution. Hanlon and Stewart made a number of recommendations for strategy, documentation and practice.

Legal and ethical issues will inevitably arise for events, including laws applying to who can be hired, on what basis applicants can be rejected (certain questions or security checks might not be permitted) or employees terminated. Another common issue is the reality and appearance of discrimination, especially on boards of directors, and the desirability of having staff and volunteers reflect the social and cultural mix of the community.

Motivation

Several theoretical approaches can be applied to the task of recruiting and motivating event workers. A quick overview is provided before getting into more detail on the volunteer.

Herzberg's Two Factor Theory

It is sometimes called the 'Motivator-Hygiene Theory', and is closely related to Maslow's hierarchy of needs. Herzberg's workplace studies (1966) caused him to conclude that 'hygiene factors' like salary, security and other benefits, do not motivate people but can cause dissatisfaction. What motivates people to work (or work better) are challenges, recognition and responsibility.

An interesting adaptation of this theory in Event Studies is its use to explain customer or guest satisfaction. In this context 'hygiene factors' like inadequate toilets, parking problems or long waits, cause dissatisfaction but do not motivate people to attend events or lead to perceptions of overall quality.

McGregor's Theory X and Theory Y

Managers who believe (consciously or instinctively) in 'Theory X' think that workers are inherently lazy, so structure and discipline (or the threat of punishment) is needed to motivate them. This is in accord with Skinner's (1938) 'behavioural modification' approach, requiring reward and discipline. However, McGregor (1960) determined that at higher levels of Maslow's hierarchy, praise, respect, recognition, empowerment and a sense of belonging are far more powerful motivators than money. Accordingly, the 'Theory Y' manager tries to remove barriers to creativity and self-fulfilment, provide a comfortable work environment, and treat employees or volunteers with a great deal of respect.

Vroom's Expectancy Theory

'Expectancy theory' (Vroom, 1964) states that workers have a variety of goals (particularly to avoid pain and experience pleasure) and that they can be motivated if they believe that there is a positive correlation between efforts and performance, that favourable performance will result in an outcome, that the outcome's value to the employee can be determined, and the desire to satisfy the need is strong enough to make the effort worthwhile. It is sometimes called expectancy-valence theory, where 'valence' refers to the emotional orientations people hold with respect to outcomes.

Professionalism

Event management is slowly becoming accepted as a quasi-profession, and this is acceptance is linked to the increasing number of graduates from various educational programmes as well as holders of designations from certifying professional associations. Getz and Wicks (1994) argued that event management can aspired to quasi-professional status on par with recreation and leisure managers, but the typical absence of government licensing prevented full professional status.

In part, the EMBOK project is intended to provide the body of knowledge necessary to permit licensing. However, Harris (2004) argued that a lack of common purpose and unity currently precludes professional status. Harris' conclusion clearly reflects the split between professional associations dedicated to specific event forms, and their rivalry for members and credibility. It is in their self-interest to perpetuate differences, but eventually they will all have to deal with the fact that 'event management' has become the academic standard, not meeting management or exhibition management and the like. They can all certainly maintain their event-specific focus to some degree, but will have to reconcile their specialization with the emerging generic professional designation of 'event manager'.

Event managers are already expected to conduct themselves as professionals, regardless of their backgrounds, affiliations, or status as volunteer, owner or employee. This expectation rests on the need for minimum standards of education, training and experience, adherence to professional codes of conduct (ethics), and legal responsibility for actions.

Harris (2004: 107) provided a model for professionalization that encompasses three approaches to defining professionals. These are the 'trait approach' (including skills based on professional, full-time occupation, provision of training, proof of competency, organization, code of conduct and altruistic service), a 'functionalist approach' (systematic knowledge, common interest, recognition by society, control of behaviour, work socialization, system of rewards and community of spirit) and a 'business approach' (commercial vision, effective response to market and client demands, managerial skills, entrepreneurial skills and success through profit).

The ethics standards, or codes of conduct prepared by major international event organizations are documented in Getz (2005), along with advice on how event professionals should create and govern their conduct by their own values and standards. Ethical issues, and how values and ethics are being used in practice throughout the event sector, require research and debate.

As professionalism increases there will be a need for more focused research on what constitutes professionalism, and on the related career issues for practitioners. Research has been done on leadership training for events (Tzelepi and Quick, 2002, regarding the Sydney Olympics), and Hanlon and Cuskelly (2002) studied generic induction (or orientation) methods for events, including the need for detailed manuals. Induction and training are particularly crucial for one-time events. Bryant and Gaiko (1999) studied the skills needed for meeting professionals, while Sheehan et al. (2000) profiled meeting planners based on hotels and conference centres. O'Brien and Shaw (2002) profiled independent meeting planners in Canada.

Research on Event Volunteer Recruitment and Motivation

Key questions for volunteer management are 'What motivates event volunteers, and how can their commitment and productivity be maximized and sustained'? Volunteering is not uniformly valued and practised, being in part a reflection of cultural norms, political systems, economic conditions and living standards. Generic information is available from many countries on who volunteers, why and for what (see e.g., United States Department of Labor, 2005; Australian Bureau of Statistics; Imagine Canada, n.d.; UK Institute for Volunteering), which is always a good starting point for any discussion of volunteers.

Volunteer management for events requires specialized knowledge within Human Resource, as well as event-specific strategies and practices, reflecting both the size and nature of the event. A lot of research has been conducted on the Olympics, but those findings are not necessarily applicable to small events or other types. Specific to events, a growing body of research evidence exists on volunteer motivation, satisfaction, commitment and experience. Studies include those by: Williams and Harrison (1988); Williams et al. (1995); Ryan and Bates (1995), Green and Chalip (1998, 2004); Elstad (1997, 2003); Farrell et al. (1998); Saleh and Wood (1998); Johnston et al. (2000); Coyne and Coyne (2001); Strigas and Newton Jackson (2003); Ralston et al. (2005) and Monga (2006). The research note below covers research on volunteer behaviour.

Research Note

Cuskelly, G., Auld, C., Harrington, M., and Coleman, D. (2004). Predicting the behavioral dependability of sport event volunteers. Event Management, 9(1/2): 73–89.

Pre- and post-event surveys gathered data on attitudes, beliefs and behavioural dependability from 391 operational-level volunteers at five sport events. Using the Theory of Planned Behaviour, Cuskelly et al. sought to predict volunteer dependability. They concluded that volunteers ought to be studied within different event categories, as there are likely to be differences between sport events and community festivals. Volunteers are apparently motivated by participation in the event itself, less than by extrinsic rewards. These intrinsic rewards include: enjoyment of being a volunteer; interacting with other volunteers and event participants and contributing to the great social good.

Underlying motivation to volunteer for events can include generic motivations like doing good ('altruism'), looking for social and career benefits (networking) and challenge. Volunteers particularly enjoy the belonging and sharing, or 'communitas' that can occur through their event experiences. Volunteering can also be one manifestation of 'serious leisure', and it is clear that some people volunteer at many events. Those who have a great experience at an event are likely to become motivated to volunteer at others.

We know from research that involvement in a sport leads to volunteering at sport events of the same type, and that the prestige of an event makes a big difference. Also, research has shown that community pride is an important factor. Monga (2006) concluded that multiple motivations apply to event volunteers, but that affiliatory reasons, or attachment to the event's theme or activity, are strongest.

There are many other issues to be considered. What are the reasons for gender and age differences, and what is the influence of location and ethnicity or race on event volunteering? How can we explain discrepancies in where and how people volunteer – are some causes more popular than others? Where volunteering is considered to be only a source of cheap labour, or is viewed as taking away paid jobs, how can it be developed?

Indoctrination, training and supervision all have to be directed towards service quality and the participation of all staff, volunteers and suppliers to facilitation of designed experiences. A serious question to be asked is the degree to which satisfactory staff/volunteer/supplier experiences contribute to guest and other stakeholder experiences. This is much more than a service quality issue, as it gets to the heart of how experiences are shaped.

Risk, Health and Safety

'Safety and health management' aims to ensure that all event participants and attendees, as well as those affected by an event, are protected from threats to their health and safety. It is people-focused, and includes the very important crowd management and security tasks. 'Risk management' can be defined as the process of anticipating, preventing or minimizing potential costs, losses or problems for the event, organization, partners and guests. Ask the question: 'What is at risk'? Is it the loss of money, reputation and survival of the event and its organizers, or personal safety and health? Risk, health and safety management has to cut across all the other systems in event management. In this section just the basic principles are covered, and some of the related issues (Figure 10.9).

Risk, health and safety	Foundations	Unique event issues and applications
• Risk planning and management integrated in all management functions • Legal liability • Insurance • Health standards • Safety standards • Security systems	• Psychology and sociology (crowding, aggression, territoriality, perception of risks) • Environmental psychology (human–setting interactions) • Operations management • Planning theory and rational decision-making	• Some events are inherently risky, and this is part of their appeal • Crowds generate risks • Some events are associated with alcohol, partying and revelry, which can lead to problems • Volunteers might not be able to cope

Figure 10.9   Risk, health and safety.

Unique Risk Elements and Challenges for Events

Numerous threats or hazards face the event producer, all of which pose risks. Protests, traffic, unruly fans, crowding, alcohol, terrorism and crime necessitate security and control measures. Bad weather and unpredictable environmental forces, including the sate of the economy, can drastically affect turnout and sales. Attracting the wrong people or incompatible segments could lead to trouble.

Many events are inherently risky, which is part of their appeal, and this imposes a dilemma on policy-makers and producers. How far can one err on the side of caution before shutting down the risks or thrills that make an event attractive? Risky activities include sports, running with the bulls and similar rites, eating and drinking, or just plain assembling in a large crowd. Celebration and revelry are hallmarks of festivals and carnivals, parties and many concerts. Any use of animals can be risky.

Risks also arise from organizational and managerial actions, such as the employment of untrained staff or volunteers, the absence of proper management systems and controls or a general lack of professionalism. Choosing the wrong setting, such as a sensitive environment or an area known for its natural hazards, can be a serious mistake. The wrong date can lead to competition and conflict, and the wrong price or programme affects image and sales. Quality control is particularly difficult at events owing to the use of many volunteers, reliance on numerous suppliers and the difficulty of retaining staff or volunteers. Systems often have to be re-invented annually.

Whatever the hazard or threat, the risks accrue to guests and participants, organizers, other stakeholders and the environment. Risks generate problems in terms of personal health and injuries, money (financial losses), marketing (tarnished image, loss of demand), the law (lawsuits for negligence), community relations and political support (owing to negative impacts).

Risk Planning and Management

Guidance is available from IFA and Argonne Productions (1992), Berlonghi (1990), the UK Event Safety Guide (1999) and Tarlow's book (2002) *Event Risk Management and Safety*. A very useful manual (*The Event Safety Guide*, revised 1999) on health and safety planning for music events has been prepared in the UK by the Health and Safety Executive of the central government. In the UK and other jurisdictions it is a requirement of law for events and facilities to produce a policy and plan for health and safety, and there are government inspectors to ensure compliance with all pertinent laws and regulations. Also, Johnson (n.d. p. 71) called for all events to have a written 'emergency action plan' to ensure that staff and volunteers will respond promptly and adequately to both predictable and unusual problems.

The planning process begins with identification of possible threats and hazards in various risk 'fields', such as finance, health or the environment. This can accompany 'task analysis' in project planning, as recommended by O'Toole and Mikolaitis (2002). Then assessment of 'risk probabilities' (how likely are they to occur) and 'severity' (how serious are the consequences) leads to a matrix analysis of Probability times Severity. Priorities can then be determined, leading to action.

According to Berlonghi (1990) there are several generic strategies for events to follow: 'avoidance' (the hazard, such as a programme activity or venue, should be eliminated); 'reduction' (some hazards can be minimized or kept to an acceptable level through better management, training, or operations, or actions focus on reducing potential severity of damage or losses); 'diffusion' (spreading risks among stakeholders or over time and space); 're-allocation' (risks can be re-allocated completely, as where a parent body or municipality absorbs risks for specific events; users have to sign waivers).

Insurance providers can help in the whole process, as they learn the risks and consequences through experience, and some have developed specific guidelines that event organizers must follow in order to even qualify for insurance. Activities and whole events have been cancelled because of the cost or lack of insurance. Professional associations and cities have resorted to self-insurance schemes just to be able to continue producing events.

Security

Security is a big part of risk planning and a key element in event operations and logistics. Understanding crowd emotions and behaviour is essential for most events, with the threat of terrorism at major events being an added worry. Tarlow (2002): 135, in the book *Event Risk Management and Safety* (Wiley), drew attention to the links between events and terrorism, specifically why they make such inviting targets:

- Proximity of events and event venues to major transportation routes and centres.
- Potentially large-scale business and tourism disruption from cancellation or postponement.
- Media attention is immediate, on-site.
- Customers at many events are unknown, and anonymous in crowds.

Goldblatt and Hu (2005) introduced the development of eSAFE, an online management knowledge system intended to help events industry professionals deal with an ongoing terrorist threat.

Research, Evaluation and Information Systems

All the management functions have to be supported by research, evaluation and information systems. The open-system model of events illustrates that information is an essential input, and that both internal and external evaluations are crucial for accountability, improvement and learning. Although fundamental research can be useful to managers, they mostly want applied research to solve immediate problems. Increasingly, accountability to external stakeholders is placing heavy information demands on event organizers.

'Pulsating' events have a special challenge to become learning organizations with solid 'memories', as they have only a few permanent staff. Can they develop partnerships for this purpose? All-volunteer event organizations are especially challenged, and probably have to rely on external sources. Owing to the chronic gap between academics and practitioners, it would make sense for institutions and professional event associations or local event groups to combine efforts (Figure 10.10).

Research, evaluation and information systems	Foundations	Unique event issues and applications
• Applied research • Internal evaluation • External evaluation and accountability • Information systems	• The field of information management • Computer science • Evaluation as a field of study • Research methods from many disciplines and fields	• The challenge of organizational learning and memory in pulsating organizations • Need for information from many, diverse sources • The gap between academics and practitioners • Many external stakeholders requiring information and demanding accountability

Figure 10.10   Research, evaluation and information systems.

The event manager first has to establish an overall process for collecting information and doing research and evaluation (i.e., be a learning organization), then determine how best to analyse, disseminate and utilize it. Storage is an issue, although more from the perspectives of security, access and convenience. Having staff responsible for information management and technology, or outsourcing the work are options.

Numerous software programs are available for aspects of event information management, especially regarding conference registration, project management and budgeting. The various specialized textbooks for event managers provide suitable starting points for developing specific research, evaluation and information systems. An article by Wood (2004) documented marketing information needs, and this is probably the most-discussed management function from a research perspective. Attention is required for all the other functions, and for an integrated event information management system.

Chapter Summary

Each of the main event management functions have been considered (programming and design excepted) with the emphasis placed on what we need to know about them, and how to do related research. Researchers have not comprehensively attacked the management functions related to events, leaving some of them very underdeveloped in terms of theory and method.

Leadership, power, organizational culture and evolution are in need of serious research in the events field. Little is known about the people who start events: Are they traditional or social entrepreneurs? What are the most effective leadership styles? Of course, with so many events being created and bid upon for strategic reasons, complete with professional event managers, we will often have to address leadership in the context of politics and negotiated mandates.

A few researchers have begun to examine what it takes for events to survive and prosper, and for event organizations to become permanent institutions. Stakeholder theory is proving to be particularly relevant, along with theories of resource dependency, population ecology and the concept of a political market square. This line of inquiry should pay off in terms of developing organizational theory for the not-for-profit sector in particular, and in terms of implications for strategic planning. A related issue is the lack of attention given to differences between events created by government agencies, private firms and not-for-profit organizations. Which structures work best, and are they interchangeable when it comes to achieving strategic goals? Different business models are available, combining elements of organization, strategy, customer-orientation and the like, but these have not been studied in the event sector.

Business and management schools teach rational planning, embodying vision, goal formulation, strategies and evaluation/feedback, but certainly within the political arena and mega events it appears that irrationality often triumphs. Why? And are we satisfied with how important decisions are made regarding events? At the scale of individual event organizations, how many and what types of decisions are being made on an ad hoc, incrementalist basis, or in response to pressure? It should be asked if non-rational approaches actually work better to ensure that all stakeholders have a voice, and for the survival and efficacy of the event. Connections with professional planners in other fields, and with policy analysts, should help advance knowledge in this area.

A great deal of expert advice is now available on project planning, logistics and operations for events, but little related research is being done to test concepts and evaluate methods specific to different types of events and event settings. Some work has been done on capacity management, and we can probably borrow a lot more from the theme park and venue managers. The field of project management is well established, and although dominated by engineers, they should be able to offer more theory and methods to events.

Marketing has received the most attention from researchers, focused on consumer motivation, segmentation and satisfaction. Work has also been done concerning the marketing orientation of festivals. Sport and entertainment marketing are quite well-developed fields of research, but are very commercial in their orientation. Event Studies also has to develop social marketing and needs assessment.

Finance is probably the most critical management function for event businesses. In the governmental and not-for-profit event sectors subsidies and other external support distort the process, but lack of resources will still constitute the main reason for failure or underachievement. Resource-based theories of the firm can be applied to event management, and resource dependency theory ties in directly with stakeholder management.

With regard to human resource management, the greatest attention has naturally been paid to volunteers as they occupy such an important place in the event sector. We now have considerable understanding of volunteer motivation, satisfaction and commitment, but not of decision-making and governance by volunteers. Another issue begging for research and theory development is the role of event staff and volunteers as performers and cast members in facilitating the event experience.

Risk, health and safety management (including security) must cut across all the management functions. There is ample advice available on risk planning and management for events, however, there has not been a concerted effort made to do related research or develop risk theory for planned events.

Research, evaluation and information systems are necessary to support all the management functions, and a good starting point is the 'open-system' model. How research and theory can support effective event management and policy-making is a big theme in this book.

Study Questions

- Define 'leadership', 'power', 'leadership styles' and 'leadership roles' in the context of planned events.
- Distinguish between 'entrepreneurship' and 'intrapreneurship' as applied to events.
- How do founders shape 'organizational culture', and why is it important?
- What are the main differences between governmental, profit and non-profit structures in the events sector?
- Explain the concept of 'institutionalization' for events, and link it to 'stakeholder theory'.
- How can events become 'learning organizations'?
- What is 'rational' planning and decision-making, and why is it not always applied to events?
- Distinguish between 'strategic', 'project' and 'business' planning for events.
- Explain the three key operation sub-systems for events and discuss key 'logistics' issues.
- What is 'capacity management' for events? Give examples.
- Should the 'marketing concept' always be fully applied to events? Explain.
- How does 'segmentation' and 'target marketing' relate to needs, motives and benefits sought?

- Should all events be run as a 'business'? What exactly would that mean?
- Discuss theories of motivation as they apply to event volunteers.
- Show how to recruit, motivate and keep committed volunteers for specific types of event.
- Why are events unique in terms of risk management? Explain the research and evaluation necessary to support risk planning and management.
- What research, evaluation and information systems should be in place to support event management? Tie your answer to the open system model.

Further Reading

Allen, J., O'Toole, W., McDonnell, I., and Harris, R. (2002). *Festival and Special Event Management* (2nd edn). Milton: Wiley Australia.

Bowdin, G., Allen, J., O'Toole, W., Harris, R., and McDonnell, I. (2006). *Events Management* (2nd edn). Oxford: Elsevier.

Hoyle, L. H. (2002). *Event Marketing: How to Successfully Promote Events, Festivals, Conventions, and Expositions*. New York: Wiley.

O'Toole, W., and Mikolaitis, P. (2002). *Corporate Event Project Management*. New York: Wiley.

Tarlow, P. (2002). *Event Risk Management and Safety*. New York: Wiley.

Tassiopoulos, D. (ed.) (2000). *Event Management: A Professional and Developmental Approach*. Lansdowne: Juta Education.

Tum, J., Norton, P., and Wright, J. (2006). *Management of Event Operations*. Oxford: Butterworth Heinemann/Elsevier.

Van der Wagen, L. (2006). *Human Resource Management for Events: Managing the Event Workforce*. Oxford: Butterworth Heinemann/Elsevier.

Chapter 11
Outcomes and the Impacted

Learning Objectives

- Know the forces and stressors which generate event-related outcomes, both intended and unintended.
- Understand the potential positive and negative social, cultural, environmental and economic impacts of events and event tourism.
- Be able to evaluate tangible and intangible costs and benefits from multiple stakeholder perspectives.
- Learn the policy implications of event outcomes.
- Be able to assess the worth of an event.

What are Outcomes and Impacts?

Planned events always have a purpose and goals. This means that certain 'outcomes' are both desired and predicted, but it is also possible that unanticipated and negative outcomes are also generated. Indeed, an event, or events collectively and cumulatively, might initiate or be part of a change process acting at a large scale on society and the environment.

The term 'outcomes' in this chapter is derived from the open system model wherein 'transforming processes' (management systems and the event itself) convert 'inputs' to 'outputs' or 'outcomes'. 'Impacts' have a more specific meaning within this approach. People who experience the outcomes of events feel 'impacted'. The economy is 'impacted' by changes related to the event.

Evaluators typically set out to demonstrate that the event was 'effective', or successful in achieving its goals, and sometimes they also assess 'efficiency' (how well resources were used). Tzelepi and Quick (2002) identified various approaches to evaluating 'effectiveness' that are relevant to events, namely: 'goal attainment' (assuming goals were pre-determined); 'systems resource approach' and 'internal process approach' (using the open-system model as a diagnostic tool); 'competing values' (within the organization); and 'strategic constituencies' (considering the views of all stakeholders).

Clients and other key stakeholders in events typically want a report on how their resources were used and the degree to which their specific objectives were met. All too often no-one is willing to examine 'externalities' – such as impacts on those not directly involved in the event's production, or environmental pollution. A full event evaluation takes into account costs and benefits and their distribution.

In 'goal-free evaluation' no assumptions are made about purposes or goals, so evaluators seek to demonstrate what happened, whether intended or unintended. Sometimes this approach is taken when long-term, expensive programmes are evaluated, as in health care and education. Government agencies will want to ensure that major policies are being implemented 'effectively' and 'efficiently', plus they want to avoid negative impacts in other policy fields.

In policy terms, the primary need is for a comprehensive events and event tourism policy, fully integrated with closely related policy domains including leisure, sport, culture, the arts, health, economic development and tourism, the environment, community, and social development. In the ensuing sections specific policy implications are discussed, related to social, cultural, economic and environmental impacts.

In each of the main sections of this chapter a figure is presented to both summarize the contents and to suggest the process at work. It starts with 'stressors', which are really 'change actors' or 'causal forces'. There is no positive or negative connotation to the term 'stressor'; the potential outcomes in the frameworks can often be interpreted as positive or negative. The third column examines possible responses, which for personal outcomes refers to individual responses, but for the others is the realm of policies and strategies.

There is nothing predictive about these figures, and they are not intended to be all-inclusive. They do provide a good starting point for considering the sources and nature of event-related outcomes, and what can be done about them. The chapter ends with a detailed discussion of 'impact assessment' and 'cost–benefit evaluation', mainly because these should be comprehensive in terms of individual, social, economic and environmental outcomes – should be, but usually are not.

Personal Outcomes

The personal dimension, from antecedents to experiences to outcomes, is the least researched and most poorly understood theme in Event Studies. Leisure theorists have a lot to offer here, but their concerns to do not apply to all types of event setting and experiences. We will have to go back to the disciplinary foundations for inspiration and guidance in pursuing knowledge of how individuals are affected by events (Figure 11.1).

Stressors, or Causal Forces

How do planned event experiences change people? Re-visit the framework for studying antecedents and choices for planned events (in Chapter 9) to see the main considerations. For the individual, the event experience can be memorable and transforming, but only in the context of anticipation/expectations, travel (if relevant), and post-event evaluation which includes assigning or modifying meanings attached to the experience.

How one 'experiences' an event is crucial. In all three experiential domains, 'conative', 'affective' and 'cognitive', the individual can direct the process, or simply go along with the flow of events. People who are interested, perceptive and engaged are going to have different kinds of experiences and outcomes.

Many environmental forces act on individual event experiences, and these too are 'stressors'. 'Social representations' are formed of events, through the media and the influence of references groups, and these shape expectations and event-related behaviour. The experiences people have at events are also in part pre-determined by the organizers, designers and managers.

Stressors or causal forces	Potential personal outcomes	Possible responses
The individual's actions in attending events are the stressors or causal factors. These actions relate to: • Anticipation • Travel to the event • The event experience • Post-event evaluation	*Negative experience:* • The event was boring or over-stimulating; did not meet expectations (in terms of quality and/or experience) • Perceived lack of value for money or a 'waste of time' *Positive experience:* • Met or exceeded expectations • Pleasantly surprised • Achieved peak or flow experience • Satisfaction; happiness • Attitude change (towards the event, sponsors, causes, or events in general) • Transformation (fundamentally changed by the experience in terms of personality, values, lifestyle)	*Negative experience:* • Loss of interest in event or event type; no intent to repeat • Negative word-of-mouth communications *Positive experience:* • Increased interest in the event or event type • Positive word-of-mouth communications • Loyalty to specific events • Higher level of involvement or specialization (in specific pursuits) resulting in increased event participation • Development of an 'event career'
• General social, economic and environmental circumstances surrounding the event (or events) as they impact on individuals • A dominant view of the event (or events) might arise through media coverage and other opinion-shaping forces • The influence of organizers, designers and managers on personal experiences at events	*Negative perceptions:* • Direct and indirect effects • The event (or events) considered to be harmful, a threat, or undesirable *Positive perceptions:* • Direct and indirect effects • The event (or events) considered to be useful, beneficial or desirable	• Perceptions affect attitudes toward the event or events in general • Political action might result

Figure 11.1   Personal outcomes.

Potential Personal Outcomes

We have to be able to determine if expectations are met, and – with greater theoretical and practical difficulty – try to understand if specific needs and motivations have been fulfilled. These can include learning, aesthetic appreciation, mastery, self actualization, or (most difficult of all) transformation. It becomes even more challenging if we want to link concepts like involvement, serious leisure, or event careers to personal outcomes, or to measure socialization and acculturation through event experiences. We also want to consider how personal meanings attached to event experiences can be measured and evaluated.

Other perspectives have to be considered as well, including those of sponsors who typically want to see changes among event consumers' awareness, image and intention towards corporations, brands and products, as well as grant givers who might want to see attitudinal changes arising from communications at events.

Both positive and negative outcomes are possible. The experience might be judged negatively if 'optimal arousal' was not achieved, quality was disappointing, or it was not as advertised. Positive experiences should follow from having expectations met or exceeded. Many contributors to positive, memorable and transforming experiences are actually beyond the control of the organizers and designers, who can only hope to suggest and facilitate great experiences.

Within a more general context, a person not attending the event might still form a perception of how he or she has been impacted, either positively or negatively. 'Social exchange theory' can explain some of this, as people believing they benefit from the event are likely to think more highly of it. Others may form a negative opinion, believing they have been harmed or impeded in some way.

Possible Responses

Satisfaction generally predicts whether people will want to repeat the experience, become loyal fans/consumers, or spread positive word-of-mouth about a service or product. Positive experiences can be expected to influence future behaviour, particularly where individuals develop event careers (or become more serious, involved, committed or specialized) as a consequence of event experiences. Dissatisfied eventgoers, on the other hand, might lose interest, stay way in the future, or try something else to achieve the same benefits.

Persons indirectly forming a negative perception of an event's impact on themselves are likely to hold negative attitudes toward it, and perhaps to events in general. This could result in political action. Support for events should increase when residents feel they benefit in some way.

Social, Cultural and Political Outcomes

Social, cultural and political outcomes of events stem from the five categories of stressors or forces show in Figure 11.2. First comes monetary 'investment' or other use of resources to create events, giving rise to economic change and a flow-through to social, cultural and environmental consequences. To the extent that tourists are attracted, or 'consume' events, their travel and presence in the host community leads to impacts. The event itself, its physical development, surrounding traffic, and on-site activities, also generate outcomes.

Stressors or causal forces	Potential social, cultural and political outcomes	Possible responses
Expenditure/investment in events	• Opportunity costs (money diverted from or not available for other purposes • Stimulation of the economy; job creation	• Exchange theory suggests that those who benefit will support events; others might feel marginalized or disadvantaged
Event tourism; host–guest interactions	• Tourism influx results in many host–guest interactions; • Demonstration effects and acculturation • Spread of disease • Possible conflict over venue and resource use	• Support for, or opposition to event tourism or visitors • Boundary maintenance (to keep tourism out of the community) • Health and safety standards imposed on events
Event-related development, activities and traffic	• Congestion, amenity loss, crime, and other disruption • Unruly behaviour at or surrounding events • Events as entertainment	• Calls for control and change • Higher or lower levels of event participation
Community involvement in events	• Feeling of ownership and control, or of exclusion and 'them versus us' • Community pride and integration, or divisiveness • Threat to authenticity or traditions • Consumer surplus or psychic benefits derived from events in the community	• Political action based on degree of perceived ownership and control • Social responses based on integration or divisiveness (participation, withdrawal) • Cultural transformation • Promote social integration and civic pride • Events become permanent institutions
Media coverage	• Changes in perceptions and attitudes resulting from media coverage (social representations formed)	• Public pressure for political action in response to dominant views of events

Figure 11.2   Social, cultural and political outcomes.

The extent and nature of community involvement in the event (such as policy involvement or volunteering) has an influence on its effects and how they are perceived. Finally, the media can have a powerful influence on how events are perceived, and even influence the impacts of events on remote audiences.

Stressors: Expenditure and Investment in Events

The first stressor or causal force is economic, relating to investments and event-related expenditures. Invested money could be spent elsewhere (i.e., events have 'opportunity costs'), resulting in a potential diminishment of social and cultural expenditure. On the other hand, new wealth created through investments and tourism could be used to enhance social and cultural programs. If the economy prospers, everyone potentially gains in social and cultural terms. Economic benefits can be maximized when money flows directly from tourists into a community-controlled event and locally owned businesses. This is usually a convincing argument made in favour of mega-events in particular, and event tourism in general.

'Social exchange theory' suggests that some groups in society will not perceive benefits, and might actually have costs or other negative impacts imposed upon them, resulting in disadvantage, dissatisfaction, and potentially political action. Researchers studying the Gold Coast (Australia) Indy races determined that where one lived in relation to the races, and respondent's occupations, helped explain positive and negative attitudes towards the event (Fredline and Faulkner, 1998, 2002a, b).

Politicians and other influential stakeholders should be explicitly accountable for the potential costs and benefits. If they have formulated sound policies, and commit to ongoing evaluation of costs and benefits, then we can say their actions are rational.

Event Tourism and Host–Guest Interactions

To the degree that events generate tourism, then direct and indirect interactions between hosts (residents) and guests (tourists) will result. Many social scientists have argued that tourism in general is a destructive force in cultural terms, and that cultural events in particular are easily 'commodified' as tourist attractions.

Some authors have worried about the negative influence of tourism on traditional cultures (e.g., Greenwood, 1972; Jordan, 1980; Wilson and Udall, 1982). Often these effects are most visible in the area of cultural productions such as rituals, music, dance and festivals, and particularly those which incorporate traditional costumes. Residents of destination areas quickly learn that culture can become a 'commodity' for which tourists will pay a great amount, resulting in either the transformation of occasional, sometimes sacred events into regular performances, or the modification of rituals into forms of entertainment which are easier to perform or please the audiences more. In both cases, the rewards become monetary and divorced from their cultural meanings.

However, there is little agreement on tourism being bad for cultural events, or on how and why negative impacts occur (see, e.g., Noronha, 1977; Macnaught, 1982; Getz, 1998b).

Some authors have argued that tourism actually helps to preserve or revive traditions and strengthen indigenous cultures (e.g., Boissevan, 1979; Cheska, 1981), and events are one of the most common mechanisms. Sofield (1991) examined a successful, traditional event in the South Pacific and drew conclusions regarding the analysis and attainment of sustainability for indigenous cultural tourism developments.

Events and event tourism can be transforming forces/processes, changing entire communities or social groups. Outcomes can be variously interpreted as positive or negative, depending on one's point of view and the information available. The entire community or society might adapt a particular stance towards them, such as events are good for the community/economy, or event tourism is bad for the environment/culture. Inevitably, a political response is necessary to perceived negatives and hostile attitudes, although it is wise to have policy and strategy in place before the problems arise.

Shaw and Williams (2004: 175) modelled 'stages in cultural commodification' for festivals and events affected by tourism. They believe that 'commodification' is part of consumer culture, that commodification and consumerism lead to dependency in tourist destination areas, and that the commodification of social and ritual events leads to '. . . an erosion of meaning, accompanied by community fragmentation.' Their stages are as follows:

1. Independent travelers take an interest in local events; they observe, but do not necessarily understand meanings.
2. Growth in organized tourism occurs.
3. Tour operators market local culture as an attraction.
4. Events become staged for tourists, leading to a loss of meaning for local people (the event is a commodity) and tourists are observing 'pseudo events'.

Shaw and Williams (2004: 177) also discussed how events negotiate or mediate commodification, drawing on a number of specific cases reported in the literature. Laxson (1991) described how Native Americans limited access by tourists to their own pueblo culture, keeping some aspects of their rituals secret. Other native communities have denied access to sacred rituals but have made other performances a regular part of pow-wows that seek to attract tourists. Picard (1996) reported that some Balinese dances performed for tourists are 'staged authenticity' because they do not contain elements that are reserved for authentic rituals.

Cultural celebrations have cultural and social impacts, perhaps reinforcing traditions or a dominant value set. The authenticity question requires careful consideration of what it means and how it can be evaluated from multiple perspectives. 'Festivalization' is both a powerful economic and tourism force in terms of its impacts, but to some observers it is a negative cultural force. Differences of opinion are the norm whenever cultural values are being discussed.

Health concerns are ever-increasing, especially because of the widespread fear that global pandemics are looming. The first things to be shut down when a serious threat is perceived will be travel and events. Ironically, to bounce back destinations will employ events and media coverage to broadcast that they are safe and open for tourism.

Conflicts over resource or venue use are a very specific form of host–guest interaction. Do residents feel deprived when tourism-oriented events are held in their parks and theatres? Or does the additional revenue generated help support local parks, recreation and cultural programming?

Community Involvement in Events

The extent to which residents are involved with events, from volunteering to ownership, and including citizen power to influence the decision-making process, can determine or moderate many social, cultural and political outcomes. To what extend can events contribute to social integration, combating social conflict or build community pride? Largely unproven claims have been made about the socially transforming power of events, so more research is definitely justified here. Similarly, do cultural events promote and enhance appreciation of, and support for the arts and other cultural pursuits?

Waitt's (2004) critical examination of the 2000 Sydney Olympic Games provides an example of how 'civic boosterism' was employed to create a dominant, positive representation of the Games, and to exclude or silence its critics. While the Games were used to reposition Sydney in the world context, they also had to be sold to the population through exploitation of Olympic symbolism and rhetoric, and through promises of major, lasting benefits. Another study, abstracted in the research note below, looked at residents of Salt Lake City.

Research Note

Gursoy, D., and Kendall, K. (2006). Hosting mega events: modelling locals' support. Annals of Tourism Research, 33(3): 603–623.

Research concerned the 2002 Winter Olympic Games in Salt Lake City. Resident support for the event was found to rely heavily on perceived benefits, which supports social exchange theory. The authors concluded that a collaborative decision-making model for events is desirable, and as an important input the residents should be consulted or canvassed on their concern for, and attachment to the community, because high levels lead to support for mega-events. Strong ecocentric values (i.e., positive towards the environment) do not necessarily translate into opposition, but such people will pay more attention to the costs.

Other researchers have found that support for mega-events varies over time, and a sampling of public opinion after an event will likely reveal a lowered impression of benefits. Euphoria and heavy political support before will persuade many people that the event is worthwhile, but afterwards they look for benefits that might not have accrued (Mihalik, 2001).

Delamere (2001) and Delamere et al. (2001) developed a scale to measure attitudes toward the social impacts of community festivals. Fredline and Faulkner (1998, 2002a, b) and Fredline (2006) noted that there are two traditions of research on event and event tourism impacts on host communities. Some studies look at broad, general impacts, while others look at how specific groups are impacted or feel about tourism and events. Recent attention has concentrated on measuring resident perceptions and attitudes towards events, as in the research by Fredline et al. (2003). Those authors argued that more effort is needed to develop consistent measures of social impacts. The concept of 'social capital' is relevant – that is what citizens, organizations, corporations and government agencies 'invest' in making more liveable, safe and healthy communities. Anything that impacts on 'quality of life' is part of the social impact concept developed by these authors.

The ultimate in community acceptance is that events become recognized as permanent 'institutions' in their community. Elsewhere we discussed this in the context of stakeholder theory and noted that key supporters have to become committed to the event, generally taking some level of ownership or at least responsibility for it. It can also be suggested that 'institutions' can only emerge through strong community support as measured by loyal attendance, committed volunteers and political support – especially in a time of crisis. Certainly a congruence of values is required between the event and its community.

Event-Related Development, Activities and Traffic

This category could be broken down into a number of forces or stressors, but they all relate to the operation of the event itself. Events generally produce positive impacts for some, and negative effects for others, often with spatial implications. Impacts of noise, congestion, crime or other disruption to community life occur in spatial and temporal patterns. For an example of research on events and crime see Barker et al. (2003).

The first comprehensive, and landmark study of event impacts (Adelaide's Grand Prix, by Burns et al., 1986) examined how residents were affected in their homes and while conducting their normal business, such as by increased commuting times. Accident rates were also analyzed, revealing a so-called 'hoon effect' attributed to the atmosphere of the races and the nature of those attracted to them. Ritchie (1984) suggested that the sociocultural impacts of events could include the benefits of an increase in activities associated with the event (e.g., arts or sports) and strengthening of regional values or traditions.

A fascinating account of a special event gone wrong was provided by Cunneen and Lynch (1988). They described how the annual Australian Grand Prix Motorcycle Races had become the scene for institutionalized rioting, despite, or perhaps because of, the efforts of organizers and police to control crowd behaviour. After some time, people came for the riots rather than the races. Obviously a major re-positioning of the event was necessitated.

Media Coverage

Media coverage of events can have global reach, influencing people around the world, and must be managed if destination promotion is to be positively enhanced (Getz and Fairley, 2004). Conversely, media attention focused on events can impact on the host community. Using events for image enhancement, branding or repositioning can also have unexpected social and cultural consequences. Do residents support the images in question, or in general favour exploitation of their culture in tourism marketing?

'Social Representation Theory' (Pearce et al., 1996) suggests that communities or societies build up representations of events based on experiences, social interaction, available information and the media. These representations are resistant to change and may influence attitudes towards new events. In some communities, therefore, we can expect to find dominant attitudes that events are good, or a threat. Such attitudes might not be strictly rational.

Hall (1992) also noted that major events, particularly those with global media coverage, tend to attract potentially violent protests and political demonstrations. This has obvious security implications and might discourage some communities from promoting their events.

Economic Outcomes

The economic impacts of events has received enormous research attention, and generated considerable controversy over methods and applications. While this has been an inevitable occurrence, given the politics of events and tourism, it also has distracted from the advancement of research tools and convincing measures of social, cultural and environmental outcomes (Carlsen et al., 2001) (Figure 11.3).

Stressors or causal forces	Potential economic impacts	Possible responses
Investment and New Money • Construction of event venues • Sponsorship and grants • Organizational expenditure	• New money flows into area and generates income and wealth • Opportunity costs mean that other development actions are not taken • Event organizers might lose money • New event venues and infrastructure builds tourism and event capacity • Inflation of prices for residents	• Perceived economic benefits drive event tourism policy and marketing; subsidies for event bidding and organizations are justified • Cost/benefit evaluation called for • Strategic planning for event tourism; partnerships with sponsors and between agencies of government • Develop and use local suppliers
Event tourism	• Mass tourism or niche markets	• Competitive strategy (bidding, producing, facilitating events) • Packaging for extended stays and spreading the benefits more widely • Leverage events for trade and development • Market to high-yield event tourists
Activities at and surrounding events	• Isolation or spread of economic benefits through tourist spending	• Planned leveraging of event benefits involves many partners
Land use changes	• Creation of event zones • Restructuring of areas has both positive and negative impacts on businesses and residents	• Integrated urban development and renewal involves events and venues
Individual and community involvement	• Capacity building for economic development	• Distribution of costs and benefits should be a major policy issue
Media coverage	• Fair coverage of costs and benefits?	• Media impact on policy

Figure 11.3 Economic outcomes.

A secondary line of economic research has examined other benefits such as urban renewal, increased trade and industrial productivity. These are usually related to large events that require substantial public and private investments. Much less-well researched and understood is the economics of organizing and producing events as a business venture (this is an application of microeconomics), or in the not-for-profit sector (where a combination of business and institutional/philanthropic values are at work).

Investment and New Money

Economic benefits are generated when events can be shown to attract new (or 'incremental') money into an area from investment, grants, sponsorship and tourists. Where the money comes from, and who is liable for ongoing operating costs or losses, is a big issue. When it comes to employment effects, typically only one-time mega-events generate a lot of construction and thereby stimulate employment growth.

It is still sometimes argued by event 'boosters' that mega-events generate huge benefits from the legacy of infrastructure and venues, but this assertion can easily be wrong. The investments in infrastructure and venues are true costs of holding events, and area residents are liable to pay for these 'investments' over many years. Perhaps the event is a catalyst for accelerating investments in infrastructure or venues that would otherwise be needed. Also, the 'investment' might have a long-term benefit in generating new tourism business through the hosting of events that could not otherwise have occurred. Remember that the term 'investment' implies a future return, and this has to be carefully scrutinized for events.

To argue that a city will gain facilities from an event that it otherwise would not have makes economic sense only if they are completely paid for (capital and future operating costs) by external agents, such as central government or sponsors. Otherwise, residents should decide if they really need, or want to pay for them. As well, if a higher level of government is paying, then one city gains at the expense of all others. The central government would have to show that the 'investment' is good for the whole country.

It is also pointless to say that needed facilities will be developed sooner, as a legacy of the event, if those facilities are not really affordable. For example, can a city really afford a new train system that is needed primarily because it will host a mega-event? This is tantamount to mortgaging the future, because it imposes higher taxation on future generations of residents. On the other hand, action now might prevent or solve future congestion problems, so it becomes a difficult decision.

A related issue is that of surplus capacity. Many communities have publicly financed parks, recreation and cultural facilities that are underutilized. To the extent that events make better use of these public assets, specifically by generating increased revenues through tourism and additional consumer spending, then some degree of public subsidy is also warranted.

Governments usually realize a substantial tax return from events, whether they 'invest' in them or not.

Research Note

Tohmo, T. (2005). Economic impacts of cultural events on local economies: an input–output analysis of the Kaustinen Folk Music Festival. Tourism Economics, 11(3): 431–451.

An example of event impact studies, but using input–output analysis rather than applying a multiplier. Results showed that it was a good investment for local government in terms of generating tax revenue (i.e., the economic benefits of tourism) and attracting funds from central government (a policy issue). Implications for regional policy are drawn.

Other studies of event impacts have clearly demonstrated the tax benefits for all layers of government (see, e.g., Taylor and Gratton, 1988; Coopers and Lybrand, 1989; Turco, 1995; Andersson and Samuelson, 2000). A major reason is that travel and events result in more consumption of heavily taxed goods and services, as well as bringing in new tourism revenue. Dimanche (1996) studied the infrastructural developments associated with the New Orleans World's Fair, saying it created a legacy in terms of new hotels, transportation and other facilities that benefited tourism – and thereby lead to future tax gains.

Event Tourism

The most-studied event impact stems from the role events play in attracting visitors to an area who would not otherwise travel there. There can be no doubt that events in general are tourist motivators, or increase a destination's appeal, but it cannot be assumed that events have tourism-related economic impacts. They have to be shown to motivate travel that would not otherwise occur. Numerous reports on tourism impacts exist, and the section on impact assessment ending this chapter provides references on how it should be done validly. Despite the state-of-the-art being well documented, some event tourism impact studies still make fundamental mistakes like failing to prove the event motivated new travel and spending, or by not discounting for time switching, casual attendees or displacement effects.

Throughout this book attention is paid to reasons for attending events, including travel motivations and event careers. Events also attract many people for generic benefits, usually entertainment and socializing in nature, but it is likely the most beneficial events from a tourism perspective are those that attract people seeking specific benefits (i.e., the niche markets). These include participation events and events organized by and for special interest groups. Mackellar (2006) examined this issue specifically by comparing nine events in one Australian region, and found they variously attracted 'community social seekers' to 'leisure fanatics'. A 'special interest event spectrum' was suggested as a way to classify events, and develop a portfolio, using the ratio of visitors to locals.

The economic benefits of event tourist segments have been studied, but not in any systematic, comparative way. Grado et al. (1998) and Dwyer (2002) looked at the convention tourist's impacts. Andersson and Solberg (1999) examined sport event tourists, and Solberg et al. (2002) studied business travelers to sport events (the media, etc.). The economic benefits derived from festival tourists have been researched by Crompton et al. (2001) and the British Arts Festivals Association (2003). Impacts of visitors to a travelling art exhibition were examined by Mihalik and Wing-Vogelbacher (1992). Major studies of festival tourism impacts have been carried out in Canada's National Capital Region (Coopers and Lybrand, 1989) and in Edinburgh (Scotinform, 1991).

Increasing attention has been given to 'leveraging' events in order to improve tourism impacts, stimulate local businesses (e.g., Chalip and Leyns, 2002) or increase trade in general (Brown, 2002). The aim of 'leveraging' strategies is to generate greater economic benefits from events, over a longer period of time, and to spread them more widely. This can be accomplished through encouraging tourism pre- and post-event, packaging event visits with wider travel itineraries, and joint marketing among attractions and destinations. Fostering trade and industrial spin-offs is another approach, and it requires sophistication in managing diverse stakeholders such as sponsors who bring their business partners to events for hospitality.

Globally, the competition for event tourism has become fierce. Destinations establish event development corporations or units, and employ professionals who bid on events that can be moved about, including world's fairs and the Olympics. In developing event 'portfolios' for the destination, thought has to be given to the individual and cumulative impacts of events, using a variety of potential measures of outcomes and value.

Activities at, and Surrounding the Event

Sometimes the concentration of economic activity at an event actually hurts other businesses. People might stay away from business areas because they fear the event-related crowds, while others are motivated to leave town or stay at home. These are all 'displacement' effects. To combat this potential problem requires 'leveraging' the event with a variety of businesses in the community to ensure they all benefit.

A paper by Chalip and Leyns (2002) showed how local businesses could increase their benefits from events through partnerships. Pennington-Gray and Holdnak (2002) researched a tourism event that was unfortunately 'disconnected' from its region, thereby minimizing the spread of benefits. They recommended ways to promote the event and destination together, for mutual benefits.

Land Use Changes

Large-scale events are typically planned with urban renewal and development in mind, thereby potentially creating permanent alterations to the landscape and civic economy. Some cities, like Gothenburg in Sweden, have developed permanent event and entertainment zones that perform important social and economic roles.

Carlsen and Taylor (2003) looked at the ways in which Manchester used the Commonwealth Games to heighten the city's profile, give impetus to urban renewal through sport and commercial developments, and create a social legacy through cultural and educational programming.

Individual and Community Involvement

Economic change in the long run, related to events, will require a strategic approach, and high levels of involvement from local businesses and the community at large. This can be called 'capacity building', or making certain that a single or multiple events lead to improved ability and willingness to attract and host higher-yielding visitors in the future.

Ways to maximize local economic benefits from events were discussed by Getz (2005). To the extent possible, 'leakages' from the local economy should be minimized by the use of resident staff and local suppliers, thereby increasing 'backward linkages'. Reinvesting profits or surplus earnings in the host community is a good way to boost support for events.

Media Coverage

We have already discussed the imputed benefits of media coverage, and how destination images and branding are potentially enhanced through events. It should not be forgotten that negative images can also be communicated widely, with potentially damaging consequences to the destination.

A common concern is the fairness and completeness of media reporting on event costs and benefits, and the related issue of how authorities and event boosters might exploit the media to achieve public support for their plans.

Environmental Outcomes

Conducting EIAs (Environmental Impact Assessments) before and after events should be the norm, but is not. The Olympics has an environmental policy that goes some way to ensuring that host cities implement green operations and sustainable design measures. But the sheer size of mega-events, especially those requiring new venue construction, ensures that claims to being green and sustainable are often met with scepticism (Figure 11.4).

Stressors or causal forces	Potential environmental impacts	Possible responses
Investment and development	• Direct impacts on land, wildlife and resources • Subsequent generation of waste and ongoing resource use • Urbanization process • Aesthetics	• Avoid sensitive areas • Regulate development for environmental sustainability • Impose full life cycle accounting • Use development to clean up damaged areas • Impose design standards
Event tourism	• Generates traffic, congestion • Consumes energy	• Favour/require mass transit • Concentrate events • Stress small-scale events
Activities	• Visitor activities and crowding can be harmful to the environment directly (e.g., trampling and erosion) or indirectly (through resource consumption and waste generated)	• Require green event practices (Reduce, Re-use, Recycle) • Clean up after events • Educate visitors (social marketing for attitude and behaviour change)
Land use changes	• Environmental legacy of positive change, or damaged ecosystems	• Community-based planning to accommodate and regulate events
Individual and community involvement	• Personal and community-felt impacts on daily life	• Enhanced pressure or support for environmental management • Lobbying by special interest groups • Multi-stakeholder inputs needed
Media coverage	• Balanced coverage of environmental issues?	• Role in shaping public opinion and policy

Figure 11.4 Environmental outcomes.

Investment and Development

The construction of new venues can have huge impacts on the physical environment and ecological systems, both immediately and in the long run. Consequently it is generally wiser to utilize existing facilities to the fullest. A full life-cycle accounting process should ensure that event facilities are planned to be waste-reducing, energy-efficient and recyclable.

Although building greener and more sustainable infrastructure for events is obviously wise, the very need for large-scale, new venues is hard to justify in environmental terms. Cities wanting the new development have to come up with integrative strategies and justifications that are convincing to many interest groups.

Event Tourism

Although highly valued for their tourism impacts, the resultant travel has an environmental cost. 'Green events' have to encompass more than on-site considerations, they have to look at the entire travel and hosting process. How can total travel be reduced by locating the event optimally, relative to the market? Can public transport be used more efficiently, especially to reduce congestion? What size of event is tolerable or sustainable in any given environment?

Tourism itself consumers vast quantities of fuel and generates untold amounts of greenhouse gasses. There are many who argue for less tourism, and therefore would approve of events that are local in orientation. Until the travel industries convert to alternative, cleaner and renewable fuels, this criticism will continue to intensify.

Activities

What do visitors do when they attend events, both on-site and in the area? Can they be educated on environmental and social responsibility, to avoid negative impacts? Specific concerns include resultant traffic and congestion, the possibility of damage to sensitive areas, and the addition to waste and pollution. The 'greening' of events will remain a major issue, with the Olympics leading the way by implementing its own environmental program. A good example of how an event can become more environmentally friendly is that of the Cherry Creek Arts Festival in Denver, Colorado (profiled in Getz, 1997, and again in 2005). Events can also be positive tools in conservation, such as festivals and shows held to raise awareness or funds.

Events will increasingly be evaluated by reference to principles of sustainable development. Currently many events are not sustainable when it comes to some or all of the following criteria:

• Minimization of waste, energy consumption, and pollution.
• Keeping private travel to a minimum.
• Protecting resources for the future.
• Fostering a positive environmental attitude.
• Re-using facilities; not building needless infrastructure.
• Avoiding damage to wildlife habitat and ecological systems.

Detailed guidelines for 'green' or 'sustainable' events are available from a number of published and online sources: www.greengold.on.ca; www.ecorecycle.vic.gov.au; www.bluegreenmeetings.org. David Chernushenko's books on green games and green sport organizations should be consulted (see Further Readings). Green and Gold Inc. also has a book describing sustainable design principles applied by the Sydney 2000 Olympic Games.

Land Use Changes

Community-based planning is needed to accommodate and regulate events, the construction of venues and establishment of event zones in cities. Mega-events resulting in large-scale venue and infrastructure development will permanently alter the landscape, and in many circumstances this is a valued and planned-for outcome. When it is not part of the initial event concept, or bid, it can be expected that long-term benefits will be harder to achieve.

Individual and Community Involvement

Economic and social impacts of events might be more obvious, but a loss of amenity, destruction of habitat, and disruption of wildlife, will be noticed by residents. Their reaction will typically be negative, stimulating a policy debate and response. In Calgary, for example, the frequent use of a city park (Princes Island) for events led to neighbourhood protests and the imposition of time and noise restrictions.

More proactive community involvement, especially in policy-making for events, should aim to prevent negative impacts and install a more comprehensive evaluation and management system for the whole event sector. A feeling of 'community ownership' in specific events should translate into better environmental management.

Media Coverage

The media might have to be educated on environmental impacts, especially regarding subtle, cumulative changes in land use, ecological processes, and amenity loss. Environmental issues tend to receive less attention than economic impacts, yet strong coverage by the media can have real influence on public environmental attitudes, as demonstrated by the building of awareness and interest in global warming issues.

Impact Assessment and Cost–Benefit Evaluation

Economic impact studies for events have often been flawed, and in some cases deliberately (Crompton and McKay, 1994). For political reasons, it can be advantageous to exaggerate benefits and minimize costs. Forecasting big benefits before an event is common practice, followed by secrecy when it comes to releasing post-event evaluations. With time, these shoddy and unethical practices will become impossible to continue in the face of public outrage and media scepticism.

The state-of-the art in economic impact assessments for events has progressed to the point where we can say there is no excuse for invalid and unreliable studies. The first comprehensive economic assessment of a major Australian event by Burns et al. (1986) laid most of the foundations, including economic cost/benefit evaluations. Crompton's (1999) report for the National Parks and Recreation Association provides specific guidelines for municipalities to do valid event impact studies.

Two landmark journal articles by Dwyer et al. (2000), published in *Event Management*, lay out the requirements for assessing and forecasting event impacts; they were based on a kind of meta-analysis of Australian event impact studies, as well as economic theory. Dwyer et al. (2006) have recommended use of 'computable general equilibrium models' for assessing the economic impacts of events beyond the local area, rather than input–output models. The input–output approach, they argued, contains an upward bias if used for broad regions or nations.

The Cooperative Research Centre in Sustainable Tourism in Australia has published a series on event impacts including the book *Economic Evaluation of Special Events: A Practitioner's Guide* by Jago and Dwyer (2006) and a kit for conducting studies (see www.crctourism.com).

The main potential error in traditional economic impact studies is a failure to clearly identify 'new' or 'incremental' income for the region, that is money that would not have entered the economy if it was not for the event. All benefits have to be 'attributed' to the event this way, and not to tourism in general. For example, only the money spent by tourists who travelled because of the event should be included.

Related measurement issues that have to be considered include the identification of 'time switching' (the visitors would have come to the destination anyway, they merely changed their time to correspond with the event) and 'casual tourists' who travelled for other reasons but also attended the event. 'Displacement' is another issue, as events might attract tourists who take rooms from regular visitors (this happens during peak travel seasons), or residents might refrain from shopping because of congestion associated with the event.

But the biggest weakness of traditional economic impact assessment is that they are too narrow in scope. Basically, such studies look for tourism-generated benefits and tend to ignore costs and negative outcomes. Hence we need comprehensive cost and benefit evaluations, as recommended by Mules and Dwyer (2006), and especially to assist public policy on financial support for events.

Comprehensive Cost and Benefit Evaluation

The main costs and benefits to be evaluated are as follows:

- *Tangible benefits*: Expenditure of sponsors and other investors (e.g., external grants); new facilities and venues (if funded externally); new employment; event tourist expenditures (and the 'multiplier' effect); positive media coverage resulting in tourism gains; general economic growth and trade; increased capacity (marketing and accommodation) resulting in future tourism growth; retained resident expenditure (this is controversial).
- *Tangible costs*: Capital and construction costs; wages and other employment costs; essential services (police, infrastructure etc.); long-term maintenance of venues.
- *Intangible benefits*: Community pride; cultural renewal; increased interest and investment in the host community or destination; enhanced real estate values.
- *Intangible costs*: Crowding and inconvenience; noise and visual pollution; personal crime and property damage; resident exodus and tourist avoidance of the area.

Costs or problems not taken into the accounts of events are termed 'externalities', and they include indirect and intangible problems like pollution and amenity loss, social and cultural disruption. 'Opportunity costs' should also be considered. These are all the alternative uses that could be made of capital, human effort, and other resources. If events constitute good investments, it has to be asked of the same resources would generate more benefits when applied to other projects.

It should always be asked 'who gains and who pays?' for events. The distribution of costs and benefits might very well be the most important issue, especially because it often seems that industry and the community's powerful elite realize huge profits at the taxpayer's expense, even while poor people are displaced or the middle class has its taxes increased to pay for the mega-event or new event venue. Is this just perception or a myth? If so, why are so few cost–benefit or post-event impact assessments conducted, and why do government agencies or event development corporations behave so secretly when it comes to accounting for expenditure on events?

The Legacy

Evaluation of events often has to consider long-term, indirect, often subtle impacts. The term 'legacy' applies to all that is left over from the event (or events) as a positive inheritance for future generations, or as problems to deal with (for discussions of event 'legacies', see Hall, 1997; Getz, 1999; Andersson et al., 1999; Ritchie, 2000).

Sometimes the true value of an element of the legacy will not be clear for a very long time, or a consensus on the value might never be achieved. The Calgary experience is informative, as this host city of the 1988 Winter Olympic Games reputedly realized a surplus of $300 million dollars (Can.) which has grown substantially and provides ongoing support for facility maintenance, amateur sport initiatives, a winter festival, and event bidding and hosting.

Mega-events especially are often 'sold' to the public (and they need selling, given the high public costs) on the basis of many benefits plus creation of a permanent legacy. To the extent that the legacy is intangible, consisting of national pride or increased legitimacy in the international community, an economic and business case does not really have to be made. But all claims made about increased tourism and the benefits of new infrastructure require careful economic assessment.

What usually happens is that mega-events are justified in advance in economic and business terms, but a full cost/benefit accounting is never forthcoming, for purely political reasons. Many costs are typically hidden, or treated as externalities, the big items being transportation improvements and security. The so-called induced tourism, supposedly generating a 'quantum leap' in tourist demand (Getz, 1999), seldom materializes, and if tourism does flourish in the aftermath it is impossible to prove that it happened because of the event.

The concepts of 'net present value' and 'future earnings' can be useful in evaluating the legacy. As pointed out by many economists, the development of new infrastructure for events is a cost of hosting the event, and not a benefit. Any derived, future benefits first have to be justified in terms of future earnings, and then discounted because of depreciation, increasing maintenance costs, and of course normal investment opportunity costs. Many so-called legacies have turned into expensive, useless 'white elephants'.

Research Project

Monitor the impacts of the 2012 Summer Olympic Games in London (or some other major event) in relation to promises made and various stakeholder expectations expressed in advance. Consider the role of the media in shaping public perceptions and attitudes toward the event. Consider how the impacts will be distributed, measured and accounted for.

What is an Event Worth?

What is an event worth? There is no absolute answer, so let's examine the different ways of addressing this question.

Economic Impact

The calculation of economic impact is generally restricted to 'new money' coming into an area because of the event, and its 'multiplier' effect. This estimate is mostly expressed in terms of 'income' or 'value added' to the area. Many authors have used multipliers, which are problematic in both theory and practical application (see, e.g, Vaughan, 1979; Archer, 1982; Burns et al., 1986; Fleming and Toepper, 1990; Crompton and McKay, 1994; Crompton, 1999; Dwyer et al., 2000; Yu and Turco, 2000; Tyrrell and Johnston, 2001; Jago and Dwyer, 2006). As noted above, this approach is narrow and often ignores costs.

Total Revenue

A simple calculation of how much revenue or 'new money' an event brings into the area is useful. Consider not just consumer spending, but also ticket and retail sales, rents and commissions, donations, grants and sponsorship revenue. This is usually going to be equal to the revenue or income side of the budget.

Return on Investment

To private investors, the 'Return on Investment' (ROI) is their measure of value. In other words, for every dollar invested, what are their profits or earnings? Tourism agencies investing in events often equate 'economic impact' with ROI. For social or cultural investments more intangible measures of ROI are required, such as changes in awareness, attitudes and behaviour.

Consumer Surplus and Existence Values

The event is worth the value that consumers assign to it in terms of 'willingness to pay'. Their 'utility value' (i.e., benefits gained from the event) might be higher than the cost they have to pay or the value of the resources consumer to produce the event. This approach to valuation is difficult, given that people are possibly unable or unwilling to talk about hypotheticals like 'what would you pay if–?' Andersson and Samuelson (2000) advised on the use of the 'contingent valuation method' for events.

Similarly, the 'existence value' of an event could be measured by asking residents what they would pay to create or keep an event, say from their own wallets or in increased taxes. The theory is that people value things even if they do not see or use them. Researchers could also ask: Who will support or rescue a threatened event: Is it worth enough to the community to bail out more than once: And what might the rescue package legitimately cost?

Sponsorship Potential

One approach is to determine the value of events to sponsors, as properties for investment and co-branding. In other words, how much will the 'title' and all other sponsors pay (or commit 'in-kind'/'contra') to the event? This is useful because a not-for-profit or public organization can put a commercial value on the event. International Events Group (IEG 1995: 19) advised event owners to consider that qualitative benefits offered to sponsors are more important than the value of tangible things like tickets and gifts. Prestige has a value, but only a surrogate measure of it can be made.

Media Value

Many events assign a dollar value to the media coverage they get by valuing the coverage at the same price you would have to pay if it was advertising. For example, news reports about the event could be given a dollar value based on the cost of an equivalent paid advertisement. But this practice ignores the fact that advertising is targeted and usually repetitive, with its timing and reach under control. It also tends to ignore the content by looking mainly at quantity. Finally, it says nothing about the potential effects of the coverage on audiences.

Shibli and the Sport Industry Research Centre (2002) took a sample of television viewers in the UK to measure the average and peak size of the live broadcast audience for a snooker championship in Sheffield, England. As well they determined its television 'rating' (i.e., the percentage of all viewers watching a single program). The volume of clearly visible or audible exposure for sponsors' logos or messages was calculated using specially trained observers and software, then a cash equivalent value was calculated based on how much it would cost to purchase television advertising in the form of 30-second messages. The same was done for messages about Sheffield. The report emphasized that there is no guarantee that such media exposure is effective.

Psychic Benefits

Burns et al. (1986) determined that the Adelaide Grand Prix imposed costs and problems on the resident population, but a large majority still thought the event was desirable and should be held again. In other words, it had 'psychic value' for them which was at least equal to the monetary value of all those personal and community-felt costs.

Multiple Perspectives on Value

As argued throughout this book, a multi-stakeholder approach is important. What does the community think about the event? Its sponsors and grant givers? Its suppliers, volunteers, staff? The tourism and hospitality sectors, and the arts community? There really is no one measure of value that sums up all these perspectives, so all their views should be solicited. Together, they constitute the community that can help an event be accepted or validated, even becoming a permanent institution.

Also, principles of 'sustainable development' can be applied to evaluating the worth of an event. Ask these questions: Did the event (or events) make it more costly or difficult for future generations to enjoy an equal or better quality of life? Were irreplaceable resources used up? Do events add to global environmental problems, or help solve them? Could the long-term impacts be predicted and, where necessary, were preventative and ameliorative actions implemented?

Chapter Summary

Outcomes should be considered in the context of the open-system model of event organizations. There are intended outcomes, with the event being a transforming process, and evaluation is required to determine the 'effectiveness' of the system in attaining these goals. 'Efficiency' also has to be evaluated, because resources are generally scarce. Some outcomes are unintended, and even 'external' to the event and the organization. External stakeholders are likely to focus on these impacts. Those who are 'impacted' by events are legitimate stakeholders, including those who represent environmental, social and cultural concerns.

When conducting impact assessments, or evaluation of outcomes, 'stressors' or 'causal factors' should first be identified. It is not just the event itself that can cause changes, so we have to consider related investments, tourism, physical developments and media effects. The degree to which the community is involved in the event, or in policy formulation related to events, will also have an important bearing on outcomes and on how people feel they have been impacted. Stressors then have to be linked to the full range of potential outcomes, both desired and unintended, internal and external. Whether impacts are positive or negative will depend on one's perspective and on the research and evaluation methods used. This analysis leads to policy, strategy and other possible responses.

'Personal outcomes' were discussed first. We believe, from theory, that people attending events can have positive and negative experiences, and these lead to potential changes within people (such as attitudes and motivations) and in their future behaviour. Partly this in the realm of generic consumer behaviour, but we have to spend more effort through research and theoretical development on understanding the unique dimensions of planned event experiences. One especially important outcome to be given more attention is the formation and implications of 'event careers'. The discussion of 'personal outcomes' also considered how general social, environmental and economic factors surrounding events can influence individuals, such as through the creation of 'social representations' of events.

In considering economic, social, cultural and political outcomes together, the first major stressor is investment and development. 'New money' that flows into an area with events can cause substantial change, and hopefully create income and wealth for residents, leading to support for events. Ideally, capacity for tourism and future events is increased and events are leveraged for additional economic growth. But opportunity costs must also be considered, as tourism can be developed in a variety of ways, plus it is not always a politically acceptable form of public-sector investment.

'Event tourism' as a stressor has several dimensions, starting with the expenditure of visitors but also extending to their activities and especially their interactions with, and influences on residents. Host–guest relations therefore becomes a policy issue, encompassing potential cultural changes. In economic terms, event tourism is a very competitive marketplace so related costs are continuously rising. Policy and strategy have to consider competitive advantages, visitor yield, and leveraging tools.

Activities at or surrounding events are social stressors, especially through noise, traffic, crime and amenity loss, often resulting in or opposition from residents. Developments surrounding events are also stressors. Permanent land use changes, including event zones in cities, can have profound consequences. Mega-events are usually conceived in the context of urban renewal or development schemes, especially when new event venues and tourism infrastructure are established; long-term maintenance costs have to be part of the cost–benefit evaluation.

Outcomes, and evaluation of whether they are positive or negative impacts, depends in part on the level of community involvement. A feeling of control, ownership, and real participation in events has to be cultivated in host communities, or else support will be lacking. Events should be viewed as a mechanism for social integration, community pride and cultural development – on par with the economic benefits. Events that want to be accepted or become permanent institutions must first satisfy diverse interests and attract strong, committed supporters. The distribution of costs and benefits is always going to be a key political issue, as criticism of major events in particular has abounded, often related to perceived gaps in what is promised versus delivered, and related to who is benefiting versus paying the price.

Lastly, we considered media coverage to be a stressor. The media not only acts as sponsor of many events, but helps establish 'social representations' that can directly impact on event success and event-related policy. The power of the media in the events sector should not be underestimated.

For environmental outcomes the same stressors were discussed. Changes result from event-related investment and development, travel and tourism, and tourist/guest activities at and surrounding events. Permanent land use changes can result, and these have environmental consequences as well. We have to evaluate not only potential direct impacts on ecosystems and wildlife, but also longer-term and cumulative change processes linked to tourism and events. Required policy responses include the integration of events and tourism with all other planning systems, and insistence upon the application of sustainable development principles and green operational standards throughout the events and tourism sectors. A lot of evaluation has to go into any decision related to mega-events, as these can have dramatic consequences in all outcome fields.

Following the discussion of key outcome fields, economic impact assessment was considered. This was not on how to do them (as plenty of good advice is available), but on some common weaknesses and research challenges. This led to the argument that comprehensive cost and benefit evaluations, including consideration of the distribution of costs and benefits and long-term changes (the 'legacy'), must be undertaken for events.

The chapter ends with the question 'what are events worth?', and a discussion of various ways to answer it. Some methods are financial, and others focus on the intangibles. In the end, a multi-perspective approach is best, so that events can be justified to all stakeholders.

Study Questions

- Discuss 'outcomes' and their evaluation in the context of the open system model of event management.
- What are 'stressors' or 'causal forces'?
- Identify the key forces that shape personal event outcomes; discuss how and why people might find their event experiences to be satisfactory or not (or positive/negative).
- How do individuals respond to their direct and indirect event experiences?
- Explain how events can cause social, cultural and political outcomes (i.e., stressors plus potential impacts). Refer specifically to 'exchange theory'.
- What is 'commodification' of culture and how is it related to authenticity in planned events?
- Why and how should we study resident perceptions and attitudes towards events?
- What generates the economic benefits attributed to events? Include 'new money'.
- How might events cause environmental impacts?
- How can events be made sustainable? Take a triple bottom-line approach.
- What research is required in order to perform an economic impact assessment for an event? In what ways is this type of assessment limited in its usefulness for policy?
- Provide a detailed explanation of cost–benefit evaluation for events, including discussion of 'opportunity costs' and the 'distribution' of impacts.
- How can you answer the question 'what is an event worth?'

Further Reading

Chernushenko, D. (2001) *Greening Our Games – Running Sports Events and Facilities that Won't Cost the Earth*. Ottawa: Centurion.

Chernushenko, D., van der Kamp, A., and Stubbs, D. (2001). *Sustainable Sport Management: Running an Environmentally, Socially and Economically Responsible Organization*. Ottawa: United Nations Environment Programme.

Dwyer, L., Mellor, R., Mistillis, N., and Mules, T. (2000). A framework for assessing 'tangible' and 'intangible' impacts of events and conventions. *Event Management*, 6(3): 175–189.

Dwyer, L., Mellor, R., Mistillis, N., and Mules, T. (2000). Forecasting the economic impacts of events and conventions. *Event Management*, 6(3): 191–204.

Fredline, L., Jago, L., and Deery, M. (2003). The development of a generic scale to measure the social impacts of events. *Event Management*, 8(1): 23–37.

Tribe, J. (2005). *The Economics of Recreation, Leisure and Tourism* (3rd edn). Oxford: Elsevier.

Chapter 12
Events and Public Policy

Learning Objectives

- Learn the ways in which planned events fit into various public policy fields.
- Be able to justify public-sector intervention in, and support for planned events.
- Understand how policy involving events is formed in a political environment.
- Know how policy affects event production and management.

What Is Public Policy?

Event managers cannot ignore the many public policies and resulting regulations or laws that impact on the event sector. Conversely, policy-makers in many public policy domains have to gain a better understanding of planned events of all types in order to ensure that events can be a sustainable force for cultural, social and economic progress. Ideally, governments at all levels will create a vision and take an integrated approach to events, or at least ensure that policies affecting events are proactive and coordinated.

We start with a discussion of the nature of public policy and the meaning of 'policy domains'. The second section examines justifications for public intervention in the event sector through discussion of the concepts of 'public goods', 'ideology', 'market failure' and 'efficiency'. Then each major policy domain related to planned events receives a more detailed examination, covering economic policy (development, tourism), social (leisure, sport, health and well-being), cultural (arts) and the environment. Finally, the chapter concludes with a look at the policy-making process as applicable to the event sector.

'Public policy' consists of a goal-directed process by governments and their agencies, manifested in laws, regulations, decisions (both actions and inaction) and intentions of governments regarding specific problems or general areas of public concern. Policy can be viewed in terms of 'power', because political parties, special interest groups and their professional lobbyists constantly seek to influence policy. Political scientists and other researchers can study inequities in who has power, and what interests are actually taken into account when event policy is established.

Policies of government are often based on 'ideology', arising from party-political manifestos. However, determining what is a government's policy in many cases has to be deduced from what they do, or avoid doing, and this might simply reflect the dominant values of society at the time. It might also be difficult to discern the rationality behind government actions, and indeed it often appears that there is no coherent policy on events.

A 'policy domain' is a broad area of government responsibility or interest, such as culture, the economy, environment or health, which usually encompass a variety of departments, agencies, laws, regulations and programmes. Planned events cross a number of policy fields, often involving two or three levels of government, so it will be necessary to develop liaison between agencies on event-related issues, and to develop integrating policies.

If a sector or sub-sector (like tourism or sport tourism, planned events in general, or cultural festivals) achieves a high enough profile, perhaps due to concerted lobbying or changes in ideology, it can become a policy domain with its own ministry, agency and explicit policy. This should result in a higher profile and more effective governmental action. Tourism has in many countries successfully lobbied governments to be considered an 'industry', and in many cases this has resulted in increased planning, better marketing, direct government involvement through funding or the establishment of industry-led tourism commissions. Nothing like this has happened for events, yet, but arts and cultural organizations have in general been fairly successful in being recognized either as an 'industry' or as a policy domain.

The Institutional Framework

Hall and Rusher (2004) noted that the policy dimensions related to events include the political nature of the policy-making process, public participation, sources of power, exercise of choice by policy-makers in a complex environment, and perceptions of the effectiveness of policy. To study event policy therefore requires knowledge of the various institutions involved, and how they interact and make policy. These include the legislators (elected or otherwise), government agencies (such as culture, tourism, sport and economic development), the courts, law enforcement, public–private partnerships, quasi-governmental organization, regulators and other organizations with power, such as trade unions and political parties.

Increasingly cities, regions and countries are creating event-specific agencies or companies to bid on, facilitate or produce events. Unfortunately, public policy gets confusing, and perhaps becomes counter-productive, when governments delegate authority to 'independent' agencies. This can result in secrecy, lack of accountability and decisions made without regard to public needs or preferences.

Each policy field will involve a different network of stakeholders, yet tourism, culture, sports, events, and other networks of agencies and interests overlap considerably. Finding one's way through these networks can be a challenge. Within them, who has power and how is it used? Intra- and intergovernmental conflicts, or lack of integration, also influence event-related policy. National governments typically promote tourism, but often it is local governments who have to provide the infrastructure; it is their voters who feel the immediate impacts. Sport and events might appear to be perfect partners, but each interest group probably wants something different and might fight over resources.

Justifying Public-Sector Involvement

At least at election time, most governments try to justify their policies. They also put forward clearly different policy platforms, based on ideology or the need for positioning. Many voters are swayed by specific proposals or measures, while others are impressed more by values and policies that suggest the general direction a government will take.

Veal (2006) observed that the critical approach to sociological research and theory has raised many public policy questions. For example, who is being served by public expenditure on festivals? Probably the most obvious public policy that relates to planned events is funding, so what is the case for public funding of events? Practice varies widely, with money coming from a variety of public agencies, all aimed at different outcomes. Increasing scrutiny of policy, or of government inaction, leads to many questions being raised in the media and at the community level.

The main lines of justification for public funding or other forms of intervention (like regulations, direct production of events or marketing) start with ideology – namely, what is a 'public good'? After that, 'market failure' or market inadequacies are often cited, and achieving greater efficiency is also used as justification. When we addressed possible responses to outcomes and the question of 'what is an event worth' in the previous chapter, we were setting up this discussion of policy justification. Some of it goes back to the disciplinary overview of economics, and there are other threads of justification running throughout the book, including 'leisure benefits'.

The Public Good Argument and Ideology

The key to this powerful argument is to demonstrate important benefits from events that accrue to society as a whole – or to the economy (which should clearly benefit us all), and to the environment (everyone supports a healthier, safer, more sustainable environment). It should also be made clear by policy-makers that the benefits from events can only be achieved through support and investment in events, or at least that the benefits of events are equal to those from other expenditure/investment opportunities. When backed by research, expert testimony and public opinion surveys showing support for events, the 'public good' argument cannot easily be refuted.

Therefore, in order to make the 'public good' argument valid and convincing, the following criteria have to be met:

- Events fit into accepted policy domains (culture, health, economics, etc.).
- Public benefits are substantial (its worth our while to get involved), inclusive (everyone gains), and they can be demonstrated or proved.
- There are rules and accountability for money spent and other actions taken.

Ideology

Political parties take different approaches to event funding or regulation, and in general to culture, economic development or leisure and sport, based on ideologies. 'Ideology' is rooted in philosophies, value sets and even religious beliefs. Seldom do political parties engage in ideologically based debate over policies towards planned events, but it does happen around specific issues and events – especially for spending on mega-events or event venues, and sometimes regarding the funding of festivals and sports.

In terms of ideological differences, observers can look for the following indicators of substantial differences between party positions, and then asses how they will affect the events sector:

- A general belief in government intervention leads to many programmes of funding as well as to many regulations – versus a general belief in free enterprise, the marketplace and individual rather than collective responsibility.
- Policies that result in governments taking a proactive lead, versus a problem-solving approach (e.g., formulating pro-event policy or merely reacting to issues).
- A belief that culture, sport and leisure are matters of health and public welfare, versus the view that they are best left to individual consumption decisions.
- A belief that tourism is business and best left to the industry, rather than being a social, environmental or cultural issue.
- Responsiveness to special interest groups (which reveals power bases).

Social Equity

The 'social equity' principle is really a part of the 'public good' justification. In the context of planned events it can be stated this way:

> *Where events provide a 'public good' (i.e., benefits accrue to society as a whole), it is justifiable for governments to intervene by way of subsidies (to events or participants) or direct provision of events, in order to ensure that everyone has the means to attend or otherwise benefit from events.*

'Social equity' literally means that access to a public good or service, and to the benefits of public investment, is based on principles of fairness, justice and need. This is not the same as 'equality', wherein everyone gets exactly the same thing. For example, 'equal access' to events or the benefits of events would mean that everyone gets the same, but that principle is not widely held to be feasible or desirable.

Equity is a serious issue for the event sector, particularly because many governments value events in the context of culture, social integration, leisure and health. If left to the free market it is probable that many people will not be able to participate in some events because of high cost, inaccessibility or lack of knowledge about opportunities. While the equity principle justifies subsidies and direct provision, the value of events to society can and should be measured. Over-development of economic impact assessment has left us weak on demonstrating social and cultural values.

Sometimes government action related to events directly violates the equity principle. I see this occur in the arts sector when heavily subsidized institutions and events (such as symphony, ballet, opera, theatre) still charge high ticket prices, making it impossible for the poor to attend. This contravenes the equity principle and has to be corrected. One solution is to maintain high nominal prices (the rich hardly notice it) but to ensure that low-cost tickets are available to those in need. Another is to proactively take art and events to the people.

Failure (or Inadequacies) of the Marketplace

This economic justification for public involvement rests on the premise (or ideological belief) that economic development in general is best left in the hands of the private sector, but in some cases the 'free market' does not provide sufficient incentive or reward to stimulate entrepreneurial activity or to generate public goods and services. Accordingly, giving money to tourism marketing organizations, participating in joint ventures with the private sector, or providing tax incentives or subsidies to investors (including events) can all be justified as a necessary means to achieve public policy aims.

This argument is sometimes extended to providing assistance for the non-profit sector. For example, non-profit organizations produce many festivals and other events in an inherently risky environment, and so they deserve assistance as long as the public good can be demonstrated.

Why Economic 'Laws' Fail in the Event Sector

Mules and Dwyer (2006) and Burgan and Mules (2000) argued that fewer sporting venues would be built and fewer events would occur without public support, because 'market forces' will not support them. Yet many of the direct benefits accrue to the hospitality and travel industry, so why should the public-sector intervene?

The supply of events would eventually reach equilibrium with demand (i.e., what consumers are willing to pay) only if a completely free market existed. At that equilibrium point there would theoretically exist the number and types of events that were 'demanded' by paying customers. But a relatively 'free market' really only exists for certain types of events: those produced by for-profit corporations for companies or consumers that are looking for specific entertainment, learning or marketing opportunities that can only be met by these types of events (perhaps weddings or private parties). But most event entrepreneurs have to compete with subsidized events and event venues in the public or non-profit domains, which distorts the marketplace.

Imagine trying to produce a private music festival for profit in a city that also hosts a dozen or more annual non-profit events, each with some degree of government subsidy. This was the case of one festival in Calgary, which only lasted 2 years and saw the private investors lose a lot of their own money. Try to imagine a free market for the Olympics, a World's Fair, or all the sporting events that are put out to bidders every year. And can there be a free market for conventions and fairs if most are produced in publicly financed convention centres?

Return on Investment and Economic Efficiency

Governments can make money! Numerous studies have shown that governments at all levels realize substantial tax gains from tourism in general, and event tourism in particular. Events stimulate consumption of goods and services that are heavily taxed. Purely on a profit basis, public-sector investment is thereby justified. However, there has to be proven feasibility, accountability and professional management in place.

Increasingly the public sector in many countries has engaged in 'downsizing' and 'outsourcing' to save the taxpayer money. Really this is a way of saying that the services need to be provided, but the private sector can do it more efficiently. Some cities have developed festivals and events, then put them out to tender. Publicly funded facilities are managed, for-profit, by private companies that use events to generate both tourism and private profits.

Efficiency is also gained when events with surplus capacity are marketed to tourists, and when events are held in public facilities and spaces that both have surplus capacity and need additional revenue. In these cases, spending a little on events can realize important benefits for residents.

Justifications Based on Intangible Benefits (Psychic and Existence Values)

'Psychic benefits' accrue to people when they value something more than its related costs, as was calculated in the landmark event impact study by Burns et al. (1986). This is similar to 'consumer surplus', meaning that people are willing to pay more than the actual cost to them.

Researchers might also be able to show that people value events even when they do not attend, because it leads to pride in their community or they anticipate indirect benefits. This 'existence' value can be given weight through use of 'contingent valuation methods'. Andersson (2006) concluded that researchers have generally found citizens to approve of public expenditure on culture, whether or not they are users.

The Law of the Commons

Culture, public lands and facilities, scenery and other natural resources exploited for tourism and events can be considered 'common' assets. Their benefits should accrue to everyone, and they need to be protected (this is the 'stewardship' principle in sustainability theory). Only government policy and action can protect common assets.

If 'common' assets are used for tourism or events without regulation, by whoever takes initiative, benefits will accrue only to a few and the resources will potentially be depleted.

Accordingly, public policy and action is justified on sustainability grounds, not necessarily in the form of investment, but at least in the form of regulation and, when needed, rationing. This is certainly a good reason for initiating public policy discussions.

Counter-arguments

Counter-arguments are also available. Money given to special interest groups often attracts opposition, especially from groups that do not get similar treatment. Sometimes there are strong cultural, even political forces opposing government spending on projects that are claimed to be 'elitist' (e.g., performing arts), 'harmful' (risky sports), 'perverse' (gay or lesbian pride) or 'narrow' (i.e., the benefits accrue only to tourism or to private companies).

A lack of involvement with tourism or events might occur because attention is turned elsewhere (So do policy-makers have the facts? Are they effectively lobbied?). And because governments are faced with virtually unlimited spending opportunities, and limits on resources, they have to constantly prioritize. It is certainly reasonable for policy-makers and political parties to say they have more important priorities than planned events, but that is not very convincing when policy already exists for directly related domains like sport, arts, tourism and economic development.

> **Research Note**
>
> Reid, G. (2006). *The politics of city imaging. A case study of the MTV Europe Music Awards Edinburgh 03. Event Management*, 10(1): 35–46.
>
> *This event became politicized because of a large public subsidy that was intended to generate local economic benefits and help portray Edinburgh in a new light. The event was part of the city's ongoing repositioning strategy. Although Reid says the event did generate some benefits, local media were very critical. Issues of power, media management, how events are justified, and what exactly is culture are all addressed in this article.*

In the sections below we look more closely at the economic, cultural, social and environmental policy domains as they relate to planned events. For each, goals are suggested, then related policy initiatives and appropriate performance measures are discussed.

Economic Policy and Events

Much of the importance attached to planned events is related to their economic benefits, leading many governments to view event development as a legitimate, strategic policy field. While this has resulted in considerable growth in the events sector, it is a limited view of planned events and does result in some negative consequences (Figure 12.1).

Possible goals	Related policy initiatives	Performance measures
• Foster event tourism • Leverage events for general economic development • Use events to maximize venue efficiency • Use events in place marketing (e.g., image enhancement)	• Establish event tourism as a policy domain • Develop an event portfolio strategy for the community or destination • Integrate event policy with venue investment and operations • Integrate event policy with place marketing and other economic development	• Measure event tourism yield relative to other tourists • Tourism growth • Demonstrable 'legacy' benefits • Evaluation of image enhancement

Figure 12.1 Economic policy and events.

Foster Event Tourism

Tourism 'boosterism' has led many policy-makers to believe that events are good, and investment in them justified, because they attract tourists and media attention. Event tourism clearly can generate foreign currency and enhance a destination's image development, but these benefits cannot be taken for granted. There are too many variables at play to ensure success, witness the downturn in tourist arrivals to Australia following the 2000 Sydney Olympic Games. The Olympics were oversold on the basis of long-term tourism benefits, but who could predict the tragedy of 9/11 the following year?

Event tourism is a truly global phenomenon, and highly competitive, but many destinations and cities do not have a specific policy or strategy for it. Event tourism policy should be fully integrated with policy for venues (e.g., convention centres, sport and cultural facilities) and for place marketing and economic development.

Developing a 'portfolio' of events (see Getz, 2005) is a good strategy. At the base of the portfolio 'pyramid' are small, local events which meet resident needs, animate the destination and perhaps have some tourism growth potential. The top of the pyramid should be an occasional mega-event, but for most destinations it is probable that enduring benefits are more attainable through development of one or more periodic 'hallmark events' that fit the brand and boost the destination's image. As well, many regional-scale events will provide tourism benefits. One essential component of the portfolio approach is to recognize that events have different value (e.g., sustainability, high yield, growth potential, market share, cost), and that portfolios can be developed for types of events and all for seasons.

Strategic consideration should also be given to the desirability and means for growing events in size and tourism significance, such as by increased marketing and lengthening of their duration. Some events can be transformed from resident to visitor dominated, although with caution to avoid displacement or disgruntlement of residents.

The selection of performance measures is important. Too many tourism organizations rely on volume measures, as if having more tourists is inherently good and without costs. Every destination should instead concentrate on yield and sustainability. Event tourists tend to be high in yield relative to mass, packaged tourists, and this has clearly been documented for convention tourists and types of participant sport tourist. The sustainability of tourists in this context refers both to their long-term demand (Will they come back?) and their appropriateness in terms of achieving sustainable development goals.

Leverage Events for General Economic Development

Event tourism policy and strategy have been expanding to focus on 'leveraging' events more comprehensively, including using events to foster trade and economic diversification. Plans also have to be in place to realize the potential urban renewal benefits of mega-events and to ensure that facilities built for events will remain viable and efficiently utilized in the long term.

The employment-creation potential of most events is small, although mega-events can generate substantial short-term growth in construction jobs. To maximize employment benefits, event policy has to be tied closely to tourism, sport and culture/arts development in general, and to venue construction and operations.

Suitable performance measures can include jobs created and sustained, the spread of event benefits in time and space, stakeholder satisfaction, new trade and business links formed, and start-up businesses related to events.

Use Events to Maximize Venue Efficiency

Funding and building convention and exhibition centres, arts and sports facilities have a major impact on events and event tourism. What is surprising is that massive infrastructure investments are frequently made without a supporting events policy. It seems to be assumed that cities need impressive facilities, and that most publicly funded event venues will be permanently subsidized by government.

How many events are held, and their economic benefits, is one measure of venue efficiency. Building them is expensive, but easy, whereas making good use of facilities in the long term is the real challenge. A balance is also desired between tourist and resident use.

Use Events in Place Marketing

Exploiting events for image building, branding, repositioning or place marketing in general requires policy and a strategy. Competitive advantages are being gained by destinations that have the knowledge and vision to integrate events with other place marketing efforts, including film development, familiarization tours, trade missions, and city or regional branding.

Because economic impact and growth measures are most in use, there needs to be more effort expended on developing and testing social, cultural and environmental performance measures in event tourism. Some intangible measures, including image enhancement, are difficult to formulate and research. Even more difficult, both in theoretical and methodological terms, is to prove that image enhancement increases tourism demand.

Cultural Policy and Events

Next to economics, events are most often seen as being in the domain of cultural policy. This relates mostly to festivals and the arts, but there is no reason why all planned events cannot facilitate cultural experiences and meet other cultural development goals (Figure 12.2).

Possible goals	Related policy initiatives	Performance measures
• Foster arts and cultural development through investment in events • Leverage events for general and traditional/indigenous cultural development • Use events to maximize venue efficiency • Foster sustainable cultural event tourism	• Integrate events in cultural policy and arts development strategies • Develop specific event funding programmes • Develop cultural themes and programming for all events	• Assess the overall effectiveness of arts and cultural development in the community • Develop and employ specific measures of cultural event success and its benefits

Figure 12.2 Cultural policy and events.

Foster Arts and Cultural Development

A number of studies have examined the aims or mandates of festivals and events. A survey of Irish festivals (Goh, 2003) asked organizers to indicate and prioritize their aims, revealing that the top goal was to promote artistic excellence. This was followed very closely by increasing tourism and area promotion (both place marketing goals). Other aims (in descending order) were to showcase local heritage or arts, boost the local economy, celebration, encourage social inclusion and education.

'Development' in the arts and cultural domains has to encompass increased awareness of what is available and its benefits to the community, audience building through direct involvement of people in the arts, generating revenue (such as by facilitating corporate sponsorship and targeting grants), fostering traditional or indigenous talent and expression, and even providing free entertainment for the public.

Radbourne (2002) said that the most common argument for government involvement is that '. . . arts and cultural activity enrich a society and that all people have the right of access and participation.' Because public benefits are generated (although these are frequently in dispute), and because the private sector will not provide the necessary supply (a 'failure of the marketplace'), direct government action is needed. Basically this is the 'social equity argument' that many people cannot afford the arts without government intervention. More recently, claims have been growing that the arts and cultural activity in general make for an attractive living and working environment, stimulating innovation and competitive advantage (e.g., Florida, 2002 and the 'creative economy').

Cultural tourism policy generally subsumes festivals and other cultural productions, witness the following excerpt from the Cultural Policy for New Brunswick (Canada) prepared by their Culture and Sport Secretariat (online at www.gnb.ca/0007/policy). Here, and in many other jurisdictions, events are recognized as having cultural value, but are also usually valued in an explicitly industrial context.

Goal #4: To maximize the economic benefits of culture in order to improve New Brunswick's position in the global economy.

Strategies to support the goal:

1. *Develop markets and audiences for New Brunswick's natural, historical and contemporary cultural products within the province and worldwide.*
2. *Improve and increase cultural tourism products (including arts, heritage and cultural products) that are authentic and of high quality.*
3. *Promote and market the province's arts and heritage facilities and cultural events to residents and visitors.*
4. *Support strategic development and entrepreneurial initiatives in the cultural industries and enterprises.*
5. *Seek financial investment and job creation through the strategic development of heritage and arts resources.*
6. *Develop new infrastructure in cooperation with other Atlantic provinces.*
7. *Invest in the cultural sector to enable artists and cultural professionals to pursue their careers in New Brunswick.*

All events can provide cultural experiences through appropriate theming and programming. There is no reason why business and political events cannot provide cultural experiences for visitors, such as through authentic entertainment, meaningful host–guest interactions, interpretation, and additional pre- or post-event cultural opportunities.

Foster Sustainable Cultural Event Tourism

Ali-Knight and Robertson (2004: 8) outlined the Edinburgh Cultural Policy, and the subsequent Festivals Strategy launched in 2001 in tandem with an Events Strategy. These policy initiatives reflected the city's commitment to its positioning as the 'festival city', in recognition of the contribution of events to both the economic and cultural viability of the city. The Festivals Strategy emerged from stakeholder consultations, in both tourism and festival sectors, discussions with core groups like the Joint Festivals Working Group and extensive desk research including benchmarking against other cities.

Some of the key goals of the Festivals Strategy were to develop a year-round programme of events, and to ensure their independence and a balance of creativity, social objectives and commercial viability. Other aims covered social inclusion (getting a broad range of residents involved) and securing adequate funding.

Research Note

Tomljenovic, R., and Weber, S. (2004). Funding cultural events in Croatia: tourism-related policy issues. Event Management, 9(1/2): 51–59.

The article provides an overview of festival funding in Croatia, revealing the existence of weak links between tourism and culture ministries until 2003 when a cultural tourism plan was formulated. Research reported in this paper examined the degree of goal congruence between cultural festival organizers and regional tourism officials on why festivals should be funded. Results showed that festival organizers poorly understood tourism and the roles they could play in its development, and they believed that funding received from tourism organizations should be based on quality programming, tradition and uniqueness, and their overall contribution to cultural development. Surprisingly, tourism officials agreed, but also wanted criteria related to the ability of festivals to attract new, high-yield visitors and improve destination image. Neither group of professionals seemed aware of the full range of benefits that cultural events could bring to the regions, and for this more education was necessary. The authors also highlighted the need for better research to support this sector and the tourism/culture partnership.

There will remain, inevitably, many tensions between culture and the growing 'instrumentalist' or 'strategic' approaches to festivals and events. Waterman (1998) highlighted latent tensions between festival as art and economics, between culture and cultural politics. He concluded that support for the arts is part of a process used by elites to establish social distance between themselves and others, and that festival development is related to place promotion, which encourages 'safe' art forms.

Traditional Culture

As illustrated in the earlier research note by Xie (2003), official Chinese policy both helped convert the Bamboo-beating dance on Hainan island to a tourist-oriented spectacle and, ironically, helped turn it into an authentic tradition for the Li people. This aspect of cultural policy is often overlooked in developed countries because traditional events and indigenous peoples are either non-existent or have been marginalized. It is more likely that native celebrations, like the North American Pow Wow, will be viewed as tourist attractions and marketed accordingly, rather than viewed as being on par with opera or theatre.

Social Policy and Events

Figure 12.3 summarizes social goals, policy initiatives and performance measures.

Possible goals	Related policy initiatives	Performance measures
• Foster social integration and community development through a programme of public events • Combat social problems at and surrounding events (hooliganism, crime, etc.) • Leverage events for urban renewal • Use events to enhance health and wellness	• Integrate events with urban renewal, social and community development policy • Integrate events with health and wellness policy • Integrate events with policy for sport, parks and recreation • Provide resources for combating social problems associated with events • Formulate policy regarding the use of public spaces for events, both formal and informal	• Assess the overall effectiveness of social policy; develop and employ specific measures of event success and its benefits

Figure 12.3   Social policy and events.

Foster Social Integration

In many communities, including small towns and city neighbourhoods, events can be catalysts for community development. Their organization and revenue-making potential can foster self-sufficiency and pride in accomplishment. Community identity and pride can be heightened through sharing with outsiders. Integration of diverse or conflicted social groups should be a specific aim, to be realized through planning and decision-making, all the way through social interaction and interpretation at events.

Public services and resources provided to events (e.g., police, fire, traffic control, transport, physical infrastructure) are often viewed as expenses to be recovered, but should be provided within the context of social and cultural policy. In many cases direct provision of events, and subsidies for using public services, is warranted.

Who should have access to public spaces and venues? Many governments license all events and ban or shut down informal gatherings, but does this policy always serve social and other goals? It can certainly be argued that in a free society people have the right to assemble and hold spontaneous events, although this has to be balanced by responsible behaviour. How should potentially conflicting aims be resolved?

Combat Social Problems

What constitutes anti-social behaviour versus permissible civil disobedience? Preventing and reacting to social problems at or surrounding events is a matter of social policy. It is not just a security issue, but should integrate public awareness and education, event management including crowd controls, venue design and travel restrictions.

Leverage Events for Urban Renewal

Mega-events in particular are viewed as opportunities for large-scale redevelopment or urban renewal projects. Cities create tangible legacies in terms of monuments and landmarks, culture and entertainment precincts, fresh design and aesthetics, and hopefully renewed residential value. History has demonstrated that these benefits must be planned in advance, not left to chance, and that events can be a powerful planning and renewal tool.

Use Events to Enhance Health and Wellness

Events can be used as social marketing tools (requiring education and thematic interpretation) and to provide activities for encouraging healthy lifestyles. There will be direct tie-ins to sport, parks and recreation. Examples include food and beverage festivals with nutritional themes, sport competitions stressing safe play, and 'edutainment' events in parks. Health concerns and regulations have to be applied across the spectrum of events and event venues, so why not make them proactive to encourage health and wellness?

'Social tourism' is a related policy field, entailing the subsidization of holidays or other leisure activities, especially for the economically disadvantaged or persons with special needs. 'Sport for All' and sport youth festivals can yield psychological as well as health benefits. Because so many sports glorify violence, policy should be directed towards the counter-message that sport can be safe, friendly and fun. Hooliganism and other social problems associated with certain sport events have to be combated through a multi-dimensional approach including legal prohibitions against travel, public education, venue design, crowd management/controls and security regimes.

Public subsidies for professional sports and private sport venues are controversial. A lot of evidence suggests it is not economically beneficial to cities, and typically it is done for reasons of prestige and political expediency. Are there any social benefits that can justify this form of subsidy?

Recreation events can be viewed as a public good, particularly when they encompass a variety of social and cultural aims. Events in parks should provide for safe social interaction and should foster environmental responsibility.

Environmental Policy and Events

Figure 12.4 summarizes environmental goals, policy initiatives and performance measures.

Possible goals	Related policy initiatives	Performance measures
• Require green and sustainable events and event venues • Leverage events for environmental education and development • Foster events with environmental themes	• Integrate event policy with planning, land use and all environmental management systems • Supply chain controls • Full life-cycle accounting	• Develop comprehensive environmental standards and evaluation measures for events and event venues • Evaluate the social marketing effectiveness of environmental messages at events

Figure 12.4   Environmental policy and events.

Require Green and Sustainable Events and Event Venues

The basic policy imperative is to ensure that all events are 'green', meeting the minimum RRR standards (i.e., reduce, reuse and recycle). Integrate events with conservation and environmental management policies, land use planning and controls, noise and traffic by-laws, and other environmental influencers. Beyond that, a policy to foster sustainable events (a 'triple bottom-line' approach: economic, social, environmental) will go much farther to conserve the environment and ensure long-term support for events.

In the UK, a Sustainable Events Management System has been developed (British Standards Institute, 2006), and this suggests a likely global trend. The document provides several reasons for developing standards, including social and client expectations, legislative compliance, and the delivery of better outcomes at lower cost. Issues to be considered under the heading of sustainable events are diverse: global climate change; air and water use and quality; land use; biodiversity; heritage; emissions and waste; product stewardship (ethics and values); health, safety and comfort. A lot of emphasis is placed on organization and management systems, including risk assessment, working with stakeholders, and supply chain controls.

Tribe (2005: 380) discussed sustainable development from an economics perspective, and we can apply these principles to events. Renewable resources are at the base of many sustainable development strategies, so what in the events sector is truly renewable? Culture is renewable, but it changes and can be impacted negatively. Cultural differences that we value, such as traditions, costumes, foods and symbols, should be protected. Events that have a negative effect on the environment, or generate excessive waste, or foster consumptive attitudes, cannot be justified in this context.

A related concept is that of 'capacity to absorb' events, or to tolerate change without detrimental impacts on culture or the environment. Each event has potential impacts, but what can we say about cumulative event impacts? Little attention has been paid to this issue. Design capacity for venues is a related concept, and event managers are forced to examine maximum attendance and the activity load of events for safety, health and experiential reasons.

The 'precautionary principle' comes up whenever sustainability is discussed, but it is controversial. Some people believe that if we can anticipate that an event might cause negative impacts, we should not produce it. This is extreme in my view, as it can be misused to preclude just about any activity or development. In the same way, the principle of 'no irreversible change' is open to considerable misuse as a way to prevent desired and necessary action. The fact is that almost any development results in irreversible changes.

Finally, we have already mentioned economic 'externalities'. A logical response to the externality problem is to require that polluters pay for their actions, and that anyone causing public costs should be held accountable. If this principle gets applied uniformly it will mean that no event organizer will be able to ignore costs and impacts that extend beyond the event. However, this principle can also be abused. Consider that events often result in traffic congestion, albeit temporarily, and some people not attending the event might lose time and money as a consequence. Should they be compensated by the event organizers? What about people impacted by event-caused noise?

Certainly it is important to consider all these costs and benefits in the feasibility study and in post-event evaluations, but also realize that society is almost always paying some price for economic activity; we tolerate congestion and noise as a normal consequence of living in cities and fostering economic growth. The same argument applies to any event that provides a 'public good' – we should be willing to collectively tolerate some degree of inconvenience or amenity loss in pursuit of social and cultural growth. To what extent we tolerate them, and how we deal with externalities, is a matter of debate and public decision-making.

Economic tools exist for influencing the marketplace and fostering sustainable development. Price mechanisms generally work well, either using high prices to discourage consumption or subsidized prices to encourage it. If society believes that attending cultural festivals is a form of sustainable development, but participation in off-road motorcycle races is not, price manipulation can be made through differential taxation, subsidies or other means. Still more effective, of course, is direct prevention of undesirable events through licensing or other regulatory devices.

Leverage Events for Environmental Education and Development

The goal here is to infuse environmental education into events, as a form of 'social marketing'. Visitors should be made aware of green operations and sustainability principles applied to the event they are attending, and they also could be informed of how to extend these actions to their home and work settings. Obviously events with environmental themes are best able to educate visitors about conservation, sustainability and other issues, but they might not attract as broad an audience.

Foster Events with Environmental Themes

Events with explicit environmental themes have been growing in number, including global movements like Earth Day and interest-specific themes like bird watching. The tools of 'thematic interpretation' should be employed to make sure the message provokes a positive reaction from guests. Many such events will be exercises in 'social marketing' by environmental agencies, but special interest groups like 'birders' are also active in this sphere.

Public Policy-Making

If events are considered a 'public good', on par with – or an element in – social, leisure, health, sport and culture policy, then there should be a planning process in place to ensure adequate provision. The following system could be put in place:

• Needs assessment, issues identification, multi-stakeholder input.
• Developing a portfolio of events to meet specific needs in specific places.

- Setting standards of provision and accessibility.
- Funding and facilitation programmes tied to public agencies and venues.
- Organizational development to ensure implementation, community capacity building.
- Research, monitoring and impact evaluation.
- Review and policy refinement.

It seems likely that most authorities will not develop such an integrated events policy, but within the closely related policy domains the same planning approach can be applied:

- Issues (Why are we interested in events? Justification for intervention?).
- Purpose and goals (What we want to accomplish with events – the desired outcomes?).
- Research, consultations and the planning process.
- Evaluation and accountability (e.g., performance measures, monitoring and feedback).
- Implementation: laws and regulations, event development or bidding agencies, event funding programmes.

Policy Considerations

Hall and Page (2006: 335) identified a number of policy-related considerations that should be applied to the events sector.

What Is the Policy Environment?

This includes the basic form of government (Is it democratic?), the distribution of power, and how society is structured. The dominant and varied values of political parties (i.e., ideology) are key forces, especially the emphasis on a free market versus interventionism.

'Institutional arrangements' must be considered. Where exactly is event-related policy formed, and how is it implemented at all levels of government and within quasi-public agencies? Unless there exists an event development agency (these are common in Australia), or an events office within city hall (e.g., in the Chicago Mayor's Office), who even speaks for events? There are many voices to be heard, and not all of them are effective in lobbying.

This introduces the notion of a 'policy arena' in which special interest groups engage in lobbying, institutions interact, individuals and groups achieve influence, and leadership might or might not be effective. The notion of a 'political market square' is pertinent, as the various stakeholders have varying degrees of power and influence, form alliances or collaborate, negotiate, and seek to influence policy. The openness of this process should be a matter of concern to everyone. In most places the policy arena for events is fractured, consisting of the often-competing voices of sport, arts, heritage, culture and tourism, and further subdivided by professional associations representing specific types of event.

Specific policy issues have to be considered within the general policy domains discussed above. Policies and programmes are formulated for specific purposes, then must be evaluated in terms of their impact, effectiveness and efficiency. Policy should be continuously reviewed and improved, and with full stakeholder input. A great deal of technical support is required for this process, including research and information dissemination. Finally, there is an important matter of accountability: How are officials and others held accountable for their policies and actions?

Research Note

Weed, M. (2003). Why the two won't tango! Explaining the lack of integrated policies for sport and tourism in the UK. Journal of Sport Management, 17(3): 258–283.

In-depth, 'informed source' interviews were conducted among agencies responsible for policy, to examine the sport and tourism policy process. Certain tensions were revealed between the two 'communities', including funding and resources, top-down policy-making, organization and professionalisation, internal focus, and project-based liaison. Results show how development of this policy network (i.e., sport plus tourism) can be made sustainable. There was a lack of perceived mutual interests, and Weed believed that improved awareness of the already-demonstrated benefits was the answer.

Agencies were unwilling to engage in activity that was peripheral to their mandate (versus their core concerns), thus requiring someone or some organization to take the lead. Wed believed this would more likely be the role of tourism agencies. Informal networking would require a common set of rules and language. In the case of disagreements, there would have to be a higher authority to defer to, otherwise each party might retreat into firm positions of opposition. Finally, policy networks will vary a great deal between countries, and presumably between the policy domain (i.e., sports tourism in general, versus sport events in particular).

Options for Events Policy and Strategy

Getz and Frisby (1991) developed a framework for local government policy-making in the events sector, and their framework can be applied to event-related policy in general. The logic also applies to other agencies, such as tourism, which get involved with events. The basic premise is the some level of policy or direct intervention in the events sector is desired and practical. First, several optional roles have to be considered:

- *'Direct provision'*: Government or agencies produce and own events.
- *'Equity approach'*: Do not produce, but invest in events (in this case 'equity' means the capital invested).
- *'Sponsorship'*: Act like corporations and make sponsorship deals for specific benefits (such as image making, social marketing).
- *'Facilitate'*: Through various policy initiatives, facilitate event creation or operations.

The 'facilitation' role leads to various assistance options:

- *Financial*: Grants, loans, lines of credit, debt relief, subsidies (e.g., for use of police, traffic services, venues), tax relief, awards and prizes.
- *Technical*: Professional advice, training, research and information, office space.
- *Marketing*: Overall or event-specific promotions, inclusion in government materials, websites, etc.
- *Regulatory*: Fast-tracking, release from onerous obligations.
- *Infrastructure*: Provision and improvement of necessary services (roads, water, etc.) and public venues (e.g., theatres, arenas, parks, plazas).

In this interventionist approach a number of other policy issues arise. To whom should assistance be given? Should all organizations and events be treated the same, or should they have to meet specific criteria like proof of managerial competence? Under what conditions should assistance be given? There could be annual applications mandated, and grants could be in the form of one-time-only seed money versus continuous support. And all systems need procedures and accountability, including formal applications, monitoring and periodic audits.

Regulating the Events Sector

Event producers have to satisfy and manage relationships with numerous regulatory agencies and their officials. A majority of these are at the local level, but sometimes multi-level approvals are needed:

- *Police*: Security requirements, police presence.
- *Traffic*: Accessibility, parking, public transport, control.
- *Fire*: Maximum capacity, accessibility and evacuation procedures, materials.
- *Health and safety*: Hazardous materials, fireworks and lasers, food and beverage preparation and storage standards, electricity, waste disposal.
- *Building inspection*: New construction or allowable temporary structures.
- *Land use*: Where events can be held, where venues can be built, size limits, site planning requirements.
- *Noise control*: Noise levels and dispersion, hours of operation.
- *Labour*: Minimum wages, age restrictions, work hours, certification of professionals and trades people.
- *Environmental*: Emission standards (smoke, pollutants), recycling, wastes.
- *Consumer protection*: Price controls, guarantees, refunds.

Policy Formulation at the Community Level: Collaboration and Consensus Building

Policy-making for events can range from a top-down approach, dictated by government or specific agencies, to bottom-up, arising from community needs assessments and the input of many stakeholders. Event tourism policy tends to be top-down (at least in Australia, as demonstrated by Whitford, 2004a, b), mainly because it is seen as legitimate economic development, but also because so much bidding on events is opportunistic.

When developing policy open to stakeholder input, a number of collaborative, consensus-building approaches can be used. Hall and Rusher (2004: 225) gave an example of effective community involvement in events policy. In New Zealand the Alexandra Blossom Festival illustrates '. . . how the complex social structures of the community have shaped the political environment and how this in turn has evolved into a relationship with local government that ensures a high degree of community input into policy development.' The festival has sought to be inclusive of various interests and values in the community.

Research, Evaluation and Public Policy

Hall and Rusher (2004: 229) concluded that '. . . there still remains relatively little analysis of the political context of events and the means by which events come to be developed and hosted within communities.' A study by Whitford (2004a: 81) in Queensland, Australia, is one of the few to address local authority policy towards events. She concluded that little recognition had been given to events '. . . as a vehicle to facilitate entrepreneurial enterprises and/or regional development' and that a '. . . more whole of government, proactive entrepreneurial approach to the development of event public policy' is needed.

What do we need to formulate and effectively administer events-related policy? Both practitioners and academics have a role to play, not just the policy-makers themselves. To analyse policy, or strategy, one should examine the following:

- Intention, or expressed purpose (is it economic and development oriented, or community and culture oriented? What are the goals and performance criteria?).
- Contents (responsibilities of the agencies involved, types of events covered, applicability in different settings).
- Implementation (programmes and schedules, funds allocated, regulations, evaluation and accountability).
- Results (multiple, independent evaluations of intended and unintended outcomes, feedback and revisions).

Research Note

Pugh, C., and Wood, E. (2004). The strategic use of events within local government: a study of London Borough Councils. Event Management, 9(1/2): 61–71.

In the UK, the public sector is responsible for a large proportion of the special events provided for the community, and most local governments (municipalities) have a substantial and varied events programme, but this entire policy field is non-mandatory. The authors argue that a more strategic approach to events would benefit urban regeneration, the local community, and place promotion.

Interviews were conducted in each of London's boroughs to determine the strategic roles played by events and how they were incorporated into the planning process. Conceptual analysis techniques were used, as well as a comparison of interview findings with the content of public documents. The researchers found that boroughs were becoming more strategic, and that they were favouring a facilitation role for events, rather than direct operations. Budget and resource limitations prevented some local authorities from fully utilizing events in strategic marketing. Identified needs included more marketing studies, better post-event evaluation, more attention to corporate sponsorship opportunities, and comprehensive stakeholder involvement in policy making.

Chapter Summary

The nature of public policy was discussed at the beginning of this chapter, leading to an exploration of how public involvement in the events sector can be justified. Specifically this included the 'public good' argument and 'equity principle', which are linked to ideology, and, borrowing from economics, the 'failure of the marketplace' justification. Additional justification is related to 'efficiency', as in getting the most out of public infrastructure and venues, and the intangible or psychic benefits that accrue to people even if they do not attend events.

Four major policy fields were examined, each beginning with a figure that identifies possible goals, related policy issues and appropriate performance measures to evaluate related policy. Starting with economics, the 'possible goals' are clearly those currently being emphasized wherever events are publicly supported: fostering event tourism, leveraging events, using events to maximize venue efficiency and incorporating events in place marketing. An obvious weakness, however, is that much of this economic activity related to events is being done without comprehensive or integrated policy, and in many cases without articulated strategies. This limitation especially applies to large-scale events that are bid on and developed in the absence of rational planning and policy-making.

Cultural policy is often applied to events, mainly because of the generally accepted roles of government in fostering the arts. Possible goals are to leverage events for indigenous cultural development, maximize arts and cultural venue efficiency, and to foster sustainable cultural tourism. There is often an emphasis on festivals or art exhibits as cultural expressions, but cultural themes and experiences can and should be facilitated throughout the planned events sector. The absence or lack of credibility assigned to performance measures in the art and cultural domains is a problem needing attention. Unfortunately, over-emphasis on economic goals has overshadowed or even stifled development of methods and measures for social, cultural and environmental evaluation.

Within the social policy domain, key goals would include the fostering of social integration and community development, combating social problems in the community and at events, leveraging events for urban renewal, and using events to enhance health and wellness. Pursuit of these goals requires that events be integrated in a number of well-established policy fields including urban planning, health, sport, recreation and public facilities. Similar to the cultural policy domain, appropriate evaluation measures and methods need development and testing. The many intangible benefits of events have to be articulated and demonstrated in justifying public intervention.

Environmentally, major policy goals should be to require all events and event venues to be green and sustainable, using a comprehensive or 'triple bottom-line' approach. Much more can be done to leverage all events for environmental education and development, and to create more environmentally themed events.

The chapter concludes with guidelines for policy-making, including the specific considerations of policy environment, institutional arrangements and policy/strategic options.

Study Questions

- What is 'public policy' and what are 'policy domains'?
- Explain how governmental intervention in the event sector can be justified, including the 'public good' and 'equity' arguments, 'market failure', and 'efficiency'.
- Discuss economic, social, cultural and environmental policy domains as they pertain to planned events. Give examples of major possible goals, related policy initiatives and performance measures.
- What factors are important in shaping the policy-making process for events? Include 'ideology' and 'institutional arrangements'.
- What process should governments follow to develop policies for events?

Further Reading

Hall, M., and Rusher, K. (2004). Politics, public policy and the destination. In: I. Yeoman et al. (eds.), *Festival and Events Management*, pp. 217–231. Oxford: Elsevier.

Radbourne, J. (2002). Social intervention or market intervention? A problem for governments in promoting the value of the arts. *International Journal of Arts Management*, 5(1): 50–61.

Chapter 13

Creating Knowledge in Event Studies

Learning Objectives

- Learn how to create knowledge in Events Studies employing research, introspection, and reflective professional practice.
- Understand the main paradigms of knowledge and knowledge formation. Be able to apply appropriate research methodologies and methods from foundation disciplines and closely related fields to Event Studies.
- Be able to formulate a sound research proposal in Event Studies.
- Be able to identify major knowledge gaps in Event Studies related to the planned event experience and meaning, planning, design and management, antecedents, patterns and processes, outcomes and the impacted.

A Framework for Knowledge Creation

This chapter is about creating knowledge in Event Studies, most of which will come from doing research. But where do good research ideas come from? How do we know if a research project is worth doing? Most event-related research has stemmed from sheer curiosity, or from a management or policy need. Because Event Studies is a new field, a lot of pertinent research has been within well-established disciplinary lines of inquiry. To progress towards interdisciplinarity, wherein Event Studies will have its own theories and methodologies, we will have to focus more on the core phenomenon and related themes.

This is not a chapter on research methods, although many are mentioned. It is intended to provide an overview of the entire knowledge creation and research process, starting with a conceptual model, then proceeding to discussion of basic research paradigms, methodologies and methods. The research notes in this chapter focus on how research is done, rather than the contents.

Figure 13.1 depicts the various ways in which knowledge can be created and a research project can begin, applied to Event Studies. At the centre is our new field of studies, and we will naturally have to rely on established disciplines and closely related profes- sional fields for ideas, theories and methods. At the moment, very few people in tradi- tional disciplines pay attention to the study *of* planned events, rather than the study of some social, economic or cultural phenomenon that happens to involve events.

Interdisciplinary Approach

Event Studies, like other immature fields of inquiry, is multi-disciplinary in nature, drawing theory, knowledge, methodologies and methods from many established disciplines. It also does this indirectly through closely related professional fields like leisure studies and tourism.

I have argued that Event Studies fits best into the Social Sciences, mainly because of its heavy reliance to the human and behavioural disciplines, but it also is eclectic in draw- ing from arts, sciences, engineering and design – really any other areas of study can offer something of value. What this means for creating knowledge in Event Studies is that a great place to start is with the knowledge contained already in the disciplines and fields discussed in this book, and to keep looking for more pertinent knowledge and how to better apply it.

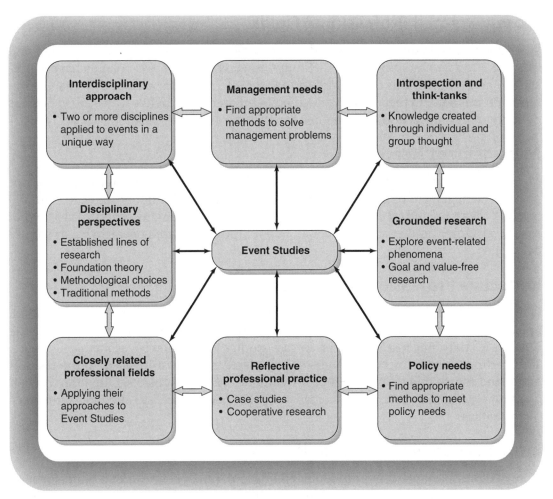

Figure 13.1   Creating knowledge and doing research in event studies.

When two or more disciplinary foundations are applied to the problem we enter the realm of interdisciplinary research, with the long-term goal being to establish unique, event-specific interdisciplinary theory and knowledge.

Disciplinary Perspectives

Anyone doing research on events should view the established disciplinary perspectives as a legitimate starting point. Even if the research problem is rooted in a policy or management need, it is highly possible that geography, economics or another discipline already provides an answer or a solid foundation for doing the research. However, within these disciplines the study of events is often incidental to a broader issue or theoretical problem, or the focus is not on the core phenomenon of the planned event experience.

Closely Related Professional Fields

Work being done in the closely related professional fields, especially leisure studies and tourism, offers a foundation for Event Studies research. These fields not only have a head start in applying various disciplines to their problems and issues, but events already figure prominently in their contents. Remember that in these fields events are viewed as delivery mechanisms and not the phenomenon of central interest.

Management Needs

Much of the event-related research done to date has been applied, related to the practice of event management or event tourism. Researchers and practitioners have to continue to work together, and to close the natural gap between them, in order to ensure that research is timely and useful. But not all Event Studies research needs to be, or should be applied.

Reflective Professional Practice

Helping to close the gap between researchers and practitioners is a two-way street. Speaking as a journal editor, I can say that it has proved close to impossible to get practitioners to contribute research papers or case studies to the refereed, academic literature. The starting point is for practitioners to be reflective, not just focused on the tasks at hand, and to use this reflection in part to initiate research projects. Often the applied needs of practitioners can dovetail nicely with the more theoretical and long-term goals of academics.

Introspection and Think-tanks

Knowledge also comes from individual reading and introspection, group brainstorming (the 'think-tank' approach) or pure serendipity (i.e., good luck). When research institutions are established, or groups of academics and research students interact at universities, a lot of new thinking and theorizing occurs almost naturally. To date, only a few such clusters of event scholars have been established. One of their aims has to be a closer link with professional practitioners.

Grounded Research

In grounded research we do not start with a problem, theory or hypothesis in mind, but with our interest in the core phenomenon (planned event experiences). The grounded approach rests on the premise that researchers should not carry pre-conceived notions into their projects, but construct research in such a way that knowledge and theories emerge from data and structured analysis. We always hope that completely fresh insights arise from grounded research. More discussion on grounded research follows in this chapter.

Policy Needs

A major theme in this book is public policy related to planned events. While general research is needed to support policy, in turn policy-makers will require a variety of studies – often evaluations – to initiate the process or support and improve their efforts.

Philosophy and Knowledge

Science and the pursuit of knowledge are not the same. 'Scientific method' is all about a prescribed process and theory building, whereas 'knowledge' can be developed from original thinking (creativity), synthesis (reflective thought by informed, wise people) and serendipity (unplanned discovery). In this section a number of important terms and concepts are examined so that Event Studies researchers will understand where their work fits into the bigger picture of science and knowledge creation. It will become clear that there is a lot of disagreement about the very meaning or usefulness of science and scientific method.

Philosophy of Science, Epistemology and Ontology

'Philosophy of science' consists of the philosophical foundations, assumptions and implications of natural and social sciences. It seeks to explain such things as the nature of scientific statements and concepts, and the formulation and use of the scientific method.

'Epistemology' specifically deals with knowledge, the relationships between the 'knower' and 'that which is to be known', and the justification of 'knowledge claims'. Modern science is dominated by 'empiricists' who believe that all knowledge is ultimately derived from some experience that requires research and analysis.

Adapting Tribe's (1997: 639) approach from tourism studies, the 'epistemology of Event Studies' should be concerned with the character of knowledge about planned events, the sources of such knowledge, the validity and reliability of claims of knowledge about planned events, the use of concepts, the boundaries of Event Studies and the categorization of Event Studies as a discipline or field.

Tribe's arguments about tourism ring true for Event Studies as well. If we limit Event Studies to the use of 'scientific method' we will miss out on large parts of the phenomenal world of planned events that are not scientifically quantifiable and are not, in fact, scientific puzzles. More appropriately, Event Studies needs greater epistemological breadth, encompassing philosophical, moral, aesthetic, historical and sociological inquiry and discourse.

'Ontology' is a branch of philosophy concerning the origins, essence and meaning of 'being', or what it means to exist. It can also be defined as dealing with conceptualizations of reality. In research, ontology usually refers to how knowledge is represented and the vocabulary being used to describe it.

In the social sciences there are four main ontological approaches. 'Realism' is based on the idea that 'the truth is out there', or that researchers can indeed discover facts and establish a true picture of reality. For example, marketing researchers might believe they can determine exactly who prefers certain types of events, and why. This leads to 'empirical research', and it can be said that 'empiricism' entails making observations about the real world which can be evaluated in relation to facts.

'Empiricism' is what separates 'science' from philosophy or theology. 'Positivism' is the scientific approach most associated with experimentation, quantitative techniques and the assumption that researchers are discovering the truth. The fourth ontological approach, 'postmodernism', rejects the notion that we discover the truth through empiricism, and proclaims that every observation or measurement is open to interpretation.

Positivism has guided most of the natural sciences and strongly influenced the social sciences, so we will discuss it in greater detail below. Later, more attention is given to postmodernism and contemporary discourse on research and knowledge.

Positivism

Similar to natural scientists, positivism adopts an external (i.e., the researcher's) perspective on discovering the truth and formulating theories that are both explanatory and predictive. Social scientists and management researchers wanting to be more like the 'hard sciences' have adopted a positivistic approach which stresses the 'scientific method' to prove cause and effect, or otherwise employs reliable and valid methods to discover the 'truth' about the world and how people and societies function in it. Positivists separate values from research. Most research done on events has been in this tradition, if only because most event-related research has been concerned with marketing and economics.

When visitor surveys are done at events, for example, researchers try to obtain a random or systematic sample so that estimates can be made about the whole population of event attendees. Conclusions are drawn regarding average spending, motivations to attend, etc. When a household survey is conducted to assess resident perceptions of, and attitudes towards events, a similar sampling process occurs and the resulting data are subjected to statistical tests to reveal patterns and explain differences. All of this can be used in theory building. Researchers assume that they are discovering, measuring or explaining the ways in which real people think and act. Are they wrong to think this?

'Experimentation' is also at the heart of positivism. Experiments are used to test hypotheses, requiring that controls be put in place to compare cause and effect among groups. While experiments are rare in applied management fields like tourism or events, the method has been widely used in some of the disciplines that contribute to our knowledge of events, especially in psychology and its sub-disciplines.

One of the oft-proclaimed advantages of scientific method is the removal of subjectivity and the imposition of strict protocols for data collection and analysis – including ethical research behaviour. For example, no student doing research for a thesis or dissertation would be allowed to draw conclusions about how events cause economic impacts without convincing supervisors and examiners that data collection and analytical techniques are sound. There is a firm understanding that researchers do not make up results, that studies can be replicated, and that conclusions can be tested.

But this scientific 'advantage' also attracts dissatisfaction and criticism when researchers study humans and societies. There is, first of all, real doubt about how well experiments and survey methods reveal the truth, or get at the complexity of individuals and groups.

Secondly, there is a concern that 'objective' research treats people as 'objects', and that the subjects of research should be part of the process and benefit from it. In fact, some research might actually do harm to people either by way of the dynamics of the research (such as observing people and thereby interfering with their lives or work) or its results (such as by exposing divisions and biases).

Schultz and Lavenda (2005) discussed how anthropologists have questioned positivism as the dominant research paradigm. Assumptions about how the world really worked, and about the ethics and politics of their research (particularly about participant observation) started to be challenged in the 1960s and 1970s. As researchers began to de-emphasize scientific detachment and entered into dialogues with informants and respondents, a greater emphasis was placed on interpretation and differences in opinion.

Schultz and Lavenda (2005: 43) believed that collaborative dialogues achieve 'intersubjective meanings' in which researchers and informants gain a new, shared understanding of the world. According to these anthropologists, researchers are to be 'reflexive', or always critically thinking about the experience of research and how it is done. Do researchers and informants share enough, in cultural terms, to really understand each other?

Postmodernism

To postmodernists, there is no single truth, and all 'meta-narratives' and 'paradigms' like religion and political doctrine are rejected. Jennings (2006: 3) said 'The postmodern paradigm disputes grand theory and views the world (its ontological perspective) as being constructed of multiple realities and that no one reality has favour over another. A central tenet is the deconstruction of the surface features of phenomena in order to expose the underlying core realities'.

'Axiology' is the study of values, value judgments and ethics. Most writers of journal articles present their data, analysis and conclusions in a way that implies complete objectivity and scientific rigour. But some academics are now trying to explain how their own values might affect their research, analysis and conclusions. And it has become fashionable to require students writing theses and dissertations to discuss their entire ontological and methodological approach, and to disclose their values or biases. That is a good idea for theses and dissertations, if only to make everyone aware of the thought and assumptions that went into the student's research and analysis. Anyone looking for this author's axiological position will have to deduce it from the contents of the whole book.

Theories and Models

Klemke et al. (1998) asserted that 'theories' have the following properties:

- May be stated as laws or assertions about existence.
- Exhibit generality or comprehensiveness.
- Explain not one law or phenomenon, but many.
- Have explanatory and predictive ability.
- Unify diverse phenomena and laws.
- Aim at deep understanding of phenomena.
- Contain terms referring to unobservable entities or properties.

I do not think Klemke's assertions about theory are applicable to Event Studies. 'Theory' is a much overused and misused term. Much of the so-called 'theory' I see in the academic literature consists not of explanatory and predictive modelling that withstands the test of time (i.e., permanence), as a good physics or chemistry theory would, but of conceptualizations and propositions. Within the social sciences, humanities and management studies I do not think we can ever have explanatory/predictive theory, nor is it a worthwhile pursuit.

A more appropriate approach to theory development comes from John Kelly (1987: 2) in his book *Freedom to Be: A New Sociology of Leisure*. Kelly argued that all theoretical models share the following:

- They are acts of explanation, communicated to others.
- They are systematic and disclose their presuppositions and evidence.
- They are always subject to question and criticism.

Theory development, to Kelly, is something we do '. . . whenever we attempt to explain to others the antecedents and conditions of occurrences'. In the context of Event Studies, each of the chapters on the five themes of Event Studies contains a lot of theory development. So too is the application of all the theories and models from other disciplines to the study of planned events.

Neuman (2003) said a 'conceptual model' is a collection of concepts that together form a web of meaning and represent a simplified description of complex phenomena. Models usually serve to depict the believed or proposed structure of interrelationships of factors which help explain a higher-order concept. Accordingly, theories in our field are never truly complete nor are they completely generalizable, but they do contribute to knowledge building and stimulate debate. Basically, we have no distinct theory of planned events. At this stage we have to reply on borrowing and adapting theories from pertinent disciplines.

Propositions and Hypotheses

'Propositions' can form the basis of a conceptual model and can be important in building theory. If we have deep understanding of some aspects of events we can legitimately propose that certain things are true, or will be discovered. Propositions need to be debated or tested, and in that sense they can be turned into 'hypotheses' for other researchers.

Propositions are generally stated in the following way:

P1: (It is proposed that) what people think of as types or forms of event, such as 'festival', 'convention' or 'sport competition', are social constructs in terms of expected setting and programme, and in terms of their meaning; these constructs will vary from culture to culture and will evolve over time.

Throughout this book there are other observations or conclusions that can easily be stated as propositions, useful either for generating research hypotheses or policy action.

Research Methodologies

Disciplines have their own methods, rules or postulates that together constitute 'methodologies', or accepted ways of conducting research and generating knowledge. Methodology is rooted in philosophical assumptions (i.e., epistemology, ontology) and provides the rationale for conducting research in accepted ways.

In 'positivism', reality is assumed to be objective, independent of the researcher/observer, and the truth can be discovered by the methodologies of the 'scientific method' such as experimentation. As discussed earlier, 'science' has been the dominant methodology and it remains the most accepted way of doing things in Event Studies. Note that many 'qualitative' methods are also part of this tradition, and indeed have considerable credibility within the social 'sciences'.

Deductive Research

In the positivistic tradition, the starting point is a proposition or hypothesis, generally derived from previous research and existing theory. Data are collected with the specific intent of testing the hypothesis through statistical techniques, such as comparing means on scores from Likert scales to 'prove' that members of one racial or cultural group hold different attitudes towards an event when compared to another group. This can, indeed, add considerable understanding to our problem of why some events do not engage all members of the community. Whether or not the resultant theory building is the same, or better/worse than that arising from inductive or grounded research, is difficult to say. In the social sciences there is no real test other than the test of time and criticism.

Inductive and Grounded Research

The starting point for 'inductive' and 'grounded research' is some kind of observation or data collection, leading to analysis. The researcher is to have no pre-conceived notion of findings. This leads to explanation or theory building. In inductive or grounded research there might emerge many possible explanations for an observed phenomenon, and they all have to be considered.

Grounded research draws mostly from the work of Glaser and Strauss (1967). In their approach, various types of coding are employed to reach a 'saturation point' where no additional understanding of relationships or abstractions is gained from the data. Theories are built upon categorized data that help to describe and explain the research focus. It should be said that many researchers find a rigorous application of the Glaser and Strauss methodology to be impractical, but the general principle of working inductively from data in steps that lead to theory is sound. The research of Xiao and Smith (2004), below, shows an application to Event Studies.

Research Note

Xiao, H., and Smith, S. (2004). Residents' perceptions of Kitchener-Waterloo Oktoberfest: an inductive analysis. Event Management, 8(3): 161–175.

This paper employs inductive analysis of answers to an open-ended question from a questionnaire survey of residents, namely: 'If you were trying to describe Kitchener-Waterloo Oktoberfest in a few words to a friend who has never attended before, what would you tell him or her?'. All 232 responses to the question were initially subjected to 'unrestricted coding' which meant that bits of data were sorted and assigned conceptual codes. These codes included phrases like fun, good time, enjoyment, excellent music, relaxation, ethnic culture, meeting strangers.

Looking at the relationships between codes, four main categories of Oktoberfest supporters emerged: seeking entertainment/fun; seeking cultural experience; seeking socialization, and vitalizing the local economy. Other categories were detected, including complaint makers, mild opponents and radical opponents. Additional emergent themes were detected, related to residents' perceptions of and support for ethnic cultural festivals.

Their findings support well-cited critics such as Boorstin (1961) on pseudo-events, staged authenticity (MacCannell, 1973) and acculturation (Nash, 2000). Culture is often exploited for fun and tourism, and in the case of KW Oktoberfest an increasingly multi-cultural population finds some degree of disconnect with the German traditions, but nevertheless has a good time.

Interpretivism

'Interpretivism' arises from the belief that the study of humans is different from the natural sciences, so positivism is not necessarily the best methodology. Sociology, for example, is split between 'structuralists' who favour positivism and 'interactionists' who favour interpretivism.

While positivism views reality as single, objective and tangible, interpretivism believes in multiple, socially constructed realities (Decrop, 2006: 47). In other words, your world view is quite different from mine. Interpretivists seek understanding, but do not make firm predictions (no explanatory/predictive models). Interpretivist research tends to focus on that which is unique, even deviant, rather than seeking global generalizability. The knowledge generated is contextual, being value and culture-bound. Researchers are likely to interact and cooperate with their subjects and to use holistic-inductive methodology (or naturalistic inquiry). 'Naturalistic inquiry' is the non-manipulative study of real-world situations, as opposed to experimentation. A lack of predetermined constraints on findings makes it similar to grounded research.

Social Constructivism

Social scientists often engage in debates about the extent to which theories are shaped by their social and political context. In this way 'social constructivism' postulates that social factors play a large role in the acceptance of new scientific theories. Jennings (2006: 3) described it this way: 'Social constructivism has an ontological position that acknowledges the multiple realities of the people (sometimes called actors) participating in the research'. It is contrary to 'postpositivists' who still perceive a reality. 'The epistemological position of social constructivism is a subjective and value-laden one. Moreover, researchers utilize primarily qualitative methodology and engage in an intrinsic, instrumental and transactional axiology'.

Semiotics

'Semiotics', or 'semiology', is the study of signs, sign systems and their meanings. 'Signs' are also symbols, standing for something else. For example, semiotics can be applied to words and texts, body movements or the clothes people wear. In contrast, 'communication' is the process of transferring data and is concerned with the media of communication. In both communications and semiotics there is a concern for how receivers interpret and give meaning to signs and communications.

According to Echtner (1999), in ontological terms the 'semiotics paradigm' views reality as being socially constructed, and consisting of systems of signs such as language. Semioticians seek to uncover recurring patterns and layers of meanings. Applied to events, we need to understand interactions among 'signs' (advertisements, branding, theming, explicit and implicit communications about the event and within the event), and the 'interpretants' – those people in attendance, or our target markets.

Ryan (2000) believed that tourist space is a locus of selected meanings where the visitor brings their own interpretations. Signs and symbols are interpreted to create meanings, with one implication being that meanings are only in part shaped by the event planner, and another implication being that multiple meanings are often the norm.

Critical Theory

Jennings (2006: 3) also described 'critical theory paradigm' as adopting '. . . an ontological position that the social world is constrained by rules, although these rules can be changed. Its epistemological position is halfway between subjectivism and objectivism. Axiologically, this paradigm should lead to transformational change, as the aim of research in this paradigm is to alter the social circumstances of those being studied'.

Research Purposes and Methods

Veal (2006: 3) provided a typology of research from the perspective of its purpose or utility. 'Exploratory' or 'descriptive' research seeks to uncover facts or describe a situation. This simplest type of research is commonplace in emerging fields like Event Studies and might consist of inventories, mapping and classifications of events, case histories, profiles of event organizations or compilations of facts about policies and regulations affecting the event sector. A trend analysis of demand for events is descriptive, whereas an analysis of factors causing the trend is explanatory.

'Explanatory' research seeks understanding. In a positivist tradition there is often an assumption of cause and effect, such as: the growth in demand for entertainment events is explained by the rise of disposable incomes enabling more people to engage in hedonistic pursuits. If we can explain why something happens, then a predictive model should be possible.

'Evaluative research' is essential in event management and in policy development. 'Internal evaluation' of an organization's effectiveness (in attaining goals) and efficiency (the best use of its resources) is a responsibility of management. 'External evaluation' is conducted by stakeholders who want to know if their 'investment' or support for the event has been worthwhile, or to otherwise examine the impacts of the event.

'Formative' evaluation includes needs assessments, feasibility studies and demand forecasting, anything to do with shaping future decisions and actions. 'Process evaluation' occurs during an event or programme, with a view to correcting mistakes or improving it while it is running. 'Outcome evaluation' includes impact assessments and other after-the-event surveys and analysis, all intended to determine accurately what happened, and why.

Quantitative Methods

Quantitative methods are associated with positivism, and qualitative with interpretivism, but there is absolutely no reason why both cannot be combined in any given piece of event-related research or evaluation. The difference is not one of good technique, but of what you need to know and how best to find out. Often an exploratory, qualitative stage, using focus groups, interviews and observation, precedes a more quantitative stage.

Secondary Data Analysis

Especially when used as a starting point in research projects, existing sources such as large datasets on leisure, travel or consumer behaviour can provide new insights. Have all analytical tools been used on the existing data? Can new hypotheses be tested? It can also be a useful exercise for students to examine general tourism data, for example, to search for event-specific behaviour and motivations.

Systematic Observation

As employed in the Getz et al. (2001) study of a surfing event, nine trained observers used temporal and areal stratification of an event to observe and record information about the setting and the audience. This is a quantitative method insofar as the data collected can be analysed in the same way as survey data. Remember that observation can also yield qualitative insights.

Questionnaire Surveys

These are probably the most popular research methods, because you can get lots of data cheaply, and sometimes quickly. In the positivistic tradition a random sample or complete census is necessary to make generalizations about a population. They can follow a number of procedures.

'Self-completion, intercept surveys' are a very common way to get immediate feedback from festival-goers, on site. 'Intercepts' can also be done of cars on roads, or of persons at airports. Usually the researcher wants a random sample (e.g., every *n*th person through the gate) but might settle for a 'systematic sample' (such as you can obtain through spatial and temporal stratification).

'Post-event, mail-back' surveys: Often a two-stage approach is best (Pol and Pak, 1994), such as getting people at the event to provide a little information and having them agree to a postal follow-up. The post-event portion is best for getting more accurate data on total expenditures and an assessment of the overall experience.

The 'telephone survey' is a good way to cover a market area, such as doing a survey of awareness of an event in a city 2 hours away by car. Sampling problems are common with this method, so often a 'quota' sample is taken (i.e., get so many males, females and families). 'Quota sampling' is useful in market research where you want a balanced response from males and females, or perhaps you only need the opinions of older tourists. Instruct canvassers to obtain a specific number from each target category.

'Convenience sampling' is generally not recommended, but is easy and cheap – just take anybody that you can get to answer your questions. It can be combined with quota sampling, and a useful variation is to sample willing people in a particular location or at an event, which has the advantage of a common frame of reference (the place or the event).

The 'captive sample': this method works well at meetings and other events where participants feel obligated to respond or cannot avoid doing the survey. Students are often a 'captive sample'!

A number of scholars have compared different survey methods applied to events, such as comparing logbooks with self-completion questionnaires (Faulkner and Raybould, 1995; Breen et al., 2001). Quite a few studies have been aimed at perfecting attendance counts and improving attendance estimates at events (e.g., Brothers and Brantley, 1993; Raybould et al., 2000).

Qualitative Methods

Qualitative methods generally do not attempt a numerical analysis, and are more focused on discovering people's attitudes, feelings, motives, or perhaps meanings attached to an event experience. Often the numbers of respondents involved is small, as the appropriate methods (e.g., participant observation, interviews, focus groups) are time-consuming. Of special interest might be the interactions between people in a focus group setting, which need to be recorded and later interpreted, or perhaps the language used by people in a self-reporting situation (e.g., Do event-goers use words like 'self-fulfilling' or 'mastery' when describing their event experiences?).

Phenomenology and Hermeneutics

'Phenomenology' as a method attempts to obtain a direct description of a person's experience, ignoring for the moment any causation or motivation. 'Hermeneutics' a Greek word for interpretation. All writing and symbolic communication (including performances and sports) can be viewed as 'text', and that text can be interpreted.

Hayllar and Griffin (2004) employed 'hermeneutic phenomenology' to explore tourists' experience of a tourist space, the 'Rocks' in Sydney. They engaged visitors in lengthy, structured interviews about the area and their experiences in it. In effect, visitors interpreted their own experiences, then researchers interpreted the 'text' of those interviews by examining themes in the recounted experiences. The results of such research are insights about experiences, but this is not 'objective' in the positivistic tradition and therefore is regarded as qualitative research. Chen's (2006) use of phenomenology (see the research note under Philosophy in Chapter 4) is one of the few examples specific to events.

A possible substitute for field research is to assess the meanings of what people say on web logs, or in other written texts. Read this first-hand account, taken anonymously from a web posting, from someone who attended a festival.

> *About fifteen years ago I went to my first (festival name and location deleted), and I fell in love with the sacred fire circle and the festival space around it. The strength and magic of this sacred container rocked my world. I can honestly say I have never experienced anything like it in my life. Those 5 days were the most memorable ones I have ever had and cannot wait to return this summer. The festival's an incredible experience. Unbelievable! I just can't explain it! I wouldn't miss it for anything in the World! It keeps me happy! It's a really intense experience if you enjoy the music because there's so much of it! Memories are made here. The kind that really make a difference in your life.*

It appears to have been a truly memorable, even transforming festival experience, and there are clues as to the nature of the experience. But what is really meant by 'magic' and 'intense'? We cannot get clarification from the written text. And how can we interpret the phrase 'rocked my world'? More questions are raised than can possibly be answered.

The following two blog quotations were from marathon runners.

> *I run because it makes me feel alive. It challenges me like nothing else. I have run each decade of my life. The pain brings me a reminder that life is not easy. The feeling when you cross the finish line reminds me that nothing worthwhile in life comes easy.*

> *I ran the first marathon to see if I could do it. I continue to run more marathons to see if I can improve my time, and maybe one day qualify for Boston…*

I run to stay in shape, get away for a while, and to compete. Compete against myself to see if I can become a better runner. It's important because it helps keep me in shape and gives me a goal to shoot for. Plus the interaction with other runners is awesome.

One cannot understand the competitive athlete who participates in many events without paying attention to their fundamental motivations. The quotations suggest these runners are creating meanings for the events in terms of mastery and self-development, with social or affiliation experiences being important.

This quote is from a student who attended a multi-cultural youth science forum.

Although this trip was academically very enriching, it is the social and cultural exchange along with the bonds we formed that will be cherished forever. This was my first trip to another country as a student and I have certainly gained a lot of confidence from it.

Clearly 'communitas' was at the core of this event experience, the sense of belonging and sharing reflected in the word 'bonds'. But it was also a learning experience and one of self-growth.

When reading first-person accounts of experiences a basic interpretive problem in that the researcher had no control over the writer. They might be posturing, lying, exaggerating, who knows? If you take them at face value they will probably mislead you. If you assume there is some grain of truth in them, collectively, it will probably result in improved understanding and maybe play a part in developing theory. It seems like a good, qualitative starting point for more in-depth phenomenological research.

There might be ethical questions to consider when analysing texts. Is it possible to identify the sources of the above blog quotes? Can they be slightly disguised while still retaining their authenticity?

Experiential Sampling

This method (see Csikszentmihalyi and Csikszentmihalyi, 1988) provides a means to collect information about the context and content of daily life, or some element of leisure such as event experiences. It can be thought of as 'systematic phenomenology', allowing people to report on the cognitive and affective elements of their lived experiences. It is particularly relevant to event experiences (although I have not found this application reported in the literature) because questions can cover the physical setting, social context, activities, thoughts, feeling, moods and other self-appraisals.

Diaries can be used, although there is the problem of recollection bias and memory failure. Getting people to write down or record their thoughts and feelings while engaged in the experience is preferable, but intrusive. Not everyone will agree to participate, and some will either do a poor job or quit.

In most experiential sampling projects the respondents have been given a signalling device such as a pager or beeper. Random beeps then trigger self-completion of a brief set of questions, the idea being to intrude as little as possible yet cover the full extent of the experience. Current technology allows for wireless internet contact and instant communication back to the researchers.

In terms of an event, it would probably be best to start experiential sampling during the anticipation and approach stage, while afterwards it might be better to address experiences through direct debriefing. Here are some ideas on what to ask:

- Where are you right now? (Perhaps requiring a map of the setting.)
- Who are you with? (Prompt with categories.)
- What are you doing? (Prompt with categories but allow for the unexpected.)
- Describe your mood. (A 7-point scale with paired opposites describing moods can be used.)
- What are you thinking about?
- Your level of concentration (e.g., paying attention to the show, or daydreaming).
- Perceived control (e.g., are you free to do what you want, or under some obligation).

Larson and Csikszentmihalyi (1983), and Hektner and Csikszentmihalyi (2002) also provided advice on how to conduct experiential sampling, including a draft instrument, and they also advised that it is probably best to use this technique in combination with other methods.

Content Analysis

What are the newspapers saying about the impacts of an event, or the wisdom of bidding on a world's fair? How have event-goers described their experiences on blogs? Content analysis can employ specific techniques such as hermeneutics to compile and interpret what has been said.

Observation and Participant Observation

Carlsen (2004) outlined a number of event evaluation methods including observation and participant observation techniques. These were used in a study by Getz et al. (2001) on a surfing event. Their direct observation employed checklists and spatially and temporally stratified sampling. Participant observation consisted of each of nine researchers 'enjoying' as much of the event as they could. Each observer then recorded their general observations and impressions, and when these qualitative (and subjective) insights were combined with systematic observation and interviews a service quality map was prepared. With three convergent methods being used, this research illustrates the principle of 'triangulation'.

Interviews

In my view you can usually learn more from a few interviews than you can from a large-scale questionnaire, but often both are desirable. 'Formal interviews' are structured, and sometimes it is best for interviewees to know the topics in advance so they can be prepared – especially if they are being consulted because of their professional position. 'Informal interviews' do not have a firm structure, although the topics have to be clear in the mind of the researcher. Interviews can be analysed systematically, using content analysis, or interpreted as to the key points.

'In-depth interviews' are a time-consuming method intended to cover a lot of ground and obtain considerable detail, usually from a few respondents. They are very useful with key informants who know a lot, such as interviewing event managers about their stake-holder relationships and strategies (see Getz et al., 2007). This method can be a part of researching the case histories of events or in conducting cross-case analysis.

'Group interviews' and 'focus groups' encourage interactions among respondents within a controlled setting. A synergistic affect is usually desired, such as getting a group of event managers together and asking them to identify all the funding issues faced by the festival sector. However, a strong personality can potentially influence everyone's opinion. Focus groups are a staple in consumer research, but of course you cannot draw generalized conclusions from the input. They are usually the starting point.

'Ethnography' traditionally involved living in a place, being submersed in a society or cultural group. Favoured by early anthropologists, this obviously time-consuming and challenging research method yields a lot of insights. But there will always be the issues of observer bias, interaction effects (changing what you are observing) and information being withheld and deliberate mis-representation by the 'observed'. 'Participant observation' can be ethnography at a small scale.

Case Studies
Getz et al. (2007) used the case study method to compare festivals in Canada and Sweden on the topics of stakeholder types, relationships, management and issues. 'Cross-case analysis' is a powerful tool in exploratory research, as it can generate numerous insights. Findings from case studies are not generalizable, but do play an important role in creating new knowledge, generating hypotheses or propositions and testing existing theory.

Time-budget Studies
How much time do people spend attending events of different kinds, or how much time do marathoners use in preparing for and travelling to races? These are classic leisure studies, as reviewed by Roberts (2006).

Action Research
'Action researchers' are usually involved in a programme or project that is intended to have specific outcomes, and the entire process continuously needs to be evaluated and revised.

There is plenty of scope for learning about what works and what does not, but also the risk of involvement bias.

Research Project

I have not seen any application of 'action research' in the events sector, but here is an idea: the researcher joins the team planning and implementing an event, all the while both contributing as an equal and observing/ analysing how decisions are made and which stakeholders have the greatest impact. Usually action research is devoted to social causes, so a more typical application would be for the participant/researcher to work with a community group to develop and evaluate a festival intended to solve some local problems.

Historical Research

The history of a specific event or class of event is the subject for historians, yet it has to be put into a social, cultural, environmental and economic context. The historical researcher has to have a point of view, or methodology. For example: How have both politics and technological innovation affected the origin and evolution of international expositions, particularly World's Fairs? Why are the Olympics such a sought-after, iconic event? Keep in mind the historiographers will assess the relevance and validity of information used and its analysis within historical research.

Research Projects

Explore the origins of professional event management starting in the mists of antiquity. For example: Who put on the Roman Games or Circus and how was their event production knowledge transferred to ensuing generations? Have festivals always been planned or did they just happen? When did not-for-profit event organizations and for-profit event companies begin?

Longitudinal Research

A great deal can be learned by time-sampling, or otherwise studying a phenomenon like an event over a long period of time. This can be an important part of historical research, but just as much an element in policy and programme evaluation. For example, looking at the impacts of event tourism on a community at one point in time is quite limiting, so why not conduct surveys every year for a decade?

Research Project

Interview event managers and other stakeholders before, during and after a planned one-time event. Measure and compare their assessment of intended and actual impacts, why things happened, and what can or should be done about it. Consider the affects of time passing on respondents' memory, attitude change and willing- ness to participate in the research. Try to explain why there is or is not consensus on event impacts, both what they were and their positive or negative interpretation.

Futures Research

Can we really conduct research on the future? There is trend extrapolation, Delphi panels and future scenarios to help envisage and plan for the future, whereas longitudinal research will tell us if we got it right. Remember that speculation and prophesy are completely different exercises.

One valuable contribution to Event Studies will be the formulation of expert and multi-stakeholder panels to periodically assess trends and possible future consequences for the world of planned events. But who will convene this?

Meta-analysis

This research method has had limited application in the events field, mainly because so few research studies yield comparable data. The work of Dwyer et al. (2000a, b) in developing an approach to event impact forecasting and evaluation was a kind of meta-analysis in that various impact studies were compared and general conclusions drawn, both about the methods employed (and how they needed to be improved and standardized) and the nature of event impacts.

Cross-cultural Research

Event Studies must also develop through cross-cultural research, and this is rarely attempted. Kay (2004) conducted a review of research 'of relevance' to cultural event tourism, but that review found that few studies systematically compared or contrasted between cultures. Kay addressed the questions of what should be the focus of cross-cultural research, and how it should be conducted, but the sphere of concern was restricted to gaining improved understanding of who attends events, and why.

The greater need is for seeking understanding of all the elements and processes in our Event Studies framework within and between different cultures (including countries) and cultural groups in society (including ethnic and affinity groups and sub-cultures). The vast majority of the available literature is Western, thereby limiting its generalizability, and in this book (and in most pertinent sources) only English-language literature has been considered.

When comparing cultures it is almost certain that the personal and social constructs attached to planned events will be different, giving rise to varying levels of significance assigned to events in a policy context. However, the power of globalization has to be taken into account, particularly through the influence of mass media and the internet, so we also have to look for diffusion and adaptation within the world of planned events.

A Research Agenda for Event Studies

Shaw and Williams (2004: 275) put forward a general research agenda for tourism studies that can readily be adapted to Event Studies. In their view, researchers have to be critical (not just a management or business-driven agenda), employ diverse disciplinary and methodological perspectives and be holistic. This means positioning Event Studies within broad social, economic and environmental discourses.

Being 'critical', as used by Shaw and Williams, means to not simply adhere to a research agenda driven by event management, event tourism or event policy. Researchers (including students) have to be free to challenge established practices and paradigms and to generate new ideas and approaches. Secondly, being 'critical' suggests adoption of a particular approach to research. Just remember that critical theory and critical thought are only useful if they help create new understanding and build better methods and skills. My point is that researchers do not have to buy into any school of thought to be critical and constructive.

Previous overviews of research in the events field have been undertaken by Formica (1998) and Getz (2000b). Within our discussion of each of the main themes of Event Studies a large number of research ideas and needs were generated, and these are summarized below. It is not useful to assign priorities to them, because depending on one's perspective any of them could be important. A starting point for doing event-related research can be disciplinary, so that only those questions framed within sociology, for example, would be important. Other starting points are management needs, policy evaluation or personal interest in a topic.

For each of the themes a few key questions are asked, and possible research methods suggested. This is not in any way to limit the range of research possibilities, but is a starting point.

A Research Agenda for Planned Event Experiences and Meanings (Figure 13.2)

This is the core of Event Studies and therefore demands constant attention from researchers and theorists. According to Borrie and Birzell (2001) there have been four common approaches to studying visitor experiences:

1. The 'satisfaction approach' is really a surrogate measure, as it asks if people were satisfied with their experiences – not what those experiences were or what they meant. This line of research has generated both practical and theoretical understanding, but does do not go far enough in exploring experiences.
2. The 'benefits approach' asks respondents to indicate level of agreement with statements regarding the benefits they might have received, such as to escape, to relax, to learn, etc. It is similar to asking about motivations to attend an event. A priority here is for examining and comparing motives/benefits at all types of events, in different cultures and settings.
3. 'Experience-based' methods involve reporting on thoughts, feelings or moods during daily life, a trip or event. Phenomenological approaches should be a top priority in Event Studies, particularly for gaining better theoretical understanding of immediate conscious experience; experiential sampling should be utilized in a variety of event circumstances.
4. A 'meanings-based' approach requires deep insights obtained through participant observation or interviews, or the application of hermeneutic phenomenology; life-enriching stories are elicited. We need considerably more research on social and personal constructs of event meanings.

Mental Exercise

Think about a recent event experience you had, or make notes the next time you go to an event. Ask yourself these questions about the entire experience:

- *What exactly were you expecting in terms of atmosphere, mood, activities, quality? What do you personally want to get out of this event?*
- *How did you feel going into the event? What was your mood?*
- *Had you been to this event (type of event) before?*
- *During the event, what did you do? With whom? What were your feelings and your mood? Describe the event experience in your own words.*
- *How do you feel now that the event is over?*
- *What have you learned?*
- *Did you/how did you change? (Personal transformation)*
- *Did you change anything? (The agent of change)*
- *Did you find what you wanted?*
- *Did the event meet your expectations? Why or why not?*

Research Project

Take any event held in your community and determine the various meanings people attach to it, including a comparison of those who attended and those who did not. You should expect that many respondents will not know, not care and not offer an opinion. Some will have a vested interest, because they benefited from the event, and others will freely attach meanings even when ignorant of the details! In this context, how is public policy toward events to be determined?

Event Studies themes	Key research questions	Possible research methods
The planned event experience and meanings	• How do people describe, explain and assign meaning to various event experiences? Within each of these dimensions: conative (behaviour); affective (emotional) and cognitive. • Describe and explain the formation of personal and social constructs regarding event experiences. • How does level of involvement or engagement affect the event experience? • Examine 'arousal' and 'flow' within different event settings. • What makes event experiences memorable and transforming? • How does 'communitas' form at events? Can it be facilitated? • Is there a measurable 'wow!' factor? • Systematically compare different event experiences (for all stakeholders, from paying customers and guests to the general public, and between types of event, from sport to carnival)	• Hermeneutics (analysis of texts; self-reporting) • Phenomenology (e.g., in-depth interviews at events) • Direct and participant observation • Experiential sampling (diary or time-sampling with standard questions)

Figure 13.2   Research agenda: planned event experience and meanings.

A Research Agenda for Antecedents and Choices (Figure 13.3)

Generic consumer research and evaluation methods have to be adapted better to event-related problems, especially because we are dealing with experiences that embody many personal, social and cultural meanings. A lot of research has been done on motivation, which gives clues as to needs, experiences and outcomes, but these are all conceptually different and their interactions are complex. For example, do people believe they 'need' events, and where do such needs come from?

Leisure constraints theory offers considerable scope for examining why some people attend events and others do not. Constraint negotiation applied to intrinsically and extrinsically motivated event attendance should be examined. Economic theories and methods should be applied to gain a better understand of supply and demand issues that influence event attendance, and particularly willingness to pay and pricing.

Research Projects

For a type of recreational or sport event examine how participants at different levels of involvement (or commitment in terms of serious leisure) develop careers that involve travel and a progression to higher levels of achievement, prestige or self-actualization. Can this concept of event careers apply to commerce and work-related events?

Ask a range of people, by age, gender and other variables, to describe their past, current and likely future participation in various types of events. Does early socialization in sport or the arts explain event interests and behaviour over the full life span? To what extent does culture and education affect interest in planned events? Do intrinsic or extrinsic motivations explain most event attendance?

Event producers and marketers need to know a whole lot about what attracts, and what keeps people away from their events. Ask people who attended an event what barriers or constraints they faced, and which were more important (use a scale). Ask them if any particular constraint was a possible 'deal breaker' (i.e., they would not pay a certain price, would not come if parking was unavailable, etc.). Now find people who did not attend and try to determine what kept them away (include awareness and interest levels, then specific constraints such as cost, accessibility, etc.).

When people say they do not have the time or money to attend a specific, upcoming event, what are they really saying? Try to determine how important those real, structural constraints are for event attendance, relative to other constraints. Use focus groups to get an initial understanding, then develop a general consumer survey. Do the results suggest marketing applications?

What types of events are 'luxury goods'? What evidence is there that free events are perceived to have lesser or greater utility to different segments of the population? Can an event change its positioning in the marketplace simply by raising or lowering its price?

Event Studies themes	Key research questions	Possible research methods
• Personal antecedents • Barriers and constraints • Decision-making • Post-event evaluation and feedback	• What are the main cultural variables affecting the perceived value and attractiveness of events? • Examine the relative importance and nature of generic versus specific (targeted) needs, motives and benefits that are sought through different planned event experiences. Develop marketing implications. • Do people believe they 'need' events? • How is economic demand for events shaped by price, competition, substitution, policy and other factors? • How are event careers developed? Use ego-involvement, recreation specialization and commitment theories • In what ways does 'serious leisure' affect events? • What constraints are most important in shaping demand and attendance at different types of event? How are constraints negotiated for intrinsically and extrinsically motivated event attendance? • How do different segments use the internet and other media for searching and decision-making in the events sector? • Can planned events be substituted by other forms of entertainment and business practices?	• General consumer and market area surveys • Focus groups • Social needs evaluation • Supply–demand assessment • In-depth interviews • Time–budget studies • Longitudinal studies of event careers and constraint negotiation

Figure 13.3 A research agenda for antecedents and choices.

Research Agenda: Management, Planning, Design and Operations of Events (Figure 13.4)

Harris et al. (2001) examined academic, practitioner and government perspectives on research needs related to events. Practitioners emphasized research on sponsorship, the

Event Studies themes	Key research questions	Possible research methods
• Leadership • Organizational culture • Planning and decision-making • Design • Marketing and communications • Finances, financial management and controls • Operations and logistics • Human Resources • Risk, health and safety • Research, evaluation and information systems	• What leadership styles are most effective for different types of events and event settings? • How can creativity and management competency be balanced in the event sector? • What strategies are most effective in achieving event sustainability and institutional status? Which stakeholder management strategies work best? • Does rational planning and decision-making work better for events than incrementalism or advocacy? Compare one-time and periodic events. • How do various stakeholders perceive and manage the risks associated with events? • What are the potential effects of sensory and emotional stimulation at events? • How can theory from environmental psychology improve event logistics and crowd management? • What are the main determinants of customer satisfaction at events? • What volunteer careers exist in the event sector, and how do they foster commitment and professionalism?	• Case studies and cross-case analysis • Historical research • Open-system audits • Stakeholder mapping • Organizational ethnography • Surveys of owners and managers • Consumer Experiments • Financial audits and return on investment (ROI) studies

Figure 13.4 Research agenda: management, planning, design and operations.

needs and motives of attendees, market segmentation and determining why events fail. Government officials wanted research on event failure and risks, as well as standard research tools and methods. Perhaps surprisingly, academics selected risk management strategy formulation as their priority, followed by valuing events and reasons for failure.

Each of the management functions, including design, suggests its own research agenda and priorities. In general, it can be said that marketing has dominated the events literature in terms of management topics, including sponsorship and motivational, satisfaction and segmentation studies. All the others are in real need of research attention, especially the application of management and foundation theory to events.

Research Projects

Adapt the Kaplan (1987) experiment by showing people a range of photos depicting one type or a variety of event settings, and manipulating the elements of coherence, legibility, complexity and mystery (i.e., more or less of each, and differently designed). Compare empty and peopled scenes. Use indoor and outdoor settings, to see if features of the natural environment affect preferences for certain types of event. The basic question to ask is: Which of these settings do you prefer for the following type(s) of event? Why? (You might need to prompt the respondents regarding the four elements.) To be more thorough, take into account a number of cultural and demographic factors among respondents.

Ask people who have been at an event (or are still there) to sketch a map of the event setting in the context of the surrounding environment. This obviously works best for large outdoor sites (such as a festival or fair) and complex indoor settings (like a trade or consumer show). Also ask them how to get from the arrival zone (e.g., where cars or busses arrive) to specific points in the event setting. Analyse their maps and wayfaring instructions using the Lynch (1960) framework. Draw implications for site design and other management systems. Theoretically, is there anything you feel is different about event settings and other urban places?

For a field project, make systematic observations at various types of events to see how people interact with the settings and with other people. Take photos or movies for later analysis. Try to find situations where people are crowded versus ones where there is little interaction. What accounts for the differences? Specifically look for cultural differences, or age, gender and other variables. Formulate recommendations for event managers, but keep in mind the specific goals for each event.

Research Agenda for Patterns and Processes (Figure 13.5)

So little historical and historiographic research has been done on planned events that it is practically an untouched theme. How has the profession of event management evolved, from the earliest times? The Olympics have been over-analysed, but what about other forms of events that have a long lineage? Multi- and cross-cultural studies are essential.

Histories of individual events are interesting, but only theoretically important if they can be systematically compared and analysed within a theoretical framework such as resource dependency or institutionalism. Historians can also make a big contribution by re-assessing history through the lens of major planned events and numerous personal events, as that is how many people remember and give meaning to the flow of time.

Geographic research on planned events has been given a solid foundation by Robert Janiskee and a few others, but there has been no consistent spatial–temporal approach. In cities, what has been the distribution and evolution of events, and how is to be explained? Have resources, culture or strategy been most responsible for the observable portfolios of events in any given area? When or how does an area or community reach saturation level in terms of the numbers and types of events? How do events interact? What are their cumulative impacts? Some of the answers will assist in event strategy formulation, policy-making and marketing.

In terms of future studies of planned events the slate is blank. There has been lots of speculation on how virtual events might evolve, possibly threatening 'live events', but I cannot believe this for a moment. There is simply no substitute for 'being there' and for 'live experiences'. However, advances in technology and communications in particular are shaping the events field, and we have to pay attention to these forces

Event Studies themes	Key research questions	Possible research methods
• History • Geography • Future studies • Policy	• In what fundamental ways have various types of events evolved, in different cultures? • Do events progress naturally through life cycles? What factors most shape their evolution? • Do communities or destinations reach event saturation? What explains different patterns of events in time and space? • What are the forces shaping the future of events? Can they be controlled? How do events adapt? • What are the ways in which stakeholders exercise power, and negotiate, to develop events and event-related policy? Who gets excluded or marginalized? • How do we know when event policies are effective and efficiently administered? • Which justifications for public involvement in events are supported, and why? • What are the ideological foundations of event policy? • How are events shaping urban form and urban society? • What measures will demonstrate the social and cultural benefits of planned events?	• Document review • Interviews with people who shaped history • Mapping • Delphi panels • Trends analysis • Scenario making • Policy reviews

Figure 13.5 A research agenda for patterns and processes.

and trends. For example, convention centres are now designed as both live and virtual event venues, to reach a global audience.

We need some 'futurists' in this field. I will play the role, for now, by offering the following propositions, each of which should suggest more than one research project:

FP 1: (Future proposition 1): Planned, live events, both personal and societal in scale and meaning, will always be a prominent feature of civilization, in all societies and cultures.

FP 2: Virtual events will gain in frequency and importance in response to advances in global technology, and because of globalization forces and the costs or risks of travel, but they will be in addition to, and not a substitute for live event experiences.

FP 3: Corporate influence on the field of planned events will continue to increase, especially in terms of events produced as manifestations of marketing and branding.

FP 4: The strategic justifications for public-sector involvement with events, especially mega-events bearing heavy costs, will be increasingly scrutinized and more difficult to defend, while social, cultural and environmental justifications will become more acceptable.

FP 5: Generic 'Event Management' professionals will become the norm, forcing the various professional associations to adapt their recruitment appeal and to demonstrate their added value.

FP 6: The event professional of the future will be competent in event management theory and applications, knowledgeable about the importance of events in society, an effective advocate for event-related policy and a constant learner within the field of Event Studies.

FP 7: Even if travel and tourism collapse, possibly because of the cascading effects of global warming, another energy crisis, war, terrorism or global pandemics, events will still remain important globally because they meet fundamental human needs.

Some Really Big Future Issues

There are strong forces shaping growth and diversification of planned events (see the force-field review in Getz, 2005), continuously spurring their development and magnifying the benefits derived from them. And there are contrary forces they might very well act against event tourism in particular, and result in major shifts in how we perceive and produce events.

There are many major forces propelling the event sector in terms of growth in numbers and diversity, the attention we pay to them, their perceived value and cumulative impacts. Both supply- and demand-side forces are at work. Leisure and tourism are driven by population and economic growth, especially personal disposable incomes. The all-pervasive and global mass media, more and more the internet, shape consumer demand for events. Economic growth and the forces of globalization (such as free trade and integrated economies) stimulate more business travel, meetings, conventions and exhibitions. Nations and cities compete heavily to attract and develop events for strategic reasons. But will all these forces continue unabated?

Global warming threatens the world's coastlines and ski resorts, and might very soon alter the ways in which we do business, travel and consume. The very mention of 'global pandemic' sends chills down the collective spines of everyone in the tourism and events industries. Why? Travel and events are the first things to be cancelled when disease breaks out, and dire predictions about the ravages of bird flu, SARS or something else abound. Add the constant threat of wars and terrorism, and the increasing inconveniences caused by security, the potential for disruption will remain high. If the world is perceived to be unhealthy or unsafe, people will stay at home. And if energy costs continue to accelerate, or shortages are experienced, many will have no choice but to stay close to home. Will that be the end of planned events?

I can foresee a future (this is scenario making) in which event tourism diminishes greatly because of the counter-forces mentioned above. Whole regions of the planet might lie devastated and mass migrations occur. The economy might suffer and consumerism disappear as a social and economic force. But, perhaps ironically, planned events will then become more important, not less. Instead of event tourism we will have to rely more on media events to stay connected globally. Instead of mega-events that move from country to country, each nation, region and community will require its own celebrations, meetings and games to bring people together for live experiences. Because events have met essential needs throughout history, in all civilizations, it is safe to conclude that they will endure and adapt.

Policy Questions

A major research priority is to examine how event policy is formulated within the context of power, negotiation, stakeholder and public input. It is equally important to determine why event policy is either not formulated, or is not integrated with other policy fields. Performance evaluation is necessary, including the developing of effectiveness and efficiency measures for policies affecting planned events. Little attention has been given to the justifications used for public-sector involvement with events, including the ideological bases, and how the public perceives the justifications (or values events in general).

Research Project

Employ a variety of methods to assess the formation or absence of event-related policy in a given jurisdiction. Use stakeholder theory, comparative ideology, the concept of a political market square, and social representation theory to help explain the situation. Consider the administrative framework and how it shapes the process.

Research Agenda: Outcomes and the Impacted (Figure 13.6)

Most event impact-related research to date has been focused on tourism and economics, leaving a huge gap in terms of social, cultural and environmental impact knowledge. Event policy and management cannot advance without addressing this issue.

There have been some specific and substantial contributions to our understanding of the social and cultural impacts of planned events, but it cannot be said that there is a comprehensive or systematic approach. Anthropologists and sociologists have paid a lot of attention to festivals in particular, and to certain event-related issues, but they have had their own theoretical agendas. Their collective contributions do not constitute sufficient knowledge about the real or potential outcomes of all planned events.

The valuation of planned events has to be completely re-evaluated and re-directed away from predominantly economic measures. Most planned events, from personal rites of passage to cultural celebrations, from trade shows to world's fairs, meet fundamental social and cultural needs. Who gives value to these meanings and roles?

Event Studies themes	Key research questions	Possible research methods
• Personal, social, cultural and political • Economic • Environmental	• How do people describe and explain why events are satisfying, memorable or transforming? • What are the personal and social consequences of negative event experiences? • What performance measures exist and are needed for the social, cultural and environmental policy domains? • How does exchange theory influence various stakeholder perceptions of event impacts? • How are social representations of events formed? • How does the nature and extent of community involvement influence event success and outcomes? • Under what circumstances are events commodified and authenticity lost, versus traditions renewed and culture revitalized? • How are the benefits and costs of events distributed through the population? What strategies work best for maximizing local economic benefits? • Who are the high-yield event tourists, and how should they be attracted? • How can events be made more environmentally sustainable? • What are the cumulative impacts of an event and events in general, within a community or ecosystem? • What is the value of any given event?	• Focus groups • In-depth interviews • Consumer and social surveys • Media content analysis • Stakeholder consultations • Ethnography • Comprehensive cost–benefit evaluations • Business surveys • Market research • Environmental audits and formal impact assessments • Valuations

Figure 13.6   Research agenda: outcomes and the impacted.

Chapter Summary

This chapter began with a framework for creating knowledge in Event Studies. The model shows that policy and management both require knowledge and generate applied research, with other sources being grounded research, introspection and think-tanks, and reflective professional practice. It also incorporates knowledge from foundation disciplines and closely related fields, and suggests that interdisciplinary research is needed.

Before beginning research it is important to consider a number of philosophical issues regarding the meaning and creation of knowledge, hence a discussion of epistemology, ontology, positivism and postmodernism. Research in Event Studies should not be confined to any particular research paradigm, rather it should be inclusive and integrative.

Positivism, associated with quantitative, scientific methods (including experimentation) has led to substantial theory development in the foundation disciplines, much of which is necessary for Event Studies. Yet the experiential nature of events and the diverse meanings attached to them necessitate alternative approaches such as phenomenology, ethnography, and inductive, grounded research in general. An interpretivist perspective, recognizing socially constructed realities, will definitely help progress the field.

Research and evaluation purposes and methods were then discussed, revealing the broad range of approaches that can be useful. Throughout the book examples of many methods have been provided, hopefully making it clear that no particular approach or technique should have pre-eminence. Finally, a research agenda for Event Studies was presented, including key research questions and appropriate methods. This agenda is really just a starting point and is not indeed to limit research. Priorities will be different depending on one's perspective on events, as outlined in our framework for creating knowledge.

Study Questions

- Is Event Studies a 'discipline', 'multi-disciplinary' or 'interdisciplinary'? Why?
- Explain the ways in which knowledge can be created for Event Studies.
- Define these terms and explain how they affect the creation of knowledge: 'epistemology', 'ontology', 'positivism' and 'postmodernism'.
- Why are 'theories' needed in Event Studies? How are they developed?
- Show how 'deductive' and 'inductive' methodologies are both appropriate in Event Studies.
- What are the main purposes and uses of research and evaluation?
- Give examples of established research methods from foundation disciplines that can be applied in Event Studies.
- Illustrate 'quantitative' and 'qualitative' research that has been applied to the study of planned events.
- Explain 'phenomenology' and why it is important in Event Studies.
- Suggest and justify research priorities for each of the main themes in Event Studies.

Further Reading

Lee, J., and Back, K. (2005). A review of convention and meeting management research. *Journal of Convention and Event Tourism*, 7(2): 1–19.

Yoo, J., and Weber, K. (2005). Progress in convention tourism research. *Journal of Hospitality and Tourism Research*, 29(2): 194–222.

Mossberg, L. (ed.) (2000). *Evaluation of Events: Scandinavian Experiences*. New York: Cognizant.

Veal, A. (2006). *Research Methods for Leisure and Tourism: A Practical Guide* (3rd edn). Harlow England: Prentice Hall.

Chapter 14
Conclusions

In this short, concluding chapter the book's 'big ideas' are reviewed. Event Studies has attempted to justify, define, build the foundations and suggest a research agenda for this academic field. The need has arisen from the global, rapidly expanding professional practice of event management and event tourism, and from the needs of policymakers who are increasingly dealing with event-related issues.

Researchers in a variety of foundation disciplines and closely related professional fields already do work that is part of Event Studies. Teachers (and they are many) who go beyond the how-to approach to inculcate their students with appreciation of the big issues surrounding events are already engaged in Event Studies. It does not exist just because of this book, rather this book is a reflection of the real world.

The Planned Event Experience

At the core of Event Studies is the planned event experience, and meanings attached to it. Event planners and designers intend that their efforts result in positive experiences and productive outcomes, leading to meanings being attached to those events that are personally, politically and socially positive. Event Studies has to focus on this experiential domain both in theoretical terms, to model and understand it, and to generate practical management applications.

It was argued that events cannot easily be classified by reference to experiences, because multiple experiences are possible within any event form. By looking at a number of 'events at the margin', such as flash mobs and gorilla gigs, we observed that planned and unplanned events can embody similar activities and experiences, which helps us understand human events in general. The question of scale was addressed, illustrating how the realm of large, public events is substantially different in several respects from small, private events.

Drawing heavily from cultural anthropology and cognitive psychology, with a tip of the hat to Tourism and Leisure Studies, a model of the planned event experience was developed. Because events can embody both the 'sacred' and the 'profane' (i.e., religious/spiritual or secular) we refer to a 'liminal/liminoid zone' (from classical anthropologists van Gennep and Turner). Two key phrases are used in our model to reflect the nature of the 'zone', that is 'time out of time' (borrowed from Falassi), and 'a special place'. Rituals and symbolism abound in the realm of planned events, and form important programmic elements of style that can be used to 'valorize' the special times and places that constitute event experiences, as well as to stimulate emotions and define the theme.

Another key experiential concept is that of 'communitas', or the sense of belonging and sharing that comes from social events, and should be a hallmark of festivals and other cultural celebrations. Communitas refers to that temporary state in which people are together as equals sharing an experience, removed from ordinary life, so they have something very specific in common. Their experience should be unstructured, relative to the outside world, and egalitarian (everyone accepted as being equal). 'Communitas' experienced at events is always clearly transient, whereas sub-cultures seek this social state on a permanent basis. A frequent motivation to attend and participate in events, and one powerful driver of 'event careers', is the emotional high that comes from being part of the group in this special place and time, and the sense of loss or sorrow upon its closure.

Three dimensions of experiences must be considered. The 'conative' or (behavioural) dimension refers to behaviour, and for the most part we are interested in purposeful behaviour, or the intent to realize specific benefits. What do people do at events that helps them have the experience they desire? How does the event programmer provide or stimulate individual activities or social interaction? At the basic level, guests simply watch and enjoy the spectacle or entertainment, or enjoy each other's company, without deep emotion or thought. The 'affective' dimension refers to emotions, and here we can talk about how designers stimulate deeper feelings, including fostering a sense of belonging and sharing. If people are emotionally 'engaged' there will be a more powerful experience. It is even possible to find 'optimal arousal' and enjoy 'flow'.

Thirdly, the 'cognitive' dimension refers to mental process, including how we perceive the setting, learn and gain understanding, appreciate beauty and form memories and attitudes. Emotional stimulation alone will not produce memorable, transforming experiences. After all, we are constantly stimulated. It takes something truly special, or an accumulation of profound experiences, to cause deep changes in values, attitudes or behaviour.

It is clear from a growing body of research that many event-goers have special interests that attract them to events, and they might even develop an event career or a lifestyle around events. 'Serious leisure', 'ego-involvement', 'recreation specialization', and 'commitment' are all theories that have bearing. There can be no doubt that highly engaged people at events want and gain different experiences from those seeking generic benefits. This fact, demonstrated in many festival and sport event research projects, points to important marketing and design implications. More work is needed, however, on how event careers, or patterns of event attendance form and evolve.

Meanings attached to planned event experiences are complex in theoretical terms. 'Social and cultural constructs', or 'social representations' of events, are part of the antecedents which shape perception of, and interest in events. Experiences at events are in part dependent on the expectations, values and meanings we bring to them, and in turn the event experience is a factor in shaping meanings attached to them. Different stakeholders have different experiences, almost by definition, ranging from the guest or paying customer to the general public and indirect effects.

Designing Experiences

Everyone involved in event planning, design, management and operations want to create satisfying, memorable, even transforming experiences, but these outcomes cannot be guaranteed. 'Design' is the combined creative and technical process of problem-solving, and in the context of events we can design the setting (e.g., site planning, décor), programming and theming, service provision (including people as cast members) and consumables (food, beverage, gifts).

Event design can benefit from traditional theatrical concepts like staging, scripting and choreography, but those applications are not suitable to all event forms and situations. Nor is it appropriate to say that all events are theatre or performance, because many are mainly business or learning-oriented in nature. Setting design can certainly benefit from greater understanding of cognitive and environmental psychology, particularly with regard to the effects of sensory stimulation, feeling of crowdedness and setting preferences.

The 'theme' suggests desired experiences, while the 'programmic elements of style' provide the activities and stimulation for people. 'Thematic Interpretation' is important in understanding and communicating the themes of planned events, and I believe it has considerable scope for enhancing all event experiences. Many people want to know more than is typically provided, while others fail to understand the significance of events because it is not interpreted to them.

Programme and service quality are important aspects of design, including the roles of staff and volunteers as 'cast members' who help shape the guests' experiences. In general, satisfaction with event experiences will be related mostly to the theme and programme (or 'product quality'), whereas service failures are potential 'dissatisfiers' that do not attract, but can repel visitors. Service 'blueprinting' can be used to shape service quality and guest experiences. Food and beverages, as well as gifts, can also be designed. The experiential elements of meals were discussed in this context.

Antecedents and Choices

The beginning point for examining event-related antecedents and choice is theory pertaining to personality, values, attitudes and lifestyle. These factors also have to be understood in social and cultural contexts. The concept of basic human needs is important, as felt needs get translated into motivation and desired experiences. We addressed the question of whether or not people 'need' planned events, and there are good reasons to conclude that at the level of society the answer is definitely yes.

'Intrinsic motivation' is a key concept, drawn from Leisure Studies and Social Psychology. For many events we tend to assume people are making free choices in order to experience the event as a form of leisure. However, there are bound to be 'extrinsic motivations' which explain event attendance, particularly work and business related but also due to the influence of significant others. And many events probably provide outlets that satisfy both forms of motivation. We know little about how motivations work across the spectrum of planned events and for specific event experiences. Cross-cultural investigations have been minimal.

Expectations are crucial, and they link back to previous experience and basic motivations, as well as to specific motives (or reasons) for attending particular events. What people bring to the event will in large part shape their experience. Some expectations are also shaped by social and cultural forces, including the influence of the media. If people are highly involved, developing event careers, their engagement with the programme and other people will be much more intense, compared to those seeking generic benefits like fun, entertainment or social opportunities.

Many barriers and constraints impede event attendance and event career development, so adaptation of 'leisure constraints theory' to events will result in greater understanding of event choices and non-attendance. 'Structural', 'personal' and 'interpersonal' constraints all remain to be studied in the context of events, while our knowledge about how people negotiate constraints and become event 'careerists' is almost non-existent.

The mechanics of decision-making for event attendance, including information searching, reliance on word of mouth or other sources, how event 'attractiveness' is perceived and loyalty versus novelty-seeking behaviour are priorities for event researchers and theorists. Also, we know little about substitution between events, or between events and other experience providers. Suffice it to say that there are change processes and feedback mechanisms in place at the personal and societal levels.

It might even be possible that experiences with one type of event, or even just one event, will shape attitudes and behaviour to whole classes of events. The meanings attached to events and event experiences, including basic satisfaction levels, will theoretically be important in shaping attitudes and future behaviour.

Conclusions on Management

Emphasis in this book has been on how to create knowledge concerning event management, planning, design and operations, not on how to do it. All the management functions were examined, drawing where possible on foundation disciplines and core management theories. Marketing has been given adequate attention in the event management literature, but business management has largely been ignored. Motivational and segmentation research in particular has been emphasized by event researchers, drawing from consumer research and underlying need and cognition theories, but theories of the firm have seldom been applied.

The roles of founders and leaders were examined, including the meaning and applications of personal and social entrepreneurship. Basically we know nothing about these people in the events context. Power has been examined to a degree, but not the organizational culture of events and how it affects experiences and other outcomes. 'Learning organization' concepts have to be applied.

The evolution, sustainability and 'institutionalization' of events are issues that must be studied more. Stakeholder theory, population ecology, resource dependency and other resource and knowledge-based theories of organization, present foundations for explaining why some events succeed and others fail. Of course the theme, programming and design of events is also crucial, but professional management of events and event organizations has to be supported by researchers and theory.

Rational planning is taught in all our event management textbooks, but appears to be lacking in the real world of event-related policy. Is this a serious problem, or can we make do with 'bounded' and flexible rationality? The biggest events seem to generate the most emotion and boosterism. When it comes to risk assessment and management, however, there is certainly no room for irrationality.

In terms of marketing, the big issues include the need for greater understanding of cross-cultural forces, and of the highly involved event careerist. Competitive advantages are going to be more and more dependent on learning how to effectively provide a mix of generic and targeted benefits. Not all events do, or should, adopt a customer or marketing orientation, as many are in the realm of public service. But should all events be run as a 'business'?

Volunteers have received a lot of attention in the literature, but other staffing and human resource management issues for events have been rather neglected. The whole future of professionalism in this field is open for research and debate. Tying staffing and volunteer issues to the event experience is a high priority.

Conclusions on Outcomes

Planned events all seek positive outcomes, usually specified in terms of organizational mandates and event goals, so an important theme in Event Studies has to be the measurement and evaluation of all outcomes. This is seldom done comprehensively, as it should be, through cost-benefit evaluation. In the public arena, narrowly-defined economic impact studies have attracted the most attention, and they have often been suspect in terms of their validity and uses. At the consumer level, most studies have employed satisfaction measures, leaving the more complex and difficult experiential and meaning outcomes under-researched.

Using the open system model for event management, it is clear that both internal and external evaluation of outcomes is important. Internally, managers engage in measurement of effectiveness (i.e., goal attainment) and efficiency (use of resources), in order to improve the event. Many stakeholders also evaluate events, form multiple perspectives, thereby necessitating different outcome and impact research but also requiring effective stakeholder management.

Personal outcomes, consisting of planned event experiences, resulting transformation of values or attitudes, the meanings attached to events, and event careers, remain the 'dark continent' in Event Studies. Our 'phenomenological core' is weak in terms of theory and research.

The 'sustainability' of events is a key issue. In the first instance this means taking a comprehensive approach to being green environmentally, socially acceptable and economically viable. From a purely business point of view it means profitability in the face of competition, while to not-for-profit and governmental event organizations it might mean becoming a permanent institution. Quite different measures and evaluation methods are needed in these contexts.

The proper conduct of economic impact studies and cost-benefit evaluations has been clearly specified in the literature, even though practice often leaves much to be desired. Over-emphasis on economic measures has resulted in a weak understanding of social, cultural and environmental outcomes and how to measure them. One exception is the assessment of resident perceptions and attitudes to events, for which we have several good theoretical and methodological approaches.

We used the device of examining 'stressors' or agents of change, and further development of this approach will help generate growth in theoretical knowledge as well as practical management implications. Events are change agents ('media' in Marshal McLuhan's terminology) in many ways, not all of which are commonly recognized and studied. Increasingly, in a policy and strategy context, they are conceptualized, justified and produced specifically to cause changes. We have to be extremely careful with the use of such power.

How much are events worth? Different perspectives and measures on 'worth' were discussed, but the really big idea is this: planned events have always been worth a great deal, in every society, and their worth is growing no matter how it is measured. Another way to put this is to say that events are needed, for many reasons, and always will be. So, by implication, event professionals and Event Studies are also growing substantially in value.

Conclusions on Events and Public Policy

Event Studies must incorporate policy considerations, in part because policy affects the dynamics of the whole event system, and in part because event outcomes increasingly require policy responses. From a public policy perspective, it has to be asked how events can be made more relevant and appealing in terms of meeting social, cultural, health and economic needs. 'Consumer marketing' has one set of aims, to attract and satisfy customers, while 'social marketing' starts with a completely different perspective – to educate, and to alter attitudes and behaviour.

Justifications for public involvement in the events sector were examined in detail, leading to the conclusion that there are sufficiently diverse and important reasons to warrant a comprehensive 'policy domain' just for events. Personally, I think the economic arguments, while often effective, have been oversold to the detriment of planned events. Equally powerful are the social, cultural and environmental justifications – but they do not yet receive the same political respect.

It probably will be the case in most jurisdictions that event policy will become more integrated with policy covering closely related fields like tourism, arts, culture, leisure and sport – all of which encompass events. It is highly desirable to make certain events are considered within the broader policy domains pertaining to the social, cultural, economic and environmental goals of governments at all levels.

Policy-making for events was considered. Often we see only regulation, not proactive, integrative policy applied to events. The environment in which such policy is created, and the process followed, is very important for the future of planned events and therefore cannot be left to chance. Those committed to events have to organize and lobby. Impacted and interested stakeholders must get involved. More and more research will be required to support policy initiatives related to events, as well as to improve strategy.

Watch for more ideological interest being taken in planned events. Its one thing to oppose or support single events, but quite another for a government or a political party to say it is committed to public celebrations, or event tourism, or realizing diverse benefits through the tool of publicly supported events.

Conclusions on Creating Knowledge

Knowledge within Event Studies will come not just from the foundation disciplines and closely related fields, but from original event-related research spurred on by policy and management needs or the academic desire for theoretical advances. As well, reflective professional practice and introspection are also important in creating knowledge.

It has been argued that Event Studies will have to utilize a variety of theories and methodologies, as contributing disciplines and fields employ both positivistic and post-modernist paradigms, quantitative and qualitative research methods, and a great variety of specific research techniques. The pursuit of explanatory and predictive theories is not really justified, but openness to the potential contributions of experiments, grounded research, ethnology or phenomenology is to be valued. Students and researchers are invited to be critical thinkers, not passively accepting of traditions and the prevailing discourse on any topic.

A research agenda was outlined for each major theme, including key questions and possible methods. This is merely a starting point for creating knowledge, as research priorities vary a great deal depending on whether the starting point is the need for policy, management or theoretical development. Because the core phenomenon of Event Studies is experiential, phenomenological research is essential. Considerable progress can be realized, both for theory development and management practice, by adopting experiential sampling, hermeneutics, ethnography, participant observation and other qualitative methods to a variety of event settings.

When Event Studies has finally 'arrived', dedicated research institutes will be created, professorships endowed and PhD students recruited to advance the field. It will not take long.

Final Comments

There is a lot more that needs to be said – I am sure I missed many things of importance in theory, or research, or policy. And there are plenty more references and research notes that could be added! But that is to be expected in a brand new field. Event Studies remains open to definition and development, drawing as it must from all the traditional disciplines and many closely related professional fields. It can never have fixed boundaries, and both knowledge creation for, and the nature of Event Studies has to remain a process of adding, refining, testing and debating.

I am convinced that Event Studies will develop legitimacy and attract both academics and students, although perhaps it will not find that respected home in the Social Sciences that I think is desirable. Most likely event management schools will add Event Studies to their curricula. But among the growing ranks of academics, policymakers and managers who make the world of planned events their career or business, there will always be the research, the reflection and the dedication to ensure that Event Studies becomes ever more sophisticated and relevant.

References

Abbott, J., and Geddie, M. (2000). Event and venue management: minimizing liability through effective crowd management techniques. *Event Management*, 6(4): 259–270.

Abrahams, R. (1987). An American vocabulary of celebrations. In: A. Falassi (ed.), *Time Out Of Time, Essays On The Festival*, pp. 173–183. Albuquerque, NM: University of New Mexico Press.

Acadia University, Theatre Studies (www.acadiau.ca).

Ahmed, Z. (1991). Marketing your community: correcting a negative image. *Cornell Quarterly*, 31(4): 24–27.

AIEST (1987). *The Role and Impact of Mega-Events and Attractions on Regional and National Tourism*. Editions AIEST, Vol. 28. Switzerland: St. Gallen.

Ajzen, I. (1985). From intentions to actions: a theory of planned behaviour. In: J. Kuhl, and J. Beckmann (eds.), *Springer Series in Social Psychology*, pp. 11–39. Berlin: Springer.

Ajzen, I. (1991). The theory of planned behavior. *Organizational Behavior and Human Decision Processes*, 50(2): 179–211.

Ajzen, I., and Fishbein, M. (1973). Attitudinal and normative variables as predictors of behaviour. *Journal of Personality and Social Psychology*, 27(1): 41–57.

Ali-Knight, J., and Robertson, M. (2004). Introduction to arts, culture and leisure. In: I. Yeoman, et al. (eds.), *Festivals and Events Management*, pp. 3–13. Oxford: Elsevier.

Allport, G. (1937). *Personality: A Psychological Interpretation*. New York: Holt, Rinehart, & Winston.

American Anthropological Association (www.aaa.net.org).

American Council for the United Nations University (2007). *State of the Future, the Millennium Project* (www.unmillenniumproject.org; www.acunu.org).

American Historical Association (www.historians.org).

Ammon, R., and Fried, G. (1998). Crowd management practices. *Journal of Convention and Exhibition Management*, 1(2/3): 119–150.

Ancient History Sourcebook (www.fordham.edu/HALSALL/ancient/asbook.html).

Andersson, T. (2006). The economic impact of cultural tourism. In: T. Andersson, B. Holmgren, and L. Mossberg (eds.), *Cultural Tourism: Visitor Flows, Economic Impact and Product Development*, pp. 33–46. Sweden: Published for the European Cultural Tourism Network at the School of Business, Economics and Law, University of Gothenburg.

Andersson, T., and Getz, D. (2007). Resource dependency, costs and revenues of a street festival. *Tourism Economics*, 13(1): 143–162.

Andersson, T., and Samuelson, L. (2000). Financial effects of events on the public sector. In: L. Mossberg (ed.), *Evaluation of Events: Scandinavian Experiences*, pp. 86–103. New York: Cognizant.

Andersson, T., and Solberg, H. (1999). Leisure events and regional economic impact. *World Leisure and Recreation*, 41(1): 20–28.

Andersson, T., Persson, C., Sahlberg, B., and Strom, L. (eds.) (1999). *The Impact of Mega Events*. Ostersund, Sweden: European Tourism Research Institute.

Archer, B. (1982). The value of multipliers and their policy implications. *Tourism Management*, 3(4): 236–241.

Arcodia, C., Whitford, M., and Dickson, C. (eds.) (2006). *Global Events Congress, Proceedings*. Brisbane: University of Queensland.

Armstrong, J. (1985). International events: the real tourism impact. *Conference on Proceedings of the Canada Chapter, Travel and Tourism Research Association*, Edmonton, pp. 9–37.

ATLAS (www.atlas-euro.org).

Australian Bureau of Statistics, Voluntary Work (www.abs.gov.au).

Axelsen, M., and Arcodia, C. (2004). Conceptualising art exhibitions as special events: a review of the literature. *Journal of Convention and Event Tourism*, 6(3): 63–80.

Backman, K., Backman, S., Uysal, M., and Sunshine, K. (1995). Event tourism: an examination of motivations and activities. *Festival Management and Event Tourism*, 3(1): 15–24.

Bailey, P. (2002). *Design for Entertaining: Inspiration for Creating the Party of Your Dreams*. Weimar, Texas: Culinary and Hospitality Industry Publications Services.

Baker, D., and Crompton, J. (2000). Quality, satisfaction and behavioral intentions. *Annals of Tourism Research*, 27(2): 785–804.

Bandura, A. (1977). Self-efficacy: toward a unifying theory of behavioral change. *Psychology Review*, 84: 191–215.

Bandura, A. (1986). *Social Foundations of Thought and Action: A Social Cognitive Theory*. Prentice-Hall, NJ: Englewood Cliffs.

Barker, M., Page, S., and Meyer, D. (2003). Urban visitor perceptions of safety during a special event. *Journal of Travel Research*, 41: 355–361.

Barker, R. (1968). *Ecological Psychology: Concepts and Methods for Studying The Environment Of Human Behavior*. Stanford, CA: Stanford University Press.

Barney, J. (1991). Firm resources and sustained competitive advantage. *Journal of Management*, 17: 99–120.

Baron, R., and Byrne, D. (2000). *Social Psychology* (9th edn). Boston, MA: Allyn and Bacon.

Bateson, J. (1989). *Managing Services Marketing: Text and Readings*. Chicago, IL: The Dryden Press.

Baum, J. (1996). Organizational ecology. In: S. Clegg, C. hardy, and W. Nord (eds.), *Handbook of Organizational Study*, pp. 77–115. London: Sage.

Baxter, M. (2001). Let's put on a show: special events and live entertainment at waterparks can make the difference between an average season and an exceptional one. *Aquatics International*, 13(8): 42.

Becker, H. (1960). Notes on the concept of commitment. *American Journal of Sociology*, 66: 32–40.

Becker, D. (2006). *The Essential Legal Guide to Events: A Practical Handbook for Event Professionals and Their Advisers*. Self published.

Bell, P., Greene, T., Fisher, J., and Baum, A. (2001). *Environmental Psychology* (5th edn). Belmont, CA: Thomson Wadsworth.

Benedict, B. (1983). *The Anthropology of World's Fairs*. Berkeley, CA: Scolar Press.

Berlonghi, A. (1990). *The Special Event Risk Management Manual*. Self-published (A. Berlonghi, P.O. Box 3454 Dana Point, California 92629) Volume 2: Special Event Security Management, Loss Prevention, And Emergency Services: The Guide for Planning and Documentation by Alexander Berlonghi

Berridge, G. (2006). *Event Design*. Oxford: Butterworth Heinemann.

Beverland, M., Hoffman, D., and Rasmussen, M. (2001). The evolution of events in the Australasian wine sector. *Tourism Recreation Research*, 26(2): 35–44.

Bloom, B. (ed.) (1956). *Taxonomy of Educational Objectives: The Classification of Educational Goals*. Susan Fauer Company, Inc.

Boella, M. (1992). *Human Resource Management in the Hospitality Industry* (5th edn). Cheltenham: Stanley Thornes.

Bohlin, M. (2000). Traveling to events. In: L. Mossberg (ed.), *Evaluation of Events: Scandinavian Experiences*, pp. 13–29. New York: Cognizant.

Boissevan, J. (1979). Impact of tourism on a dependent island: Gozo, Malta. *Annals of Tourism Research*, 6: 76–90.

Boo, S., and Busser, J. (2006). Impact analysis of a tourism festival on tourists' destination images. *Event Management*, 9(4): 223–237.

Boorstin, D. (1961). *The Image: A Guide to Pseudo-Events in America*. New York: Harper and Row.

Borrie, B., and Birzell, R. (2001). Approaches to measuring quality of the wilderness experience. In: W. Freimund, and D. Cole (eds.), *Visitor Use Density and Wilderness Experience: Proceedings*, pp. 29–38. Ogden, UT: US Department of Agriculture, Forest Service, Rocky Mountain Research Station.

Bos, H. (1994). The importance of mega-events in the development of tourism demand. *Festival Management and Event Tourism*, 2(1): 55–58.

Botterill, D., and Crompton, J. (1996). Two case studies: exploring the nature of the tourist's experience. *Journal of Leisure Research*, 28(1): 57–82.

Bouchet, P., LeBrun, A., and Auvergne, S. (2004). Sport tourism consumer experiences: a comprehensive model. *Journal of Sport Tourism*, 9(2): 127–140.

Bourdieu, P. (1986). The forms of capital. In: J. G. Richardson (ed.), *Handbook of Theory and Research in the Sociology of Education*. New York: Greenwald Press.

Bowdin, G., and Church, I. (2000). Customer satisfaction and quality costs: towards a pragmatic approach for event management. In: J. Allen, R. Harris, and L. Jago (eds.), *Events Beyond 2000 – Setting the Agenda*. Sydney: Australian Centre for Event Management, University of Technology.

Bowdin, G., Allen, J., O'Toole, W., Harris, R., and McDonnell, I. (2006). *Events Management* (2nd edn). Oxford: Elsevier.

Bramwell, B. (1997). Strategic planning before and after a mega-event. *Tourism Management*, 18(3): 167–176.

Bramwell, B., and Lane, B. (1993). Interpretation and sustainable tourism: the potential and the pitfalls. *Journal of Sustainable Tourism*, 1(2): 71–80.

Breen, H., Bull, A., and Walo, M. (2001). A comparison of survey methods to estimate visitor expenditure at a local event. *Tourism Management*, 22: 473–479.

Bristow, D., and Sebastion, R. (2001). Holy cow! Wait 'til next year! A closer look at the brand loyalty of Chicago Cubs baseball fans. *The Journal of Consumer Marketing*, 18(3): 256–275.

British Arts Festivals Association (2003) (www.artsfestivals.co.uk).

British Columbia Sports Branch (www.tsa.gov.bc.ca/sport).

British Standards Institute (2006). *Sustainable Event Management System: Specification with Guidance for Use*. Bristol: British Standards Institute.

Brothers, G., and Brantley, V. (1993). Tag and recapture: testing an attendance estimation technique for an open access special event. *Festival Management and Event Tourism*, 1(4): 143–146.

Brown, G. (2002). Taking the pulse of Olympic sponsorship. *Event Management*, 7(3): 187–196.

Brown, G., Chalip, L., Jago, L., and Mules, T. (2001). The Sydney Olympics and Brand Australia. In: N. Morgan, A. Pritchard, and R. Pride (eds.), *Destination Branding: Creating the Unique Destination Proposition*, pp. 163–185. Oxford: Butterworth-Heinemann.

Brown, G., Havitz, M., and Getz, D. (2007). Relationships between wine involvement and wine-related travel. *Journal of Travel and Tourism Marketing*, 21(1).

Brown, S., and James, J. (2004). Event design and management: ritual sacrifice? In: I. Yeoman, et al. (eds.), *Festivals and Events Management*, pp. 53–64. Oxford: Elsevier.

Brunson, M., and Shelby, B. (1993). Recreation substitutability: a research agenda. *Leisure Sciences*, 15: 67–74.

Bryan, H. (1977). Leisure value systems and recreation specialization: the case of trout fisherman. *Journal of Leisure Research*, 9(3): 174–187.

Bryant, S., and Gaiko, S. (1999). Determining skills necessary for meeting planners. In: W. Roehl (ed.), *Proceedings, The Convention/Expo Summit VII*, Las Vegas. Department of Tourism and Convention Administration, William F. Harrah College of Hotel Administration, University of Nevada at Las Vegas.

Bureau International des Expositions (www.bie-paris.org).

Burgan, B., and Mules, T. (2000). Sampling frame issues in identifying event-related expenditures. *Event Management*, 6(4): 223–230.

Burns, J., Hatch, J., and Mules, T. (eds.) (1986). *The Adelaide Grand Prix: The Impact of a Special Event*. Adelaide: The Centre for South Australian Economic Studies.

Burr, S., and Scott, D. (2004). Application of the recreational specialization framework to understanding visitors to the great salt lake bird festival. *Event Management*, 9(1/2): 27–37.

Butler, R., and Grigg, J. (1987). The hallmark event that got away: the case of the 1991 Pan American Games in London, Ontario. *PAPER 87, People and Physical Environment Research Conference*. Perth: University of Western Australia.

Calgary Herald (2005). *Our Alberta, A Calgary Herald Magazine Series Celebrating Alberta's Centennial*.

Cameron, C. (1989). Cultural tourism and urban revitalization. *Tourism Recreation Research*, 14(1): 23–32.

Campbell, S., and Fainstein, S. (eds.) (2003). *Readings in Planning Theory*. Blackwell.

Canadian Heritage (www.canadianheritage.gc.ca).

Can West News Service. December 14, 2005, p. A3. Santarchists (www.canada.com/calgaryherald).

Carlsen, J. (2000). Events industry accreditation in Australia. *Event Management*, 6(2): 117–121.

Carlsen, J. (2004). The economics and evaluation of festivals and events. In: I. Yeoman, et al. (ed.), *Festivals and Events Management*, pp. 246–259. Oxford: Elsevier.

Carlsen, J., and Taylor, A. (2003). Mega-events and urban renewal: the case of the Manchester 2002 Commonwealth Games. *Event Management*, 8(1): 15–22.

Carlsen, J., Getz, D., and Soutar, G. (2001). Event evaluation research. *Event Management*, 6(4): 247–257.

Catherwood, D., and Van Kirk, R. (1992). *The Complete Guide to Special Event Management*. New York: Wiley.

Cavalcanti, M. (2001). The Amazonian Ox Dance Festival: An anthropological account. *Cultural Analysis*, 2 (www.socrates.berkeley.edu).

Center for Exhibition Industry Research. March 26, 2003, news release. CEIR (www.ceir.org).

Chalip, L., and Costa, C. (2006). Building sport event tourism into the destination brand: foundations for a general theory. In: H. Gibson, (ed.), *Sport Tourism: Concepts and Theories*, pp. 86–105. London: Routledge.

Chalip, L., and Leyns, A. (2002). Local business leveraging of a sport event: managing an event for economic benefit. *Journal of Sport Management*, 16: 132–158.

Chalip, L., and McGuirty, J. (2004). Bundling sport events with the host destination. *Journal of Sport Tourism*, 9(3): 267–282.

Chalip, L., Green, B. C., and Hill, B. (2003). Effects of sport media on destination image and intentions to visit. *Journal of Sport Management*, 17: 214–234.

Chen, P. (2006). The attributes, consequences, and values associated with event sport tourists' behaviour: a means-end chain approach. *Event Management*, 10(1): 1–22.

Chernushenko, D. (1994). *Greening Our Games – Running Sports Events and Facilities That Won't Cost the Earth* (1st ed.). Ottawa: Centurion.

Chernushenko, D., van der Kamp, A., and Stubbs, D. (2001). *Sustainable Sport Management: Running an Environmentally, Socially and Economically Responsible Organization* (2d ed.). Ottawa: United Nations Environment Programme.

Cheska, A. (1981). Antigonish Highland Games: An ethnic case study. Paper presented at the *North American Society of Sport History, ninth annual convention*, Hamilton.

Citrine, K. (n.d.). Site planning for events. In: *Event Operations*, pp. 17–19. Port Angeles, WA: International Festivals and Events Association.

Clarke, J. (2003). How journalists judge the 'reality' of an international 'pseudo-event': a study of correspondents who covered the final withdrawal of Vietnamese troops from Cambodia in 1989. *Journalism*, 4(1): 50–75.

Club Managers Association of America (www.cmaa.org).

Cohen, E. (1979). A phenomenology of tourist experiences. *Sociology*, 13: 179–201.

Coleman, J. (1988). Social capital in the creation of human capital. *American Journal of Sociology*, 94: S95–S120. In the supplement: Organizations and Institutions: Sociological and Economic Approaches to the Analysis of Social Structure.

Coleman, J. (1990). *Foundations of Social Theory*. Cambridge, Mass: Belknap Press of Harvard University Press.

Columbia University, Arts Administration (www.tc.columbia.edu).

Coopers and Lybrand Consulting Group (1989). *NCR 1988 Festivals Study Final Report*, Vol. 1. Ottawa: Report for the Ottawa-Carleton Board of Trade.

Coughlan, D., and Mules, T. (2002). Sponsorship awareness and recognition at Canberra's Floriade festival. *Event Management*, 7(1): 1–9.

Coyne, B., and Coyne, E. (2001). Getting, keeping and caring for unpaid volunteers for professional golf tournament events. *Human Resources Development International*, 4(2): 1999–214.

Crawford, D., Jackson, E., and Godbey, G. (1991). A hierarchical model of leisure constraints. *Leisure Sciences*, 9: 119–127.

Crespi-Vallbona, M., and Richards, G. (2007). The meaning of cultural festivals: stakeholder perspectives. *Journal of Cultural Studies* (forthcoming).

Crompton, J. (1979a). Motivations for pleasure vacation. *Annals of Tourism Research*, 6(4): 408–424.

Crompton, J. (1979b). An assessment of the image of Mexico as a vacation destination and the influence of geographical location upon that image. *Journal of Travel Research*, 17(4): 18–23.

Crompton, J. (1993). Understanding a business organization's approach to entering a sponsorship partnership. *Festival Management and Event Tourism*, 1(3): 98–109.

Crompton, J. (1995). Factors that have stimulated the growth of sponsorship of major events. *Festival Management and Event Tourism*, 3(2): 97–101.

Crompton, J. (1999). *Measuring the Economic Impact of Visitors To Sports Tournaments and Special Events*. Ashburn, VA: Division of Professional Services, National Recreation and Park Association.

Crompton, J., and Love, L. (1995). The predictive validity of alternative approaches to evaluating quality of a festival. *Journal of Travel Research*, 34(1): 11–24.

Crompton, J., and McKay, S. (1994). Measuring the economic impact of festivals and events: some myths, misapplications and ethical dilemmas. *Festival Management and Event Tourism*, 2(1): 33–43.

Crompton, J., and McKay, S. (1997). Motives of visitors attending festival events. *Annals of Tourism Research*, 24(2): 425–439.

Crompton, J., Lee, S., and Shuster, T. (2001). A guide for undertaking economic impact studies: *The Springfest example. Journal of Travel Research*, 40(1): 79–87.

Crouch, G., Perdue, R., Timmermans, H., and Uysal, M. (eds.) (2004). *Consumer Psychology of Tourism, Hospitality and Leisure*, Vol. 3. Cambridge, MA: CABI.

Crouch, G., Perdue, R., Timmermans, H., and Uysal, M. (eds.) (2004). Building foundations for understanding the consumer psychology of tourism, hospitality and leisure. In: G. Crouch, R. Perdue, H. Timmermans, and M. Uysal (eds.), *Consumer Psychology of Tourism, Hospitality and Leisure*, Vol. 3. pp. 1–10. Cambridge, MA: CABI.

Csikszentmihalyi, M. (1975). *Beyond Boredom and Anxiety: The Experience of Play in Work and Leisure*. San Francisco, CA: Jossey-Bass.

Csikszentmihalyi, M. (1990). *Flow: The Psychology of Optimal Experience*. New York: Harper Perennial.

Csikszentmihalyi, M., and Cikszenmihalyi, I. (1988). *Optimal Experience: Psychological Studies of Flow on Consciousness*. Cambridge, MA: Cambridge University Press.

Cunneen, C., and Lynch, R. (1988). The social meanings of conflict in riots at the Australian Grand Prix Motorcycle Races. *Leisure Studies*, 7(1): 1–19.

Cuskelly, G., Auld, C., Harrington, M., and Coleman, D. (2004). Predicting the behavioral dependability of sport event volunteers. *Event Management*, 9(1/2): 73–89.

Daniels, M., and Norman, W. (2005). Motivations of equestrian tourists: an analysis of the Colonial Cup races. *Journal of Sport Tourism*, 10(3): 201–210.

Dann, G. (1977). Anomie, ego-involvement and tourism. *Annals of Tourism Research*, 4: 184–194.

Dann, G. (1981). Tourist motivation: an appraisal. *Annals of Tourism Research*, 8(2): 187–219.

Darcy, S., and Harris, R. (2003). Inclusive and accessible special event planning: an Australian perspective. *Event Management*, 8(1): 39–47.

Davidson, R. (2003). Adding pleasure to business: conventions and tourism. *Journal of Convention and Exhibition Management*, 5(1): 29–39.

Deci, E., and Ryan, R. (1985). *Intrinsic Motivation and Self-Determination in Human Behavior*, New York: Plenum.

Deci, E., and Ryan, R. (2000). The "what" and "why' of goal pursuits: human needs and the self-determination of behavior. *Psychological Inquiry*, 11: 227–268.

Decrop, A. (2006). *Vacation Decision Making*. Wallingford, CT: CABI.

Deighton, J. (1992). The consumption of performance. *Journal of Consumer Research*, 19: 362–372.

Delamere, T. (2001). Development of a scale to measure resident attitudes toward the social impacts of community festivals, Part 2: Verification of the scale. *Event Management*, 7(1): 25–38.

Delamere, T., Wankel, L., and Hinch, T. (2001). Development of a scale to measure resident attitudes toward the social impacts of community festivals, Part 1: Item generation and purification of the measure. *Event Management*, 7(1): 11–24

Denton, S., and Furse, B. (1993). Visitation to the 1991 Barossa Valley Vintage Festival: Estimating overall visitor numbers to a festival encompassing several venues and events. *Festival Management and Event Tourism*, 1(2), 51–6.

Derrett, R. (2004). Festivals, events and the destination. In: I. Yeoman, et al. (eds.), *Festivals and Events Management*, pp. 33–50. Oxford: Elsevier.

De Young, R. (1999). Environmental psychology. In: D. Alexander, and R. Fairbridge (eds.), *Encyclopedia of Environmental Science*, Hingham, MA: Kluwer Academic Publishers.

Dietz-Uhler, B., and Murrell, A. (1999). Examining fan reactions to game outcomes: a longitudinal study of social identity. *Journal of Sport Behavior*, 22(1): 15–27.

Dietz-Uhler, B., Harrick, E., End, C., and Jacquemotte, L. (2000). Sex differences in sport fan behavior and reasons for being a sport fan. *Journal of Sport Behavior*, 23(3): 219–231.

Diller, S., Shedroff, N., and Rhea, D. (2006). *Making Meaning*. (Pearson) Upper Saddle River, NJ: New Riders.

Dimanche, F. (1996). Special events legacy: the 1984 Louisiana World Fair in New Orleans. *Festival Management and Event Tourism*, 4(1): 49–54.

Donaldson, L. (1996). The normal science of structural contingency theory. In: *Handbook of Organizational Studies*, pp. 57–77.

Donaldson, T., and Preston, L., (1995). The stakeholder theory of the corporation: concepts, evidence, and implications. *Academy of Management Review*, 20(1): 65–91.

Drummond, S., and Anderson, H. (2004). Service quality and managing your people. In: I. Yeoman, et al. (eds.), *Festival and Events Management*, pp. 80–96. Oxford: Elsevier.

Duke University, Theatre Studies (www.duke.edu/web/theaterstudies).

Dungan, T. (1984). How cities plan special events. *The Cornell Hotel and Restaurant Administration Quarterly* (May): 83–89.

Durkheim E. (1978). Sociology and the social sciences. In: M. Traugott (ed.), *Emile Dukheim on Institutional Analysis*. Chicago, IL: University of Chicago Press.

Dwyer, L. (2002). Economic contribution of convention tourism: conceptual and empirical issues. In: K. Weber, and K. Chon (eds.), *Convention Tourism: International Research and Industry Perspectives*, pp. 21–35. New York: Haworth.

Dwyer, L., Mellor, R., Mistillis, N., and Mules, T. (2000a). A framework for assessing 'tangible' and 'intangible' impacts of events and conventions. *Event Management*, 6(3): 175–189.

Dwyer, L., Mellor, R., Mistillis, N., and Mules, T. (2000b). Forecasting the economic impacts of events and conventions. *Event Management*, 6(3): 191–204.

Dwyer, L., Forsyth, P., and Spurr, R. (2006). Assessing the economic impacts of events: a computable general equilibrium approach. *Journal of Travel Research*, 45(1): 59–66.

Eagleton, T. (1981). *Walter Benjamin: Towards a Revolutionary Criticism*. London: Verso.

Echtner, C. (1999). The semiotic paradigm: implications for tourism research. *Tourism Management*, 20: 47–57.

Echtner, C., and Jamal, T. (1997). The disciplinary dilemmas of tourism studies. *Annals of Tourism Research*, 24(4): 868–883.

Economic Planning Group and Lord Cultural Resources (1992). Strategic Directions for the Planning, Development, and Marketing of Ontario's Attractions, Festivals, and Events. Toronto: Ministry of Culture, Tourism, and Recreation.

Ellis, M. (1973). *Why People Play*. Englewood Cliffs NJ: Prentice Hall.

Elstad, B. (1997). Volunteer perceptions of learning and satisfaction in a mega-event: the case of the XVII Olympic Winter Games in Lillehammer. *Festival Management and Event Tourism*, 4(3/4): 5–83.

Elstad, B. (2003). Continuance commitment and reasons to quit: a study of volunteers at a jazz festival. *Event Management*, 8(2): 99–108.

Ekman, A. (1999). The revival of cultural celebrations in regional Sweden: aspects of tradition and transition. *Sociologia Ruralis*, 39: 280–293.

Emery, P. (2001). Bidding to host a major sports event. In: C. Gratton, and I. Henry (eds.), *Sport in the City: The Role of Sport in Economic and Social Regeneration*, pp. 91–108. London: Routledge.

Encyclopedia Britannica Online (www.britannica.com).

End, C., Dietz-Uhler, M., and Demakakos, N. (2003). Perceptions of sport fans who BIRG. *International Sports Journal*, 7(1): 139–150.

Fairley, S. (2003). In search of relived social experience: group-based nostalgia sport tourism. *Journal of Sport Management*, 17, 284–304.

Fairley, S., and Gammon, S. (2006). Something lived, something learned: Nostalgia's expanding role in sport tourism. In: H. Gibson. (ed.), *Sport Tourism: Concepts and Theories*, pp. 50–65. London: Routledge.

Falassi, A. (ed.) (1987). *Time Out of Time: Essays on the Festival*. Albuquerque, NM: University of New Mexico Press.

Farber, C. (1983). High, healthy and happy: Ontario mythology on parade. In: F. Manning (ed.), *Celebration of Society: Perspectives on Contemporary Cultural Performance*, pp. 33–50. Bowling Green, KY: Bowling Green Popular Press.

Farrell, J., Johnston, M., and Twynam, D. (1998). Volunteer motivation, satisfaction, and management at an elite sporting competition. *Journal of Sport Management*, 12: 288–300.

Faulkner, B., and Raybould, M. (1995). Monitoring visitor expenditure associated with attendance at sporting events: an experimental assessment of the diary and recall methods. *Festival Management and Event Tourism*, 3(2): 73–81.

Faulkner, B., Chalip, L., Brown, G., Jago, L., March, R., and Woodside, A. (2000). Monitoring the tourism impacts of the Sydney 2000 Olympics. *Event Management*, 6(4): 231–246.

Federation European Carnival Cities (www.carnivalcities.com).

Federman, M. (www.mcluhan.utoronto).

Fenich, G. (2005). *Meetings, Expositions, Events, and Conventions: an Introduction to the Industry*. Upper Saddle River, NJ: Pearson.

Festinger, L. (1957). *Theory of Cognitive Dissonance*. Stanford: Stanford University Press.

Fishbein, M. (1980). A theory of reasoned action: some applications and implications. In: H. Howe, and M. Page (eds.), *Nebraska Symposium on Motivation*, Vol. 27, pp. 65–116. Lincoln, NE: University of Nebraska Press.

Fishbein, M., and Ajzen, I. (1975). *Belief, Attitude, Intention, and Behavior: An Introduction to Theory and Research*. Reading, Mass: Addison-Wesley.

Flashmobs (www.flashmob.com).

Fleck, S. (1996). *Events without barriers: Customer service is a key in complying with the Americans With Disabilities Act. Festivals*, March, pp. 34–35. International Festivals and Events Association.

Fleming, W., and Toepper, L. (1990). Economic impact studies: relating the positive and negative impacts to tourism development. *Journal of Travel Research*, 29(1): 35–42.

Florida, R. (2002). *The Rise of the Creative Class: And How It's Transforming Work, Leisure, Community and Everyday Life*. New York: Basic Books.

Formica, S. (1998). The development of festivals and special events studies. *Festival Management and Event Tourism*, 5(3): 131–137.

Formica, S., and Murrmann, S. (1998). The effects of group membership and motivation on attendance: an international festival case. *Tourism Analysis*, 3(3/4): 197–207.

Formica, S., and Uysal, M. (1998). Market segmentation of an international cultural-historical event in Italy. *Journal of Travel Research*, 36(4): 16–24.

Foucault, M. (1972). *Archaeology of Knowledge*. London: Tavistock Publications.

Fredline, E., and Faulkner, B. (1998). Resident reactions to a major tourist event: the Gold Coast Indy car race. *Festival Management and Event Tourism*, 5(4): 185–205.

Fredline, E., and Faulkner, B. (2002a). Residents' reactions to the staging of major motorsport events within their communities: a cluster analysis. *Event Management*, 7(2): 103–114.

Fredline, E., and Faulkner, B. (2002b). Variations in residents' reactions to major motorsport events: why residents perceive the impacts of events differently. *Event Management*, 7(2): 115–125.

Fredline, L. (2006). Host and guest relations and sport tourism. In: H. Gibson (ed.), *Sport Tourism: Concepts and Theories*, pp. 131–147. London: Routledge.

Fredline, L., Jago, L., and Deery, M. (2003). The development of a generic scale to measure the social impacts of events. *Event Management*, 8(1): 23–37.

Freeman, L., White, D., and Romney, A. (1992). *Research Methods in Social Network Analysis*. New Brunswick, NJ: Transaction Publishers.

Freeman, R. (1984). *Strategic Management: A Stakeholder Approach*. Boston, MA: Pitman.

Freedman, J. (1975). *Crowding and Behavior*. San Francisco, CA: Freeman.

Frisby, W., and Getz, D. (1989). Festival management: a case study perspective. *Journal of Travel Research*, 28(1): 7–11.

Funk, D., and Bruun, T. (2007). The role of socio-psychological and culture-education motives in marketing international sport tourism: A cross-cultural perspective. *Tourism Management*, 28(3): 805–819.

Gabrenya, W., and Hwang, K. (1996). Chinese social interaction: Harmony and hierarchy on the good earth. In: H. Bond (ed.), *The Handbook of Chinese Psychology*, pp. 309–322. Hong Kong: Oxford University Press.

Gammon, S. (2004). Secular pilgrimage and sport tourism. In: B. Ritchie, and D. Adair (eds.), *Sport Tourism: Interrelationships, Impacts and Issues*. Clevedon: Channel View.

Geertz, C. (1993). *The Interpretation of Cultures*. London: Fontana Press.

Getz, D. (1993a). Corporate culture in not-for-profit festival organizations: concepts and potential applications. *Festival Management and Event Tourism*, 1(1): 11–17.

Getz, D. (1993b). Case study: Marketing the Calgary Exhibition and Stampede. *Festival Management and Event Tourism*, 1(4), 147–156.

Getz, D. (1997). *Event Management and Event Tourism* (1st edn). New York: Cognizant Communications Corp.

Getz, D. (1998a). Information sharing among festival managers. *Festival Management and Event Tourism*, 5(1/2): 33–50.

Getz, D. (1998b). Event tourism and the authenticity dilemma. In: W. Theobald (ed.), *Global Tourism* (2nd edn), pp. 409–427. Oxford: Butterworth-Heinemann.

Getz, D. (1999). The impacts of mega events on tourism: strategies for destinations. In: T. Andersson, C. Persson, B. Sahlberg, and L. Strom (eds.), *The Impact of Mega Events*, pp. 5–32. Ostersund, Sweden: European Tourism Research Institute.

Getz, D. (2000a). Festivals and special events: life cycle and saturation issues. In: W. Garter and D. Lime (eds.), *Trends in Outdoor Recreation, Leisure and Tourism*, pp. 175–185. Wallingford, UK: CABI.

Getz, D. (2000b). Developing a research agenda for the event management field. In: J. Allen, et al. (eds.), *Events Beyond 2000: Setting the Agenda, Proceedings of Conference on Event Evaluation, Research and Education*, pp. 10–21. Sydney: Australian Centre for Event Management, University of Technology.

Getz, D. (2001). Festival places: a comparison of Europe and North America. *Tourism*, 49(1): 3–18.

Getz, D. (2004). Bidding on events: critical success factors. *Journal of Convention and Exhibition Management*, 5(2):1–24.

Getz, D. (2005). *Event Management and Event Tourism* (2nd edn). New York: Cognizant.

Getz, D., and Carlsen, J. (2006). Quality management for events. In: B. Prideaux, G. Moscardo, and E. Laws (eds.), *Managing Tourism and Hospitality Services*, pp. 145–155. Wallingford: CABI.

Getz, D., and Fairley, S. (2004). Media management at sport events for destination promotion. *Event Management*, 8(3): 127–139.

Getz, D., and Frisby, W. (1988). Evaluating management effectiveness in community-run festivals. *Journal of Travel Research*, 27(1): 22–27.

Getz, D., and Frisby, W. (1991). Developing a municipal policy for festivals and special events. *Recreation Canada*, 19(4): 38–44.

Getz, D., and McConnell, A. (2006). *The Effective Use of Stakeholder Management in Event Projects*. Unpublished case study, University of Calgary.

Getz, D., and Wicks, B. (1994). Professionalism and certification for festival and event practitioners: trends and issues. *Festival Management and Event Tourism*, 2(2): 103–109.

Getz, D., Anderson, D., and Sheehan, L. (1998). Roles, issues and strategies for convention and visitors bureaux in destination planning and product development: a survey of Canadian bureaux. *Tourism Management*, 19(4): 331–340.

Getz, D., O'Neil, M., and Carlsen, J. (2001). Service quality evaluation at events through service mapping. *Journal of Travel Research*, 39(4): 380–390.

Getz, D., Andersson, T., and Larson, M. (2007). Festival stakeholder roles: Concepts and case studies. *Event Management, 10*(2/3): 103–122.

Gibson, H. (1998). Sport tourism: a critical analysis of research. *Sport Management Review*, 1: 45–76.

Gibson, H. (2004). Moving beyond the "what is and who" of sport tourism to understanding "why". *Journal of Sport Tourism*, 9(3): 247–265.

Gibson, H. (2005). Understanding sport tourism experiences. In: J. Higham (ed.), *Sport Tourism Destinations: Issues, Opportunities and Analysis*. Oxford: Elsevier.

Gibson, H. (ed.) (2006a). *Sport Tourism: Concepts and Theories*. London: Routledge.

Gibson, H. (2006b). Towards an understanding of 'why sport tourists do what they do'. In: H. Gibson (ed.), *Sport Tourism: Concepts and Theories*, pp: 66–85. London: Routledge.

Gibson, H., Willming, C., and Holdnak, A. (2003). Small-scale event-sport-tourism: fans as tourists. *Tourism Management*, 22(3): 181–190.

Gitelson, R., Kerstetter, D., and Kiernan, N. (1995). Evaluating the educational objectives of a short-term event. *Festival Management and Event Tourism*, 3(1): 9–14.

Glaser, B., and Strauss, A. (1967). *Discovery of Grounded Theory: Strategies for Qualitative Research*. Chicago, IL: Aldine.

Gleick, J. (2000). *Faster: The Acceleration of Just About Everything*. Pantheon Books.

Glenn, J., and Gordon, T. (eds.). *Futures Research Methodology* (www.acunu.org/ millennium).

Goffman, E. (1959). *The Presentation of Self in Everyday Life*. Garden City, NY: Doubleday.

Goffman, E. (1974). *Frame analysis: An Essay on the Organization of Experience*. New York: Harper and Row.

Goh, F. (2003). *Irish Festivals – Irish Life: Celebrating The Wealth of Ireland's Festivals. Executive Summary*. Dublin: Association of Irish Festival Events.

Goldblatt, J. (2004). *Special Events: Event Leadership for a New World*. New York: Wiley.

Goldblatt, J., and Hu, C. (2005). Tourism terrorism, and the new world for event leaders. *E-Review of Tourism Research*, 3(6): 139–144.

Grado, S., Strauss, C., and Lord, B. (1998). Economic impacts of conferences and conventions. *Journal of Convention and Exhibition Management*, 1(1): 19–33.

Graham, S., Goldblatt, J., and Delpy, L. (1995). *The Ultimate Guide to Sport Event Management and Marketing*. Chicago, IL: Irwin.

Grant, R. (1991). Toward a knowledge-based theory of the firm. *Strategic Management Journal*, 17: 109–122.

Gratton, C., and Kokolakakis, T. (1997). *Economic Impact of Sport in England 1995*. London: The Sports Council.

Green, B. C., and Chalip, L. (1998). Sport tourism as the celebration of subculture. *Annals of Tourism Research*, 25(2), 275–291.

Green, B. C., and Chalip, L. (2004). Paths to volunteer commitment: lessons from the Sydney Olympic Games. In: R. Stebbins, and M. Graham (eds.), *Volunteering as Leisure/Leisure as Volunteering: An International Assessment*. Wallingford, UK: CABI.

Greenwood, D. (1972). Tourism as an agent of change: a Spanish Basque case study. *Ethnology*, 11: 80–91.

Gregson, B. (1992). *Reinventing Celebration: The Art of Planning Public Events*. Orange, CT: Shannon Press.

Grippo, R. (2004). *Macy's Thanksgiving Day Parade*. Arcadia.

Gursoy, D., and Kendall, K. (2006). Hosting mega events: modelling locals' support. *Annals of Tourism Research*, 33(3): 603–623.

Gustafsson, I., Ostrom, A., Johansson, J., and Mossberg, L. (2006). The five aspects of meal model: a tool for developing meal services in restaurants. *Journal of Foodservice*, 17: 84–93.

Haahti, A., and Komppula, R. (2006). Experience design in tourism. In: D. Buhalis, and C. Costa (eds.), *Tourism Business Frontiers: Consumers, Products and Industry*, pp. 101–110. Oxford: Elsevier.

Habermas, J. (1973). *The Theory of Communicative Action: Reason and Rationalization of Society*. Boston, MA: Beacon.

Hall, E. (1966). *The Hidden Dimension*. New York: Doubleday.

Hall, M. (1992). *Hallmark Tourist Events: Impacts, Management and Planning*. London: Belhaven.

Hall, M. (1994). *Tourism and Politics: Policy, Power and Place*. Chichester: Wiley.

Hall, M. (1997). Mega-events and their legacies. In: P. Murphy (ed.), *Quality Management in Urban Tourism*, pp. 75–87. Chichester: Wiley.

Hall, M. (2005). *Tourism: Rethinking the Social Science of Mobility*. Harlow, England: Pearson.

Hall, M., and Page, S. (2006). *The Geography of Tourism and Recreation: Environment, Place and Space* (3rd edn). London: Routledge.

Hall, M., and Rusher, K. (2004). Politics, public policy and the destination. In: I. Yeoman, et al. (eds.), *Festival and Events Management*, pp. 217–231. Oxford: Elsevier.

Ham, S., Housego, A., and Weiler, B. (2005). *Tasmanian Thematic Interpretation Planning Manual* (available online at www.tourismtasmania.com).

Hanlon, C., and Cuskelly, G. (2002). Pulsating major sport event organizations: a framework for inducting managerial personnel. *Event Management*, 7(4): 231–243.

Hanlon, C., and Stewart, B. (2006). Managing personnel in major sport event organizations: what strategies are required? *Event Management*, 10(1): 77–88.

Hannan, M., and Freeman, J. (1977). The population ecology of organizations. *American Journal of Sociology*, 82: 929–64.

Hannan, M., and Freeman, J. (1984). Structural inertia and organizational change. *American Sociological Review*, 49(2): 149–164.

Hannam, K., and Halewood, C. (2006). European Viking themed festivals: an expression of identity. *Journal of Heritage Tourism*, 1(1), 17–31

Harris, M. (2003). *Carnival and Other Christian Festivals: Folk Theology and Folk Performance*. Austin: University of Texas Press.

Harris, R., Jago, L., Allen, J., and Huyskens, M. (2001). Towards an Australian event research agenda: first steps. *Event Management*, 6(4): 213–221.

Harris, V. (2004). Event management: a new profession. *Event Management*, 9(1/2): 103–109.

Harvey, M., Loomis, R, Bell, R., and Marino, M. (1998). The influence of museum exhibit design on immersion and psychological flow. *Environment and Behavior*, 30: 601–627.

Hayllar, B., and Griffin, T. (2004). The precinct experience: a phenomenological approach. *Tourism Management*, 26(4): 517–528.

Havitz, M., and Dimanche, F. (1999). Leisure involvement revisited: drive properties and paradoxes. *Journal of Leisure Research*, 31(2): 122–149.

Hede, A. (2005). Sports-events, tourism and destination marketing strategies: an Australian case study of Athens 2004 and its media telecast. *Journal of Sport Tourism*, 10(3): 187–200.

Hede, A., and Jago, L. (2005). Perceptions of the host destination as a result of attendance at a special event: a post-consumption analysis. *International Journal of Event Management Research*, 1(1) (www.ijemr.org).

Hede, A., Jago, L., and Deery, M. (2004). Segmentation of special event attendees using personal values: relationships with satisfaction and behavioural intentions. *Journal of Quality Assurance in Hospitality and Tourism*, 5(2/3/4): 33–55.

Heimer, C. (2001). Law: new institutionalism. In: *International Encyclopedia of the Social and Behavioral Sciences*, pp. 8534–8537. Oxford: Elsevier.

Hektner, J. M., and Csikszentmihalyi, M. (2002). The experience sampling method: measuring the context and content of lives. In: R. Bechtel, and A. Churchman (eds.), *Handbook of Environmental Psychology*, pp. 233–243. New York: Wiley.

Herzberg, F. (1966). *Work and the Nature of Man*. Cleveland, OH: World Publishing Co.

Higham, J. (ed.) (2005). *Sport Tourism Destinations: issues, opportunities and analysis*. Oxford: Elsevier.

Hiller, H. (2000a). Mega-events, urban boosterism and growth strategies: an analysis of the objectives and legitimations of the Cape Town 2004 Olympic bid. *International Journal of Urban and Regional Research*, 24(2): 439–458.

Hiller, H. (2000b). Toward an urban sociology of mega-events. *Research in Urban Sociology*, 5: 181–205.

Hilliard, T. (2006). Learning at conventions: integrating communities of practice. *Journal of Convention and Event Tourism*, 8(1): 45–68.

Hinch, T., Jackson, E., Hudson, S., and Walker, G. (2006). Leisure constraint theory and sport tourism. In: H. Gibson (ed.), *Sport Tourism: Concepts and Theories*, pp. 10–31. London: Routledge.

Hofstede, G. (1980). *Culture's Consequences: International Differences in Work Related Values*. Beverly Hills, CA: Sage Publications.

Hormans, G. (1958). Social behavior as exchange. *American Journal of Sociology*, 63(6): 597–606.

Hover, M., and van Mierlo, J. (2006). Imagine your event: imagineering for the event industry. Unpublished manuscript. Breda University of Applied Sciences and NHTV Expertise, Netherlands: Event Management Centre.

Hoyle, L. (2002). *Event Marketing: How to Successfully Promote Events, Festivals, Conventions, and Expositions*. New York: Wiley.

Hudson, S., Getz, D., Miller, G.A., and Brown, G. (2004). The future role of sporting events: evaluating the impacts on tourism. In: K. Weiermair, and C. Mathies (eds.), *The Tourism and Leisure Industry – Shaping the Future*, pp 237–251. Binghamton, NY: Haworth.

Hughes, G. (1999). Urban revitalization: the use of festival time strategies. *Leisure Studies*, 18: 119–135.

Hughes, H. (1993). Olympic tourism and urban regeneration. *Festival Management and Event Tourism*, 1(4): 157–162.

Huizinga, J. (1955). *Homo Ludens: A Study of the Play Element in Culture*. Boston, MA: Beacon Press.

Hultkrantz, L. (1998). Mega-event displacement of visitors: the world championship in athletics, Goteborg 1995. *Festival Management and Event Tourism*, 5(1/2).

Imagine Canada (www.imaginecanada.ca).

International Association of Assembly Managers (www.IAAM.org).

International Association for Exhibition Management (www.IAEM.org).

International Association of Fairs and Expositions (IAFE) (www.fairsandexpos.com).

International Events Group (1995). *IEG's Complete Guide to Sponsorship*. Chicago, IL: IEG Inc.

International Festivals Association (n.d.). *IFA's Official Guide to Sponsorship*. Port Angeles, WA: IFA.

International Festivals Association (IFA) and Argonne Productions (1992). *Festival Sponsorship Legal Issues*. Port Angeles, WA: IFA.

International Festivals and Events Association (IFEA) (n.d.). *Event Operations*. Port Angeles, WA: IFEA.

International Festivals and Events Association (IFEA) (2000). *Parades*. Port Angeles, WA: IFEA.

International Special Events Society (www.ISES.com)

Iso-Ahola, S. (1980). *The Social Psychology of Leisure and Recreation*. Dubuque, IA: Brown.

Iso-Ahola, S. (1983). Towards a social psychology of recreational travel. *Leisure Studies*, 2(1): 45–57.

Iso-Ahola, S., Jackson, E., and Dunn, E. (1994). Starting, ceasing and replacing leisure activities over the life-span. *Journal of Leisure Research*, 26: 227–249.

Jackson, E. (ed.) (2005). *Constraints on Leisure*. State College, PA: Venture Publishing.

Jackson, E., Crawford, D., and Godbey, G. (1992). Negotiation of leisure constraints. *Leisure Sciences*, 15: 1–12.

Jafari, J. (1987). Tourism models: the sociocultural aspects. *Tourism Management*, 151–159.

Jafari, J. (1990). Research and scholarship: the basis of tourism education. *Journal of Tourism Studies*, 1(1).

Jago, L., and Dwyer, L. (2006). *Economic Evaluation of Special Events: A Practitioner's Guide*. Gold Coast, Australia: Cooperative Research Centre for Sustainable Tourism.

Jago, L., and Harris, R. (2003). Introduction. *Event Management*, 8(1): 1–2.

Jago, L., and Shaw, R. (1999). Consumer perceptions of special events: a multi-stimulus validation. *Journal of Travel and Tourism Marketing*, 8(4): 1–24.

Jago, L., Chalip, L., Brown, G., Mules, T., and Ali, S. (2002). The Role of Events in Helping to Brand a Destination. Paper presented at the *Events and Placemaking Conference*, Sydney.

Jago, L., Chalip, L., Brown, G., Mules, T., and Shameem, A. (2003). Building events into destination branding: insights from experts. *Event Management*, 8(1): 3–14.

Jamal, T., and Getz, D. (1995). Collaboration theory and community tourism planning. *Annals of Tourism Research*, 22(1): 186–204

James, J., and Ridinger, L. (2002). Female and male sport fans: a comparison of sport consumption motives. *Journal of Sport Behavior*, 25: 260–278.

Janiskee, R. (1980). South Carolina's harvest festivals: rural delights for day tripping urbanites. *Journal of Cultural Geography* (October): 96–104.

Janiskee, R. (1985). Community-Sponsored Rural Festivals in South Carolina: A Decade of Growth and Change. Paper presented to the Association of American Geographers, Detroit.

Janiskee, R. (1991). Rural festivals in South Carolina. *Journal of Cultural Geography*, 11(2): 31–43.

Janiskee, R. (1994). Some macroscale growth trends in America's community festival industry. *Festival Management and Event Tourism*, 2(1): 10–14.

Janiskee, R. (1996). The temporal distribution of America's community festivals. *Festival Management and Event Tourism*, 3(3): 129–137.

Janiskee, R., and Drews, P. (1998). Rural festivals and community reimaging. In: R. Butler, M. Hall, and J. Jenkins (eds.), *Tourism and Recreation in Rural Areas*, pp. 157–175. Chichester: Wiley.

Jarvie, G. (1991). *Highland Games: The Making of the Myth*. Edinburgh: Edinburgh University Press.

Jawahar, I., and McLaughlin, G. (2001). Toward a descriptive stakeholder theory: an organizational life cycle approach. *Academy of Management Review*, 26(3): 397–414.

Jaworski, A., and Pritchard, A. (eds.) (2005). *Discourse, Communication and Tourism*. Clevedon: Channel View.

Jennings, G. (2006). Perspectives on quality tourism experiences: an introduction. In: G. Jennings and N. Nickerson (eds.), *Quality Tourism Experiences*, pp. 1–21. Oxford: Elsevier.

Jennings, G., and Nickerson, N. (eds.) (2006). *Quality Tourism Experiences*, pp. 81–98. Oxford: Elsevier.

Johnson, D. (n.d.). Festival risk management: success with safety. In: *Event Operations*, pp. 71–73. Port Angeles, WA: International Festivals and Events Association.

Johnston, M., Twynam, G., and Farrell, J. (2000). Motivation and satisfaction of event volunteers for a major youth organization. *Leisure*, 24(1): 161–177.

Jones, H. (1993). Pop goes the festival. *Marketing Week*, 16(23): 24–27.

Jones, I., and Green, B. C. (2006). Serious leisure, social identity and sport tourism. In: H. Gibson (ed.), *Sport Tourism: Concepts and Theories*, pp. 32–49. London: Routledge.

Jordan, J. (1980). The summer people and the natives: some effects of tourism in a vermont vacation village. *Annals of Tourism Research*, 7(1): 34–55.

Jung, M. (2005). Determinants of exhibition service quality as perceived by attendees. *Journal of Convention and Event Tourism*, 7(3/4): 85–98.

Kang, Y., and Perdue, R. (1994). Long term impact of a mega-event on international tourism to the host country: a conceptual model and the case of the 1988 seoul olympics. In: M. Uysal (ed.), *Global Tourist Behavior*, pp. 205–225. International Business Press.

Kaplan, S. (1987). Aesthetics, affect, and cognition: environmental preference from an evolutionary perspective. *Environment and Behavior*, 1: 3–32.

Katz, A. (1981). Self help and mutual aid: an emerging social movement. *Annual Review of Sociology*, pp. 129–155.

Kay, P. (2004). Cross-cultural research issues in developing international tourist markets for cultural events. *Event Management*, 8(4): 191–202.

Kelly, J. (1985). *Recreation Business*. New York: Macmillan.

Kelly, J. (1987). *Freedom to Be: A New Sociology of Leisure*. New York: Macmillan.

Kerstetter, D., and Gitelson, R. (1995). Perceptions of sponsorship contributors to a regional arts festival. *Festival Management and Event Tourism*, 2(3/4): 203–209.

Kim, S., Scott, D., and Crompton, J. (1997). An exploration of the relationships among social psychological involvement, behavioral involvement, commitment, and future intentions in the context of birdwatching. *Journal of Leisure Research*, 29(3): 320–341.

Klemke, E., Hollinger, R., and Rudge, D. (eds.) (1998). *Introductory Readings in the Philosophy of Science*. New York: Prometheus Books.

Kotler, P., Haider, D., and Rein, I. (1993). *Marketing Places*. New York: The Free Press.

Kyle, G., and Chick, G. (2002). The social nature of leisure involvement. *Journal of Leisure Research*, 34(4): 426–448.

Larson, M. (2002). A political approach to relationship marketing: case study of the storsjöyran festival. *International Journal of Tourism Research*, 4(2): 119–143.

Larson, M., and Wikstrom, E. (2001). Organising events: managing conflict and consensus in a political market square. *Event Management*, 7(1): 51–65.

Larson, R., and Csikszentmihalyi, M. (1983). The experience sampling method. In: H. Reis (ed.), *Naturalistic Approaches to Studying Social Interaction*, pp. 41–56. San Francisco, CA: Jossey-Bass.

Lashley, C., Morrisson, A., and Randall, S. (2004). My most memorable meal ever! hospitality as an emotional experience. In: D. Sloan (ed.), *Culinary Taste, Consumer Behaviour in the International Restaurant Sector*. Oxford: Butterworth Heinemann.

Laurent, G., and Kapferer, J. (1985). Measuring consumer involvement profiles. *Journal of Marketing Research*, 22(1): 41–53.

Laverie, D., and Arnett, D. (2000). Factors affecting fan attendance: the influence of identity salience and satisfaction. *Journal of Leisure Research*, 32(2): 225–246.

Laxson, J. (1991). How "we" see "them": tourism and native American Indians. *Annals of Tourism Research*, 21: 406–409.

Laybourn, P. (2004). Risk and decision making in events management. In: I. Yeoman, et al. (eds.), *Festivals and Events Management*, pp. 286–307. Oxford: Elsevier.

Lee, C., Lee, Y., and Wicks, B. (2004). Segmentation of festival motivation by nationality and satisfaction. *Tourism Management*, 25(1): 61–70.

Lee, H., Kerstetter, D., Graefe, A., and Confer, J. (1997). Crowding at an arts festival: a replication and extension of the outdoor recreation crowding model. In: W. Kuentzel (ed.), *Proceedings of the 1966 Northeastern Recreation Research Symposium (USDA Forest Service Ge. Tech. Rep. NE-232)*, pp. 198–204. Radnor, PA: Northeastern Forest Experiment Station.

Lee, J. (1987). The impact of Expo '86 on British Columbia markets. In: P. Williams, J. Hall, and M. Hunter (eds.), Conference papers of the *Travel and Tourism Research Association, Canada Chapter, Tourism: Where is the Client.*

Lee, J., and Back, K. (2005). A review of convention and meeting management research. *Journal of Convention and Event Tourism*, 7(2): 1–19.

Lee, S., and Crompton, J. (2003). The attraction power and spending impact of three festivals in Ocean City, Maryland. *Event Management*, 8(2): 109–112.

Leibold, M., and van Zyl, C. (1994). The summer olympic games and its tourism marketing: city tourism marketing experiences and challenges with specific reference to Cape Town, South Africa. In: P. Murphy (ed.), *Quality Management in Urban Tourism: Balancing Business and the Environment, Proceedings*, pp. 135–151. University of Victoria.

Leiper, N. (1981). Towards a cohesive curriculum in tourism. the case for a distinct discipline. *Annals of Tourism Research*, 8(1): 69–84.

Leiper, N. (1990). Tourist attraction systems. *Annals of Tourism Research*, 17(3): 367–384.

Li, R., and Petrick, J. (2006). A review of festival and event motivation studies. *Event Management*, 9(4): 239–245.

Li, Y. (2000). Geographical consciousness and tourism experience. *Annals of Tourism Research*, 27: 863–883.

Locke, E. (1991). *The Essence of Leadership*. New York: Lexington Books.

Long, P. (2000). After the event: perspectives on organizational partnership in the management of a themed festival year. *Event Management*, 6(1): 45–59.

Love, L., and Crompton, J. (1996). A Conceptualization of the relative roles of festival attributes in determining perceptions of overall festival quality. Paper presented to the *Research Symposium, Annual Conference of the International Festivals and Events Association* (unpublished).

Lynch, K. (1960). *The Image of the City*: Cambridge, MA: MIT Press.

MacAloon, J. (1984). Olympic games and the theory of spectacle in modern societies. In: J. MacAloon (ed.), *Rite, Drama, Festival, Spectacle: Rehearsals Towards a Theory of Cultural Performance*, pp. 241–280. Philadelphia, PA: Institute for the Study of Human Issues.

MacCannell, D. (1973). Staged authenticity: arrangements of social space in tourist settings. *American Journal of Sociology*, 79(3): 589–603.

MacCannell, D. (1976). *The Tourist: A New Theory of the Leisure Class*. New York: Schocken Books.

Mackellar, J. (2006). Special interest events in a regional destination – exploring differences between specialist and generalist events. In: C. Arcodia, M. Whitford, and C. Dickson (eds.), *Global Events Congress Proceedings*, pp. 176–195. Brisbane: University of Queensland.

Macnaught, T. (1982). Mass tourism and the dilemmas of modernization in pacific island communities. *Annals of Tourism Research*, 9: 359–81.

Madrigal, R. (1995). Cognitive and affective determinants of fan satisfaction with sporting event attendance. *Journal of Leisure Research*, 27(3): 205–207.

Madrigal, R. (2003). Investigating and evolving leisure experience: antecedents and consequences of spectator affect during a live sporting event. *Journal of Leisure Research*, 35(1): 23–45.

Mahony, D., Madrigal, R., and Howard, D. (1999). The effect of self-monitoring on behavioral and attitudinal loyalty towards athletic teams. *International Journal of Sport Marketing and Sponsorship*, 1: 146–167.

Mahony, D., Madrigal, R., and Howard, D. (2000). Using the psychological commitment to team (PCT) scale to segment sport consumers based on loyalty. *Sport Marketing Quarterly*, 9(1): 15–25.

Malouf, L. (2002). *Parties and Special Events: Planning and Design*. Culinary and Hospitality Industry Publications Services.

Mandelbaum, S., Mazza, L., and Burchell R.W. (eds.) (1996). *Explorations in Planning Theory*. New Brunswick, NJ: Center for Urban Policy Research, Rutgers University.

Mannell, R., and Iso-Ahola, S. (1987). Psychological nature of leisure and tourist experiences. *Annals of Tourism Research*, 14: 314–331.

Mannell, R., and Kleiber, D. (1997). *A Social Psychology of Leisure*. State College, PA: venture Publishing Inc.

Mannell, R., and Zuzanek, J. (1991). The nature and variability of leisure constraints in daily life: the case of the physically active leisure of older adults. *Leisure Sciences*, 13: 337–351.

Manning, F. (ed.) (1983). *The Celebration of Society: Perspectives on Contemporary Cultural Performance*. Bowling Green, OH: Bowling Green University Popular Press.

Markus, H., and Kitayama, S. (1991). Culture and the self: implications for cognition, emotion, and motivation. *Psychological Review*, 98: 224–253.

Marris, T. (1987). The role and impact of mega-events and attractions on regional and national tourism development: resolutions of the 37th congress of the AIEST, Calgary. *Revue de Tourisme*, (4): 3–12.

Maslow, A. (1954). *Motivation and Personality* (2nd edn). New York: Harper and Row.

Maslow, A. (1968). *Toward a Psychology of Being* (2nd edn). Toronto: Van Nostrand Rheinhold.

Masterman, G. (2004). *Strategic Sports Event Management: An International Approach*. Oxford: Elsevier.

Masterman, G., and Wood, E. (2006). *Innovative Marketing Communications: Strategies for the Events Industry*. Oxford: Butterworth-Heinemann.

Mayfield, T., and Crompton, J. (1995). The status of the marketing concept among festival organizers. *Journal of Travel Research, Spring*: 14–22.

McGehee, N., Yoon, Y., and Cardenas, D. (2003). Involvement and travel for recreational runners in North Carolina. *Journal of Sport Management*, 17(3): 305–324.

McGregor, D. (1960). *The Human Side of Enterprise*. New York: McGraw Hill.

McKercher, B., and du Cros, H. (2002). *Cultural Tourism*. New York: Haworth.

McKercher, B., Mei, W., and Tse, T. (2006). Are short duration festivals tourist attractions? *Journal of Sustainable Tourism*, 14(1): 55–66.

McLuhan, M. (1964). *Understanding Media: The Extensions of Man*. New York: McGraw Hill.

McMahon-Beattie, U., and Yeoman, I. (2004). The potential for revenue management in festivals and events. In: I. Yeoman, et al. (eds.), *Festivals and Events Management*, pp. 202–214. Oxford: Elsevier.

McPhail, T. (2006). *Global Communication: Theories, Stakeholders, and Trends* (2nd edn). Blackwell Publishers.

Meeting Professionals International (2003). *Meetings and Conventions: A Planning Guide*. Mississauga: MPI.

Mehmetoglu, M., and Ellingsen, K. (2005). Do small-scale festivals adopt 'market orientation' as a management philosophy? *Event Management*, 9(3): 119–132.

Mendell, R., MacBeth, J., and Solomon, A. (1983). The 1982 world's fair – a synopsis. *Leisure Today, Journal of Physical Education, Recreation and Dance* (April): 48–49.

Merrilees, B., Getz, D., and O'Brien, D. (2005). Marketing stakeholder analysis: branding the brisbane goodwill games. *European Journal of Marketing*, 39(9/10): 1060–1077.

Meyersohn, R. (1981). *Tourism as a Socio-Cultural Phenomenon: Research Perspectives*. University of Waterloo, OPTIUM Publications, Research Group on Leisure and Cultural Development.

Mifflin, K., and Taylor, R. (2006). Stakeholder theory and youth event tourism in Western Australia. In: C. Arcodia, M. Whitford, and C. Dickson (eds.), *Global Events Congress Proceedings*, pp. 227–240. Brisbane: University of Queensland.

Mihalik, B. (1994). Mega-event legacies of the 1996 Atlanta Olympics. In: P. Murphy (ed.), *Quality Management in Urban Tourism: Balancing Business and Environment. Proceedings*, pp. 151–162. University of Victoria.

Mihalik, B. (2001). Host population perceptions of the 1996 Atlanta Olympics: support, benefits and liabilities. *Tourism Analysis*, 5(1): 49–53.

Mihalik, B., and Wing-Vogelbacher, A. (1992). Travelling art expositions as a tourism event: a market research analysis for ramesses the great. *Journal of Travel and Tourism Marketing*, 1(3): 25–41.

Miller, L., Jago, L., and Deery, M. (2004). Profiling the special event nonattendee: an initial investigation. *Event Management*, 8(3): 141–150.

Mintzberg, H. (1983). *Power in and Around Organizations*. Englewood Cliffs, NJ: Prentice Hall.

Mintzberg, H. (1994). *The Rise and Fall of Strategic Planning*. New York: The Free Press.

Mitchell, R., Agle, B., and Wood, D. (1997). Towards a theory of stakeholder identification and salience: defining the principle of who and what really counts. *Academy of Management Review*, 22(4): 853–886.

Mitler, B., van Esterik, P., and van Esterik, J. (2004). *Cultural Anthropology, Second Canadian Edition*. Toronto, Canada: Pearson Education.

Mohr, K., Backman, K., Gahan, L., and Backman, S. (1993). An investigation of festival motivations and event satisfaction by visitor type. *Festival Management and Event Tourism*, 1(3): 89–97.

Monga, M. (2006). Measuring motivation to volunteer for special events. *Event Management*, 10(1): 47–61.

Morrison, A. (1995). *Hospitality and Travel Marketing, Second Edition*. Albany, NY: Delmar.

Morrow, S. (1997). *The Art of the Show: An Introduction to the Study of Exhibition Management*. Dallas, TX: International Association for Exhibition Management.

Mossberg, L. (ed.) (2000a). *Evaluation of Events: Scandinavian Experiences*. New York: Cognizant Communication Corp.

Mossberg, L. (2000b). Effects of events on destination image. In: L. Mossberg (ed.), *Evaluation of Events: Scandinavian Experiences*, pp. 30–46. New York: Cognizant Communication Corp.

Mossberg, L. (2006). Product development and cultural tourism. In: T. Andersson, B. Holmgren, and L. Mossberg (eds.), *Cultural Tourism: Visitor Flows, Economic Impact and Product Development*, pp. 47–59. Sweden: Published for the European Cultural Tourism Network at the School of Business, Economics and Law, University of Gothenburg.

Mossberg, L., and Getz, D. (2006). Stakeholder influences on the ownership and management of festival brands. *Scandinavian Journal of Hospitality and Tourism*, 6(4).

Mount, J., and Niro, B. (1995). Sponsorship: an empirical study of its application to local business in a small town setting. *Festival Management and Event Tourism*, 2(3/4): 167–175.

Mowen, A., Vogelsong, H., and Graefe, A. (2003). Perceived crowding and its relationship to crowd management practices at park and recreation events. *Event Management*, 8(2): 63–72.

Moyer, K. (1968). Kinds of aggression and their physiological basis. *Communications in Behavioral Biology*, 2A: 65–87.

Mules, T. (1993). A special event as part of an urban renewal strategy. *Festival Management and Event Tourism*, 1(2): 65–67.

Mules, T., and Dwyer, L. (2006). Public sector support for sport tourism events: the role of cost-benefit assessment. In: H. Gibson (ed.), *Sport Tourism: Concepts and Theories*. London: Routledge.

Mules, T., and McDonald, S. (1994). The economic impact of special events: the use of forecasts. *Festival Management and Event Tourism*, 2(1): 45–53.

Nash, D. (2000). Acculturation. In: J. Jafari (ed.), *Encyclopedia of Tourism*. New York: Routledge.

National Association for Interpretation (www.interpnet.com).

National Outdoor Events Association (UK) (www.noea.org.uk).

Neulinger, J. (1974). *Psychology of Leisure: Research Approaches to the Study of Leisure*. Springfield, IL: Charles C. Thomas.

Neuman, W. (2003). *Social Research Methods: Qualitative and Quantitative Approaches* (4th edn). Boston, MA: Allyn and Bacon.

New Brunswick Culture and Sport Secretariat (www.gnb.ca).

New South Wales. *Traffic Management for Special Events* (www.rta.nsw.gov.au).

Ngamsom, B., and Beck, J. (2000). A pilot study of motivations, inhibitors, and facilitators of association members in attending international conferences. *Journal of Convention and Exhibition Management*, 2(2/3): 97–111.

Nickerson, N., and Ellis, G. (1991). Traveler types and activation theory: a comparison of two models. *Journal of Travel Research*, 29: 26–31.

Nickerson, R. S. (1999). Enhancing creativity. In: R. Sternberg (ed.), *Handbook of Creativity*. Boston, MA: Cambridge University Press.

Nicholson, R., and Pearce, D. (2001). Why do people attend events: A comparative analysis of visitor motivations at four South Island events. *Journal of Travel Research*, 39: 449–460.

Nogawa, H., Yamaguchi, Y., and Hagi, Y. (1996). An empirical research study on Japanese Sport Tourism in Sport-for-All Events: case studies of a single-night event and a multiple-night event. *Journal of Travel Research*, 35: 46–54.

Noronha, R. (1977). Paradise reviewed: tourism in Bali. In: E. de Kadt (ed.), *Tourism: Passport to Development?*, pp. 177–204. Oxford: Oxford University Press.

North American Society for Sport Management (www.nassm.com).

Nurse, K. (2004). Trinidad carnival: festival tourism and cultural industry. *Event Management*, 8(4): 223–230.

Oakes, S. (2003). Demographic and sponsorship considerations for jazz and classical music festivals. *The Service Industries Journal*, 23(3): 165–178.

Oakley, E., and Krug, D. (1991). *Enlightened Leadership: Getting to the Heart of Change*. New York: Simon and Schuster.

O'Brien, D. (2005). Event business leveraging: The Sydney 2000 Olympic Games. *Annals of Tourism Research*, 33(1): 240–261.

O'Brien, E., and Shaw, M. (2002). Independent meeting planners: a Canadian perspective. *Journal of Convention and Exhibition Management*, 3(4): 37–68.

O'Dell, T. (2005). Management strategies and the need for fun. In: T. O'Dell, and P. Billing, (eds.), *Experience-scapes: Tourism, Culture, and Economy*, pp. 127–42. Copenhagen Business School Press.

O'Dell, T., and Billing, P. (eds.) (2005). *Experience-scapes: Tourism, Culture, and Economy*. Copenhagen Business School Press.

Oldberding, D., and Jisha, J. (2005). 'The Flying Pig': building brand equity in a major urban marathon. *Sport Marketing Quarterly*, 14: 191–196.

Oliver, R. (1977). Effect of expectation and disconfirmation on postexposure product evaluations – an alternative interpretation. *Journal of Applied Psychology*, 62(4): 480–486.

Oliver, R. (1980). A cognitive model of the antecedents and consequences of satisfaction decisions. *Journal of Marketing Research*, 17(3): 460–469.

Olson, J., and Reynolds, T. (2001). *Understanding Consumer Decision Making: A Means End Approach to marketing and Advertising Strategy*. Mahwah, NJ: Lawrence Erlbaum Associates, Inc.

Ooi, C. (2005). A theory of tourism experiences. In: T. O'Dell, and P. Billing (eds.), *Experience-scapes: Tourism, Culture, and Economy*, pp. 51–68. Copenhagen Business School Press.

Oppermann, M., and Chon, K. (1997). Convention participation decision-making process. *Annals of Tourism Research*, 24(1): 178–191.

O'Sullivan, E., and Spangler, K. (1998). *Experience Marketing: Strategies for the New Millennium*. State College, PA: Venture Publishing.

Otnes, C. (2003). *Cinderella Dreams: The Allure of the Lavish Wedding*. University of California Press.

O'Toole, W. (2000). The integration of event management best practice by the project management process. *Australian Parks and Leisure*, 3(1): 4–8.

O'Toole, W., and Mikolaitis, P. (2002). *Corporate Event Project Management*. New York: Wiley.

Paluba, G., and Neulinger, J. (1976). Stereotypes based on free time activities. *Loisir et Societe/Society and Leisure*, 35: 515–525.

Parasuraman, A., Berry, L., and Zeithaml, V. (1988). SERVQUAL: A multiple-item scale for measuring consumer perceptions of service quality. *Journal of Retailing*, 64(1): 12–40.

Pearce, P. (2005). *Tourist Behaviour: Themes and Conceptual Schemas*. Clevedon: Channel View.

Pearce, P., Moscardo, G., and Ross, G. (1996). *Tourism community relationships*. Oxford: Pergamon.

Pennington-Gray, L., and Holdnak, A. (2002). Out of the stands and into the community: Using sports events to promote a destination. *Event Management*, 7(3): 177–186.

Penrose, E. (1959). *The Theory of the Growth of the Firm*. New York: Wiley.

Pfeffer, J. (1981). *Power in Organizations*. London: Pitman.

Pfeffer, J., and Salancik, G. (1978). *The External Control of Organizations: A Resource Dependence Perspective*. New York: Harper and Row.

Picard, M. (1996). *Bali. Cultural Tourism and Touristic Culture* (2nd edn). Singapore: Archipelago Press.

Picard, D., and Robinson, M. (eds.) (2006). *Festivals, Tourism and Social Change: Remaking Worlds*. Clevedon: Channel View.

Picard, D., and Robinson, M. (2006). Remaking worlds: Festivals, tourism and change. In: D. Picard, and M. Robinson (eds.), *Festivals, Tourism and Social Change: Remaking Worlds*, pp. 1–31. Clevedon: Channel View.

Pine, B., and Gilmore, J. (1999). *The Experience Economy: Work is Theatre and Every Business a Stage*. Boston: Harvard Business School Press.

Pitts, B. (1999). Sports tourism and niche markets: Identification and analysis of the growing lesbian and gay sports tourism industry. *Journal of Vacation Marketing*, 5(1), 31–50.

Plog, S. (1972). *Why destination areas rise and fall in popularity*. Paper presented to the *Travel Research Association Southern California Chapter*, Los Angeles.

Plog, S. (1987). Understanding psychographics in tourism research. In: J. Ritchie, and C. Goeldner (eds.), *Travel, Tourism and Hospitality Research*, pp. 302–213. New York: Wiley.

Pol, L., and Pak, S. (1994). The use of a two-stage survey design in collecting data from those who have attended periodic or special events. *Journal of the Market Research Society*, 36(4): 315–326.

Porter, M. (1980). *Competitive Strategy: Techniques for Analyzing Industries and Competitors*. New York: The Free Press.

Preda, P., and Watts, T. (2003). Improving the efficiency of sporting venues through capacity management: The case of the Sydney (Australia) Cricket Ground Trust. *Event Management*, 8(2): 83–89.

Prentice, R., and Anderson, V. (2003). Festival as creative destination. *Annals of Tourism Research*, 30(1): 7–30.

Prideaux, B., Moscardo, G., and Laws, E. (eds.) (2006). *Managing Tourism and Hospitality Services: Theory and International Applications*. Wallingford: CABI.

Przeclawski, K. (1985). The role of tourism in contemporary culture. *The Tourist Review*, 40: 2–6.

Pugh, C., and Wood, E. (2004). The strategic use of events within local government: A study of London Borough councils. *Event Management*, 9(1/2): 61–71.

Putnam, R. (2004). *Democracies in Flux: The Evolution of Social Capital in Contemporary Society*. New York: Oxford University Press.

Pyo, S., Cook, R., and Howell, R. (1988). Summer Olympic tourist market – Learning from the Past. *Tourism Management*, 9(2), 137–144.

Quinn, B. (2000). Whose festival? Whose place? An insight into the production of cultural meanings in arts festivals turned festival attractions. In: M. Robinson, N. Evans, and P. Callaghan (eds.), *Expressions of Culture, Identity and Meaning in Tourism*. Sunderland, UK: Centre for Travel and Tourism Research/Business Education Publishers Ltd.

Quinn, B. (2006). Problematising 'festival tourism': arts festivals and sustainable development in Ireland. *Journal of Sustainable Tourism*, 14(3): 288–306.

Radbourne, J. (2002). Social intervention or market intervention? A problem for governments in promoting the value of the arts. *International Journal of Arts Management*, 5(1): 50–61.

Raj, R. (2004). The behavioural aspects of financial management. In: I. Yeoman, et al., (eds.), *Festivals and Events Management*, pp. 273–285. Oxford: Elsevier.

Ralston, L., Ellis, D., Compton, D., and Lee, J. (2006). Staging memorable events and festivals: An integrated model of service and experience factors. In: C. Arcodia, M. Whitford, and C. Dickson (eds.), *Global Events Congress Proceedings*, pp. 268–285. Brisbane, Queensland: University of Queensland.

Ralston, R., Lumsdon, L., and Downward, P. (2005). The third force in events tourism: Volunteers at the XVII Commonwealth Games. *Journal of Sustainable Tourism*, 13(5): 504–519.

Ravenscroft, N., and Mateucci, X. (2002). The festival as carnivalesque: Social governance and control at Pamplona's San Fermin fiesta. *Tourism Culture & Communication*, 4(1): 1–15.

Raybould, M. (1998). Participant motivation in a remote fishing event. *Festival Management and Event Tourism*, 5(4): 231–241.

Raybould, M., Mules, T., Fredline, E., and Tomljenovic, R. (2000). Counting the herd: Using aerial photography to estimate attendance at open events. *Event Management*, 6(1): 25–32.

Reid, G. (2006). The politics of city imaging: a case study of the MTV Europe Music Awards in Edinburgh 03. *Event Management*, 10(1): 35–46.

Reisinger, Y. (2006). Travel/tourism: spiritual experiences. In: D. Buhalis, and C. Costa (eds.), *Tourism Business Frontiers: Consumers, Products and Industry*, pp. 148–167. Oxford: Elsevier.

Reunion Network (www.reunionfriendly.com).

Richards, G. (1996). European cultural tourism: Trends and future prospects. In: G. Richards (ed.), *Cultural Tourism in Europe*, pp. 311–333. Wallingford UK: CABI.

Richards, G. (ed.) (2006). *Cultural Tourism: Global and Local Perspectives*. New York: Haworth.

Richards, P., and Ryan, C. (2004). The Aotearoa Traditional Maori Performing Arts Festival 1972–2000: a case study of cultural event maturation. *Journal of Tourism and Cultural Change*, 2(2): 94–117.

Riggio, M. (ed.) (2004). *Carnival: Culture in Action: The Trinidad Experience*. New York: Routledge.

Ritchie, B. (1984). Assessing the impacts of hallmark events: Conceptual and research issues. *Journal of Travel Research*, 23(1): 2–11.

Ritchie, B. (2000). Turning 16 days into 16 years through Olympic legacies. *Event Management*, 6(2): 155–165.

Ritchie, B., and Adair, D. (2004). *Sport Tourism: Interrelationships, Impacts and Issues*. Clevedon: Channel View.

Ritchie, B., and Smith, B. (1991). The impact of a mega-event on host region awareness: A longitudinal study. *Journal of Travel Research*, 30(1): 3–10.

Ritchie, B., Sanders, D., and Mules, T. (2006). Televised events: Shaping destination images and perceptions of capital cities from the couch. In: C. Arcodia, M. Whitford, and C. Dickson (eds.), *Global Events Congress, Proceedings*, pp. 286–299. Brisbane, Queensland: University of Queensland.

Rittichainuwat, B., Beck, J., and LaLopa, J. (2001). Understanding motivations, inhibitors, and facilitators of association members in attending international conferences. *Journal of Convention and Exhibition Management*, 3(3): 45–62.

Roberts, K. (2006). *Leisure in Contemporary Society* (2nd edn). Wallingford: CABI.

Robinson, M., Hums, M., Crow, R., Philips, D. (2001). *Profiles of Sport Industry Professionals: The People Who Make the Games Happen*. Gaithersburg, Maryland: Aspen Publishers.

Robinson, M., Picard, D., and Long, P. (2004). Festival tourism: Producing, translating, and consuming expressions of culture(s). *Event Management*, 8(4): 187–189.

Roche, M. (2000). *Mega-Events and Modernity: Olympics and Expos in the Growth of Global Culture*. London: Routledge.

Roche, M. (2006). Mega-events and modernity revisited: Globalization and the case of the Olympics. *Sociological Review*, 54: 25–40.

Rogers, E. (1995). *Diffusion of Innovations*. New York: The Free Press.

Rogers, T. (1998). *Conferences : a twenty-first century industry*. Harlow: Addison Wesley Longman.

Rogers, T. (2003). *Conferences and Conventions: A Global Industry*. Oxford: Butterworth Heinemann.

Rogers, T., and Davidson, R. (2006). *Marketing Destinations and Venues for Conferences, Conventions and Business Events*. Oxford: Butterworth Heinemann.

Rojek, C. (1995). *Decentring Leisure*. London: Sage.

Rojek, C., and Urry, J. (eds.) (1997). *Touring Cultures: Transformation of Travel and Theory*. London: Routledge.

Rozin, S. (2000). The amateurs who saved Indianapolis. *Business Week*, April 10.

Runners World (www.runnersworld.co.uk).

Russell, J. (2004). Celebrating culture, energising language, transforming society. In: M. Robinson, D. Picard, I. Schneider, and O. Haid (eds.), *Conference on Proceedings of the Journeys of Expression III*. Centre for Tourism and Cultural Change, Sheffield-Hallam University (Compact Disc).

Russell, J., and Lanius, U. (1984). Adaptation level and the affective appraisal of environments. *Journal of Environmental Psychology*, 4: 119–135

Rutley, J. (n.d.) Security. In: *Event Operations*, pp. 75–83. Port Angeles: International Festivals and Events Association.

Ryan, C. (2000). Tourist experiences, phenomenographic analysis, post positivism and neural network software. *International Journal of Tourism Research*, 2(2): 119–131.

Ryan, C. (2002). *The Tourist Experience* (2nd edn), London: Continuum.

Ryan. C., and Bates, C. (1995). A rose by any other name: The motivations of those opening their gardens for a festival. *Festival Management and Event Tourism*, 3(2): 59–71.

Ryan, C., and Lockyer, T. (2002). Masters' Games – The nature of competitors' involvement and requirements. *Event Management*, 7(4): 259–270.

Ryan, C., and Trauer, B. (2005). Sport tourist behaviour: the example of the Masters games. In: J. Higham, (ed.), *Sport Tourism Destinations: Issues, Opportunities and Analysis*. Oxford: Elsevier.

Ryan, C., Smee, A., Murphy, S., and Getz, D. (1998). New Zealand events: a temporal and regional analysis. *Festival Management and Event Tourism*, 5(1/2), 71–83.

Sahlins, M. (1976). *Culture and Practical Reason*. Chicago, IL: University of Chicago Press.

Saleh, F. and Ryan, C. (1993). Jazz and knitwear: Factors that attract tourists to festivals. *Tourism Management*, 14(4): 289–297.

Saleh, F., and Wood, C. (1998). Motives and volunteers in multi-cultural events: the case of Saskatoon Folkfest. *Festival Management and Event Tourism*, 5: 59–70.

Sandercock, L. (1998). *Making the Invisible Visible, A Multicultural Planning History*, pp. 1–30. Berkely: University of California Press.

San Francisco State University. *Hospitality Management* (www.sfu.edu/hm).

Selznick, P. (1957). *Leadership in Administration*. Evanston, IL: Row, Peterson.

Schechner, R. (1988). *Performance Theory*. New York: Routledge.

Schechner, R. (2002). *Performance Studies: An Introduction*. New York: Routledge.

Schein, E. (1985). *Organizational Culture and Leadership*. San Francisco: Jossey-Bass.

Schultz, E., and Lavenda, R. (2005). *Cultural Anthropology: A Perspective on the Human Condition*. New York and Oxford: Oxford University Press.

Scotinform Ltd. (1991). *Edinburgh Festivals Study 1990–91: Visitor Survey and Economic Impact Assessment, Final Report*. Edinburgh: Scottish Tourist Board.

Scott, D. (1996). A comparison of visitors' motivations to attend three urban festivals. *Festival Management and Event Tourism*, 3(3): 121–128.

Scott, J. (2000). *Social Network Analysis: A Handbook* (2nd edn), London: Sage.

Scott, W. (2001). *Institutions and Organizations*. Thousand Oaks, CA: Sage.

Senge, P. (1990). *The fifth discipline: The art and practice of the learning organization.* New York: Doubleday.

Senge, P., Roberts, C., Ross, R., Smith, B., and Kleiner, A. (1994). *The fifth discipline fieldbook: Strategies and tools for building a learning organization.* New York: Doubleday.

Severt, D., Wang, Y., Chen, P., and Breiter, D. (2007). Examining the motivation, perceived performance, and behavioral intentions of convention attendees: evidence from a regional conference. *Tourism Management,* 28(2): 399–408.

Shackley, M. (2001). *Managing Sacred Sites: Service Provision and Visitor Experience.* London: Continuum.

Shaw, G., and Williams, A. (2004). *Tourism and Tourism Spaces.* London: Sage.

Shedroff, N. (2001). *Experience Design.* (Pearson) Upper Saddle River, NJ: New Riders.

Sheehan, A., Hubbard, S., and Popovich, P. (2000). Profiling the hotel and conference center meeting planner: A preliminary study. *Journal of Convention & Exhibition Management,* 2 (2/3): 11–25.

Shibli, S., and the Sport Industry Research Centre (2002). *The 2002 Embassy World Snooker Championship, An evaluation of the economic Impact, Place Marketing Effects, and Visitors' Perceptions of Sheffield,* for Sheffield City Council.

Shone, A. and Parry, B. (2001). *Successful Event Management.* London: Continuum.

Silvers, J. (2004). *Professional Event Coordination.* Hoboken, NJ: Wiley.

Silvers, J., Bowdin, G., O'Toole, W., and Nelson, K. (2006). Towards an international event management body of knowledge (EMBOK). *Event Management,* 9(4): 185–198.

Singh, R. (2006). Pilgrimage in Hinduism: Historical context and modern perspectives. In: D. Timothy, and D. Olsen (eds.), *Tourism, Religion and Spiritual Journeys,* pp. 220–236. London and New York: Routledge.

Singh, S. B. (1989). *Fairs and Festivals in Rural India: A Geospatial Study of Belief Systems.* Varanasi: Tara Book Agency.

Skinner, B. (1938). *The Behavior of Organisms.* New York: Appleton-Century-Crofts.

Skinner, B., and Rukavina, V. (2003). *Event Sponsorship.* New York: Wiley.

Smith, M. (2006). Entertainment and new leisure tourism. In: D. Buhalis, and C. Costa, (eds.), *Tourism Business Frontiers: Consumers, Products and Industry,* pp. 220–227. Oxford: Elsevier.

Smith, E., and Mackie, D. (2000). *Social Psychology* (2nd edn), New York: Worth Publishers.

Sociology (www.sociology.org.uk.).

Sofield, T. (1991). Sustainable ethnic tourism in the South Pacific: some principles. *Journal of Tourism Studies,* 1(3): 56–72.

Sofield, T., and Li, F. (1998). Historical methodology and sustainability: an 800-year-old festival from China. *Journal of Sustainable Tourism,* 6(4): 267–292.

Sofield, T., and Sivan, A. (2003). From cultural festival to international sport – the Hong Kong Dragon Boat Races. *Journal of Sport Tourism,* (81): 9–20.

Solberg, H., Andersson, T., and Shibli, S. (2002). An exploration of the direct economic impacts from business travelers at world championships. *Event Management*, 7(3): 151–164.

Solomon, J. (2002). *An Insider's Guide to Managing Sporting Events*. Champaign, IL: Human Kinetics.

Spiller, J. (2002). History of convention tourism. In: K. Weber, and K. Chon (eds.), *Convention Tourism: International Research and Industry Perspectives*, pp. 3–20. Binghampton, NY: Haworth.

Spilling, O. (1998). Beyond intermezzo? On the long-term industrial impacts of mega-events: the case of Lillehammer 1994. *Festival Management and Event Tourism*, 5(3): 101–122.

Spiropoulos, S., Gargalianos, D., and Sotiriadou, K. (2006). The 20th Greek Festival of Sydney: a stakeholder analysis. *Event Management*, 9(4): 169–183.

Sports Business Market Research Inc. (2000). *The 2001 Sports Business Market Research Handbook*. Loganville GA: Richard K. Miller and Associates.

Stear, L. (1981). Design of a curriculum for destination studies. *Annals of Tourism Research*, 8(1): 85–95.

Stebbins, R. (1982). Serious leisure: a conceptual statement. *Pacific Sociological Review*, 25(2).

Stebbins, R. (1992). *Amateurs, Professionals, and Serious Leisure*. Montreal: McGill-Queen's University Press.

Stebbins, R. (2001). *New Directions in the Theory and Research of Serious Leisure*. Lewiston, NY: Edwin Mellen.

Stebbins, R. (2006). *Serious Leisure: A Perspective for Our Time*. Somerset, NJ: Aldine Transaction Publications.

Stebbins, R. and Graham, M. (eds.) (2004). *Volunteering as Leisure/Leisure as Volunteering: An International Assessment*. Wallingford, Oxon: CABI.

Sternberg, R. J. *Handbook of Creativity*. Boston, MA: Cambridge University Press.

Stokes, R. (2004). A framework for the analysis of events – tourism knowledge networks. *Journal of Hospitality and Tourism Management*, 11(2): 108–123.

Stott, C. J., Hutchison, P., and Drury, J. (2001). 'Hooligans' abroad? Inter-group dynamics, social identity and participation in collective 'disorder' at the 1998 World Cup Finals. *British Journal of Social Psychology*, 40, 359–384.

Strigas, A., and Newton Jackson, E. (2003). Motivating volunteers to serve and succeed: Design and results of a pilot study that explores demographics and motivational factors in sport volunteerism. *International Sports Journal*, 7(1): 111–123.

Supovitz, F., and Goldblatt, J. (2004). *The Sports Event Management and Marketing Playbook*. New York: Wiley.

Tapp, A. (2004). The loyalty of football fans – we'll support you evermore? *Journal of Database Marketing and Customer Strategy Management*, 11(3): 203–215.

Tarlow, P. (2002). *Event Risk Management and Safety*. New York: Wiley.

Tassiopoulos, D. (ed.) (2000). *Event Management: A Professional and Developmental Approach*. Lansdowne: Juta Education.

Taylor, P., and Gratton, C. (1988). The Olympic Games: An economic analysis. *Leisure Management*, 8(3): 32–34.

Taylor, R., and Shanka, T. (2002). Attributes for staging successful wine festivals. *Event Management*, 7(3): 165–175.

Teigland, J. (1996). *Impacts on Tourism From Mega-Events: The Case of Winter Olympic Games*. Sogndal: Western Norway Research Institute.

Tellstrom, R., Gustafsson, I., and Mossberg, L. (2006). Consuming heritage: The use of local food culture in branding. *Place Branding*, 2(2): 130–143.

Thrane, C. (2002). Music quality, satisfaction, and behavioral intentions within a jazz festival context. *Event Management*, 7(3): 143–150.

Tilden, F. (1957). *Interpreting our Heritage*. Chapel Hill: University of North Carolina Press.

Timothy, D., and Boyd, S. (2006). Heritage tourism in the 21st century: valued traditions and new perspectives. *Journal of Heritage Tourism*, 1(1): 1–16.

Timothy, D., and Olsen, D. (eds.) (2006). *Tourism, Religion and Spiritual Journeys*. London and New York: Routledge.

Tohmo, T. (2005). Economic impacts of cultural events on local economies: An input-output analysis of the Kaustinen Folk Music Festival. *Tourism Economics*, 11(3): 431–451.

Tomlinson, G. (1986). The staging of rural food festivals: some problems with the concept of liminoid performances. *Paper presented to the Qualitative Research Conference on Ethnographic Research*, University of Waterloo.

Tomljenovic, R., and Weber, S. (2004). Funding cultural events in Croatia: Tourism-related policy issues. *Event Management*, 9(1/2): 51–59.

Toohey, K., and Veal, T. (2007). *The Olympic Games: A Social Science Perspective*. Wallingford: CABI.

Trail, G., and James, J. (2001). The motivation scale for sport consumption: assessment of the scale's psychometric properties. *Journal of Sport Behavior*, 24(1): 109–127.

Travel Industry Association of America (1999). *Profile of Travellers Who Attend Sports Events*. Washington DC: TIAA.

Travel Industry Association of America, and Smithsonian Magazine (2003). The Historic/Cultural Traveller.

Tribe, J. (1997). The indiscipline of tourism. *Annals of Tourism Research*, 24(3): 638–657.

Tribe, J. (2002). The philosophic practitioner. *Annals of Tourism Research*, 29(2): 338–357.

Tribe, J. (2004). Knowing about tourism – epistemological issues. In: L. Goodson, and J. Phillimore (eds.), *Qualitative Research in Tourism: Ontologies, Epistemologies and Methodologies*, pp. 46–62. London: Routledge.

Tribe, J. (2005). *The Economics of Recreation, Leisure and Tourism* (3rd edn). Oxford: Elsevier.

Tribe, J. (2006). The truth about tourism. *Annals of Tourism Research*, 33(2): 360–381.

Tum, J., Norton, P., and Wright. J. (2006). *Management of Event Operations*. Oxford: Butterworth Heinemann/Elsevier.

Turco, D. (1995). Measuring the tax impacts of an international festival: Justification for government sponsorship. *Festival Management and Event Tourism*, 2(3/4): 191–195.

Turco, D., Riley, R., and Swart, K. (2002). *Sport Tourism.* Morgantown, WV: Fitness Information Technology Inc.

Turner, V. (1969). *The Ritual Process: Structure and Anti-Structure.* New York: Aldine de Gruyter.

Turner, V. (1974). Liminal to liminoid, in play, flow and ritual: an essay in comparative symbology. In: E. Norbeck (ed.), *The Anthropological Study of Human Play*, pp. 53–92. Houston: Rice University Studies.

Turner, V. (ed.) (1982). *Celebration: Studies in Festivity and Ritual.* Washington: Smithsonian Institution Press.

Turney, M. (www.nku.edu/~turney/).

Tyrrell, T., and Johnston, R. (2001). A framework for assessing direct economic impacts of tourist events: Distinguishing origins, destinations, and causes of expenditures. *Journal of Travel Research*, 40: 94–100.

Tzelepi, M., and Quick, S. (2002). The Sydney Organizing Committee for the Olympic Games (SOCOG) "Event Leadership" training course – an effectiveness evaluation. *Event Management*, 7(4): 245–257.

UK Health and Safety Executive (1999). *The Event Safety Guide* (www.hsebooks.com).

UK Institute for Volunteering Research (www.ivr.org.uk).

UK National Outdoor Events Association (www.noea.org.uk).

UK Sport. Major Sport Events: The Guide (online at www.uksport.gov.uk).

University of North Carolina, Greensboro (www.uncg.edu.rth).

Urry, J. (1990). *The Tourist Gaze: Leisure and Travel in Contemporary Societies.* London: Sage.

Urry, J. (1995). *Consuming Places.* Routledge: London.

Urry, J. (2002)*The Tourist Gaze: Leisure and Travel in Contemporary Societies* (2nd edn). London: Sage.

US Department of Labor (2005). *Volunteering in the United States, 2005.* (http://www.bls.gov/news.release/volun.nr0.htm).

US Embassy Japan. *Matsuri: The Festivals of Japan* (www.us.emb-japan.go.jp/jicc/spot festivals.htm).

Uysal, M., Gahan, L, and Martin, B. (1993). An examination of event motivations: A case study. *Festival Management and Event Tourism*, 1(1):5–10.

Van der Wagen, L. (2004). *Event Management for Tourism, Cultural, Business and Sporting Events* (2nd edn). Frenchs Forest NSW: Pearson Education Australia.

Van der Wagen, L. (2006). *Human Resource Management for Events: Managing the Event Workforce.* Oxford: Butterworth Heinemann.

Van Gennep, A. (1909). *The Rites of Passage* [1960 translation by M. Vizedom and G. Coffee]. London: Routledge and Kegan Paul

Vanhove, D., and Witt, S. (1987). Report of the *English-Speaking Group on the Conference Theme. Revue de Tourisme*, 4: 10–12.

Vaughan, R. (1979). *Does a Festival Pay? A Case Study of the Edinburgh Festival in 1976.* Tourism Recreation Research Unit, Working Paper 5, University of Edinburgh.

Veal, A. (2006). *Research Methods for Leisure and Tourism: A Practical Guide* (3rd edn). Harlow, England: Prentice Hall.

Verhoven, P., Wall, D., and Cottrell, S. (1998). Application of desktop mapping as a marketing tool for special events planning and evaluation: a case study of the Newport News Celebration. In: *Lights. Festival Management and Event Tourism*, 5(3): 123–130.

Voss, T. (2001). Institutions. In: *International Encyclopedia of the Social and Behavioral Sciences*, pp. 7561–7566. Oxford: Elsevier.

Vroom, V. (1964). Work and Motivation. New York: Wiley.

Waitt, G. (2004). A critical examination of Sydney's 2000 Olympic Games. In: I. Yeoman et al (eds.), *Festivals and Events Management*, pp. 391–408. Oxford: Elsevier.

Walker, G, Deng, J, and Dieser, R. (2005). Culture, self-construal, and leisure theory and practice. *Journal of Leisure Research*, 37(1): 77–99.

Walker, G., and Virden, R. (2005). Constraints on outdoor recreation. In: E. Jackson (ed.), *Constraints to Leisure*, Chapter 13. State College, PA: Venture Publishing.

Walle, A. (1994). The festival life cycle and tourism strategies: the case of the Cowboy Poetry Gathering. *Festival Management and Event Tourism*, (2), 85–94.

Wang, N. (1999). Rethinking authenticity in tourism experience. *Annals of Tourism Research*, 26(2): 349–70.

Wang, P., and Gitelson, R. (1988). Economic limitations of festivals and other hallmark events. *Leisure Industry Report* (August): 4–5.

Wanhill, S. (2006). Some economics of staging festivals: the case of opera festivals. *Tourism, Culture and Communication*, 6(2): 137–149.

Wann, D. (1995). Preliminary validation of the sport fan motivation scale. *Journal of Sport and Social Issues*, 19: 377–396.

Wann, D. (1997). *Sport Psychology*. Upper Saddle River, NJ: Prentice Hall.

Wann, D., and Branscombe, N. (1993). Sport fans: measuring degree of identification with their team. *International Journal of Sport Psychology*, 24: 1–17.

Wann, D., Schrader, M., and Wilson, A. (1999). Sport fan motivation: Questionnaire validation, comparisons by sport, and relationship to athletic motivation. *Journal of Sport Behaviour*, 22(1): 114–139.

Wann, D., Royalty, J., and Rochelle, A. (2002). Using motivation and team identification to predict sport fans' emotional responses to team performance. *Journal of Sport Behavior*, 25(2): 207–216.

Waterman, S. (1998). Carnivals for elites? The cultural politics of arts festivals. *Progress in Human Geography*, 22(1): 54–74.

Waters, H. (1939). *History of Fairs and Expositions*. London, Canada: Reid Brothers.

Weber, K., and Chon, K. (2002). *Convention Tourism: International Research and Industry Perspectives*. New York: Haworth.

Weber, K., and Ladkin, A. (2004). Trends affecting the convention industry in the 21st century. *Journal of Convention and Event Tourism*, 6(4): 47–63.

Weed, M. (2003). Why the two won't tango! Explaining the lack of integrated policies for sport and tourism in the UK. *Journal of Sport Management*, 17(3): 258–283.

Weppler, K., and McCarville, R. (1995). Understanding organizational buying behaviour to secure sponsorship. *Festival Management and Event Tourism*, 2: 139–148.

Whitford, M. (2004a). Regional development through domestic and tourist event policies: Gold Coast and Brisbane, 1974–2003. *UNLV Journal of Hospitality, Tourism and Leisure Science*, 1: 1–24.

Whitford, M. (2004b). Event public policy development in the Northern Sub-Regional Organisation of Councils, Queensland Australia: Rhetoric or realisation? *Journal of Convention and Event Tourism*, 6(3): 81–99.

Whitson, D., and Macintosh, D. (1996). The global circus: International sport, tourism, and the marketing of cities. *Journal of Sport and Social Issues*, 20(3): 275–295.

Wickham, T., and Kerstetter, D. (2000). The relationship between place attachment and crowding in an event setting. *Event Management*, 6(3): 167–174.

Wicks, B. (1995). The business sector's reaction to a community special event in a small town: A case study of the Autumn on Parade Festival. *Festival Management and Event Tourism*, 2(3/4): 177–183.

Wicks, B. and Fesenmaier, D. (1993). A comparison of visitor and vendor perceptions of service quality at a special event. *Festival Management and Event Tourism*, 1(1): 19–26.

Wicks, B., and Fesenmaier, D. (1995). Market potential for special events: a midwestern case study. *Festival Management and Event Tourism*, 3(1): 25–31.

Wiersma, B., and Strolberg, K. (2003). *Exceptional Events: Concept to Completion* (2nd edn). Weirmar, Texas: Culinary and Hospitality Industry Publications Services.

Wikipedia, *The Free Encyclopedia* (www.wikipedia.org).

Williams, P., Dossa, K., and Tompkins, L. (1995). Volunteerism and special event management: a case study of Whistler's Men's World Cup of Skiing. *Festival Management and Event Tourism*, 3(2): 83–95.

Williams, P., and Harrison, L. (1988). *A Framework for Marketing Ethnocultural Communities and Festivals*. Unpublished report to the Secretary of State Multiculturalism, Ottawa.

Wilson J., and Udall, L. (1982). *Folk Festivals: A Handbook for Organization and Management*. Knoxville: The University of Tennessee Press.

Wood, D., and Gray, B. (1991). Toward a comprehensive theory of collaboration. *The Journal of Applied Behavioural Science*, 27(1): 3–22.

Wood, E. (2004). Marketing information for the events industry. In: Yeoman I., Robertson, M., Ali-Knight, J., Drummond, S., and McMahon-Beattie, U., *Festival and Events Management: An International Arts and Culture Perspective*, pp. 130–157. Oxford: Elsevier.

Xiao, H., and Smith, S. (2004). Residents' perceptions of Kitchener-Waterloo Oktoberfest: an inductive analysis. *Event Management*, 8(3): 161–175.

Xie, P. (2003). The Bamboo-beating dance in Hainan, China. Authenticity and commodification. *Journal of Sustainable Tourism*, 11(1): 5–16.

Xie, P. (2004). Visitors' perceptions of authenticity at a rural heritage festival: a case study. *Event Management*, 8(3): 151–160.

Yeoman, I., Robertson, M., Ali-Knight, J., Drummond, S., and McMahon-Beattie, U. (2004). *Festival and Events Management: An International Arts and Culture Perspective*. Oxford: Elsevier.

Yoo, J., and Weber, K. (2005). Progress in convention tourism research. *Journal of Hospitality and Tourism Research*, 29(2): 194–222.

Yoon, S. Spencer, D., Holecek, D., and Kim, D. (2000). A profile of Michigan's festival and special event tourism market. *Event Management*, 6(1): 33–44.

Young, H. (1998). *Individual Strategy and Social Structure*. Princeton, NJ: Princeton University Press.

Yu, Y., and Turco, D. (2000). Issues in tourism event economic impact studies: the case of Albuquerque International Balloon Fiesta. *Current Issues in Tourism*, 3(2): 138–149.

Zaichkowsky, J. (1985). Measuring the involvement construct. *Journal of Consumer Research*, 12(December): 341–352.

Zaltman, G., and Coulter, R. (1995). Seeing the voice of the customer: Metaphor-based advertising research. *Journal of Advertising Research*, 35(July/August): 35–51.

Zuckerman, M. (1979). *Sensation Seeking: Beyond the Optimal Level of Arousal*. Hillsdale, NJ: LEA.

Index

Abbott, J., 119
Abrahams, R., 41, 199
Acadia University, 163
accountability, 285–286
action research, 368–369
activity(ies), 30, 226, 308, 313, 316
aesthetic(s), 76–78, 185, 216
affect(ive) quality of places, 219–220
    dimension of experience (see experience)
affordance (setting), 67, 212, 248–249
agency theory, 94–95
agenda (see research agenda)
aggression, 64, 200, 210, 222, 291
Ahmed, Z., 14
AIEST, 25
Ajzen, I., 70, 143, 238
Alberta, 107–108
Ali-Knight, J., 339
Allen, J., 297
Allport, G., 238
American Anthropological Association, 55
American Council for the United Nations
    University, 123
American Historical Association, 106
Ammon, R., 291
Ancient History Sourcebook, 112
Anderson, H., 228
Anderson, V., 282
Andersson, T., 82, 88, 268, 285, 312, 313, 319,
    321, 333
animation/animator, 13, 25, 33, 139,
    141–142, 188, 202, 335
antecedents (and choices), 10, 12–13,
    179–180, 236–255, 373–374, 387–388
anthropology, 50–55

anti-social behaviour, 64, 341
Archer, B., 321
Arcodia, C., 186
Argonne Productions, 292
Armstrong, J., 271
Arnett, D., 188
art(s),
    and cultural management, 158–159
    and cultural development, 337–339
    and entertainment, 37, 185–186
    visual, 38
    performing, 37
    performance, 11, 45, 157
    installation, 38, 157–158
assembly, 39, 213, 217, 162–163
ATLAS (Association for Tourism and
    Leisure Education), 140
attitudes, 238
attraction, 136, 140–141
attraction gradient, 216
attractiveness, 116–117, 140–141, 250–251
Auld, C., 290
Australian Bureau of Statistics, 289
authenticity, 113–114, 200–203
award(s), 34, 37, 53, 182, 185, 189, 193, 224,
    334, 347
Axelson, M., 186
axiology, 358

Back, K., 243
Backman, S., 242
Backman, K., 242
Bailey, P., 213
Baker, D., 227
Bandura, A., 69

Barker, M., 286
Barker, R., 68
Barney, J., 91
Baron, R., 68, 70
barriers and constraints, 236, 245–249, 374, 387
Bates, C., 290
Bateson, J., 218
Baum, A. 74
Baum, J., 95, 96
Baxter, M., 142
Beck, J., 242
Becker, D., 102, 104
Becker, H., 137
behaviour/behavioural
    aggressive, 222
    and experiential influences, 66–67
    anti-social, 64, 222, 341
    approach-avoidance, 65
    consistent, 137
    constraints, 220
    consumer, 12, 64, 73, 81, 323, 363
    crowd, 72, 309
    dangerous, 79
    deviant/elicit, 59, 103
    ethical, 78
    fan, 188
    geography, 114
    learned, 51
    leisure, 69, 137
    modification, 288
    organizational/inter-organizational, 72, 160, 262, 264, 269–270
    political, 98
    ritualistic, 47, 51–53
    setting, 68, 219
    sciences, 5
    social, 55, 59
    socially accepted, 244
    strategies, 247
    theory, 186
    theory of planned, 70–71, 238, 244, 253, 290
    travel/tourist, 143, 212, 242, 253
    type A, 64
    volunteer, 290
Bell, P., 65, 66, 74, 221, 222

Benedict, B., 41
benefits
    and costs, 60, 72, 89, 101–102, 117–118, 161, 266, 273, 300–301, 305, 307–308, 310, 314, 317–320, 324, 325, 330, 343, 380, 389
    cultural, 337–338
    economic/tourism, 4, 25, 87–88, 99, 103, 117, 140, 189, 196, 305, 310–314, 324, 334–336
    environmental, 134
    generic, 182, 204, 209, 250, 281–282, 312, 385, 387, 388
    leisure, 57, 129, 133–134, 251, 330
    personal, 166, 181–182, 198–199, 239–240, 244, 252, 290, 303, 372, 385
    political, 113
    public, 263, 330–331, 338
    psychic, 192, 186, 322, 333, 349
    social, 59, 341–342
    targeted, 27, 250, 251, 312, 388
Berlonghi, A., 222, 292
Berridge, G., 203, 209
Beverland, M., 111
Birzell, R., 371
Bloom, B., 149
blueprinting, 212, 228–230, 386
Boella, M., 259
Bohlin, M., 116
Boissevan, J., 306
Boo, S., 143
Boorstin, D., 113, 125, 201, 361
Borrie, B., 371
Bos, H., 141
Botterill, D., 197
Bouchet, P., 186, 187
Bourdieu, P., 58
Bowdin, G., 15, 266, 297
Boyd, S., 201
Bramwell, B. , 150, 271
brand(ing)/co-branding, 142–143, 282–284
Branscombe, N., 188
Brantley, V., 345
Breen, H., 364
Breiter, D., 190
Bristow, D., 188
British Arts Festivals Association, 33, 313
British Columbia Sport Branch, 42, 118

British Standards Institute, 266, 342
Brothers, G., 364
Brown, G. , 136, 142, 313
Brown, S., 208, 209, 215, 225,
Brunson, M., 251
Bruun, T., 242, 243
Bryan, H., 136
Bryant, S., 289
Bureau International des Expositions (BIE), 41
bureaucracy/bureaucratization, 95, 104,
    259, 264–267
Burgan, B., 332
Burns, J., 308, 318, 321, 322, 333
Burr, S., 136
business
    management, 90
    plan(ning), 271–274
    travel/tourist, 140, 313, 378
    venture, 90, 260, 283–285, 310
    and trade events, 38, 42, 190, 225, 244
Busser, J., 143
Butler, R., 271
Byrne, D., 68, 70

Calgary Herald, 45, 107
Cameron, C., 142
Campbell, S., 272
Canadian Heritage, 34–35
CanWest News Service, 45
capacity
    building, 21, 85, 195, 310, 314, 319, 345
    design/site, 66, 219, 223, 278, 343, 347
    management, 163, 278, 295
    surplus, 88, 285, 311, 333
    to absorb events, 119, 323, 343
Cardenas, D., 249
Carlsen, J., 123, 226, 266, 309, 314, 367
carnival, 33–34, 52, 53, 64, 79, 178, 180, 181,
    183, 204, 292, 372
case study(ies), 80, 90, 138, 149, 152, 267, 270,
    282, 334, 353, 354, 368, 375
careers
    event, 12, 13, 179, 181, 203, 236, 243, 248,
        253, 254, 302, 303, 312, 323, 374, 385, 387,
        388, 389
    leisure, 133

travel, 133, 181, 241, 244, 248, 254
    professional, 3, 6, 22, 90, 128, 138, 147, 160,
        289, 290, 392
    volunteer, 137, 375
catalyst, 13, 33, 60, 144, 202, 311, 340
Catherwood, D., 283
causal factors/forces (stressors), 13, 301–302,
    304–305, 310, 315, 323
cause-related, 26, 175, 261
Cavalcanti, M., 54
celebration (cultural), 30–36, 183–185
Center for Exhibition Industry Research
    (CEIR), 40, 190
Chalip, L., 142, 143, 161, 179, 186, 193, 238,
    242, 290, 313
Chen, P., 76–77, 187, 188, 190, 365
Chernushenko, D., 101, 316, 325
Cheska, A., 306
Chick, G., 135
choice(s)
    antecedents and, 235–255, 373–374, 387–388
    theory of, 82
    freedom of, 172
Chon, K., 189, 242
choreography, 224–225, 386
Church, I., 266
Citrine, K., 177
Clarke, J., 113
closely related fields, 5, 9, 10, 11, 15, 90,
    127–167, 352, 354, 380, 384, 390–392
club management, 162–163
Club Managers Association of
    America, 163
cognitive
    dissonance theory, 65, 247, 251
    mapping, 66, 77, 114, 218
    psychology, 61–62, 64, 148, 150, 171, 175,
        186, 215, 231, 232, 384, 386
    strategies, 247
Cohen, E., 132, 201
collaboration, 58, 92–93, 104, 119, 259, 260,
    264, 270–272, 307, 345, 347–348, 357
Coleman, D., 290
Coleman, J., 58, 268
colour, 66, 67, 212, 215–217
Columbia University, 158

commemoration, 19, 31, 34–35, 52, 107–109, 143, 183, 232
commitment, 137
communications
  live, 203
  mix, 278–282
  studies, 152–154
  theory, 57–58
communitas, 179–182, 184, 187–189, 191–193, 198, 203, 204, 290, 366, 385
community
  development, 60, 159, 340, 350
  involvement, 304, 307–308, 314, 317, 347–348
  sense of, 181, 200
comparative advantage, 94
competition(s), 186–187
competitive and comparative advantage, 94
competitive sport/recreation event experience, 186–187
complex(ity)
  in settings, 68, 218
  or over-stimulation, 217
conative (see experience)
conference (defined), 39
consensus building, 347
constraint(s) (and barriers), 10–12, 57, 64, 67, 82, 95, 103, 129, 130, 135, 137, 166, 189, 198, 220, 236–237, 245–250, 251, 253, 254, 265, 267, 272, 275, 361, 373, 374, 387
  structural, 245–246
  personal, 246
  interpersonal, 246
constructivism, 361
consumables, 12, 21, 210, 212, 228, 230–231, 279, 386
consumer
  show, 39–40
  surplus, 82, 321, 333
content analysis, 367
contested culture, 202
contingent(cy) valuation, 321, 333
controls and accountability, 285–286
convention(s), 18, 21, 25, 27, 36, 38, 39 ,40, 46, 54, 67, 85, 86, 103, 114, 116, 123, 146, 147,

149, 166, 189–190, 193, 224, 227, 243, 251, 313, 332, 36, 359, 379
convention centres/venues, 39, 53, 86, 141, 144, 146, 147, 162, 179, 213, 214, 332, 335, 336, 377
convention and meeting experiences, 189–190, 217
Coopers and Lybrand Consulting Group, 84, 312, 313
core phenomenon and major themes, 9–12
corporate
  events, 26, 39
  meanings, 203
cost-benefit analysis/evaluation, 317–323
Costa, C., 142
Coughlan, D., 284
Coulter, R., 77
counter arguments, 334
Coyne, B., 290
Coyne, E., 290
Crawford, D., 245
creating knowledge, 391–392
creativity and design, 210–211
Crespi-Vallbona, M. 202
critical
  path analysis, 277
  social theory, 57, 362, 371
Crompton, J., 117, 197, 227, 228, 242, 280, 283, 313, 317, 318, 321
cross-cultural, 20, 51, 56, 78, 370
Crouch, G., 74, 237
crowd(ing), 221–222
  management and control, 223
Csikszentmihalyi, M., 180, 237, 239, 243, 366, 367
Csikszentmihalyi, I., 366, 367
culture, 51–52
  traditional, 340
cultural
  authenticity, 200–202
  celebration, 30–36
  development, 337–339
  differences, 135
  event tourism, 144–145, 339
  experiences, 183, 337

identity, 202
meanings, 200–202
outcomes/impacts, 303–309
performances, 188–189
policy, 337–340
Cunneen, C., 309
Cuskelly, G., 269, 289, 290
customer, 192, 228–229
actions, 228–229
orientation, 279–280

Daniels, M. 161
Dann, G., 242
Darcy, S., 219
Davidson, R., 47, 189
Deci, E., 69, 134
Decrop, A., 237, 238, 240, 255, 361
decision to attend or participate, 251–252
decision-making, 249–252, 271–275
deductive research, 360
Deery, M., 246, 281, 326
Deighton, J., 156
definitions of design, 208–209
defining experience, 170–177
Delamere, T., 308
Delphi, 122–123, 370
demand
for goods and services, 82–83
for events, 83–85, 250
demonstration effect, 46
Deng, J., 135
Denton, S., 119
Derrett, R., 200
describing and classifying events, 18–27
design, 173–176, 208–212, 374–376
destination, 97, 140
development, event-related, 308–309, 315
De Young, R., 66
Dieser, R., 135
Dietz-Uhler, B., 188
diffusion of innovation theory, 58–59
Diller, S., 197, 198, 205
Dimanche, F. 135, 312
direct and induced demand, 85
discipline or field of study, 8

disciplinary perspectives, 353
discourse, 154
displacement, 117–118
Donaldson, L., 93
Donaldson, T., 91
Downward, P., 194
Drews, P., 60
Drummond, S., 228
Du Cros, H., 145
Duke University, 163
Dungan, T., 163
Durkheim, E., 267
Dwyer, L. 88, 117, 313, 318, 319, 321, 326, 332, 370

Eagleton, T., 32
Echtner, C., 8, 362
economic(s), 80–89
development, 85–87, 336
efficiency, 333
laws, 332
impacts, 88–89
meanings, 202
outcomes, 309–314
policy, 334–337
Economic Planning Group, 141
education and interpretation, 147–152
educational and scientific events, 42
effectiveness and efficiency, 336
ego involvement, 135–136
Ekman, A., 32
elements of style, 225–226
Ellingsen, K., 280
Ellis, M., 131
Elstad, B., 195, 290
EMBOK, 2–3, 211, 288
Emery, P., 141
Encyclopedia Britannica, 80, 98
End, C., 188
Ensor, J., 120
entertainment (arts and), 37, 173
entrepreneurs, 90, 260–261
environmental
education, 344
impacts/outcomes, 314–317

environmental (*Continued*)
   policy, 342–344
   preferences, 68
   psychology, 65–68
   sociology, 60
   themes, 344
epistemology, 355–356
Epting, F., 197
equity (social), 331–332
ethics, 55, 78, 357, 366
ethnography, 54–55
evaluation, 236, 253–254, 281, 293–294, 348, 363
event(s)
   and ordinary life, 109
   and society, 109–110
   and the economy, 110
   as theatre, 214–215
   at the margin, 44–47
   defined, 18
   design, 208–232
   education, 3–4
   experiences and meanings, 9–12
   history of, 110–112
   life-cycle, 110–111
   places, 118–119
   settings, 213–214
   studies, 2–3, 6–7, 9–14
   tourism, 116–118, 140–146, 305–307, 312–313, 316, 335–336
   typology of forms, 30–46
exhibitions, 39–40, 189, 214
existence value, 321, 333
expectations, 244–245
expectation-confirmation theory, 71
expenditure, 305
experience
   economy, 172–175
   defining, 170–177
   design, 386
   leisure, 131–132, 172
   nature of, 76–77, 384–386
   research agenda, 371–373
   touristic, 175
experience factor model, 230
experiential sampling, 366–367

failure of the marketplace, 332
fairs, 40–42
Fairley, S., 179, 181, 192, 309
Falassi, A., 31, 47, 53, 178, 179, 183, 384
Fainstein, S., 272
Farber, C., 32
Farrell, J., 195, 290
Faulkner, B., 305, 308, 364
Federation European Carnival Cities, 34
Federman, M., 155
Fenich, G., 47
Fesenmaier, D., 116, 228
Festinger, L., 65
festival(s), 31–33, 183
field(s) of study, 4–6, 8
Fishbein, M., 143
Fisher, J., 74
flash mobs, 44–45
Fleck, S., 219
Fleming, W., 321
Florida, R., 211, 338
Formica, S., 242, 371
forms of event (typology), 30–46
forms of theatre, 165–166
Foucault, M., 154
founders, 258–264
Fredline, E., 305, 308, 326
freedom (of choice), 130, 172
Freeman, J., 95
Freeman, L., 58
Freeman, R., 91
Freedman, J., 222, 223
frequency of events, 29–30
Fried, G., 291
Frisby, W., 111, 267, 340
Funk, D., 242, 243
functions of planned events, 23–24,
Furse, B., 119
future(s)
   intentions, 253–254
   issues, 378–379
   research, 370
   studies, 119–123

Gabrenya, W., 135
Gaiko, S., 289
Gammon, S., 179, 181, 185
gap between practitioners and
    researchers, 7–8
gastronomy, 230–231
Geddie, M., 119
Geertz, C., 32, 200
generic
    benefits, 204, 250, 251, 312, 385, 387
    event settings, 213–214
    and specific experiences, 182–196
geography, 114–119
Getz, D., 15, 26, 71, 81, 90, 92, 95, 111, 114,
    117, 119, 123, 214, 224, 226, 228, 241, 262,
    265, 267, 268, 269, 270, 273, 275, 277, 282,
    283, 285, 287, 288, 289, 305, 309, 314, 316,
    319, 320, 335, 340, 367, 368, 371, 378
Gibson, H.,187, 188, 205, 242, 253, 255
Gilmore, J., 164, 165, 172–175, 205
Gitelson, R., 142, 284
Glaser, B., 360
Gleick, J., 20
Glenn, J., 125
global challenges, 123
Goffman, E., 57, 337
Goh, F., 337
Goldblatt, J., 43, 260, 293
Goodson, L., 15
Gool, 181
Gordon, T., 125
governance, 264–265
Grado, S., 313
Graham, S., 43, 160
Grant, R., 91
grant givers, 194
Gratton, C., 202, 312
Gray, B., 92
Green, B.C., 179, 186, 238, 242, 248, 290
Green and Gold Inc., 317
green events, 342–344
Greene, T., 74
Greenwood, D., 305
Gregson, B., 214
Griffin, T., 365

Grigg, J., 271
Grippo, R., 35
grounded research, 354, 360–361
guaranteed and safe experience, 176–177
guests, 192
guerrilla gigs, 44–45
Gursoy, D., 307
Gustafsson, I., 231

Haahti, A., 215
Habermas, J., 57, 154
Halewood, C., 179
Hall, E., 221
Hall, M., 13, 42, 98, 100, 101, 309, 319, 329,
    345, 348, 350
hallmark and iconic events, 24–25
Ham, S., 151
Hanlon, C., 269, 287, 289
Hannan, M., 95
Hannam, K.179
Harrington, M., 290
Harris, M., 33
Harris, R., 7, 219, 297, 374
Harris, V., 288, 289
Harrison, L., 290
Harvey, M., 218
Havitz, M., 135
Hayllar, B., 365
health, 291–293, 341–342
Hede, A., 144, 281
Heimer, C., 268
Hektner, J., 367
heritage commemorations, 34–35
hermeneutics, 76–77, 365–366
Herzberg, F., 227, 287
Higham, J., 253
Hill, B., 143
Hiller, H., 60, 101
Hilliard, T., 149
Hinch, T., 237, 248
history, 106–114
historical research, 369
historiography, 106–107, 369
Hofstede, G., 262
Holdnak, A., 313

Hormans, G., 72
hospitality management and studies, 146–147
host-guest interactions, 305–307
Housego, A., 151
Hover, M., 181
Hoyle, L., 297
Hu, C., 293
Hudson, S.,143
Hughes, G., 32
Hughes, H., 119
Huizinga, J., 131
Hultkrantz, L., 118
Hwang, K., 135
human
    geography, 114–119
    resources and volunteer management,
        286–291
hypotheses, 359

iconic events, 24–25
ideology, 330–331
inductive research, 360–361
image making, 142–144
Imagine Canada, 289
impacts (and outcomes), 300–326
individual involvement in events, 314
information
    management, 281
    search and use, 249–250
installation art, 157–158
institutions/institutionalism/
    institutionalization, 96–98, 266–269, 329
integrated marketing, 280
interdisciplinary, 352–353
interpersonal constraints, 246–247
International Association for Exhibition
    Management (IAEM), 39
International Events Group (IEG), 283, 322
International Association of Fairs and
    Expositions (IAFE), 41
International Festivals Association (IFA), 292
International Festivals and Events
    Association (IFEA), 214
International Special Events Society (ISES), 26
inter-organizational behaviour, 269–271

interpersonal factors, 244
interpretation, 150–152
interpretivism, 361
interviews, 367–368
intrapreneurship, 261
intrinsic motivation, 172
invisible management processes, 230
investment, 305, 311–312, 315
involvement, 135–136
Iso-Ahola, S., 173, 240, 241

Jackson, E., 135, 247, 255
Jafari, J., 8, 178
Jago, L., 7, 26, 142, 143, 246, 281, 318, 321,
    326
Jamal, T., 8, 92
James, Jeffrey, 188
James, Jane, 209, 215, 225
Janiskee, R., 60, 116, 125, 376
Jarvie, G., 111
Jawahar, I., 91
Jaworski, A., 152, 154
Jennings, G., 357, 361
Jisha, J., 282
Johnson, D., 292
Johnston, R., 321
Johnston, M., 195, 290
Jones, H., 116
Jones I., 248
Jordan, J., 305
Jung, M., 189
justifying
    market intervention, 98–108
    public sector involvement, 329–334

Kang, Y., 85
Kaplan, S., 68, 218, 375
Kapferer, J., 136
Katz, A., 267
Kay, P., 370
Kelly, J., 142, 358, 359
Kendall, K., 307
Kerstetter, D., 119, 221, 284
Kim, S., 137
Kitayama, S., 135

Kleiber, D., 62, 63, 64, 68, 74, 131, 172
Klemke, E., 358
knowledge
    and philosophy, 355–359
    domains, 2–3
    based theory of the firm, 91
    creation, 10, 14, 122, 352–381, 391–392
Kokolakakis, T., 202
Komppula, R., 215
Kotler, P., 142
Krug, D., 259
Kyle, G., 135

Ladkin, A., 123
land use changes, 314, 317
Lane, B., 150
Lanius, U., 219, 220
Larson, M., 58, 91, 271
Larson, R., 367
Lashley, C., 230
Laurent, G., 136
law(s), 101–103, 332
law of the commons, 333–334
Laws, E., 233, 281
Laybourn, P., 271, 272
Lavenda, R., 50, 51, 74, 357
Laverie, D., 188
Laxson, J., 306
leadership, 258–264
learning
    organization, 269
    theory, 148–149
Lee, C., 242
Lee, H., 221
Lee, J.M., 243, 381
Lee, J., 118
Lee, S., 117
Lee, Y., 242
Leibold, M., 242
Leiper, N., 8, 139
legacy, 319–320
legal considerations, 102–103
legitimacy, 202
leisure studies, 128–138 (see also serious
    leisure)

leisure constraints, 135, 245
leveraging, 336, 341, 344
Leyns, A., 313
Li, F., 111
Li, R., 242, 255
Li, Y., 175
life-cycle, 110–111
life stage, 132–133
lifestyle, 130–131, 238, 281
light, 216
liminal and liminoid, 178–181
linear-nodal settings, 214
literature, 38
Locke, E.,
Lockyer, T., 227
logistics, 273, 275–278
Long, P., 93
longitudinal research, 369
Lord Cultural Resources, 141
Love, L., 227, 228
loyalty, 252
Lumsdon, L., 194
Lynch, K., 218–219, 376
Lynch, R., 309

MacAloon, J., 188, 189, 205
MacCannell, D., 132, 201, 361
Macintosh, D., 199
Mackellar, J., 312
Mackie, D., 188
Macnaught, T., 305
macro and micro economics, 81–82
Madrigal, R., 188
Mahony, D., 188
Malouf, L., 213
management, 10, 13, 89–98, 388–389
    research agenda, 374–376
    needs, 354
Mandelbaum, S., 272
Mannell, R., 62, 63, 64, 68, 74, 131, 172, 241,
    247
Manning, F., 32
margin (events at the), 44–47
market(ing), 2, 87–88, 145, 278–282
Markus, H., 135

Marris, T., 25
Maslow, A., 61, 239, 241, 287, 288
Masterman, G., 43, 280
Mateucci, X., 32
Mayfield, T., 280
McCarville, R., 283
McConnell., A., 241
McDonald, S., 85
McDonnell, I., 297
McGehee, N., 136, 242, 248, 249
McGregor, D., 288
McGuirty, J., 161
McKay, S., 242, 317, 321
McKercher, B., 145
McLaughlin, G., 91
McLuhan, M., 155, 390
McMahon-Beattie, U., 285
McPhail, T., 155
meanings, 9–12, 196–203, 253, 371–373, 384–386
means-end theory, 76–77
media, 193, 196
    coverage, 309, 314, 317
    events, 25
    studies, 155
    value, 322
meetings and conventions, 38–39, 189
Meetings Professionals International (MPI),
        39, 213
Mehmetoglu, M., 280
Mei, W., 145
mega-events, 25, 60, 199
Mellor, R., 326
memorable experiences, 181
Mendell, R., 144
Merrilees, B., 92
meta analysis, 370
methods, 362–370
methodology, 8, 54–57, 359–362
Meyersohn, R., 132
microeconomics, 81–82
Mifflin, K., 92
Mihalik, B., 308, 313
Mikolaitis, P., 262, 273, 292, 297
Miller, L., 246
Mintzberg, H., 258, 259

Mitchell, R., 91
Mitler, B., 51, 52, 200
Mistillis, N., 326
models, 358–359
model of the planned event experience, 177–181
Mohr, K., 242
Monga, M., 290
Morrison, A., 280
Morrow, S., 39, 47
Moscardo. G., 233
Mossberg, L., 143, 172, 282, 381
motive, 240
motivation, 190, 240–244, 287–290
motivator-hygiene theory, 287
Mount, J., 284
Mowen, 221–223
Moyer, K., 64
Mules, T., 85, 88, 119, 284, 319, 326, 332
Murrmann, S., 242
Murrell, A., 188

Nash, D., 361
National Association for Interpretation, 150
National Outdoor Events Association, 219
need for Event Studies, 6–7
needs, 239–240
Neimeyer, R., 197
new money, 311–312
Nelson, K., 15
Neulinger, J., 130, 134
Neuman, W., 359
Newton Jackson, E., 290
Nickerson, N., 63
Nickerson, R., 211
Nicholson, R. 182, 242
Ngamsom, B., 242
Niro, B., 284
Nogawa, H., 242
Norman, W., 161
North American Society for Sport
        Management, 160
Norton, P., 297
not for profit, 96–97
Noronha, R., 46
Nurse, K., 33

Oakes, S., 281
Oakley, E., 259
observation, 367
O'Brien, D., 97
O'Brien, E., 289
O'Dell, T., 181
officials, 194
Oldberding, D., 282
Oliver, R., 71
Olsen, D., 36, 184, 205
Olson, J., 76
one-time events, 269
ontology, 355–356
Ooi, C., 175
open space settings, 214
open system theory, 265
operations and logistics, 275–278, 374–376
Oppermann, M., 189, 242
ordinary life, 109
organization(al)
    behaviour, 264–271
    culture, 261–263
    evaluation, 266–269
    quality, 266
    structure, 264–265
O'Sullivan, E., 176
Otnes, C., 44
O'Toole, W. 15, 262, 273, 292, 297
outcomes and impacted, 10, 13–14, 300–326,
    379–380, 389–390
overstimulation, 217
ownership, 264–265
Oxford English Dictioanry, 173

Page, S., 345
Pak, S., 364
Paluba, G., 134
parades and processions, 35, 112–113
Parasuraman, A., 229
parks and recreation, 128–129
Parry, B., 44
participants, 193
participant observation, 367
participation events, 27, 193
patterns and processes, 10, 14, 376–379

peak experience, 239
Pearce, D., 182, 242
Pearce, P., 181, 212, 241, 255, 309
Pennington-Gray, L., 313
Penrose, E., 91
people movement, 276
Perdue, R., 74, 85
performance
    art, 157
    studies, 156–157
performers, 193
performing art events, 37–38
permanent event organizations, 269
personal
    and interpersonal factors, 244
    construct theory, 197
    outcomes, 301–303
    meanings, 197–198
    space, 220–221
personality, 62–64, 237, 260
Petrick, A., 242, 255
Pfeffer, J., 93
phenomenology, 76–77, 365–366
Phillimore, J., 15
philosophy
    and knowledge, 355–359
    of planned events, 78
    of science, 355–356
Picard, D., 33
Picard, M., 306
pillow fight club, 44–46
pilgrimage, 36, 184–185
Pine, B. , 172–175, 205
Pitts, B. 34, 242
place,
    marketing, 142, 337
    affective quality of, 219–220
    time and, 20–21
planning,
    and decision-making, 271–275
    business, 273–274
    project, 273
    research agenda, 374–376
    strategic, 274
    theory, 272–273

planned
    event experience model, 177–181
    versus unplanned, 27–28
    behaviour theory, 70–71, 238, 244, 253, 290
    event typology, 21–23, 384–386
    event functions, 23–24
play theory, 131
Plog, S., 63, 237
Pol, L., 364
policy,
    considerations, 345
    domains, 93, 97, 328
    environment, 345–346
    making, 344–349
    needs, 355
    questions, 379
political
    and state events, 36, 185
    outcomes and impacts, 303–309
    science, 98–101
population ecology theory, 95–96
Porter, M., 94
positioning, 282
positivism, 356–357, 359–360, 362
post experience evaluation and feedback,
    253–254
postmodernism, 357–358
preferences (setting), 218
Preda, P., 163, 278
Prentice, R., 282
premier or prestige events, 25
Preston, L., 91
Prideaux, B., 228
Pritchard, A., 152, 154
private events, 44
procession settings, 213–214
procurement, 277–278
product
    orientation, 279–280
    quality, 226–227
professional(ism), 288–289, 354
programming, 223–227
propositions, 359
protests, 46
Przeclawski, K., 132

psychic benefits, 322, 333
psychology, 61–62
public
    administration, 96
    at large, 196
    goods, 82, 88, 330, 331, 344
    policy, 263–264, 328–329, 390–391
    relations, 113
publicity stunt, 26
Pugh, C., 348
pulsating events, 269, 286, 294
Putnam, R., 58
Pyo, S., 85

qualitative research, 364–370
quality, 226–230
quantitative methods, 363
questionnaire surveys, 363–364
queuing theory, 277
Quick, S., 289, 300
Quinn, B., 33, 200, 262

Radbourne, J., 338, 350
Ralston, L., 230
Ralston, R., 195, 240
Raj, R., 285
Ravenscroft, N., 32
Raybould, M., 119, 242, 364
recreation(al)
    events, 443–444
    experiences, 186–187
    specialization, 136–137
reflective professional practice, 354
Reid, G., 334
Reisinger, Y., 184
regulators, 194, 270
regulations, 347
religious
    events, 36
    experiences, 183–184
    studies, 78–80
research
    and evaluation and public policy, 348–349
    agendas, 371–380
    evaluation, and information systems, 293–294

for marketing, 281
gap between practitioners and academics, 7–8
methods, 54–55, 362–370
methodologies, 359–362
on political science of events, 101
purposes, 362–363
traditions, 54–55
resource(s)
and financial management, 282–286
based theory of the firm, 91
dependency theory, 93–94, 284
return on investment, 285, 321, 333
Reunion Network, 44
revenue
sources, 283–284
or yield management, 285
total, 321
Reynolds, T., 77
Rhea, D., 205
Richards, G., 33, 116, 202
Richards, P., 267–268
Ridinger, L.,188
Riggio, M., 33
riot, 46
risk, 291–293
Ritchie, B., 144
Ritchie, J.R., 143, 144, 308, 319
rites and rituals, 52–54
rites de passage, 44, 109, 177–178, 197
Rittichainuwat, B., 189
Roberts, K., 132, 308
Robertson, M., 339
Robinson, Mike., 33
Robinson, M., 160
Roche, M., 199
Rogers, E., 58
Rogers, T., 39, 47
Rojek, C., 132, 139
Rozin, S., 202
Rukavina, V., 283
Runners World, 250
rural sociology, 60–61
Rusher, K., 329, 348, 350
Russell, J., 219, 220

Russell, Julie, 199
Rutley, J., 223
Ryan, C., 116, 178, 227, 237, 242–243, 267, 268, 290, 362
Ryan, R., 69, 134

safety, 291–293
Sahlins, M., 268
Salancik, G., 93
Saleh, F., 194, 227, 290
Sandercock, L., 272
Samuelson, L., 312, 321
San Francisco State University, 147
Santacons, 44–45
satisfaction, 253
scale, 28–29
scenario making, 122
Schechner, R., 164, 165, 167
Schein, E., 261, 262, 267
Schultz, E., 51, 74, 357
Scotinform Ltd., 313
Scott, D., 136, 242
Scott, J., 58
Scott, W., 94, 97, 104
script(ing), 164–165, 224–225
Sebastion, R., 188
secondary data analysis, 363
security, 293
seeking and escaping theory, 132, 220, 241
segmentation and target marketing, 281–282
self
actualization, 239–240
construal, 135
determination theory, 69–70, 134–135
Selznick, P., 267
semiotics, 361–362
Senge, P., 269
sense
of community, 200
of place, 200
sensory stimulation, 216–218
serious leisure, 241, 245, 247, 137–138
service(s)
blueprinting, 228–230
design and quality, 228–230

setting
    affordances, 248–249
    design, 212–213
Severt, D., 189, 190
Shackley, M., 36
Shanka, T., 281
Shedroff, N., 205, 208
Sheehan, A., 289
Shelby, B., 251
Shaw, G., 114, 125, 131, 306, 371
Shaw, M., 289
Shaw, R., 26
Shibli, S. 322
Shone, A., 44
Singh, R., 36, 184
Singh, S., 80
Silvers, J., 2, 15
Sivan, A., 111
Skinner, Bruce, 283
Skinner, B.F., 288
smell, 217
Smith, B., 143
Smith, E., 188
Smith, M., 180
Smith, S., 243, 360
social
    capital theory, 58
    cognition and social cognitive theory,
        69–70, 73
    construct, 120–121, 199
    constructivism, 361–362
    cultural, and political outcomes, 303–309
    equity, 331–332
    exchange theory, 72
    integration, 340–341
    meanings, 199–200
    network theory, 58
    policy, 340–342
    psychology, 68–72
    problems, 341
sociology, 55–61
Sofield, T., 111, 306
Solberg, H., 313
Solomon, J., 42, 43
sound, 216

Soutar, G., 123
Spangler, K., 176
spatial patterns, 10, 14, 115–116
special events, 26–27
specialization, 136–137
spectacle (theory of), 188–189
spectator and interactive events, 26, 187–188
Spiller, J., 38
Spilling, O., 85, 87
spiritual experiences, 183
Spiropoulos, S., 92
sponsors, 194
sponsorship, 283, 321
sport
    as cultural expression, 200
    events, 42–43
    experiences, 186–187
    management and studies, 160–162
    sociology, 59
    spectators/fans, 187–188
    tourism, 43, 121, 160, 161, 167, 181, 187,
        242–243, 253, 328, 346
staff(ing), 194, 229
staging, 215
stakeholder
    and network theory, 91–93
    experiences, 190–196
    management, 202, 270–271
Stear, L., 139
Stebbins, R., 63, 137, 241,
Sternberg, R., 211
Stewart, B., 287
Stokes, R., 92
Stott, C., 64
strategic
    event creation, 263–264, 266
    planning, 274–275, 346–347
Strauss, A., 360
stressors, 222–223, 301–302
Strigas, A. 290
Strolberg, K., 211
style, 225–226
subsidizing events, 87–88
substitution, 251
Supovitz, F., 43

supply chain management, 277–278
suppliers, 194, 270
sustainable, 316, 339, 342–344
symbolic interactionists, 57–58
systematic observation, 363

tangible evidence, 229
Tapp, A. 188
target market(ing), 281–282
Tarlow, P., 292, 293, 297
Tassiopoulos, D., 297
taste, 217
Taylor, P., 312
Taylor, R., 281
Taylor, Ruth, 92, 314
Teigland, J., 85, 117
Tellstrom, R., 230
temporal
    patterns, 115–116
    process, 10, 14
theatre
    events as, 214–215
    forms, 165–166
    studies, 163–166
theme and programme design, 223–237
thematic interpretation, 150–151
theory,
    and models, 358–359
    of allocation, 82
    of choice, 82
    of planned action/behaviour, 70–71, 238,
        244, 253, 290
    of spectacle, 188–189
    on experience and meaning, 11–12
    X and theory Y, 287
Thrane, C., 227
Thyne, M., 281
Tilden, F., 150
time
    budget studies, 368
    is of the essence, 19–20
    and a place, 201
    switching, 117–118
timing and build, 225
Timothy, D., 36, 184, 201, 205

Timmermans, H., 74
Toepper, L., 321
Tohmo, T., 312
Tomlinson, G., 35
Tomljenovic, R. 339
Toohey, K., 43, 47
tools of interpretation, 151–152
touch, 217
tourism (see also event tourism)
    body of knowledge, 140
    experiences, 175
    management and studies, 138–146
trade show, 39–40
traffic, 308–309
Trail, G., 188
training, 260
transformation, 253
Trauer, B., 242, 243
travel career trajectory, 241–242
Travel Industry Association of America,
        145, 187
trend extrapolation, 121–122
Tribe, J., 5, 6, 15, 80, 84, 104, 326, 343, 355
Tse, T., 145
Tum, J., 276, 277, 278, 297
Turco, D., 43, 312, 321
Turner, V., 32, 33, 47, 52–53, 177, 178, 183,
        184, 189, 239, 384
Turney, M., 113
Twynam, D., 195
typology
    of event forms, 30–46
    of planned events, 212–213
Tyrell, T., 321
Tzelepi, M., 289, 300

Udall, L., 305
UK Health and Safety Executive, 292
UK Institute for Volunteering, 289
UK National Outdoor Events Association, 219
University of North Carolina, Greensboro, 128
unique risk elements, 291–292
urban
    renewal, 341
    sociology, 60

Urry, J., 175, 186
US Department of Labor, 289
Uysal, M., 74, 242

value, 322–323
values, 237–238
Van der Kamp, A., 325
Van der Wagen, L., 211, 259, 260, 286, 287, 297
Van Gennep, 177, 178, 189, 384
Vanhove, D., 25
Van Kirk, R., 283
Van Mierlo, J., 181
Van Zyl, C., 242
Vaughan, R., 321
Veal, A., 43, 47, 56, 64, 330, 362, 381
vendors, 194
venue(s)
    efficiency, 336
    management, 162–163
    sustainable, 342–344
Verhoven, P., 117
Virden, R., 237
VIPs, 194
visual arts, 38
visible staff contacts, 229,
volunteer(s), 194, 286–291
Voss, T., 267
Vroom, V., 288

Waitt, G., 307
Walker, G., 135, 237
Walle, A., 111
Wang, N., 201
Wang, P., 142
Wang, Y., 190
Wanhill, S., 284–285
Wann, D., 187, 188
Waters, H., 40
Watts, T., 163, 278
Weber, K., 381
Weber, S., 339

Waterman, S., 339
wayfinding, 218
Weed, M., 346
Weiler, B., 150
wellness, 341
Weppler, K., 283
Whitford, M., 87, 348
Whitson, D., 199
Wickham, T., 119, 221
Wicks, B., 116, 228, 283, 288
Wiersma, B., 211
Wijngaarden, 181
Wikipedia Online Encyclopedia, 45, 122
Wikstrom, E., 58, 91, 271
Williams, A., 114, 125, 131, 306, 371
Williams, P., 290
Wilson, J., 305
willingness to pay, 83–85, 250, 321
Wing-Vogelbacher, A., 313
Witt, S., 25
Wood, C., 195, 290
Wood, D., 92
Wood, E., 153, 167, 280, 281, 294, 348
world's fairs, 41–42
worth of events, 320–323
wow factor, 177
Wright, J., 297

Xiao, H., 242, 360
Xie, P., 54–55, 152, 340

Yeoman, I., 163, 285, 350
yield management, 285
Yoo, J., 381
Yoon, S., 116, 249
Young, H., 268
Yu, Y., 321

Zaichkowsky, J., 135
Zaltman, G., 77
Zuckerman, M., 63
Zuzanek, J., 247